CRITICS OF EMPIRE

CRITICS OF EMPIRE

British Radicals and the Imperial Challenge

BERNARD PORTER

LONDON · NEW YORK

Published in 2008 by I.B.Tauris & Co Ltd
6 Salem Road, London W2 4BU
175 Fifth Avenue, New York NY 10010
www.ibtauris.com

In the United States of America and Canada distributed by
Palgrave Macmillan a division of St. Martin's Press,
175 Fifth Avenue, New York NY 10010

ISBN (HB): 978 1 84511 506 7
ISBN (PB): 978 1 84511 507 4

A full CIP record for this book is available from the British Library
A full CIP record is available from the Library of Congress

Library of Congress Catalog Card Number: available

Printed and bound in Great Britain by TJ International Ltd, Padstow, Cornwall

To the memory of my parents

Contents

List of Illustrations

Preface

THE history of British imperial expansion in the late nineteenth century has been well worked in recent years. Its interpretation is still controversial, and doubtless always will be, but the details are familiar. Not so the reverse side of the coin. The dissent within Britain which accompanied this expansion has been less closely examined – partly, perhaps, because it has seemed too feeble and insignificant to merit more detailed treatment.

At the turn of the twentieth century the dissentients were a small minority, and their voices were all but drowned in the general imperialist clamour of the Chamberlainite era. It would be falsifying the historical record to claim for them any great potency in their own time. Yet to ignore them completely, or to treat them merely as riders to the main imperialist assertion, is to create a serious blind spot in our view of the political situation of the 1890s and after. An exploration of their attitudes, which is the purpose of the present study, will tell us much about Radical thinking at the turn of the century, its merits and its defects, and much also about the origins of certain ideas about empire which were to grow in strength towards the end of our period and in the first half of the twentieth century: chief among them the policy of 'indirect rule', and the 'economic interpretation' of imperialism. Such considerations bestow on this small group of political non-conformists a somewhat wider significance than seemed to attach to them in their own time.

The scope of this book is necessarily restricted to one or two aspects of a broad and diffuse subject. The omissions will manifest themselves during the course of it: India and the issue of imperial federation, for example, are treated hardly at all, and missionary and humanitarian opinion only cursorily. But the criterion used for selection has not been altogether arbitrary. The subjects on which contemporary Radical opinion has been sought have been those which Radicals themselves selected as the most vital and pressing. Africa was the battle-ground both for the chief imperial rivalries of the period and also for the main colonial controversies within Britain: so Africa will figure largest of all in our discussions. The argument of this book will revolve around the Radical debate on issues raised by colonial expansion in Africa.

Foremost among these, of course, was the issue of 'imperialism', its motivation and morality, and much of what we have to say will be concerned with the different 'anti-imperialist' ideologies which flourished at the turn of the century. J. A. Hobson's most pregnant 'capitalist theory' will be subjected to particularly detailed examination, with the object neither of ratifying nor of disputing it, but of explaining its origin and form, and so providing a basis from which criticism of it may proceed. The present author has no simple and coherent 'theory of imperialism' to offer in its place, and he has tried as far as possible to suppress any views of his own as to the historical viability of Hobson's. This may be deplored: but the fact is that any authoritative view of imperialism must be grounded not in a reading of other men's interpretations, but in a wide and detailed knowledge of the facts – and such knowledge the author does not profess.

'Imperialism' was one issue emphasised by the colonial events of the turn of the century; but our terms of reference are not confined exclusively to its enemies. Many who called themselves 'imperialists' were nevertheless highly critical of the conduct of colonial affairs, and their views should not be neglected merely because they appear somewhere in the middle of the 'imperial/ anti-imperial' spectrum. It was these men (and women) who offered some of the most radical solutions to another problem raised by African expansion – the problem of tropical government, of how to rule alien peoples. This body of critical but imperially constructive ideas will constitute our other prime concern. The whole book will attempt to present a picture, albeit incomplete, of political Radicalism's response to African empire in the 1890s and early 1900s.

Much of it is based upon hitherto unpublished material. Consequently the list of those to whom I should like to acknowledge my gratitude for allowing me to consult collections of private papers in their care, and to publish extracts from them, is a long one. Mr Patrick Monkhouse and Mr David Ayerst went to great trouble to supply me with copies of letters from J. A. Hobson in the *Guardian* archives, and Mrs Mabel Scott and Mr Harold Hobson have given their approval to my publication of them, and helped me considerably in other ways. For permission to use and quote from John Holt's correspondence I am grateful to Mr C. R. Holt; for the Ramsay MacDonald Papers, to the Rt. Hon. Malcolm MacDonald, P.C. and Mr David Marquand, M.P.; for the Samuel Papers to Viscount Samuel, the Hon Godfrey Samuel and the Clerk of the Records of the House of Lords; for the Campbell-Bannerman Papers to Lady Pentland; for the Passfield Papers to the Directors of the Passfield Trust; for the G. B. Shaw Papers to the Public Trustee and the Society of Authors; for the Wedgwood Papers to Miss C. V. Wedgwood and the Wedgwood Museum Trust; for the Casement and A. S. Green Papers to the Trustees of the National Library of Ireland; for the Fabian Society Papers to Mr Tom Ponsonby, General Secretary of the Fabian Society; and for the Morel Papers to the Directors of the London School of Economics. I have quoted briefly from a few other manuscript collections, and many more correspondents, whose descendants or executors I have been unable to trace: I hope that all of them will forgive my lack of courtesy in not consulting them. Messrs Allen & Unwin have kindly allowed me to quote extensively from J. A. Hobson's *Imperialism: a Study.*

A great deal of the manuscript material I have consulted is in the British Library of Political and Economic Science, whose Keeper of Manuscripts, Mr C. G. Allen, has been exceptionally helpful. Other libraries whose staffs have greatly facilitated the research for this book are the British Museum Library; the University Library, Cambridge; the National Library of Ireland, Dublin; the House of Lords Record Office; Rhodes House, Oxford; and the libraries of Transport House and Congress House, London.

The substance of the present study has appeared in two

previous guises: as a fellowship dissertation in 1966, and as a Ph.D. thesis in the following year. In the early stages of its preparation I benefited greatly from the guidance of Professor P. N. S. Mansergh, and thereafter from that of Dr R. E. Robinson. To both of them I owe more than I can express. Dr H. M. Pelling, Dr A. F. Madden, Dr J. E. Flint and Mr Frank Davey have read an earlier version of the manuscript, and made many helpful suggestions. The responsibility for any opinions expressed in this book, of course, and for any errors which remain in it, is entirely my own. Lastly I must thank the Department of Education and Science – whose assistance is usually taken for granted – for supporting me in my research; and the Master and Fellows of my college for enabling me to prepare this book for publication by electing me into a Research Fellowship, and for being a constant source of wise and friendly advice.

BERNARD PORTER

Corpus Christi College, Cambridge

Introduction to the Second Edition

CRITICS of Empire first appeared at the height of the Vietnam War, which was widely criticised at the time as an imperialist venture. Its reappearance now coincides with two other American-led wars, in Afghanistan and Iraq, which many regard in much the same way. That might be thought to give it a contemporary relevance at both times. I do not recall this relevance influencing me greatly, or even at all, when I wrote the book originally. I saw it merely as an academic study in the history of political thought and colonial policy – and as a means of getting a Ph.D. (The book grew out of my thesis.) When I was researching it, in the mid-1960s, the Vietnam War was not as big an issue in America and Britain as it became a few years later. In any case, I was not greatly interested in it. Today, however, it is much more difficult to ignore the modern resonances. The reason for this is not that the *events* of the present day are necessarily repeating the history of the turn of the twentieth century, which is the period this book covers – I have my views on this, the comparison between old British and modern American 'imperialisms', which I have aired elsewhere[1] – but that much of the *rhetoric* surrounding those events is. (This book, of course, is about rhetoric.) This applies on both sides of the argument: to modern 'imperialists', who are much more open about their imperialism today than they were in the 1960s (put on the defensive as they were then by the critique whose origins are described in this book, the 'capitalist' one); as well as to the 'antis'. Reading *Critics of Empire* again, even with a proper historian's caution against exaggerating superficial parallels, I have been constantly struck by this. It has all been said (if not done) before. Often – in my view – the discussion was far more sophisticated then. This is one good reason to reissue the book today. Another is that it is still, even after all these years, the only

[1] Bernard Porter, *Empire and Superempire: Britain, America and the World* (Yale University Press, 2006).

book-length treatment of turn-of-the-twentieth-century 'anti-imperialism', an important subject in its own historical right; and is almost impossible to get hold of, even second-hand.

That it is being reissued now in exactly its original form requires some explanation. No history book can stand the test of nearly forty years. This was a pioneering work; pioneers usually make mistakes. Much has been written since 1968 that has modified my views and my perspective on many of the topics covered here – I shall be coming to this shortly. If I were starting out to write *Critics of Empire* now, I would write it very differently. That was one of the reasons I preferred not to edit the existing text: it would have required unravelling almost entirely. Luckily for me, my publishers and their advisers had also decided against this, partly for this reason, and partly because they thought the original version of the book was worth publishing not only as a history book, but also as a historical document – a reflection of the times in which it was written. Reading this text again, I found it to be exactly that (it made me quite nostalgic) – but not *only* that. Most of its conclusions, I think, still stand, and some may be even more 'relevant' to the present day than they were to the era of Vietnam. I hope that new readers today will also be able to view it in this treble way: as a source of knowledge and understanding of the early 1900s (of course), of the 1960s, and for our present times. This new Introduction will seek to bridge the gap between those last two points. A lot has happened in the meantime.

* * *

One thing that has happened is, of course, that academic research in several of the areas covered by this book has moved on. This is particularly true of some of my leading *dramatis personae* and organisations: J. A. Hobson (the main individual), J. M. Robertson, E. D. Morel, Mary Kingsley, the Ethical movement, the 'Progressives', the 'New Liberals' and the 'Rainbow Circle'. The place of these people and groups in the evolution of a new critique of imperialism in the 1890s and early 1900s is explained below, together with the broader influences and earlier precedents that were also crucial to this process; most of these, however, were almost totally unknown in the 1960s – the main exception was Hobson, and he was not known *about* much – which is why I regard myself as their discoverer (a 'pioneer'). Since then a great amount of published work has appeared on some of them. Hobson studies have especially flourished.[1] The 'New Liberals' are now a fixture in the British historical firmament, with fine studies by Peter Clarke, Michael Freeden and Stefan Collini in particular.[2] The Rainbow Circle's minutes have been published.[3] Robertson now has a volume of essays devoted to him.[4] There is a book about the Ethical Movement.[5] E. D. Morel and his Congo Reform Association are the subject of at least three post-1968 studies.[6] There are several books and articles on the 'Pro-Boers'.[7] Mary Kingsley has been the subject of at least eight new biographies, and her own major work has been reprinted (by a

[1] The most recent and best book on Hobson is Peter Cain, *Hobson and Imperialism: Radicalism, New Liberalism, and Finance 1887–1938* (2002), whose bibliography lists six other post-1968 books and collections specifically on Hobson, scores of articles, and about a dozen other books that feature him prominently. Particularly noteworthy are H. V. Emy, *Liberals, Radicals and Social Politics, 1892–1914* (Cambridge, 1973); Norman Etherington, *Theories of Imperialism: War, Conquest and Capital* (1984); David Long, *Towards a New Liberal Internationalism: The International Theory of J. A. Hobson* (1986); Michael Freeden (ed.) *Reappraising J. A. Hobson: Humanism, and Welfare* (1990); J. A. Townshend, *J. A. Hobson* (1990); and J. Pheby (ed.) *J. A. Hobson after Fifty Years* (1994).

[2] Peter Clarke, *Lancashire and the New Liberalism* (1971), and *Liberals and Social Democrats* (1978); Michael Freeden, *The New Liberalism: An Ideology of Social Reform* (1978); and Stefan Collini, *Liberalism and Sociology: L. T. Hobhouse and Political Argument in England 1880–1914* (1979).

[3] Michael Freeden (ed.) *Minutes of the Rainbow Circle, 1894–1924* (1989).

[4] G. A. Robertson (ed.) *J. M. Robertson (1856–1933), Liberal, Rationalist, and Scholar* (1987).

[5] I. D. McKillop, *The British Ethical Societies* (1986).

[6] Wm Roger Louis and Jean Stenger, *E. D. Morel's History of the Congo Reform Movement* (1968); Catherine Ann Cline, *E. D. Morel, 1873–1924: The Strategies of Protest* (1980); Jules Marchal, *E. D. Morel contre Léopold II: l'histoire du Congo, 1900–1910* (1996).

[7] Stephen Koss (ed.) *The Pro-Boers: The Anatomy of an Antiwar Movement* (1973); Arthur Davey, *The British Pro-Boers 1877–1902* (1978); John W. Auld, 'The Liberal pro-Boers', in *Journal of British Studies*, vol. 14 (1975) pp. 78–99; R. Gott, 'Little Englanders', in Raphael Samuel (ed.) *Patriotism: The Making and Unmaking of British National Identity*, vol. I (1989) pp. 90–102; Keith Surridge, '"All you soldiers are what we call pro-Boer": the military critique of the South African War, 1899–1902', in *History*, vol. 82 (1997) pp. 582–600; Paul Laity on 'The British peace movement and the war', in David Omissi and Andrew Thompson (eds) *The Impact of the South African War* (2002).

feminist publisher).[1] These were empty gaps in the historiography before 1968; now they are being filled. I would ask readers of the following to bear this in mind before criticising me too harshly for the imperfections in my own treatment of them: remember that I was working in the dark (or early dawn); my successors have at least had my poor guttering candle to lead them some of the way. As well as all this, there have also been some major new studies of 'anti-imperialism' in the periods both preceding mine,[2] and after-wards.[3] For my pre-1890s historical background, I had to rely largely on a single and very old work by the Dane, C. A. Bodelsen, which I now see as deficient in many ways, and for the same reason as *Critics of Empire* was: because Bodelsen was a pioneer.[4] Anti-imperialism in the contemporary USA, which closely mirrored that in Britain, has also become the subject of books and articles since 1968.[5] So

[1] Jean Gordon Hughes, *Invincible Miss: The Adventures of Mary Kingsley* (1968); Signe Höjer, *Mary Kingsley, forskningsresande I Västafrika: en biografi* (Stockholm, 1975); Deborah Jane Birkett, *An Independent Woman in West Africa: The Case of Mary Kingsley* (1987), and *Mary Kingsley: Imperial Adventuress* (1992); Valerie Grosvenor Myer, *Victorian Lady in Africa: The Story of Mary Kingsley* (1989); Robert D. Pearce, *Mary Kingsley: Light and the Heart of Darkness* (1990); Alison Blunt, *Travel, Gender and Imperialism: Mary Kingsley and West Africa* (1994); Katherine Frank, *A Voyager Out: The Life of Mary Kingsley* (2005); and Mary Kingsley, *Travels in West Africa* [1897] republished by Virago press in 1982.

[2] Ged Martin, '"Anti-imperialism" in the mid-nineteenth century', in Ronald Hyam and Ged Martin (eds) *Reappraisals in British Imperial History* (1975); A. J. Durrans, 'A two-edged sword: the liberal attack on Disraelian imperialism', in *Journal of Imperial and Commonwealth History*, vol. 10 (1982) pp. 262–84; Miles Taylor, 'Imperium et Libertas? Rethinking the radical critique of imperialism during the nineteenth century', in *Journal of Imperial and Commonwealth History*, vol. 19 (1991) pp. 1–23; Mira Matikkala, 'Anti-imperialism, Englishness, and empire in late-Victorian Britain' (Cambridge Ph.D. dissertation, 2006).

[3] Partha Sarathi Gupta, *Imperialism and the British Labour Movement, 1914–1964* (1975); Stephen Howe, *Anticolonialism in British Politics: The Left and the End of Empire, 1918–64* (1993); Nicholas Owen, 'Critics of empire in Britain', in Wm Roger Louis (ed.) *Oxford History of the British Empire*, vol. 4, *The Twentieth Century* (1999) pp. 188–211.

[4] G. A. Bodelsen, *Studies in Mid-Victorian Imperialism* (1924). The deficiencies I think lie in the way he measured 'pro' and 'anti' imperialism mainly in terms of people's attitudes to the question of colonial 'separation'.

[5] Edward Berkeley Tompkins, *Anti-Imperialism in the United States: The Great Debate, 1890–1920* (Philadelphia, 1970); Gerald E Markowitz (ed.) *American Anti-Imperialism 1895–1901* (1976); and see Stephen C. Call, 'Protesting against modern war: a comparison of issues raised by anti-imperialists and pro-Boers', in *War in History*, vol. 3 (1996) pp. 66–84.

the whole subject has opened up; as one would expect, in such an interesting area – and one with such seemingly modern resonances – after nearly forty years.

Despite this, none of these studies has altered the basic picture I painted of turn-of-the-twentieth-century 'anti-imperial' ideology in 1968. Most of them elaborate and amplify what I wrote then, always usefully; very few, that I have noticed, take serious issue with any of it. The main exception to this concerns my analysis of Hobson's 'anti-imperial' thinking (those inverted commas, incidentally, are important: we shall return to this), with which a couple of subsequent historians have taken issue, mainly on the ground that I made too much of what I saw as a tension between the 'conspiratorial' side of his theory (imperialism as a capitalist 'plot'), and his 'structural' explanation (imperialism as the result of domestic market imbalances). David Long, for one, thinks these can be reconciled.[1] It is possible that I also rather underplayed the anti-Semitic aspect of the 'conspiratorial' part of the theory (p. 202n), though the best recent scholarship on this is *almost* as charitable to Hobson as I was. Crucially, none of it believes that anti-Semitism was at all central to his 'capitalist theory', or is a reason for distrusting that.[2] As for the 'conspiracy' *versus* 'structure' thing, I feel less qualified to pronounce on this than more expert economic historians, like Long and Peter Cain. But it does not really matter to my main argument. *Critics of Empire* sought to explain the *origins* of the major 'anti-imperial' ideologies of the early twentieth century. My purpose in distinguishing between

[1] David Long, *Towards a New Liberal Internationalism*, pp. 92–94.

[2] See Colin Holmes, 'J. A. Hobson and the Jews' in Holmes (ed.) *Immigrants and Minorities in British Society* (1978) pp. 125–57; and J. Allett, 'New liberalism, old prejudices: J. A. Hobson and the "Jewish question"', in *Jewish Social Studies*, vol. 49, no. 2 (Spring 1987) pp. 99–114. The burden of these pieces is that Hobson was guilty of attacking the Jews, sometimes in 'emotional' terms, as a personification of the kinds of economic activities of which he most disapproved; but that (a) any anti-Semitism exhibited here was casual, and secondary to his economic views; (b) it did not exhibit the characteristics of what Holmes calls 'classical' and Allett 'stereotypical' anti-Semitism; and (c) he ditched even this degree of anti-Semitism later: indeed, from the time of *Imperialism: A Study* (1902). My own original comment on this I now think was very superficial (as Holmes implies, p. 138). I may have been over influenced here by an interview I conducted with Hobson's daughter Mabel Scott, who assured me that Jews – and in particular the Liberal politician Herbert Samuel – were some of her father's 'best friends'.

these two kinds (as I saw them) of 'capitalist theory' in Hobson's case was to highlight two of the latter's major roots: his earlier 'underconsumptionist' theory (applied much more generally than to imperialism), and his personal experience in South Africa in 1899. These were both clearly crucial but also quite distinct influences.[1] That is so, whether the theory of imperialism to which they gave rise has this tension in it, or not.

The fact that the fundaments of my analysis seem to have weathered most of the later scholarship on these particular issues does not, of course, indicate that I was right on everything. One of the problems with this book, as I see now (and I think sensed even then), is that it is somewhat confined in its scope: both chronologically, to the 20-year period, only, between 1895 and 1914 (inclusive), though there is a sizeable preliminary chapter of earlier 'background'; and geographically, covering only 'British Radical attitudes to colonialism in *Africa*' (the book's original subtitle), and so scarcely mentioning, for example, India, which was by far the most important part of the British empire at this time, and had a powerful critical tradition of its own. That may appear an extraordinary omission. (Ireland is scarcely less so.) I remember my reasons for setting these limits – but they may not seem adequate. One was that I needed to keep my topic 'manageable' for Ph.D. purposes – a doctoral dissertation is supposed to be completed in three years – and two decades of debates over African colonialism was just about as much as I could manage in that time. (Remember, again, that this was mainly an unploughed field. And we had no xerox machines.) My research supervisor, the late great Ronald ('Robbie') Robinson, was mainly an Africanist, so he did not – so far as I can recall – object. It is interesting how at this time the Indian subcontinent and the other British colonies were nearly always studied separately, by different groups of scholars, just as they had been *administered* separately – by different government Offices – when they had been parts of the empire. Maybe this was a hangover from that time, and from the tradition of imperial history's being mainly written about and taught by ex-colonial hands. So, scarcely any Indian expert knew anything about Africa, and vice versa. Ireland was something else again, with its own specialists. That was one reason for this book's (literal) limitations.

---

[1] Crucial, that is, to the way his ideas were framed and presented after 1900. I make it clear that the essential features of his theory were already in place before the Boer War.

My *rationale*, however, was different. 1895–1914 was chosen because it appeared to me to be the period of the most virulent popular and ideological imperialism in Britain: when the 'imperial challenge' – to quote my new subtitle – was at its height. That made it a particularly interesting period in which to examine the *reaction* to this phenomenon, and also a discrete one: rather like studying the phenomenon of pacifism during – rather than before or after – a war. As I came to work on it, it also became clear to me that it was the very heat of the imperialism of the time that largely forged the distinctive kind of anti-imperialism that became so ubiquitous afterwards (Hobson, again); which made even more sense of this choice of dates. In fact I have few regrets today about that.

I have more regrets over my concentration on Africa; which also had its rationale, but – as I now think – a much weaker one. The excuse for that was that Africa was where all the 'imperialism' of the time seemed to be 'happening' then: the expansion, wars, annexations, experiments in 'native policy'; where most Britons' attention was most obviously focussed – in those 'jingo' demonstrations, for example, during the South African War; and where the public debate – in Parliament, journals, newspapers, meetings, various societies and pressure groups – was mainly concentrated. Joseph Chamberlain, the most charismatic imperialist of the age, and a major hate figure for my Critics, was chiefly interested in Africa. By contrast other imperial theatres – with the brief exception of China, *circa* 1898–1900 – scarcely featured. India seemed stable and placid. Ireland had passed through its major period of turmoil after 1886. The West Indies were simply stagnating. Events in the 'white' dominions, momentous though some of these may have been – Australian federation, for example – were simply not contentious. There was no heat there; nothing to draw me in like the heroics (or villainies) that were being acted out in the jungles and deserts of tropical Africa, or the thud and blunder (the Spoonerism a very apt one in this case) of the great Anglo–Boer War. Africa was also, of course, very much a centre of attention in the 1960s, when the book was written, with the main contemporary phase of decolonisation going on there (Nigeria 1960, Sierra Leone and Tanzania 1961, Uganda 1962, Kenya 1963 ...), and a bitter and very high-profile conflict over *apartheid* in the very country where the major crisis of that earlier period had taken place (South

Africa's withdrawal from the Commonwealth, 1961). (India and Ireland, again, had passed through all that.) This may have been one way in which the events of the 1960s impinged on my view of the 1890s and 1900s; events in Africa, however, rather than Vietnam.

This was short sighted. Ireland was still in fact bubbling during the 1900s, as I should have realised from reading the 'pro-Boer' speeches of Irish Nationalists in the British House of Commons during the South African War, which clearly did not stem from a purely objective view of the rights and wrongs of *that* conflict. India started showing serious signs of rebellion in the late 1900s, including terrorism, which on one occasion spilled over on to British soil (with the assassination of Sir William Curzon Wyllie in London in 1909). I do not mention that. Nor do I mention the terrible Indian famines of the later 1870s and 1890s, from which millions of poor Indians died: as important an event in human terms, surely, as the South African War (around 75,000 deaths in all); but then famines were not usually included in British histories of the *raj* in the 1960s – or else were treated as 'merely' natural catastrophes. That was not the case in the period covered by my book. Famines loomed large in the considerable critical literature directed against British rule in India in the 1880s and 1890s, much of it published for a British readership,[1] and reinforced by a number of committed Members of the British House of Commons, including the Indian Dadabhai Naoroji (MP for Central Finsbury from 1892 to 1895):[2] all of which, again, I ignored. Once more, part of the reason for this was that very few of the critics of Britain's Indian empire took any interest in Africa – that division of labour

---

[1] For example, James Geddes, *The Logic of Indian Deficit* (1871); William Digby, *Indian Problems for English Consideration* (1881); *India for the Indians – And for England* (1885); *British Rule in India: Has it Been, is it Still, a Good Rule for the Indian People?* (1891); and *'Prosperous' British India: A Revelation from Official Records* (1901); Dadabhai Naoroji, *Poverty of India* (1878), and *Poverty and Un-British Rule in India* (1901); and see Mira Matikkala, 'William Digby and the British radical debate on India from the 1880s to the 1890s' (M.Phil. dissertation, Cambridge, 2004).

[2] Other Indophile MPs included Charles Bradlaugh, John Seymour Keay, Samuel Smith, W. S. B. McLaren, and the brothers William and David Wedderburn. I have taken this information, and most of the rest of the material and references in this paragraph, from Mira Matikkala, 'Anti-imperialism, Englishness, and empire in late-Victorian Britain'.

again – which meant that I did not pick up on them from my African reading.[1] That is not a good enough excuse, however, and is a great shame, because much of the critical work on India was more sophisticated, and raised other issues, than that on Africa. The 'drain theory', for example – referring to the transfer of wealth from India to Britain under the *raj* – was a crucial brick in the total edifice of anti-imperialist ideology at that time.[2] It must have informed the African debate too. Readers of the present book should be aware of this, and allow for it while following me through these very Afro-centred ideas. My account of these, I think, still stands up and remains important; but it does not tell the whole story.

* * *

The other new factor that has come into the picture since the original publication of this book is the rise of what is called the 'New' imperial history. One of its objectives has been to show how much more affected by 'imperialism' British society was from the eighteenth to the twentieth centuries than many more parochial British historians used to assume; which of course is manna from heaven to non-parochial historians like myself, struggling for years on what used to be regarded as the margins of British history, but are now almost universally seen as essential to a full understanding of it. There are, I believe, a couple of problems with some recent products of this 'New' history. One is a rather loose and inclusive use of the word 'imperial', to cover any *foreign* feature in British society irrespective of whether it was the result of Britain's overseas dominance or not. (The idea of 'dominance' is surely essential to any useful definition of 'imperialism'.) The second is a tendency, especially among literary and cultural 'theorists', who do not usually know much history, to *assume* an imperial dimension to just about everything in British society, and so to impose an imperialist reading on it whether the empirical evidence for it is there or not. In the particular area of study covered by this book,

---

[1] Two exceptions were the eccentric radical Wilfred Scawen Blunt, and the Marxist H. M. Hyndman (who both feature in the book, but not their Indian interests).

[2] See Geddes's *Logic of Indian Deficit*; Digby, *'Prosperous' British India*; Naoroji, *Poverty and Un-British Rule* (all cited fully above); and B. H. Ganguli, *Dadabhai Naoroji and the Drain Theory* (1965).

one of the effects of this has been to downplay the significance of 'anti-imperialism' in British society, especially at this time (when the imperial mood seems to have been at its height), but also at all other periods (including, in one case, before the British empire was even born),[1] on the grounds that almost everyone in Britain *must* have been 'imbricated' with empire,[2] whether he or she knew it or not. Even 'anti-imperialists' were imperialists really. Edward Said, one of the chief proponents of this view, actually cited *Critics of Empire* in support of it.[3] But it is a fair point – or a fair possibility, at any rate. I was aware of it when I wrote *Critics of Empire*. That is why I called it that, rather than *The Anti-Imperialists*, which I toyed with at an early stage but soon jettisoned, when it became clear to me how problematical that expression was.

It was problematical because many of my 'Critics' were by no means out-and-out anti-imperialists: in the sense of condemning every kind of domination of one people over others, calling for imperial withdrawal in all circumstances, and abjuring every one of the attitudes that are commonly associated with imperialism, like the prejudice that their cultures were in some ways superior to others. Many of them simply wanted to *reform* the existing European empires: ensure that the Congo 'Free State' – to anticipate an example that features prominently in this book – was ruled with more concern for the welfare of its native inhabitants than was the case at that time under the (personal) suzerainty of the notorious King Leopold II of the Belgians; or that colonies generally were 'exploited' for their own people's interests rather than – or as well as – those of Western capitalists. Even Hobson held this latter view. (He was against 'native' peoples allowing their lands to go to waste.)[4] This was why I could not, in all conscience, use the word 'anti-imperialist' as a collective term for these

---

[1] Martin Green, *Dreams of Adventure, Deeds of Empire* (1979) p. 49 (reading 'imperialism' into Shakespeare's *Richard II*).

[2] 'Imbricated' is Catherine Hall's word, in *Civilizing Subjects: Metropole and Colony in the English Imagination, 1830–1867* (2002).

[3] Edward Said, *Culture and Imperialism* (1993) p. 291.

[4] I thought that I had nailed the misapprehension about Hobson's absolute 'anti-imperialism' in this book. In 1982, however, Julian Townsend could still state, probably correctly: 'That Hobson was an anti-imperialist is a widely held assumption', which consequently required nailing again in his own article, 'J. A. Hobson: anti-imperialist?' *International Review of History and Political Science*, vol. 19 (1982) pp. 28–41.

people; especially for the most interesting of them, who had the greatest influence on thinking and policy later on. Edward Said I think picked up the wrong messages from this. First, he thought it must indicate a general state of 'imperialism' among the British people as a whole: if even Hobson, the anti-imperialist *par excellence* – the great guru of the faith in later years – was flecked with it, then it followed that everyone else must be soaked in the stuff. Second, he assumed that if Hobson (and the others) did have 'imperialist' spots, it must have been for 'imperialistic' reasons. Try as they might, they simply could not throw off the dominant imperialist 'discourse' of the day. That showed just how powerful and pervasive the latter was. But that is not my reading of it.

In fact *Critics of Empire* said very little about the prevalence of anti-imperialism in Britain in the 1890s and 1900s, because that was not its subject. Other historians took that on later: most notably Richard Price, whose *An Imperial War and the British Working Class*, casting doubt on the ubiquity of 'popular' imperialism, came out in 1972;[1] and John Mackenzie, whose hugely influential *Propaganda and Empire*, approaching the same question from another angle and coming to an almost diametrically opposite conclusion, appeared in 1984.[2] If I had been inclined to offer an opinion on this question then, it would probably have been closer to Mackenzie's than to Price's: my brief allusions to the 'popular mood' in the book (for example, p. xi) imply that. Like my contemporary 'Critics', I was impressed by the *noise* that the pro-imperialist forces made around the time of the Boer War into thinking that they must have constituted the vast majority. I have changed my mind on that since. This is not to say that I now believe that *anti*-imperialists were in the majority. There were certainly more of them around then than there seemed to be – even by stricter criteria of 'anti-imperialism' than any that Hobson might fit. Said mentions two of them: Wilfred Scawen Blunt, and William Morris.[3] Others kept their heads down during the war,

---

[1] Richard Price, *An Imperial War and the British Working Class: Working-Class Attitudes and Reactions to the Boer War 1899–1902* (1972).

[2] John Mackenzie, *Propaganda and Empire: The Manipulation of British Public Opinion 1880–1960* (Manchester, 1984); which was closely followed by his edited volume *Imperialism and Popular Culture* (1986).

[3] Said, *Culture and Imperialism*, p. 291. Morris died before the Boer war.

out of a feeling of the hopelessness of their cause which may have been over-pessimistic (just as my own initial estimate was). Two examples are John Morley, the politician, despite repeated requests to him to lead the anti-war movement, which if he had responded positively to them might have encouraged more to brave the gunfire; and Herbert Spencer, the philosopher.[1] Scores of other Liberal MPs behaved in the same cowardly – or prudent? – way (below, p. 76). Beyond these, there were undoubtedly *millions* of Britons who were left entirely cold by the war, and by the phenomenon of imperialism – however defined – generally; not anti-imperialists in an activist sense – but then there were not all that many activist *imperialists* around, either – but more passively; simply *non*-imperialists: men and women, especially of the working classes, who had other priorities and value systems that crowded any kind of significant 'imperial' feeling out entirely.[2]

This should not be surprising, in a society that had long *believed* itself to be 'anti-imperialist'; against much of the evidence, it has to be said, and partly because of the particular baggage that came with the word during most of the nineteenth century (connected with the Napoleons), but still quite genuinely. For very many Britons (or English, at any rate) this was an essential part of their 'national identity': their liberalism, or libertarianism; the quality that was drummed into their heads in their schools as the factor that distinguished them from every other European people, and in which they were supposed to take most pride. This was what the imperialist J. R. Seeley was inveighing against in 1883, when he besought his compatriots to shut up about their wretched 'liberty' for a moment, and start taking pride in their overseas exploits.[3] Of course 'liberalism' can be harnessed to imperialism[4] – as can almost any political

[1] Matikkala, 'Anti-imperialism, Englishness, and empire', pp. 150–3, 165–9. I now think I gave too little space and credit to Spencer in my book.

[2] See chapters 6 and 9 of my *The Absent-Minded Imperialists: Empire, Society in Culture in Britain* (2004).

[3] J. R. Seeley, *The Expansion of England* (1883) pp. 7–10.

[4] There is an extensive literature on the 'imperialism' implicit in John Stuart Mill's works: for example, Eileen P. Sullivan, 'Liberalism and imperialism: J. S. Mill's defence of the British Empire', *Journal of the History of Ideas*, vol. 44 (1983) pp. 599–617; Lynn Zastoupil, *John Stuart Mill and India* (1994); Bhikhu Parekh, 'Liberalism and colonialism: a critique of Locke and Mill', in Jan Nederveen Pieterse and Bhikhu Parekh (eds) *The Decolonisation of Imagination: Culture, Knowledge and Power* (1995) pp. 81–98; Uday Singh Mehta, *Liberalism and Empire: A Study in Nineteenth Century British Liberal Thought* (1999); Martin I. Moir et al. (eds) *J. S. Mill's Encounter with India* (1999). Then, of course, there were the turn-of-the-century 'Liberal Imperialists', treated below, pp. 79–84.

idea one can think of (even 'anti-imperialism': *vide* the Spanish-American War); but in this case, in nineteenth-century Britain, it was widely supposed to be its antithesis (Richard Cobden, quoted below, pp. 14–15, is an example); and Disraeli's overt imperialism, when it burst onto the scene briefly in the 1860s, was seen as an alien, un-British, even 'Oriental' incubus (Disraeli's Jewish origins of course came in here),[1] to be resisted for that reason; and also because it was believed to directly threaten British 'liberties': what might be termed the 'Empire strikes back' effect. This was an old concern; it was Pitt the Elder, for example, who feared imperialism's bringing 'Asiatic principles of government' in its train: that is, to the metropole.[2] We need to be mindful of this powerful *anti*-imperial strain in nineteenth-century English patriotism. Patriotism (or nationalism) is often confused or conflated with imperialism, assumed to ride in harness with it; in Britain, however (certainly before Disraeli), they are more often found galloping in opposite directions.[3]

Socialism, which came into the picture (effectively) a little later, and spread significantly among both the skilled working classes and the middle-class intelligentsia in the 1880s and 1890s, was also largely resistant to the 'jingo' virus, though not completely so, as this book shows. These were powerful rival discourses to the imperial one. There were others too: certain versions of Christianity, for example (the more Christian ones). These rarely manifested themselves in general or catch-all 'anti-imperialist' movements or writings: but then, again, there were scarcely any *pro*-imperialist movements or writings then either.[4] 'Imperialism' was not an issue; not because it was widely accepted, but because the different phenomena that later became combined together under this rubric – overseas conquest, settlement, ruling alien people – were generally *disaggregated* at this time. Thus, there were powerful anti-aggression, pacifist and what Paul Laity

---

[1] Anthony S. Wohl, '"Dizzi-Ben-Dizzi": Disraeli as alien', *Journal of British Studies*, vol. 34 (1995) pp. 375–411.

[2] Quoted in Stanley Ayling, *The Elder Pitt* (1976) p. 367.

[3] On this see Miles Taylor, 'Imperium et Libertas?'; and Mira Matikkala, 'Anti-imperialism, Englishness, and empire in late-Victorian Britain', *passim*.

[4] The Royal Colonial Society, which later on became an imperialist pressure-group, certainly was not this in its early years: see Edward Beasley, *Empire as the Triumph of Theory: Imperialism, Information, and the Colonial Society of 1868* (2005).

calls 'pacific-ist' movements[1]– these were the ones most likely to use the 'i'-word then (as a term of abuse); anti-emigration writings (arguing that the poor should be given the means to live at home rather than be forced into exile), and anti-slavery and 'aborigines protection' societies, directed against the exploitation of non-Europeans. Essentially, these can be seen to have formed a powerful tradition of *effective* British anti-imperialism. That did not simply curl up and die when the imperial hurricane of the late 1890s came along.

What happened was that it ducked down behind the levees, briefly, and then stood up again when the storm seemed to have passed. The Boer War if anything strengthened it: first by tempering J. A. Hobson's great critical sword, to be brought out of its scabbard later (Peter Cain thinks much later);[2] and second by sickening many Britons with this particular manifestation of imperialism: the dog's dinner their army had made of it, for example, which introduced them to the idea that the empire might in fact be a source of weakness rather than strength (there were rumours of continental powers plotting to exploit Britain's woes in South Africa), and some of the 'atrocities' it had been forced to resort to in order to end it at all.[3] After it, very few imperial activists remained as confident as they had been at the height of the war – the time of the relief of Mafeking and the patriotic demonstrations that it had set off in Britain – of the enduring imperialism of most of their compatriots. (Hence, perhaps, their activism.) Some thought they could descry 'the vermin of anti-imperialism' spreading alarmingly

---

[1] Paul Laity, *The British Peace Movement, 1870–1914* (2001).

[2] Both Peter Cain, *Hobson and Imperialism*, pp. 161–4, and Ian Smith, in David Omissi and Andrew Thompson (eds.), *The Impact of the South African War*, p. 61, believe that the impact of *Imperialism: A Study* was not really felt until the later 1930s.

[3] See Peter Cain's and Ian Smith's chapters in David Omissi and Andrew S. Thompson, *The Impact of the South African War* (2002); and Paula Krebs, *Gender, Race and the Writing of Empire: Public Discourse and the Boer War* (Cambridge, 1999). Bertrand Russell was one person who turned against the war during the course of it, though he of course was hardly typical. One of the reasons he later gave was the scandal of the concentration camps, but David Blitz has found that he was in fact won over from 'liberal imperialism' when a French philosopher caught him out in a logical contradiction: 'Russell and the Boer War: from imperialist to anti-imperialist', *Russell: The Journal of Bertrand Russell Studies*, vol. 19 (2000) pp. 117–42.

among the lower orders then, threatening the very existence of the empire in the years to come. (This was 1909.)[1] If Britain was 'imperialistic' then, it was certainly not imperialistic enough for the likes of these.

Of course we cannot trust these alarmists, any more than we should rely on the word of those of the opposite political persuasion who had seen the vermin of *imperialism* scurrying over everything just a few years before. In both cases, one can see why they could have exaggerated. What the evidence suggests, however – but *not* the evidence presented in *Critics of Empire*, which, to repeat, was not concerned with this question – is that, firstly, most contemporary Britons were probably not very *enthusiastic* imperialists, and maybe not imperialists at all, in any sense, but unconcerned and apathetic, even in the years covered by this book, which were surely the most 'imperialistic' in British history; and, secondly, that those who were concerned about imperial matters were deeply divided over them. They were also divided over most of the other issues that have usually attached themselves to (modern) imperialism: race, capitalism, modernisation, 'civilisation', the rights and duties of peoples towards one another, and so on, where turn-of-the-century educated opinion was far more varied than one would imagine from the writings of those who only see one or two 'dominant' discourses there; possibly more open and varied, indeed, than today. (This was an amazingly fecund period in political thinking.) Imperialism, in other words, was a *controversial* issue in contemporary Britain. And the controversy was more complex than to permit it to be reduced to a simple 'imperial/anti-imperial' polarity. At least, it was to anyone who thought at all deeply about it; like my 'Critics'.

* * *

This was why Critics of empire could not be out-and-out anti-imperialists; and why I preferred writing about the former than the latter, who tended to be predictable and boring. It was easy enough to inveigh against imperialism then, just as it is today (I know: I do it). Just a moment's reflection, however, will show what an inadequate response that is, however good it may make

---

[1] Walter Frewen Lord, 'The creed of imperialism', *Nineteenth Century*, vol. 66 (1909) p. 33.

one feel. An obvious consideration a century ago was the presence of other predator-nations waiting in the wings to snaffle up any colony that any other country might let go of, and who might prove to be worse masters – this was most Britons' view – than Britain was. There was certainly some myopia involved here (about the relative beneficence of British rule), and some hypocrisy (with the argument being used merely as an excuse in many cases); but the problem was a genuine one, objectively. Predators did not even have to be *nations*. One of the inferences that was later drawn from Hobson's 'capitalist imperialist' theory (it is made less of in his version of it) was that you did not need to have a state involved for international capitalism itself to behave imperialistically; indeed, capitalist companies could be far more so if they were freed from formal colonial restraints (below, p. 231). In theory, at least, an imperial relationship with a country could protect it from 'capitalist imperialism' in this sense; in practice this did not happen very often, but it did sometimes. (The British Colonial Office's obstruction of Sir William Lever's plans for large-scale exploitation of Nigeria, after the revelation of the Congo scandals, described below – p. 280 – is one example.) The main point, however, is that simply taking away an empire – or even all of them, if that had been possible – would not guarantee the end of imperial*ism*. It might even make it worse. The true alternative to 'imperialism', therefore, was not 'anti-imperialism', but had to be something else. This was one of the problems my 'Critics' were struggling with.

The dilemma was well expressed by the Positivist Frederic Harrison in 1880. Harrison is a good example to take, because his anti-imperialist credentials appear solid from almost everything else he wrote and said on colonial questions. (He was a supporter of Egyptian nationalism, for example.) But this is how he saw the overall situation.

> We have no crude project for abandoning the empire today like a leaky ship, or handing it over to confusion or chance, as a prey to new conquerors. … We do not pretend that the blind conquests of former ages can be resettled in a day, or that we ought to fling off the tremendous responsibilities with which ages of history have burdened us. But this we do say: the heterogeneous empire must be regarded as a passing

responsibility, and not as a permanent greatness of our country. To increase its burdens and its limits should be a public crime. … In the meantime it must be governed in the sole interest of the countless millions who compose it … until the time shall arrive when, part by part, it may be developed into normal and national life of its own.[1]

That reads to me like a genuine case of 'reluctant imperialism', for non-imperialistic motives. There is much more of this in this book (for example p. 231). It does not apply to everyone covered here. Mary Kingsley, for example, was a far more positive imperialist than this. Hobson was much less of a formal imperialist – it is difficult to find any hint of enthusiasm for the thing anywhere in his writings – but he was certainly a believer in what today we would call 'globalisation', even if it had to be imposed on inefficient peoples (the industrialised world had a right to the products of the tropics, for example), so long as it was managed in a fair and humanitarian way (pp. 230–2). That – the 'imposition' part of it – arguably implied 'imperialism' of a sort. George Bernard Shaw, one of the most trenchant contemporary critics of imperialism, including on his own soil (Ireland), was nonetheless obviously genuinely fond of the somewhat eccentric plan he produced in 1900 for a *socialist* empire to replace the present capitalist one (p. 114). Some of the other hand-wringing – 'How I'd like us to get out. But we can't!' – may have been insincere. With people's motives, who can tell? But in view of the patriotic-liberal and pacific traditions that were still as 'dominant' in British society then as most other 'discourses' of the time, it is at least possible that most of the traces of 'imperialism' that can be discerned in these 'Critics' were not the results of any residual enthusiasm for empire, but because the Critics – unlike the extreme 'antis' – were rationally aware of the inherent contradictions of the 'anti' position.

A second real problem was the 'native question'. Put like that, it looks bad to modern eyes – the very word 'native', for example (though in truth that is not literally deprecatory but has come to seem so latterly because of the way it was used in colonial times); the generalisation that is implied by the use of the phrase (as if

---

[1] Frederic Harrison, 'Empire and humanity', *Fortnightly Review*, vol. 27 (1880) pp. 298–9, quoted in Mira Matikkala, 'Anti-imperialism, Englishness, and empire in late-Victorian Britain', p. 76. On Harrison's anti-imperialism, see ibid., pp. 22, 42, 218–27.

indigènes everywhere were a single category); and the indignity that being defined as a 'question' clearly involves. (The British did the same with 'the Irish Question'; until one clever historian thought of standing it on its head – 'Ireland's English Question' – to show them how it felt.)[1] But there was, again, a genuine problem here. There *were* peoples in the world which were not at the same level of material progress and sophistication as Europeans, Americans and some others; not necessarily to their moral detriment, in some eyes – the 'noble savage' ideal was one that persisted long into the nineteenth century (see below p. 32) – but in a way that, for a start, made them particularly vulnerable to our 'predators'. Some of them may also have been unhappy – starving, warring, diseased, tyrannised and so on; unless you believed in primitive idylls – that all these folk had been contentedly coexisting in Shangri-Las until the wicked Europeans happened upon them – which was another part of the 'noble savage' myth. Those that had been subjected to colonialism already had probably had their indigenous social and political structures so badly damaged as to make them even more vulnerable and unhappy. What was to be done with these? The traditional anti-imperialist reply had always been 'nothing': either on the grounds that there was nothing you *could* do for 'lower races', they were just too irredeemably backward or inferior – racism was as common a reason for anti-imperialism during the nineteenth century as it was for imperialism (Charles Dickens is an example)[2] – or because 'liberation' was sufficient on its own. Anti-slavers, for example, used to assume that the market would take good care of all their emancipated blacks. That no longer seemed plausible. Both J. A. Hobson and E. D. Morel, from different directions (South Africa and the Congo), had shown what the 'market' could mean, if it was not at least regulated, for vulnerable Africans. This brought the whole question of what was 'best' for native people into the spotlight.

Of course, speculating on what is 'best' for people 'below' you – in common with most other people at the time Hobson referred to them as the 'lower races', though we must be careful not to read

---

[1] Patrick O'Farrell, *Ireland's English Question: Anglo–Irish Relations 1534–1970* (1971).

[2] For example, his treatment of the character of Mrs Jellyby in *Bleak House*; and, for a more overt example, see 'The noble savage', *Household Words*, no. 168 (11 June 1853) pp. 337–9.

any necessary rac*ism* into that: the word was often used loosely then, and 'lower' could just mean less 'advanced' in one way or another, and not necessarily a bad way – is patronising, and so implicitly 'imperialistic', perhaps, by one possible definition of that very flexible term. It was also patronising, incidentally, when it involved the welfare of the working classes back home in Britain, who were the victims of capitalism who were nearest to hand at the turn of the twentieth century, and were speculated about in much the same way, though in this case, of course, without the 'i'-word coming into it. But that was no reason not to think and advise about these questions, particularly if it was you – your imperial nation, or privileged class – that had the power actually to make a difference. The basic question was this: how should 'weaker' people – 'natives' or the workers – be expected to adapt to *modernisation*: to the inexorable march, as it seemed at the time, of international capitalism everywhere, not always in the hands of the 'best' capitalists; which Hobson had shown to be the underlying 'taproot' of imperialism, and which had been the fundamental dynamic of British domestic economic and social progress for years? Did you allow them simply to go under, become its victims (if you did not take the utopian view of capitalism, like Cobden's: below pp. 14–15), on the grounds that this was 'inevitable', and that natives and workers deserved no better? Or did you trust the natives and workers to turn *against* capitalism eventually, as its 'internal contradictions' started biting, after the brief respite Lenin believed imperialism represented ('the highest stage of capitalism'), when the system would implode, and the socialist 'stage' of history take over? Or, thirdly, did you try to do something about it, either with a view to protecting the natives *from* modernity, or at least easing and adapting their transition to it? If the last – which was the one my Critics favoured – then it would clearly involve some degree of 'imperialism', or intervention by the 'greater' powers; and some difficult philosophical choices, between different kinds of adaptation, and about the extent to which indigenous, pre-modern cultures should be 'respected' during the process of it.

There are problems, of course, with 'respecting' native (or for that matter working-class) cultures: patronisation (again); the artificiality of it in some places, where indigenous cultures had already gone under, and so would need to be essentially reinvented; its convenience for those imperialists who merely wanted to use it to keep the natives 'down'; and the resentment it could give rise to among some of those natives who actually wanted to embrace the 'higher' culture. All these problems clearly attached to the colonial policy of 'indirect rule', which was one of the offshoots of this kind of thinking in the early twentieth century, as this book shows (see below, pp. 313–24). None of this, however, was the fault of any of the Critics who explored these ideas initially; nor does it automatically undermine the latters' *theoretical* validity. On the 'patronisation' issue: yes, Mary Kingsley's admiration for West African cultures smacks of this, but she was patronising towards her own gender too (see below, p. 152); and I defy anyone to read Hobson's and Ramsay MacDonald's thoughts about culture and 'civilisation' quoted here (pp. 181, 187–8), and find any of that in them. If you believed that capitalist imperialism (in the form practised then) was not only bad for Britain, but also damaging to its subjects; and if you were at all concerned about the latter – not content, that is, to allow the process to continue, either because natives deserved what was coming to them, or in the hope of the socialist revolution their extreme exploitation might provoke: the two *most* anti-imperialist approaches to this – then you needed to give some sympathetic thought to these matters, mildly 'imperialistic' though that might make you seem.

The great problem with using 'imperialistic' methods to do 'good' for more vulnerable peoples, however, was that imperial nations could not be trusted with this task. That was Hobson's and MacDonald's answer to those who argued for a 'liberal' imperialism in their own time: that however well meaning the call for it might be (and MacDonald was generous in acknowledging that it could be this), it was (a) not the existing imperial powers that were necessarily the best fitted for this work: they were there because they were the strongest, not because they were the most enlightened; (b) too easily hijacked by other interests with less elevated (more capitalist) designs; and (c) unlikely to accord to other cultures the 'respect' that was due to them. (Below pp. 185–9.) Hobson was also greatly concerned about the 'empire strikes back' effect: what he feared was the reactionary impact that imperialism was having back home. 'Jingoism' was a sign of that (see pp. 202–3). This was why his ultimate answer to these questions was neither to sanction what was called 'liberal' imperialism then, nor to abandon the idea of intervention by the strong in the affairs of the weak entirely (the anti-imperialist solution), but a 'third way': to spread the responsibility for that intervention, by internationalising it. This became his next major task in this field: helping (theoretically) towards the creation of a *world* government, or 'League of Nations', that could – as well as preserving the peace – undertake these duties disinterestedly. That project, however, came outside the scope of the present work.[1]

* * *

In the nearly forty years since *Critics of Empire* was originally published, these latter aspects of my Critics' thought have received less attention than Hobson's famous attack on 'capitalist imperialism'. One of the reasons for this was the leading place that the 'capitalist theory' came to take in the major ideological debate of the Cold War years. Another may have been that the question of the adaptation of 'weaker' peoples to the 'modern world' seemed to be taken out of the hands of the 'stronger' peoples when the former were progressively decolonised during those forty years – transformed into nation states of their own – leaving the problem now theirs to cope with. Both these circumstances have changed since. The end of the Cold War had a surprising effect on the 'capitalist theory': making it *less* contentious, less necessary to counter it, that is, than in the days when it was stained by its association with an alien and threatening political creed; and so more widely accepted, at least in broad outline. When the latest major explanation for British imperialism was published in the 1990s, rehabilitating Hobson to a great extent – Cain and Hopkins's 'gentlemanly capitalist' theory – no one attacked *that* on the grounds that it was a dangerously 'left-wing' line.[2] At the same time, the idea that the national independence that most colonies had now won from their old masters would automatically safeguard them against modernisation and effective domination, by those masters or by others, or would put everything right for them in other ways – always challenged by those (Lefties) who regarded 'economic imperialism' as something that did not necessarily require the formality of a political bond

[1] See Hobson's *Towards International Government*, and *A League of Nations* (both 1915); and Bernard Porter, 'Hobson and internationalism', in Michael Freeden (ed.) *Reappraising J. A. Hobson: Humanism and Welfare* (1990), pp. 167–81.

[2] Peter Cain and A. G. Hopkins, *British Imperialism: Innovation and Expansion 1688–1914*, and *Crisis and Deconstruction 1914–1990* (1993).

for it to work – was further undermined when it came to be
realised how little independence any country could really enjoy, in
the face of the trend that now went under the name of 'globalisation'.
'Imperialism' did not stop just because empires seemed to. This, of
course, was what the old 'pure' anti-imperialists had always been
blind to. It is also why the ideas whose geneses are explored in this
book – Hobson's, Morel's and the rest – are still 'relevant', a
hundred years on.

If, that is, *Lenin* isn't right. Lenin needs to be brought in here,
briefly, because his theory of imperialism is so often conflated with
Hobson's (the 'Hobson–Lenin theory'), but in fact was different
in at least one crucial respect. It is well known that Lenin got his
'capitalist theory of imperialism' from Hobson (at least in part).
He then however added a Marxist gloss to it, by claiming that
imperialism was a *necessary and inevitable* outcome of capitalism,
whereas Hobson had always seen it as a matter of choice (see
below, pp. 190–1). This is significant, because of its bearing on
what could be 'done'. Hobson believed that by modifying capitalism at home – distributing wealth more widely, for example,
to boost domestic purchasing power – the need for and consequently the incidence of aggressive imperialism would lessen.
Lenin on the other hand thought that the inherent and ultimately
self-destructive dynamic of the capitalist 'system' made that
impossible. Hobson's belief in 'reforming' capitalism also
extended, incidentally, to domestic policy – indeed, this was
where it started out (see pp. 168–72); it is this that made him a
'New Liberal' and (in Lenin's derisive word) a 'bourgeois', and
later a supporter of Ramsay MacDonald's moderate Labour Party,
rather than a communist. He was, in fact, a Keynesian before
Keynes's time (as the latter acknowledged: below, p. 169). In the
1960s, when the present book was written, most of us – certainly
on the moderate British left, but also much more widely than that
– thought he was right. Both at home and abroad, capitalism and
imperialism had shown themselves capable of being reformed or
modified – through the welfare state, for example; the granting
of self-government to colonies; and the 'Commonwealth': a
socialist or at least 'social' ideal if ever there was one – in time to prevent their both blowing up in our faces. By the same token, Lenin,
with all his talk of the inevitability of ever-increasing capitalist and
imperialist exploitation, seemed to have been discredited. But that

was then. Now, on the occasion of the reissue of this book, things look very different. 'Reformist' solutions to the intrinsic problems of capitalism are collapsing all over the world. Red-in-tooth-and-claw capitalism is stalking the land again. It is ironic that the collapse of 'Marxist' regimes in eastern Europe should have given rise to this: the vindication of the Marxist prediction of the inexorable march of capitalism, and, arguably, imperialism; though not its prediction of the (revolutionary) end of this process – yet.

But that may be too pessimistic (or optimistic, if you like what is happening). We should never be too impressed by the fashions of our own day; historians in particular should always be aware of the transience of the 'inevitable' – or irreversible trends that *are* then reversed: like the 'imperialist' one that appeared so unstoppable to its opponents round about 1900, discouraging them so mightily, but then faded away. If Lenin was wrong, and what seems at present to be the 'end of history' proves to be merely a temporary setback,[1] then it may be worth looking at some of these old Critics again, to see what guidance they might have to offer the present day.

For the present does seem to suggest some intriguing parallels with what was being done and said a hundred years ago. The big events of those years – and the ones that had most impact on the critical theories of empire that form the subject of this book – were the British invasion of Egypt in 1881, and the Anglo–Boer War of 1899–1902. Several historians have noted the uncanny superficial resemblances between the first of these events, especially, and the American–British invasion of Iraq in 2003 (both to remove a tyrant, both intended to be temporary but in fact exacerbating local nationalism and Muslim fundamentalism, so that the invading countries were dragged in further. ... The only missing element in the Egyptian case is the chimera of 'weapons of mass destruction'). More generally, American 'hegemony' can be seen as the direct successor to British imperialism, with the differences often claimed here being narrower than they are usually perceived – for example, Britain *preferred* 'informal', commercial dominance, just as the US does. 'Globalisation' is simply 'free trade' under another name.[2] *Plus ça change, plus c'est* virtually *la même chose*. Surely Hobson and Co. must still have something to say about this, from beyond their graves?

---

[1] Francis Fukuyama, *The End of History and the Last Man* (1992).

[2] On this, see the long final footnote to Peter Cain, *Hobson and Imperialism*, p. 284.

In fact it only needs the substitution of a word or two – 'oil' for 'gold', for example – to make it seem almost as though these Critics were writing in and for the present day. The 'capitalist theory' of imperialism is clearly just as plausible now as it was then (which is not to say it is necessarily right). Instead of citing Gladstone's investment portfolio in 1881 (largely Egyptian stocks), we can point to Bush and Cheney's oil interests. There are obvious modern equivalents to the military–industrial interests and the great press barons Hobson singled out for blame as early as 1902. His writings on the 'empire strikes back' effect – political and social reaction at home – seem as applicable to the USA today as they were to Britain then. Even the Jews are back: as much part of the present-day radical critique of the Iraq War – see John Mearsheimer's and Stephen Walt's famous 2006 piece on 'The Israel Lobby'[1] – as they were of Hobson's early strictures on the power of Jewish finance in South Africa. 'Methods of barbarism' was a phrase that could as easily be applied to Abu Ghraib, Guantanamo Bay and aerial bombing, as it was to the farm-burning, concentration camps and (alleged) shooting of Boer prisoners that the British Liberal leader was so appalled by in 1901.[2] Ramsay MacDonald's wise words on cultural relativity – 'any civilisation has some political, social or ethical excellence which in that respect may place it superior to the propagandist's [i.e. imperialist's] civilisation itself' (below, p. 187) – cannot be repeated too often to people who hold that, for example, the only 'model to the world' is the American one. (That is George W. Bush.)[3] And the 'liberal imperial' excuse for empire, first uttered by Lord Rosebery in the early 1900s (see pp. 79–80), and now revived by a number of modern newspaper columnists and even historians in order to persuade the USA to shoulder its imperial responsibilities more

---

[1] John Mearsheimer and Stephen Walt, 'The Israel Lobby', *London Review of Books*, vol. 28 no. 6 (23 March 2006); and later issues, for the furore occasioned by that.

[2] This is the phrase Sir Henry Campbell-Bannerman used in the House of Commons on 14 June 1901 to describe Kitchener's tactics in the war; quoted in J. A. Spender, *The Life of the Rt Hon. Sir Henry Campbell-Bannerman* (1923), vol. 1, p. 336. On rereading *Critics of Empire*, I was surprised to find I had not quoted it there. In the context of the time, it was a brave statement.

[3] Speech to B'nai B'rith International, on 28 August 2000.

'formally',[1] could be said to be just as amenable now to the objections that were made to it by our Critics then.

Much of the force of these Critics' opposition to 'liberal imperialism', then and now, derives from the fact that, unlike the 'purer' anti-imperialists, they took on board the case *for* it as well. Both Hobson and MacDonald, for example, acknowledged, firstly, that there *were* problems in the world that could only be settled by outside intervention – the 'native question' then, 'failed states' today; and, secondly, that you could have honourable motives for wishing to intervene for this sort of purpose: insofar as the 'underlying spirit of imperialism' was the wish to do 'good' for people, MacDonald wrote, it 'cannot not be condemned'. 'Morality is universal'. (Below, p. 185.) National 'sovereignty' did not come into it, because international society was interdependent, just as MacDonald (as a socialist) believed domestic societies were. That was the case for liberal imperialism. It is, in fact, very close indeed to the case that British prime minister Tony Blair made for 'humanitarian intervention', in a famous speech in Chicago in April 1999,[2] which was widely read at the time as a kind of 'imperialism', and may be so (it depends on your definition). There can be little doubt that Blair's *motives* for this would have been applauded by MacDonald. (Coincidentally, MacDonald was of course one of Blair's predecessors as Labour prime minister. This is very much a 'Labour' thing.)

But MacDonald would not have stopped there. OK, he would have said – at least, this is what he said around 1900 – your motives might be of the best; these are good theoretical justifications for 'liberal imperialism': but *it rarely turns out like that*. Powers that find themselves in a position to exert this kind of authority in the world are not usually the ideal ones to do it sensitively (often the opposite); and their better sides are too easily hijacked by disreputable special interests in any case. (Below, pp. 185–8.) Hobson would have added his fears of the 'empire strikes back' effect; others would point to the *atrocities* that

---

[1] See for example Niall Ferguson, *Empire: How Britain made the Modern World* (2003) and *Colossus: The Rise and Fall of the American Empire* (2004), taken both together, and with numerous of his articles in the American press; and the American commentators quoted in my *Empire and Superempire: Britain, America and the World* (2006), pp. 4–5.

[2] This speech can be found on the internet, at www.pbs.org/newshour/bb/international/jan–june99/blair doctrine4–23.html.

so often seem to accompany even the best-intentioned imperialisms. These were the clinching arguments against unilateral forms of imperialism, and the reason why most of these constructive Critics insisted that if 'humanitarian intervention' were thought to be necessary, it would need to be implemented not by single nations, but *internationally*. This is clearly what Tony Blair intended originally – it is why he pushed the US president to seek a new UN resolution to legitimise the invasion of Iraq in March 2003, for example; but then, when that failed, he decided to back the unilateralist United States regardless.[1] The outcomes of this, in Iraq and elsewhere, could be said to bear out MacDonald's and Hobson's warnings, almost to the letter. This is why those warnings, and much of the rest of these Critics' agenda, still have a resonance today, a hundred years after they were uttered, and forty years after I first wrote about them. Hence the republication of this book.

* * *

I have few acknowledgments to add here to the list that appeared at the end of my original Preface. Professor Roger Louis and Dr Lester Crook are the main ones: the former for suggesting the book's republication (and for his kind help and advice throughout), and the latter for taking it on. It was Lester who also came up with the new subtitle. I wrote this Introduction in the splendid environment of the University of Sydney, where I was teaching at the time, at the invitation of Professor Robert Aldrich. I should like to thank him and my other colleagues in the Sydney History Department warmly both for their society and for their intellectual stimulation; my terrific new Australian students for very similar reasons; the University of Sydney Fisher Library for its great resources and friendly help; and my partner Kajsa for – everything.

Enskede, Stockholm
February 2007

---

[1] The Iraq invading force was called a 'coalition', of course ('of the willing'); but it is clear that the USA made all the original decisions unilaterally, and the 'coalition' was merely of powers that went along with these. This is not 'internationalism' in the normal sense of the word.

Abbreviations

A.P.S.	Aborigines Protection Society
A.R.	*Annual Register*
A.S.G.P.	A. S. Green Papers
B.M. Add. MS.	British Museum Additional Manuscript
B.S.A.C.	British South Africa Company
C.B.P.	Campbell-Bannerman Papers
C.F.S.	Congo Free State
C.H.B.E.	*Cambridge History of the British Empire*
C.H.J.	*Cambridge Historical Journal*
C.O.	Colonial Office
C.R.	*Contemporary Review*
C.R.A.	Congo Reform Association
C19th	*The Nineteenth Century*
D.N.B.	*Dictionary of National Biography*
E.D.M.P.	E. D. Morel Papers
E.H.R.	*Economic History Review*
H.G.P.	Herbert (Viscount) Gladstone Papers
H.L.R.O.	House of Lords Record Office
H. of C.	House of Commons
I.J.E.	*International Journal of Ethics*
I.L.C.	Imperial Liberal Council
I.L.P.	Independent Labour Party
J.A.A.	*Journal of African Administration*
J.A.H.	*Journal of African History*
J.A.I.	*Journal of the Anthropological Institute of Britain and Ireland*
J.A.S.	*Journal of the African Society*
J.H.I.	*Journal of the History of Ideas*
J.H.P.	John Holt Papers
J.H.S.N.	*Journal of the Historical Society of Nigeria*
J.M.H.	*Journal of Modern History*

J.P.E.	*Journal of Political Economy*
J.R.S.A.	*Journal of the Royal Society of Arts*
L.R.C.	Labour Representation Committee
L.S.E.	London School of Economics
M.G.	*Manchester Guardian*
N.L.I.	National Library of Ireland
P.D.	Parliamentary Debates ('Hansard')
	[e.g. 4 P.D. 53, c. 1234 = Parliamentary Debates, fourth series, volume 53, column 1234]
P.P.	Parliamentary Paper
P.S.Q.	*Political Science Quarterly*
P.R.	*The Progressive Review*
S.-D.F.	Social-Democratic Federation
T.U.C.	Trades Union Congress

I

Introductory:
The Nineteenth-century Legacy

I. INTRODUCTION

IN 1900 the British Empire was approaching its zenith, ostentatiously and noisily. Imperial expansion was becoming more difficult – there were too many people at the table, and the food was running short. Soon there would be nowhere left to expand into. But there was no serious prospect of contraction either: the civilised nations were overspilling – economically and politically, if not physically – into the waste places of the earth, by some sort of natural law, like air drawn into a vacuum; and if Britain were to opt out of the process then others were eager to take her place. It seemed inevitable; the 'backward' countries were destined to come within Europe's embrace, willingly or unwillingly, and they had better be English than French or German.

So it appeared to many men at the time, and they accepted their fate, cheerfully or otherwise. But not everyone; in Britain the imperial theme had always had its counterpoint of protest, and the critics were as vocal in 1900 as ever before. The Boer War threw each side into exaggerated relief: the imperialists with their Union Jacks and their bluster, the Little Englanders with their white flags and their moral scruples. The battle between them was, in its own way, as bitter as the military one in South Africa, and as unequal. The anti-imperialists could make no kind of impression on the forces arrayed against them; for the time being, imperialism was a little too fervent. But the dissatisfaction was there. England was by no means unanimous in her imperialism.

Late nineteenth-century imperialism generally meant what was happening in Africa; this was where the imperial drama of the

1880s and 1890s was acted out. In a few short years the continent was carved up and distributed among the European powers, its boundaries determined by the strength and interests of its de-spoilers. 'Spheres of influence' were drawn on maps, and colonial officers and troops sent out to make them secure. The work of 'civilising the native' and 'developing' his country began in earnest.

For imperialists this was a political necessity and a moral duty; for the dissentients it raised questions of grave and disturbing import. The fundamental problem was this: what was, and what should be, the position of tropical countries and peoples in rela-tion to the industrial civilisation of the West? The question could be answered at a number of different levels. For the extreme anti-imperialists – the critics most in evidence during the Boer War years – the solution was simple. Imperial expansion was morally wrong and the process must be reversed. The question of *how* to rule colonies was therefore an irrelevance. There was no point in discussing what to do with the money before the chips were gathered in, particularly if you were against gambling. And in any case, the methods of colonial government were points of detail, of technique; you learnt them at Haileybury or apprenticed to a District Commissioner, like learning how to drive a tram. All that mattered was imperialism and its destruction. This was the Little Englander view, idealistic and impractical perhaps, but consistent and passionately adhered to. For others the problem was more complex. Imperial expansion in Africa, they said, was possibly regrettable, but it was a fact. It had to be explained in more sophisticated terms before it could be effectively combated, and in the meantime it necessitated a careful rethinking of basic assumptions about the dissemination of culture and civilisation. The methods of colonial administration were more controversial than those of tram-driving, and there was room here for construc-tive criticism. The number of people who felt this way was very small. Not all of them could be dubbed 'anti-imperialists', but all were deeply critical of the way the Empire was being run. They went to make up that body of disaffection which is the subject of the present study. Their influence was negligible in 1900. But they were to come into their own during the following years, gaining allies on the anti-imperial front, and influence even among those who directed imperial policy.

It was largely by these critics that the stage was set for the imperial debate of the twentieth century. The 'economic theory' of imperialism, which ascribes colonial expansion to capitalist exploitation, was their creation. Afterwards reiterated or embellished by a succession of writers from Lenin to Nkrumah, it has now come to be accepted in one form or another by the whole communist world and, to a lesser extent, by a significant minority outside. Whenever there is discussion of imperialism, whether as a historical or a modern phenomenon, the economic theory, though it may be disputed, cannot be ignored. This was, perhaps, their most important – certainly their most notorious – contribution; but it was not the only one. The imperialism which was forced, in the twentieth century, to come to terms with nationalism in Asia and Africa was itself the product of change. It was more self-consciously philanthropic than it had been before, though often its philanthropy was misdirected. For whatever reason (perhaps because they foresaw the inevitable), colonial secretaries and administrators had begun to take a more constructive interest in the welfare of their African and Asian wards, and such phrases as 'indirect rule', 'trusteeship', 'native paramountcy' and 'local self-government' became the commonplaces of discussion and sometimes the orthodoxy of policy. Many of these new approaches to the problems of colonial government stemmed from, or were anticipated by, the imperial criticism of the 1890s and 1900s. Shouted down at the time, or else ignored, its influence in the long run was comparable, at least, with that of the jingoes.

All this came out of a reaction to a specific situation: to what was called the 'New Imperialism' of the 1890s. What imperialism is or was is not our concern. It is an ambiguous and contentious term, whose meaning at any one time is determined by its etymological history, by the political circumstances in which it is used and to which it is popularly applied, and by the interpretation which those who write about it wish to give it. As a policy which is accepted and actively pursued by a government in power it can, perhaps, be defined comparatively easily by its concrete application, and as such it leaves less room for disagreement and confusion. But as a word used by men who oppose or criticise it, or who advocate it in opposition to a non- or insufficiently imperialistic ministry – when it is employed as an abstract idea or a doctrine – it becomes surrounded and obscured by various accretions which may seem to have little relevance to the thing itself. In such circumstances it can be a policy, an emotion, a slogan, or a combination of all three, and the simple definition becomes lost in a medley of apparently extraneous factors. If we had to say what imperialism was, then we should wish to extricate it from such factors in the interests of clarity. But we are not interested in imperialism *per se*, nor even in anti-imperialism: only in what men *understood* by these terms in so far as this affected their response to certain of its specific manifestations. So the extraneous factors will have to remain, for they were real to contemporaries, sometimes more real than the 'facts' of Empire. It was a thing called the New Imperialism which provoked men to protest; and the form their protest took depended largely on how they saw and interpreted it.

It depended also on a number of other factors. Ideas have a curious and complex genesis. Sometimes they are inherited from past generations, in which case they usually undergo transformation in the process of transmission from one generation to the next. The form can be the same, but the content different; or the essence of an idea can persist, but under a new name. Always ideas are carried on – or revived, or reinterpreted, or invented or discarded – according to how far they fit the conditions, fulfil the needs, of an age or a group of men within it. These considerations all have to be investigated if we are to explain the genesis, and thereby the nature, of late-nineteenth-century critical theories about empire: firstly the inheritance from the past, and the way it was distorted; then the political situation of the time and the particular features of it which stimulated certain lines of thinking; and lastly the individual preconceptions and preferences which predisposed men to pursue these lines rather than others. These things combined and interacted to produce the distinctive imperial ideologies of *fin-de-siècle* Radicalism. But at their centre, furnishing a large and fruitful credit-account of ideas and attitudes for Radicals to draw on, there was the legacy left by their ancestors: and this must be our first concern.

II. ANTI-IMPERIALISM AND THE 'LIBERAL TRADITION'

Like all systems of thought, the imperial theories of 1900 were built on foundations whose materials were familiar, sometimes recast to serve new functions, but in great part quarried from the ruins of older structures. The Radicals' plundering was selective, and very often they misinterpreted the past. An outline of the historical precedents and sources for their theories, therefore, will by no means furnish a balanced description of imperial attitudes in the nineteenth century: we shall be concerned more for the past as it appeared to Radicals than the past as it really was. These Radicals went for ideological sustenance to three main traditions. The first was anti-imperialism itself, the separatist doctrines which grew out of the events immediately preceding American independence and provided a large corpus of arguments, chiefly economic, for later Radicals to use. But the first British Empire was different in many ways from the second, and criticism of late-nineteenth-century imperialism was to a great extent directed against phenomena which did not seem to attach themselves to the earlier variety; so we must also consider certain other features of the Radical outlook which originated independently of any controversy about empire – the pacifist and internationalist doctrines of Cobden and Bright. Thirdly, there was the humanitarian strain in eighteenth- and nineteenth-century opinion – not only independent of the anti-imperialist tradition, but often incompatible with it, yet contributing in large measure to the views of later colonial critics. These three systems of thought together comprised the nineteenth-century inheritance of twentieth-century Radicalism.

The first was particularly tenacious in Radical thought. Since the middle of the seventeenth century the profitability of overseas 'plantations' had aroused a certain amount of scepticism among a small minority of English writers.[1] It was not, however, until serious doubts were cast on the wisdom of the mercantile system in the later eighteenth century that any strong exception was taken to the colonies by polemicists. 'It was then', says one historian, 'that British anti-imperialism had its origin.'[2] During the second half of the century increasing numbers of pamphleteers and propagandists were to be found advocating the emancipation of the American colonies. Men like Joseph Priestley, John Cartwright and Richard Price argued that their retention was incompatible with civil liberties and human rights: 'It is high time', wrote Cartwright, 'that we opened our eyes to the unintentional encroachments we have been making upon the liberties of mankind.'[3] But more popular, and more telling, were those economic arguments which found their 'most voluble and most consistent' expression in the writings of Josiah Tucker, Dean of Gloucester,[4] and their most impressive exposition in Adam Smith's *Wealth of Nations*. The case put forward by these men was aimed chiefly at the mercantile system. But it was a case which could be adapted, later, to a non-mercantilist empire.

Many of the points they made were inapplicable to a later situation. Tucker's worried concern about the drain on the population of the mother-country could have little meaning in an age when the problem was rather how to dispose of a surplus population than how to find more. Similarly, the fears expressed by retentionists, and which Tucker and others spent much of their time countering, about naval stores and colonial manufacturing rivalry were irrelevant to the late-nineteenth-century

[1] See Richard Koebner, *Empire*, pp. 65–6; and Klaus E. Knorr, *British Colonial Theories 1570–1850*, pp. 59–62.
[2] R. L. Schuyler, 'The Rise of Anti-Imperialism in England', in *P.S.Q.*, vol. 37, no. 3 (Sept 1922), p. 440.
[3] Quoted in Koebner, op. cit. p. 201. See also Schuyler, art. cit. pp. 456–9 (on Cartwright and Price), and Knorr, op. cit. pp. 195–200 (on Price and Priestley).
[4] Knorr, op. cit. p. 117; and see also Koebner, op. cit. pp. 197–9, and Schuyler, art. cit. pp. 440–51.

Empire, as was Tucker's warning that retention was facilitating the spread of 'the Contagion of Republicanism'.[1] All these things applied exclusively to the 1770s and to the specific problem of America. Yet the economic case which Adam Smith in particular advanced against the Navigation Acts, and which formed the corner-stone of his argument, did not lose its validity when the Navigation Acts were repealed. Smith was concerned to demonstrate that from the point of view of national self-interest the possession of colonies (though not colonial trade itself) was unprofitable and unbusinesslike. By diverting more capital to the colonies than in the ordinary course of things would go there, they were artificially encouraging a trade which was of less value to the nation than that European and Mediterranean commerce which was more 'natural' to her, and the returns on which were more frequent and hence more productive. The colonial system rendered the country precariously dependent upon one or two unnaturally bloated enterprises; by raising the rate of profit it discouraged parsimony and thus the accumulation of capital; and in the sole interest of a minority it cost the taxpayer millions of pounds, for civil and military establishments in the colonies, on which he would see no return.[2] 'Under the present system of management, therefore', Great Britain derived 'nothing but loss from the dominion which she assumes over her colonies'.[3]

The imperial annexations of the 1880s and 1890s were not bolstered in the same way by a mercantilist system. Yet they were essentially artificial stimuli to colonial trade, and were beset by many of the same drawbacks which attended mercantilism: exclusive companies, imperfect competition, and a kind of preference in the guise of expensive civil and military establishments, the whole benefiting the few at the expense of the many. The same gibe which Adam Smith applied to America could be applied later to East and West Africa: 'England purchased for some of her subjects, who found themselves uneasy at home, a great estate

[1] Knorr, op. cit. p. 124.
[2] Adam Smith, *Wealth of Nations*, bk. IV, ch. vii, pt. iii.
[3] Ibid. (Everyman ed., 1910), vol. ii, p. 112.

in a distant country.'¹ That the transaction was not hedged about to the same extent with monopolistic regulations was of no special import: Smith had laid the foundations for all those subsequent Liberal arguments which pleaded emancipation on the grounds of national economic self-interest.

The loss of the American colonies, and the fact that – for whatever reason – trade did not seem to suffer by their loss,² served to strengthen anti-imperialist sentiment.³ The school of 'Political Economy' nurtured on the *Wealth of Nations* followed Adam Smith's lead in attacking the colonial system,⁴ and Philosophic Radicalism kept closely in step. Jeremy Bentham pulled out all the anti-imperialist stops in his pamphlet *Emancipate Your Colonies*, written in 1793 to demonstrate to the French nation 'the Uselessness and Mischievousness of distant Dependencies to an European State'.⁵ They were costly in time of peace, and would be even more so in the event of war.⁶ They did not benefit commerce, for 'it is *quantity of capital*, not *extent of market*, that determines the quantity of trade'.⁷ Their subjection was contrary to political morality: 'You choose your own government: why are not other people to choose theirs? Do you seriously mean to govern the world, and do you call that *liberty*? What is become of the rights of men?'⁸ Furthermore, he claimed somewhat cynically, the possession of colonies was attended by the evil of slavery and the bitter controversies which went with it: 'emancipation throws all these heartburnings and difficulties out of doors'.⁹ In sum,

> give up your colonies – because you have no right to govern them, because they had rather not be governed by you,

¹ Ibid. p. 111.
² Schuyler, 'Rise of Anti-Imperialism', *P.S.Q.*, pp. 460–1. Even Adam Smith had predicted *some* short-term ill-effects: *Wealth of Nations*, ii 103.
³ Schuyler points out that the Napoleonic Wars temporarily checked this process (op. cit. p. 464). See also C. A. Bodelsen, *Studies in Mid-Victorian Imperialism*, ch. i.
⁴ Knorr, *British Colonial Theories*, ch. viii.
⁵ Printed in Bowring (ed.), *The Works of Jeremy Bentham*, vol. iv, pp. 407–18.
⁶ Ibid. p. 410.   ⁷ Ibid. p. 411.   ⁸ Ibid. p. 408.   ⁹ Ibid. p. 416.

because it is against their interest to be governed by you, because you get nothing by governing them, because you cannot keep them, because the expense of trying to keep them would be ruinous, because your constitution would suffer by your keeping them, because your principles forbid your keeping them, and because you would do good to all the world by parting with them.[1]

Five years later Bentham was to modify his stand a little. In *A Manual of Political Economy* he rehearsed once more the economic arguments against colonies; but, he said,

> it is necessary to examine what is due to colonial establishments – to a family which has been created, and which ought not to be abandoned. Can they maintain themselves? Will not their internal tranquillity be interrupted? Will not one class of the inhabitants be sacrificed to another? for example, the free men to the slaves, or the slaves to the free men? Is it not necessary that they should be protected and directed, in their condition of comparative weakness and ignorance? Is not their present state of dependence their safeguard against anarchy, murder, and pillage?[2]

The conflict between national self-interest and national responsibility – between economy and humanitarianism – was in later years to prove a constant source of difficulty for anti-imperialist Radicals. For the moment, however, Political Economy gained the upper hand. Adam Smith's profit-and-loss assessment of colonial ties found devoted champions in the persons of Richard Cobden and John Bright, whose writings and speeches in turn provided inspiration for the Radicals of a later age.

Soon after Cobden and Bright arrived on the scene, the battle against mercantilism was fought and won. Although it found

---

[1] Ibid. p. 417.

[2] Bentham, *A Manual of Political Economy* (1798), in Bowring, *Works of Jeremy Bentham*, iii 56. In the same work Bentham extols the value of colonies 'as a means of relieving the population – of preventing its excess, by providing a vent for those who find themselves over-burthened upon their native soil . . .'.

some defenders during the 1840s,[1] on the whole the unprofitability of the old colonial system came to be accepted, and the Navigation Acts were finally repealed in 1849. Repeal did not, however, put an end to the Empire. It did not dispose of the contention that a nation profited in some way by the possession of colonies; nor did it prevent in later years the implementation of policies which were designed to do precisely what the mercantile system had done: to protect and subsidise a favoured sector of commerce. Railways built by the state in Africa, and exclusive charters granted to African companies, were as incompatible with free trade as anything outlawed by the 1849 Act, and as vulnerable to the classical economic arguments. Hence Cobden and Bright, in applying the theories of the 1770s to the conditions of the 1840s and 1850s, were later found to be no less relevant in the 1890s. It was they who gave completest expression to that critique of empire which became elevated and enshrined in the Liberal–Radical canon as the 'Liberal Tradition'.

This tradition was a curious mixture of moralism and materialism. It was a common complaint of later imperialists that the 'Manchester School' was small-minded when it came to treat foreign affairs, too insular and commercial. And certainly Cobden and Bright concentrated greatly on the English end of the colonial question, neglecting more than Adam Smith or Bentham the interests of the dependencies. Bright's restatement of the classical economists' case was typical: 'I am inclined to think that, with the exception of Australia, there is not a single dependency of the Crown which, if we come to reckon what it has cost in war and protection, would not be found to be a positive loss to the people of this country.'[2] Cobden's argument was the same. The colonies imposed a military burden on Britain which she could not afford: 'Our colonies must maintain their own establishments. We cannot keep armies in Canada and elsewhere – we cannot afford it.'[3]

[1] See R. Koebner and H. D. Schmidt, *Imperialism*, p. 60.

[2] Bright, speech of 29 Oct 1858; printed in *Selected Speeches of the Rt. Honble John Bright, M.P., on Public Questions*, p. 208.

[3] Cobden in H. of C., 13 Dec 1852; printed in John Bright and Thorold Rogers (ed.), *Speeches on Questions of Public Policy by Richard Cobden, M.P.*, vol. i, p. 551.

Still less could we afford to extend our rule. 'The present Government are taking possession in Asia, as well as Africa, of tracts of tropical territory, which, I believe, ... are only calculated to entail additional expense upon us, instead of benefiting us, as a free-trading community.'[1] Such empire brought military as well as financial dangers. ' We are governing India. The world never saw such a risk as we run, with 130 or 140 millions near the antipodes, ruling them for the sake of their custom, and nothing else. ... You might have something happen to you there at any time.'[2] But it was not only the expense or the military risks which worried Cobden. Large standing armies were a reactionary force, hostile to reform and detrimental to peace. They and the colonies were retained as a 'great preserve of the landlord class for their younger sons';[3] to 'preserve the patronage which the system afforded to the minister';[4] or to satisfy 'certain parties, who are interested in clothing regiments'.[5] Both he and Bright felt that franchise reform must remedy this.

> If you had a thorough representation in Parliament, you could not persuade the people of this country to spend half the money which is now spent under the pretence of protecting them, but which is really spent in order that certain parties may get some sort of benefit out of it.[6]

John Bright shared Cobden's feeling that war-scares were 'got up' in the interests of the few and against the interests of public welfare.

> You should condemn this foolish and wicked jealousy of Russia, which springs from ignorance among our people, and is fostered by writers in the press. It suits those who live out of the 25,000,000£ spent annually, and for the most part wasted on our monstrous armaments, to keep up this feeling,

---

[1] Cobden at Manchester, 23 Jan 1851; ibid. ii 463.
[2] Cobden at Rochdale, 23 Nov 1864; ibid. ii 357–8.
[3] Cobden at Leeds, 18 Dec 1849, ibid. ii 424–5; and cf. ibid. i 486.
[4] Cobden in H. of C., 8 Mar 1850; ibid. i 505.
[5] Cobden at Manchester, 10 Jan 1849; ibid. i 480–1.
[6] Cobden at Rochdale, 29 Oct 1862, ibid. ii 336–7; and cf. Bright, quoted in Asa Briggs, *Victorian People* (1965 ed.), pp. 205, 231, 233.

and the influential among them are constantly acting on the proprietors, editors, and writers of the London newspapers.[1]

Foreign policy was 'nothing more nor less than a gigantic system of outdoor relief for the aristocracy of Great Britain'.[2] The cost of it fell on those people who were least able to afford it, and hindered their material advancement.

> You have to make up your mind to one thing – you cannot afford all this waste. . . . The more you waste of the capital of the country, the more people will be wanting employment . . . in proportion as the extravagance of Government increases, poor-rates and the expenses of a repressive police increase also.[3]

Bright went so far as to claim that 'great revenues' tended towards 'the corruption of a government'.[4] The lesson was plain: the people must 'unite in supporting the principles of peace, as the only means of improving their temporal condition'.[5]

Neither Cobden nor Bright entirely left out of account the interests of the dependencies themselves, despite Bright's assertion that 'Our dear friend Cobden would never touch India in any shape, always giving as his reason that we have no business there.'[6] Yet when Cobden did speak or write on India, it was in a deeply pessimistic vein. We could not govern 100 million Asiatics, he wrote, and if we could we would not gain by it. The only way we could rule in India was despotically, and this would react malevolently on British democracy.[7] So he de-

---

[1] Bright, 25 Nov 1876; printed in H. J. Leech (ed.), *The Public Letters of the Right Hon. John Bright, M.P.*, p. 195.

[2] Bright, speech of 29 Oct 1858; in *Selected Speeches*, p. 204.

[3] Cobden at Manchester, 10 Jan 1849, *Speeches on Public Policy by Cobden*, i 487; and cf. Cobden, speaking on the despatch of troops to Nova Scotia, H. of C., 1 Aug 1862: 'To spend a million of money in that way – money which would have solaced the hearts and homes of the famishing people in Lancashire – was a wanton waste of public treasure.' (Ibid. ii 272.)

[4] Bright, speech of 29 Oct 1858, in *Selected Speeches*, p. 210.

[5] Cobden at Wrexham, 14 Nov 1850 (*Speeches on Public Policy by Cobden*, ii 404–5).

[6] Bright, letter to Thomas Bayley Potter, 4 Dec 1877, quoted in G. M. Trevelyan, *The Life of John Bright*, p. 262, n. 1.

[7] See Cobden's letters to Mr Ashworth, 16 Oct 1857, and to G. Combe, 16 May 1868, in J. Morley, *The Life of Richard Cobden*, vol. ii, pp. 206–8 and 216.

spaired. 'It is . . . from an abiding conviction in my mind that we have entered upon an impossible and hopeless career in India, that I can never bring my mind to take an interest in the details of its government.' [1] Bright was a little less fatalistic. He condemned the way in which Britain had taken possession of India, but 'I accept that possession as a fact. There we are; we do not know how to leave it, and therefore let us see if we know how to govern it.'[2] Bright, therefore, was more forthcoming than his colleague with schemes of reform:[3] their aim should be, he said, to do for our empire what the Romans did for theirs, and civilise the vanquished.[4] Yet still the note of criticism was sharpest in his speeches: he spoke eloquently of the poverty and suffering which Britain tolerated in India, the excessive and oppressive taxation, bad finances, bad roads, almost non-existent education, and incompetent and corrupt administration;[5] and he was never sanguine of any real change for the better.[6]

Cobden and Bright were chiefly concerned, however, with the interests of England, and retrenchment and domestic reform remained the guiding principles behind their opposition to military expenditure, imperial defence and interference in the affairs of other countries (even of nations 'struggling to be free').[7]

[1] Cobden, letter to William Hargreaves, 4 Aug 1860; ibid. ii 360–1. When Cobden spoke in the H. of C. on the East India Bill, 27 June 1853, his tone was similarly pessimistic (*Speeches on Public Policy by Cobden*, ii 377–99).

[2] Bright, speech of 11 Dec 1877; *Selected Speeches*, p. 51.

[3] See Bright, speech in H. of C., 3 June 1853, in Thorold Rogers (ed.), *Speeches on Questions of Public Policy by the Right Honourable John Bright, M.P.*, pp. 1–17; and speeches of 24 June 1858, 1 Aug 1859 and 11 Dec 1877, in *Selected Speeches*, pp. 1–51. His solutions to the Indian problem were (*a*) to divide India up into at least five presidencies; (*b*) to employ more non-European officials; (*c*) greater toleration for religion and liberty, and more respectful treatment of the natives (see Trevelyan, op. cit. p. 267); (*d*) all this with a view to eventual Indian self-government.

[4] Bright in H. of C., 3 June 1853; in *Speeches on Public Policy by Bright*, p. 17.

[5] See n. 3 above.   [6] Letter of 14 Jan 1860, in *Public Letters*, p. 179.

[7] See Cobden in H. of C., 28 June 1850; *Speeches on Public Policy by Cobden*, ii 224–7: 'I claim for myself as much sympathy for foreigners struggling for liberty as anyone in this House; but it is not true, as [Roebuck] . . . said, that I ever attended a public meeting, and said I was in favour of going to war. . . . I never in public advocated interference in the Government of foreign countries. . . .'

Neither of them set much store by moral pacifist arguments.[1]
Yet we often find in their speeches an appeal to ethical considerations which went far beyond mere material interest; especially
in the more emotionally charged orations of John Bright. 'I
believe there is no permanent greatness to a nation except it be
based upon morality . . . the moral law was not written for men
alone in their individual character . . . it was written as well for
nations.'[2] 'It may seem Utopian,' said Cobden, 'but I don't feel
sympathy for a great nation, or for those who desire the greatness
of a people by the vast extension of empire. What I like to see is
the growth, development, and elevation of the individual man.'[3]
Both of them believed that the best hope for the peace of the
world and the happiness of mankind lay in free trade; the spread
of commerce among nations, the gradual erosion of national
barriers and the destruction of imperial animosities. It was a
materialist solution, but a moral ideal.

> I have been accused of looking too much to material in-
> terests. Nevertheless I can say that I have taken as large and
> great a view of the effects of this mighty principle as ever did
> any man who dreamt over it in his own study. I believe that
> the physical gain will be the smallest gain to humanity from
> the success of this principle. I look farther; I see in the Free-
> trade principle that which shall act on the moral world as the
> principle of gravitation in the universe, – drawing men to-
> gether, thrusting aside the antagonism of race, and creed,
> and language, and uniting us in the bonds of eternal peace.
> I have looked even farther. I have speculated, and probably
> dreamt, in the dim future – ay, a thousand years hence – I
> have speculated on what the effect of the triumph of this
> principle may be. I believe that the effect will be to change
> the face of the world, so as to introduce a system of govern-
> ment entirely distinct from that which now prevails. I believe
> that the desire and the motive for large and mighty empires;

[1] Neither Cobden nor Bright was an extreme pacifist. See Knorr, *British
Colonial Theories*, p. 167.
[2] Bright, speech of 29 Oct 1858; *Selected Speeches*, pp. 218, 220.
[3] Cobden at Rochdale, 29 Oct 1862; *Speeches on Public Policy by Cobden*,
ii 315–16.

for gigantic armies and great navies – for those materials which are used for the destruction of life and the desolation of the rewards of labour – will die away; and I believe that such things will cease to be necessary, or to be used when man becomes one family, and freely exchanges the fruits of his labour with his brother man. I believe that, if we could be allowed to reappear on this sublunary scene, we should see, at a far distant period, the governing system of this world revert to something like the municipal system; and I believe that the speculative philosopher of a thousand years hence will date the greatest revolution that ever happened in the world's history from the triumph of the principle which we have met here to advocate.[1]

Even Richard Cobden could rise to oratorical heights; and it was this kind of utopian vision which sustained his disciples half a century later.

Yet Cobden and Bright were no more representative of 'the Liberal tradition' than Disraeli was of the Tory. Later Radicals could not see this. J. M. Robertson illustrates the extent to which Manchesterism had, by 1909, become embedded in Radical mythology. In a foreign affairs debate in the House of Commons he said: ' A great deal has been said as to the traditions of Liberal foreign policy. What is the Liberal tradition as to foreign policy? ... The practical tradition of Liberal foreign policy is non-intervention in foreign affairs.' A Member interrupted him: 'Was that Palmerston's policy?' Robertson replied: 'Palmerston's is exactly a case which is rejected as really representative of Liberal tradition. If any man is to be taken as representative of Liberal foreign policy, it is Richard Cobden. He is a higher authority on Liberal traditions.' [2] From the point of view of the practical politics of sixty years before, this was patently absurd. Whenever Cobden's party was in power between 1835 and 1865, Palmerston had effective control of foreign affairs, and to discount him as unrepresentative of 'the practical tradition of Liberal

[1] Cobden at Manchester, 15 Jan 1846; ibid. i 362–3.
[2] H. of C., 22 July 1909; 5 P.D. 8 (Commons), c. 717.

foreign policy' was like describing Senator Fulbright as representing the practical foreign policy of the American Democratic
Party in the 1960s. In the colonial field Cobden was by no means
typical either of his party or of his age. It has been shown that
in the middle of the nineteenth century 'anti-imperialism' was
never more than a minority attitude, that all governments
persisted in trying to secure at least a commercial hold on foreign
countries and that very often this 'informal imperialism' culminated in formal annexation.[1] The Liberal Tradition and 'mid-
Victorian separatism'[2] were both to a great extent mythical.
How did they come to have so strong a hold on later Radicals?

One of the aspects of colonial expansion most prominent in
the later nineteenth century was the 'forward' policy in tropical
Africa. Here there was a certain amount of evidence that, in the
1860s, the Cobdenites had triumphed. The *Report of the Select
Committee on Africa (Western Coast)*, published in 1865, was
thoroughly permeated with Manchesterism. The Committee
deprecated

> the needless employment of English officers and military on
> such a shore as costly to this country.... The scattering of
> forces, both naval and military, in such parts of the world, is
> an additional evil, which, in case of general war, would be of
> serious consideration.[3]

Because of this they advocated the evacuation, as far as was
practicable, of all Britain's West African possessions except
Sierra Leone.[4] The Report was never implemented. But it remained among the Parliamentary Blue Books as evidence of the
mid-Victorians' good intentions.

[1] J. Gallagher and R. E. Robinson: 'The Imperialism of Free Trade', in
E.H.R., vol. vi, no. 1 (1953). According to this article, between 1841 and
1851 Britain occupied or annexed New Zealand, the Gold Coast, Labuan,
Natal, the Punjab, Sindh and Hong Kong; in the next twenty years she
asserted control over Berar, Oudh, Lower Burmah, Kowloon, Lagos,
Sierra Leone, Basutoland, Griqualand and Transvaal, and established new
colonies in British Columbia and Queensland.

[2] C. A. Bodelsen's expression, in *Studies in Mid-Victorian Imperialism*,
ch. i.

[3] P.P. (1865), i, Draft Report, p. xiv, paras. 45 and 46.

[4] Ibid. p. iii, 3rd Resolution.

This alone, however, would have been insufficient to create a legend. The responsibility for this must rest partly on the shoulders of Disraeli. It was he who, in his Crystal Palace speech of June 1872, created the myth that the Liberals had been plotting for years to dismember the Empire: it was a lie, but it lived.[1] And it was nurtured by the Radicals themselves. Some years earlier John Bright had sought to persuade his countrymen that the creed of 'Peace, Retrenchment, Reform' had been the cornerstone of Liberal foreign policy for over a century:

> I appeal to this audience, to every man who knows anything of the views and policy of the Liberal party in past years, whether it is not the fact that up to 1832, and indeed to a much later period, probably to the year 1850, those sentiments of Sir Robert Walpole, of Mr Fox, of Earl Grey, and of Sir Robert Peel, the sentiments which I in humbler mode have propounded, were not received unanimously by the Liberal party as their fixed and unchangeable creed?[2]

The power of Cobden and Bright's personalities lived on long after they had left the political scene: their writings and doctrines were lovingly preserved and perpetuated by the Cobden Club, and the legend was perpetuated with them. When the flow of their published speeches came to an end, another man was there to take over and carry Cobdenism into the twentieth century: Goldwin Smith.[3] Smith began writing in the 1860s and continued through until the end of the Boer War. His intellectual roots were sunk deep in Political Economy and Manchesterism, and he lived long enough to contribute to the debate on the New Imperialism. He was able, therefore, to keep the Liberal Tradition alive for a later generation. There was no propagandist – unless it be Sir Charles Dilke – to do this for the *real* Liberal tradition of foreign and colonial policy.

The myth was strengthened by the political events of the 1870s and 1880s. Home Rule and Gladstone's Bulgarian agitation of

---

[1] Koebner and Schmidt, *Imperialism*, pp. 109–10.
[2] Bright, speech of 29 Oct 1858; *Selected Speeches*, p. 199.
[3] See Elisabeth Wallace, *Goldwin Smith, Victorian Liberal*. Smith's first important work was *The Empire*, a collection of letters published in 1863.

B

1876–7 somehow stamped the whole Liberal Party with the mark of 'moralism' and anti-imperialism. His bellicosity in defence of oppressed Bulgars (and later Armenians) was far removed from Cobden's non-interventionism: yet it was an attempt to conduct foreign affairs according to the rules of morality, and this was in general accord with Manchester's ideals. By doing so, Gladstone 'diverted the Liberal party from its logical path'.[1] Liberalism became personified by its leader, and its foreign policy was identified with his Christian moralism. The cabinet and party split of 1886 only served to emphasise this: the old Whigs and 'imperialists' had been shed, and the main stem of Liberalism stood out clearly as the party of Home Rule, morality in foreign affairs, evacuation in the Sudan and appeasement in South Africa.[2] This may not have been too mistaken a view of what became known as the 'Gladstonian Party' of the late eighties and the nineties – although, as we shall see, there remained within it a powerful 'Roseberyite' section to impede the designs of the self-styled 'old school'.[3] The error lay in trying to project this situation back into the past, to draw a broad and straight line from Adam Smith through Cobden and Bright to the later Gladstone and call it the Liberal Tradition.

Yet this was the myth. We shall see how in the 1890s one section of anti-imperialist opinion went to Adam Smith and Cobden for its arguments, took its stand first of all on the precepts of 'national economic self-interest' and secondly on the grounds of international morality, and justified its position against the taunts of its 'imperialist' colleagues by appealing to a Liberal Tradition which was of more recent manufacture than it realised.

III. THE ABORIGINE QUESTION

A case which rested entirely on considerations of profitability could have little to say about the government of native races within the British Empire. Before any concern could be shown

---

[1] R. T. Shannon, *Gladstone and the Bulgarian Agitation 1876*, p. 273.
[2] See below, pp. 70, 84–7.   [3] See below, pp. 79–84.

for the welfare of these peoples, it was necessary to cultivate a feeling of responsibility. Manchester felt very little in the way of responsibility. She tended to assume that men were best improved by being left alone to 'help themselves': this was the Cobdenites' reply to those who accused them of having too little regard for Indians and Africans. Consequently anti-imperialists and colonial reformers were seldom the same men. The anti-imperialist solution to colonial problems was that of the 1865 West Africa Committee – withdrawal. The remedy of the humanitarians was that of the Niger Expedition of 1841 – expansion.

There were, of course, exceptions to this rule. Bright occasionally took a constructive interest in the plight of the Indians; Bentham came to see that there were other considerations to be taken into account than that of 'expense'. A more notable case is that of the writer Richard Congreve, whose anti-imperialism, as we shall see, combined Political Economy with an unusual and unorthodox Indocentrism. In general, however, the two things did not converge until a later age, and the colonial reformers, some of whose doctrines anticipated that age, must be considered independently of the anti-imperialists.

Broadly speaking, humanitarian interest in native races can be said to have begun in the 1770s.[1] Before then the 'aborigine question' was 'apparently never discussed in Parliament'; Englishmen concerned themselves only with trade matters and neglected the interests of their colonial wards.[2] The first phase of the discussion of this question began with the rise of the anti-slavery movement in the 1770s, and ended with the Bill of 1833.

The history of Wilberforce's anti-slavery agitation is too familiar to need recapitulation. For our purposes legal slavery and the slave trade are special cases which have only a slight relevance to the 1890s, and the importance of this early period lies more

[1] In 1670 Charles II issued a directive to the Council of Foreign Plantations, imploring them to treat the American Indians humanely; and, of course, the roots of the anti-slavery movement go back to the seventeenth century. Locke began his *Two Treatises of Civil Government* with an indictment of slavery: 'Slavery is so vile and miserable an estate of man...' (Everyman ed., 1924, p. 3).

[2] *C.H.B.E.*, vol. ii, p. 188.

in some of the attendant features of the movement. The first is the doctrine of 'trusteeship' which Burke adumbrated in a famous speech of 1783:

> all political power which is set over men, and ... all privilege claimed or exercised in exclusion of them, being wholly artificial, and for so much, in derogation from the natural equality of mankind at large, ought to be some way or other exercised ultimately for their benefit ... such rights or privileges, or whatever else you choose to call them, are all in the strictest sense a *trust*; and it is of the very essence of every trust to be rendered *accountable*. ...[1]

The practice of 'trusteeship' was to have an uneven career during the following century. At this time, however, the concept appeared to have injected a new sense of moral purpose into the government of Asia. Pitt's India Act of 1784 has been described as an attempt to implement its principles there;[2] Dundas's reforms in Ceylon as indicating the 'general recognition' of the principle that 'Imperialism is stultified unless like the quality of mercy itself it becomes mutually beneficial'.[3] The first quarter of the nineteenth century saw the 'first age of reform' in India, the application of Utilitarian and Evangelical ideas to the problem of 'elevating' – that is, uprooting and remoulding in a Western image – native races.[4]

> Let us endeavour to strike our roots into the soil by the gradual introduction and establishment of our own principles and opinions; of our laws, institutions and manners; above all, as the source of every other improvement, of our religion, and consequently of our morals.[5]

So the easy-going tolerance of Indian institutions characteristic of the old East India Company administration was to be superseded by the self-confident reformism of Bentham and James Mill.

---

[1] Burke on Fox's East India Bill, 1 Dec 1783; quoted in G. R. Mellor, *British Imperial Trusteeship 1783–1850*, p. 22.
[2] *C.H.B.E.*, ii 193.   [3] Ibid. p. 168.
[4] Eric Stokes, *The English Utilitarians and India*, ch. i.
[5] Wilberforce (1818), quoted in ibid. p. 35.

Self-confidence was the mark also of the new initiatives taken during the same period by humanitarian and missionary organisations in Africa. All the main missionary societies were founded around the turn of the century.[1] It was their efforts, together with Buxton's, that secured for the Hottentots of South Africa the amelioration in their conditions which helped to produce the Great Trek.[2] It was members of the Clapham Sect who in 1786 conceived the idea of founding a new colony in Sierra Leone to provide a new home for those 14,000 English slaves recently liberated by the Somerset judgment: a colony which would provide a base for the progressive civilisation of the whole of Africa. And 'civilisation' to the humanitarians in Africa meant the same as it did to Wilberforce in India: all the appurtenances of British, industrial, protestant culture. 'Most Europeans', writes Philip Curtin, 'thought their own way of life represented values of universal application.' Humanitarianism, egalitarianism and the Englishman's new-found pride in the industrial marvels he had lately accomplished all merged to produce 'the easy assumption that the good life was possible only within the framework of Western culture'.[3] The greatest blessing that could be conferred on the African, therefore, was to make him more like an Englishman; 'To wash the Blackamoor white.'[4]

While slavery remained the chief evil to be combated, however, such policies could claim only a small fraction of the humanitarians' attention; and it was not until the later 1830s that the 'aborigine question' came into its own. For a short time there was a bout of agonised soul-searching regarding the treatment of natives under British rule, particularly those in New Zealand and South Africa.[5] The 'high-mark of this self-accusatory line of argumentation'[6] was the *Report of the Select Committee on Aborigines (British Settlements)*, drawn up by Thomas Fowell Buxton

[1] Wesleyan Missionary Society 1785, Baptist 1792, London 1795, Scottish 1796, Church 1800, and the British and Foreign Bible Society 1803.

[2] *C.H.B.E.*, viii 276–90.

[3] Philip D. Curtin, *The Image of Africa*, pp. 259–60; and cf. p. 143, and ch. x.

[4] Quoted in ibid. p. 261.

[5] See Knorr, *British Colonial Theories*, pp. 382–5.   [6] Ibid. p. 383.

and published in 1837; its indictment of the conduct of colonists towards native races was uncompromising.

> It is not too much to say, that the intercourse of Europeans in general, without any exception in favour of the subjects of Great Britain, has been, unless when attended by missionary exertions, a source of many calamities to uncivilised nations.
>
> Too often, their territory has been usurped; their property seized; their numbers diminished; their character debased; the spread of religion impeded. European vices and diseases have been introduced amongst them, and they have been familiarised with the use of our most potent instruments for the subtle or the violent destruction of human life, viz. brandy and gunpowder.[1]

The remedies suggested by the Committee were comprehensive, and many of them anticipated those of later generations of colonial reformers. Missionary activity, of course, was to be encouraged, but the education of aborigines was not to be confined to the Gospel – 'with plans of moral and religious improvement should be combined well-matured schemes for advancing the social and political improvement of the tribes'. Land-alienation and the acquisition of new territories should be strictly regulated, and treaties with native races discouraged. Our justice should be both fair and comprehensible to them. The 'sale of ardent spirits' should cease. Labour-contracts must be so regulated as to proscribe 'the growth of a servile relation, differing little from slavery'. And the administration of native affairs should be withdrawn from the control of colonial legislatures and reserved to the British Crown.[2]

These were in the main regulatory and restrictive solutions. The Report, however, also stressed repeatedly the value to both parties in Africa of trade and commerce, and it was this notion which gave the greatest cause for hope to those humanitarians who in 1841 inaugurated the Niger scheme.

Philanthropic optimism was almost unbounded in the mid 1830s. Despite its financial failure, the Sierra Leone experiment

---

[1] P.P. (1837), vii (1), p. 5.　　　　[2] Ibid. pp. 77–81.

had convinced the 1837 Commissioners of 'the capacity of the negro race ... for mental culture, and their good average intellect';[1] and Thomas Fowell Buxton and Saxe Bannister both took considerable pains to show that natives could be induced to work, improve themselves and put on 'trowsers'.[2] The only thing holding them back was the slave trade. This was Buxton's problem in particular: that the slave trade was so profitable to Africa herself as well as to the European agents that it was difficult to eradicate. In 1837 the answer came to him: 'the deliverance of Africa was to be effected, *by calling out her own resources*'.[3] In 1840 he published *The Remedy; being a Sequel to the African Slave Trade*. In it he presented his scheme: to persuade the African native that legitimate trade was more profitable than the slave trade – 'that the wealth readily to be obtained from peaceful industry, surpasses the slender and precarious profits of rapine' – and to teach the Spaniard likewise that legitimate commerce would be of more benefit to *him*. 'If we cannot be persuaded to suppress the slave trade for the fear of God, or in pity to man, it ought to be done for the lucre of gain.' To this effect a company was to be formed to set up agricultural stations and model farms on the west coast, show the natives how to exploit their natural resources and encourage them to exchange their products for the manufactured goods of Europe. At the same time the naval squadrons off the coast were to be strengthened against the slave-trader.[4] For these proposals Buxton secured the approval and support of the British Government, and in 1841 an expedition sailed for the mouth of the Niger to put them into practice.[5]

[1] Ibid. p. 58; and cf. p. 44, on Christian instruction: 'every tribe of mankind is accessible to this remedial process'.

[2] S. Bannister, *Humane Policy; or Justice to the Aborigines of New Settlements essential to a due Expenditure of British Money, and to the Best Interests of the Settlers*, pp. 191 ff.; and T. F. Buxton, *The Remedy; being a Sequel to the African Slave Trade*, pp. 175–235.

[3] Charles Buxton (ed.), *Memoirs of Sir Thomas Fowell Buxton, Baronet, with Selections from his Correspondence*, p. 429.

[4] T. F. Buxton, *The Remedy*, pp. 1–18, 20, 23, 238–9.

[5] See Charles Buxton, op. cit. pp. 439–549; and J. Gallagher, 'Fowell Buxton and the New African Policy', in *C.H.J.*, vol. x, no. 1 (1950), pp. 36–58.

The commercial solution to the aborigine problem was of course another aspect of that same visionary Free Trade philosophy which so inspired Cobden and Bright. For them free trade was the path to peace, and it precluded 'imperialism'. The humanitarians, however, saw it primarily as the means of civilising the savage,[1] and at that stage in Africa's history, at any rate, this involved colonial expansion.[2] It was a form of commercial imperialism. Indeed, in talking of 'opening new fields for British capital and enterprise, and creating a vent and employment for that industry and intelligence which is stagnant at home',[3] the humanitarian Standish Motte was anticipating the 'imperialist' arguments of the next generation. Buxton himself mentioned in support of his scheme the consideration that 'New markets for the sale of our manufactured articles are urgently required . . .'.[4] But the beauty of free trade was that it benefited all parties, and the humanitarians were interested in its possibilities for the African. Africa was to be saved by her own efforts, and by the encouragement Europe gave to those efforts in fostering a free and legitimate commerce.

The expedition of 1841 was accompanied by expansion in other parts of West Africa, always for the purpose of spreading civilisation and combating the slave trade.[5] But the Niger scheme failed,[6] and with it went much of the wind in the humanitarians' sails. For some, 'free commerce' still appeared the answer to the problem of the slave trade,[7] the 'trust' remained the ruling

[1] See Bannister, *Humane Policy*, p. 109: 'It is universally agreed that trade is an important means of civilisation.'

[2] Gallagher, art. cit. p. 36.

[3] Standish Motte, *Outline of a System of Legislation, for Securing Protection to the Aboriginal Inhabitants of All Countries Colonised by Great Britain . . .*, p. 9.

[4] T. F. Buxton, *The Remedy*, p. 243.

[5] Gallagher, art. cit. p. 55; and see P.P. (1842), xi, which recommended the resumption of direct control over forts on the Gold Coast, where for years George Maclean had been extending his influence over the West African hinterland (*C.H.B.E.*, ii 654–68).

[6] Gallagher, art. cit. pp. 56–7.

[7] See P.P. (1865), v (1), p. xiii; and J. F. A. Ajayi, 'Henry Venn and the Policy of Development', in *J.H.S.N.*, vol. i, no. 4 (Dec 1959), pp. 331–42.

principle behind West African policy, and politicians continued to profess the 'white man's burden' into the 1850s.[1] But concern for the aborigine appears to have waned after the mid-century. The British experience with coloured races was not such as to encourage optimism. The results of Livingstone's second expedition, organised in 1858 under government auspices with the professed object of civilising the African native, were disappointing.[2] Humanitarians were losing faith in the civilising value of commerce.[3] The transatlantic slave-trade had practically ceased (except to Cuba), thus reducing the humanitarians' chief incentive to action – until the following century, when another kind of slavery was to suggest the same, commercial, solution.[4] And the Taiping Rebellion and Indian Mutiny disillusioned many with the 'white man's burden'. 'During the generation after 1850', writes one historian, '... Tropical and sub-tropical colonies, their relative economic importance having greatly declined, faded into the background of public consciousness.'[5] Hence the Report of the 1865 West African Committee which, however unrepresentative it may have been of opinion vis-à-vis 'imperialism', illustrates, by its utter contrast to (for example) the 1837 Committee, the poverty of humanitarian zeal in the sixties.

IV. MID-CENTURY DISILLUSION

If the official and humanitarian momentum had spent itself by 1865, the missionaries still soldiered on, and clung to the ethnocentric assumptions of their forebears. In East Africa during the later nineteenth century, for example, there was a new proselytising initiative, stimulated by Livingstone's exploration of the Zambesi region, his stirring appeals to the young men of Cambridge to spread the light of civilisation and commerce there, and even more by his death and the wave of popular enthusiasm

---

[1] See P. Knaplund, *Gladstone and Britain's Imperial Policy*, pp. 202–3; and Earl Grey, *The Colonial Policy of Lord John Russell's Administration*, vol. i, pp. 13–14.

[2] *C.H.B.E.*, ii 629–30.   [3] Curtin, *Image of Africa*, p. 429.

[4] See below, Ch. 8.   [5] Mellor, *British Imperial Trusteeship*, p. 28.

which followed it in England.[1] Missionaries flocked to do the
Christian hero's bidding, often raw and ignorant recruits,
naïvely happy in the assurance that they could earn the gratitude
of Africa's millions, and credit in heaven, by spreading the
blessings of their own English civilisation. Explorers and administrators shared the same outlook. It was a matter of filling a
void, replacing 'ignorance and superstition' by knowledge,
decency, industry and Christian enlightenment. To these men,
the African's mind was 'a blank sheet whereon we may write as
we will, without the necessity of first deleting old impressions'.[2]
It was as easy as that: a question of giving to the African what (if
he only knew his own mind) he most desired.

Yet there were traces of a new, less self-confident approach.
The Indian Mutiny had provoked men like Cobden to despair
of ever properly ruling or reforming India. In India itself the first
flush of reforming zeal had passed away long before. In some
circles, the second half of the nineteenth century was marked by a
growing lack of faith in the ability of non-European nations to
become moulded and perfected in a Western pattern. As Cobden
said – and the italicised passage is significant –

> Hindoostan must be ruled by those who live on that side of
> the globe. Its people will prefer to be ruled badly – *according
> to our notions* – by its own colour, kith and kin, than to sub-
> mit to the humiliation of being better governed by a suc-
> cession of transient intruders from the antipodes.[3]

For those who had become disillusioned with the concept of
the 'civilising mission', at least as public policy, there were three
possible alternatives. The first was Indirect Rule. As a broad
principle of government with theoretical backing, Indirect Rule
was not to take coherent shape until the twentieth century; but
in effect it had been practised for some time past by individual

---

[1] Roland Oliver, *The Missionary Factor in East Africa*, ch. i.
[2] H. Duff quoted in H. A. C. Cairns, *Prelude to Imperialism*, p. 165. The
generalisations in this paragraph are based on the same book. Cf., for the
eighteenth century, Curtin, op. cit. p. 89.
[3] Cobden, 16 Oct 1857; quoted in Morley, *Life of Cobden*, ii 208 (italics in
the original).

colonial administrators as an expedient born of material and political weakness.[1] In the second half of the nineteenth century George Maclean on the Gold Coast and Sir Arthur Gordon in Fiji ruled indirectly – through native customary institutions and laws.[2] This was one possibility. A second was Lord Cromer's. Cromer was deeply impressed by the cultural gulf which existed between Europeans and those men he treated together under the single heading of 'Orientals'. The gulf, he thought, was unbridgeable. The only thing an imperial power could do was to govern despotically and confine its benevolent attentions to the raising of the material standards of its subjects.[3] This was the basis of his conduct in Egypt. But there was a third alternative: withdrawal from the dependencies. In order to be willing to advocate this as a practical policy, however, one had to be convinced first of all that evacuation would be to Europe's interest; and, secondly, that a country like India would not lapse into barbarism and anarchy once the imperial grip were relaxed. Richard Congreve,[4] who published his pamphlet on *India* immediately after the Mutiny, was one of a very small minority which could bring itself to accept both these conditions. His analysis of British commercial and political interests was drawn from the Manchester tradition.[5] His reasons for believing that India could survive the transition to independence were founded upon a belief that some kind of guarantee could be elicited from other European powers that her stability and security would be safeguarded by them.[6] But most significant of all were the

[1] See Margery Perham, *Native Administration in Nigeria*, p. 345; and Lord Hailey, *An African Survey*, pp. 527–8.

[2] On Maclean, see Curtin, op. cit. pp. 474–5, and *C.H.B.E.*, ii 635–68; on Gordon, see J. D. Legge, *Britain in Fiji 1858–1880*, pp. 154 *et passim*.

[3] Lord Cromer, 'The Government of Subject Races' (1908), and 'The French in Algeria' (1913), printed in *Political and Literary Essays*, pp. 3–53 and 250–63.

[4] A brief assessment of Congreve's life and writings is to be found in Pierre Guiral, 'Observations et Réflexions sur un Prophète de la Décolonisation', in *Études Maghrébines*, 1964, pp. 211–16.

[5] Richard Congreve, *India* (1907 ed.), pp. 21–2.

[6] Ibid. pp. 13–14. He suggested the setting up of a Commission representing the other powers interested in India, together with Brahminism and Islam, to 'constitute the germ of a European protectorate'.

reasons he gave for the justice and advisability of withdrawal.

Congreve called himself a Positivist; and the aim of Positivism, he said, was to 'subordinate politics to morals'.[1] Our occupation of India was clearly selfish and immoral – those who denied this were deluding themselves – and so ethical considerations dictated that we return what we had stolen.[2] This was the point to which he returned most frequently. But, beyond this, Congreve insisted that our attempt to change Indian society and culture, however well-meaning it might sometimes be, was presumptuous and 'unnatural'. Indian civilisation was something to be respected, not looked down upon as 'primitive'. When England arrived on the scene it was 'in decay';[3] but this was no reason for us to try to replace it with a totally different culture. 'Like an unskilful physician, we interfered with the course of nature, and suspended its healing action.' [4] The effect was irreparably harmful to the Indians – 'the decomposition of their whole mental framework.' Our social organisation was unsuited to them, our religion alien to their mentality. Our sin in India was that same 'reckless want of sympathy' which was now condemned in the old Spanish Empire.[5]

This sympathetic approach to alien civilisations was something new in English colonial criticism. It might have been expected, perhaps, to grow naturally out of the mass of infor-

---

[1] Ibid. p. 7. On Positivism, see below, pp. 158–9.

[2] Ibid. p. 12. His moral argument in favour of impartial arbitration of Britain's case in India bears a striking resemblance to Hobson's forty years later: 'When the interest of the weaker, as viewed by the stronger, so entirely coincides with the power and pride of the stronger; when the duty of the stronger so entirely coincides with his own views of his interest; in the case of individuals, it would be clearly right to call in some third judgment, not for the stronger to act at once as judge and party. As between nations, I believe the same rule holds good . . .' (p. 12. See below, p. 181).

[3] Ibid. p. 23.

[4] Ibid. p. 15. Congreve's assessment of the relative merits of Western Christian and Eastern Hindu society seems to have been based on his Comteist belief in spiritual (political) power. Hinduism, he thought, was far closer to this ideal (for Comte, the ideal of the thirteenth-century Catholic Church) than was modern Western Christianity, which had irrevocably lost its hold on the people of Europe.

[5] Ibid. pp. 23–8.

mation about those civilisations which had been accumulated in the recent past by travellers and scientists, and particularly from the contributions of the infant science of anthropology – *tout comprendre c'est tout pardonner*. But the anthropologists were surprisingly unhelpful. The eighteenth century had added much to European knowledge of alien peoples; its information was more accurate, less sensationalist, than ever before; and the popular concept of the 'noble savage' did much to place the African and the Amerindian in a favourable, even flattering, light.[1] Polygenesis – the doctrine that different races were created separately, that the cultural discrepancies between them, therefore, were ineradicable – was a minority view, and the alternative hypothesis of monogenesis, which at least conceded the black man's humanity and capacity for progress, held the field. But even monogenesis tended to assess 'progress' ethnocentrically, to judge alien cultures by a standard derived from Western preconceptions.[2] In the following century anthropology became more 'scientific' and better organised, but its methods and hypotheses were even less conducive to cultural empathy. From the beginning of the century anthropology was the preserve of the biologist,[3] and the biologist, however 'empirical' he claimed to be, was concerned to study other races not for their own sake, but in order to elucidate their 'place in nature'. His first aim was 'to examine, classify, and arrange the whole order of nature in a rational pattern'.[4] The existence of 'savages' offended against his sense of rational propriety, and they had somehow to be brought into the confines of the tidy world-picture which, he felt, was necessary if he were to retain intellectual control over nature.

[1] Sometimes, also, the eighteenth century could display a refreshing cynicism which might counter ethnocentric assumptions of superiority. Henry Home wrote in 1761: 'Barbarians are slaves to custom: Polite people to fashions. The Hottentots are an instance of the former: the French of the latter.' (Quoted in J. S. Slotkin, *Readings in Early Anthropology*, p. 89.)

[2] Katherine George, 'The Civilized West Looks at Primitive Africa, 1400–1800', in *Isis*, vol. xlix (1958), pp. 69–72; Curtin, *Image of Africa*, chs. i and ii; H. N. Fairchild, *The Noble Savage, passim*; and A. C. Haddon, *A History of Anthropology* (1934), *passim*.

[3] Curtin, op. cit. pp. 329–32, 363.

[4] Ibid. p. 36.

This was his reason for studying them at all.[1] The solution was to organise the races of man hierarchically, with the 'Caucasian' at the top and the 'Negro' at the bottom – a little higher than the monkeys.[2] The schema was neat and regular, and in the 1860s Darwin's evolutionary theory (adopted in a form more unilinear than Darwin himself had hypothesised) gave new support to it. Evolutionary anthropology posited one single scale of civilisation, with Western Europe at its summit. The cultural differences between contemporary societies were ascribed to 'the achievement of different stages of essentially the same process'.[3] So, in so far as a culture was different from that of nineteenth-century England, it followed that it was 'lower' in the scale, and if there were elements in it which did not fit into the evolutionary pattern, then they could be explained away as 'survivals' from a previous stage of culture.[4] This was the orthodoxy of English anthropology until well into the twentieth century. Anthropologists had added considerably to the corpus of knowledge about alien civilisations. But they were not interested in those civilisations *per se*, only in the way they fitted into a pattern, or in the light they shed, by comparison, on the origins of Western culture. Further, the evolutionist basis of their science shackled them as firmly as anyone else to Anglocentrism. A culture could not be respected for itself if it were seen merely as a lower rung in the ladder of uniform progress; and when puzzling features of it were dismissed as pointless anachronisms, then their social functions could not be properly and usefully appreciated. The scientist was the worst enemy – or the most embarrassing friend – of the native.

Tolerance of alien institutions would not come from this quarter; mere knowledge of them was not enough. In order to arrive at a position from which strange cultures could be considered objectively and sympathetically, a certain degree of

[1] J. W. Burrow, *Evolution and Society*, pp. 2–3 *et passim*; and A. O. Lovejoy, *The Great Chain of Being*, ch. viii.

[2] See, for example, Lamarck cited in Curtin, op. cit. p. 230.

[3] Burrow, op. cit. p. 116.

[4] Ibid. *passim*, and R. H. Lowie, *The History of Ethnological Theory*, p. 82. The concept of 'survivals' was Sir Edward Tylor's.

'cultural relativism' was necessary. This would mean, in the later nineteenth century, adhering to one of two points of view. On the one hand, one could deny categorically the ability of the native to achieve the standards demanded by Western civilisation, or at least insist that his progress along Western lines must be slow and laborious. This view rarely coincided with a benevolent regard for native interests, but it was not necessarily antipathetic to them. The explorer Joseph Thomson, for example, strongly refuted the charges of those, who, 'under the influence of fevers and the thousand troubles attendant on African travelling, have much maligned and unjustly abused the natives';[1] yet he himself doubted the African's capacity for improvement, and urged his readers 'not to be carried away with the idea that it is possible to graft the civilisation of Europe on to the low mind of the negro in either one or two generations'.[2] Christianity, he claimed, was unsuited to his 'low undeveloped mind'; Mohammedanism, an inferior religion, fitted him better.[3] Others – a small minority in an aggressively Christian England – urged the same point.[4] This

[1] Joseph Thomson, *To the Central African Lakes and Back* (1881), vol. i, p. 238.

[2] Joseph Thomson, 'East Central Africa, and its Commercial Outlook', in *The Scottish Geographical Magazine*, vol. ii (1886), pp. 77–8.

[3] Joseph Thomson, 'Note on the African Tribes of the British Empire', in *J.A.I.*, vol. xvi (1886), p. 184; and 'The Results of European Intercourse with the African', in *C.R.*, Mar 1890, pp. 348–52.

[4] Cairns, *Prelude to Imperialism*, pp. 209–13. John Stuart Mill had said much the same thing in 1840, in a letter to the Positivist Gustave d'Eichthal: 'Islamism is a fortunate thing for the Africans . . .' (Francis E. Mineka (ed.), *The Earlier Letters of John Stuart Mill, 1812–1848*, vol. ii, p. 456). The relativist implications of this are confirmed elsewhere in Mill's writings and correspondence: see ibid. i 37, 41, 43, and ii 404; his *Autobiography* (1961 ed.), p. 101; and his article on 'Civilization' (1836), printed in *Dissertations and Discussions*, vol. i, p. 161. Yet Mill's solution to the Indian problem was a despotic rule by resident officials: see *Considerations on Representative Government* (Everyman ed.), pp. 197–200, 377–93; and his later letters criticise the tendency 'd'attribuer toutes les variétés dans le caractère des peuples et des individus à des différences indélébiles de nature, sans se demander si les influences d'éducation et du milieu social et politique n'en donnent pas une explication suffisante' (letter of 1860, quoted in H. S. R. Elliot, *Letters of John Stuart Mill*, vol. ii, p. 235). He makes the same criticism of Charles Dilke's *Greater Britain* (letter to Dilke, 9 Feb 1869; B.M. Add. MS. 43897, f. 1). Richard Congreve was guilty of just this 'tendency'.

outlook was not a relativistic one; it still held out European culture as the African's ultimate goal. But it was at least gradualist, granting alien civilisations a brief respite and a gentle initiation.

The second alternative was more promising. Ethnocentrism rested on cultural arrogance, a belief not only in the inferiority of other civilisations, but also in the excellence of one's own. If this could be undermined, Victorian euphoria dissipated and Western Europe displaced from the top of the cultural ladder, then there would be less tendency to undervalue other cultural systems. There were signs in England during the 1880s of dissatisfaction with European civilisation; Edward Carpenter's *Civilisation, Its Cause and Cure* (1889) marks its extreme limit. Applied specifically to Africa, this way of thinking generally took the form of a return to the old eighteenth-century 'noble savage' myth. Contrasting the 'uncivilised' African with his European brother, Edward Carpenter, Joseph Thomson and an East African missionary, Duff MacDonald, described and lauded his natural virtue, his happiness, his freedom from disease, and the harmony of his social life.[1] Such reports were generally highly romanticised. A more sober view was expressed by an ex-Indian civil servant, Robert Needham Cust, who appealed to missionaries to confine their attentions to religious matters and desist from cultural proselytising:

> Civilization is the *incidental*, not the primary, object of a Mission. . . . The Missionary should place before his eyes as the model, which he aims at, *not* the British, or New England, village, with all its surroundings of European culture, but the villages of Palestine, such as they were, when our Lord passed through them. Nothing is so bad as to turn a Negro into a Pseudo-Englishman. What has a particular stage of Human Culture to do with the Everlasting Gospel?[2]

[1] Edward Carpenter, *Civilisation, Its Cause and Cure* (11th ed., 1910), pp. 6–11; Joseph Thomson and (Miss) E. Harris-Smith, *Ulu: An African Romance* (1888), *passim*; and Rev. Duff MacDonald, *Africana; or, the Heart of Heathen Africa* (1882), vol. i, pp. 39–42.

[2] Robert Needham Cust, *Notes on Missionary Subjects*, pt. i, pp. 17–18.

The Gospel ... should not be accompanied by a spurious admixture of European non-essentials.[1]

It distresses me to hear National Customs, not only criminal, but actually legalised under British Law, and profitable, and which could not be abandoned without great evils, denounced by those, who do not understand them.[2]

Cust was not denigrating Western civilisation. But by denying its integral connexion with Christianity he was able to relegate it to the background of missionary ambition, and so regard alien cultures from a standpoint quite apart from the ethnocentric one.

Congreve, Cust and the others were in a small minority in late-nineteenth-century Britain. Their different degrees of 'cultural relativism' fitted very poorly into the Victorian *Weltanschauung*. Yet we shall see how the same kind of disillusion with the 'civilising mission of the West' was to inculcate in later Radical writers a similar hostility towards 'cultural imperialism', and an alternative Indirect Rule philosophy.

These constituted the fund of historical arguments on which late-nineteenth-century Radicals could draw. There was the Free Trade anti-imperialism of Adam Smith, Bright and Cobden, aiming to show that empire, and especially a protective empire, was uneconomic. There was the Liberal 'tradition' of non-intervention, concerned to demonstrate that Liberals had always felt this way. On the other side there was that other branch of free-trade theory, which saw the salvation of the African in unrestricted commerce but insisted that he be introduced to its benefits by means of state action. And lastly, there was the vacuum left by the failure of this policy, which for most Radicals served only to emphasise the wisdom of non-interference, but which for some might suggest new ways of doing good to the African without proselytising him. It was the first two which were most conspicuous in the 1890s, when all the emphasis in the debate over

---

[1] Cust, *Essays on the Prevailing Methods of the Evangelization of the Non-Christian World*, p. 272.

[2] Cust, *Notes on Missionary Subjects*, pt. i, p. xiii.

imperialism was on its implications for the imperialising power. The more Afrocentric attitude was only to appear prominently in political discussions after the turn of the century. All these arguments were to be modified by, and adapted to, the new circumstances of the late nineteenth century and the preoccupations of its Radicals.

CHAPTER TWO

The Imperial Challenge, 1895

WHILE much of the Radicals' case against the Empire in 1900 was familiar from long before, their critique was more original than the sum of its parts. For the novelty of an ideology depends less upon the intrinsic originality of its different ingredients than on the way in which these ingredients are combined together, and the circumstances in which the ideology arises and to which it is applied; and at the turn of the century such considerations produced an ideological synthesis which was, in effect, unprecedented. This is particularly true of the *explanations* they offered for the imperialist phenomenon. If the Radicals' arguments against imperialism, and sometimes the alternatives they proposed for it, were 'traditional' ones, yet their analysis of its causes was often founded upon the assumption that the imperialism they saw around them in the 1890s was 'new' and had its roots, therefore, in circumstances peculiar to the age. It can be said in criticism of them that they stressed too greatly the contrast between their generation and the last; that they ignored those features of imperialism which were ever-present and attributed too much to 'new' political and economic factors. To a great extent the 'New Imperialism' was as mythical as that 'Liberal Tradition' from which it had sprung. Nevertheless, certain features attendant upon the imperialism of the late nineteenth century appeared sufficiently novel to merit concern, and to provoke a reaction among its opponents which differed markedly from that of their predecessors.

The form this reaction took varied according to the preconceptions of different political groups. But there were certain features common to them all, certain problems inherent in the imperial situation of the 1890s which were felt by every Radical to be fundamental. These problems fall into three broad categories. First, there was the sentimental aspect of the 'new' imperialistic movement, the recrudescence of such irrational phenomena as 'jingoism', militarism and the emotional ethos which surrounded them. Secondly, there was the economic issue, the signs which appeared towards the end of the century that the nation's policy was being shaped by capitalists to an extent unknown before, and with little concern for the interests of anyone but themselves. And lastly, there was the problem of Africa herself, of her 'development' or 'exploitation', and of the interests (for those who took any notice of them) of her inhabitants. These three groups of interrelated problems, which together characterised – in the eyes of Radicals – the New Imperialism, must be considered briefly here.

I. JINGOISM

The story of the 'rise of Empire sentiment' has been told often enough before.[1] Whether or not the contrast between mid-Victorian 'separatism' and late-Victorian 'imperialism' was as significant from a practical point of view as some have made out, there can be little doubt that the emotional accretions to the name of the Empire became thicker and more beguiling as the last thirty years of the century wore on. Indeed, this is partly the reason why misunderstanding ever arose as to the nature of earlier imperial policy. While there were few to shout about it, people failed to notice it. Towards the end of the century there was considerably more shouting. 'Imperialists' themselves boasted of it. W. E. Henley wrote that

it would seem that, at last, after years of stupor – years in which the blind were content to be led by the insane – the British Empire is by way of realising the fact that it is the

[1] e.g. Koebner and Schmidt, *Imperialism*, pp. 81–134; A. P. Thornton, *The Imperial Idea and its Enemies*, ch. 1; Bodelsen, *Studies in Mid-Victorian Imperialism*, pt. ii; Richard Faber, *The Vision and the Need*, ch. ii.

greatest and strongest which the world has ever seen. . . .
We have renewed our old pride in the Flag, our old delight
in the thought of a good thing done by a good man of his
hands, our old faith in the ambitions and traditions of the
race. . . .[1]

In its early days this sentiment was associated almost exclusively
with the white dominions: in one instance it embraced the whole
of Anglo-Saxondom within and outside the Empire.[2] This was
the kind of imperialism preached by the John the Baptists of
the new movement, Dilke, Seeley and Froude.[3] In later years it
was still to retain this enthusiasm for the dominions, and to
channel it into grand schemes for union and federation;[4] but when
the political spotlight began to focus more and more closely on
the tropical and alien parts of the Empire, imperial sentiment was
to broaden out and include these too. With the extension of the
Empire into the tropics went a corresponding sense of glory and
power, and an emotion which took the name of jingoism.

Jingoism rarely acknowledged that it was 'irrational' by the
criterion of the Manchester School – that it flew in the face of
economic facts. Imperialists insisted, as we shall see, that trade
followed the flag and that the flag, therefore, was an economic
asset. But the emotional aspect of it was independent of such
considerations, and this made it difficult for free-trade Liberals,
brought up to argue from political economy, to find common
ground on which they could join issue with imperialists. An
early sonnet by William Watson illustrates the irrelevance of the
jingo way of thinking for Cobdenites:

> In cobwebb'd corners dusty and dim I hear
> A thin voice pipingly revived of late,
> Which saith our India is a cumbrous weight,
> An idle decoration, bought too dear.
> The wiser world contemns not gorgeous gear;
> Just pride is no mean factor in a State;

[1] W. E. Henley, Introduction to C. de Thierry, *Imperialism*, pp. vii–viii.
[2] Charles Dilke, *Greater Britain*.
[3] Ibid.; J. R. Seeley, *The Expansion of England*; and J. A. Froude, *Oceana*.
[4] See J. E. Tyler, *The Struggle for Imperial Unity*.

A HANDSOME OFFER.

Boxa (*considerably damaged*). "I DIDN'T LIKE TO MENTION IT BEFORE, BUT NOW THAT 'YOU 'VE RECOVERED YOUR PRESTIGE,' GIVE ME EVERYTHING I WANT AND ALL SHALL BE FORGIVEN!"

THE AVENGER!

These two imperialist self-portraits, by Sir John Tenniel in Punch *(21 March and 25 July 1900), illustrate the arrogance and the idealism of 'jingoism' at its zenith*

The sense of greatness keeps a nation great;
And mighty they who mighty can appear.
It may be that if hands of greed could steal
From England's grasp the envied orient prize,
The tide of gold would flood her still as now:
But were she the same England, made to feel
A brightness gone from out those starry eyes,
A splendour from that constellated brow?[1]

Watson conceded the economic case yet stuck to his imperialist guns. And 'splendour' and 'pride', which formed his own rationale for the Empire, were the least alarming aspects of jingoism.

The jingo psychology of the *fin-de-siècle* still awaits its analyst. Most of its noisier features, however, are well known: the swagger and bluster of the music-halls and the 'yellow press', of Kipling and Alfred Austin, and of the mafficking crowds in the London streets. These were disturbing enough, but to those who feared such things they were only the surface manifestations of a deeper and more insidious evil. Beneath them there lay a complex of emotions and prejudices, and occasionally of clear and deeply pondered argument, which presaged ill for the future: race-pride and chauvinism, the worship of war and aggression, Social Darwinism and 'manifest destiny', impatience with 'sentimental' liberalism and humanitarianism, and a political realism which could turn quickly into cynical amoralism. The popular poetry of the time was full of such features. Kipling mirrored most of them, with his talk of 'the Pride of the Race' and the 'Sons of The Blood',[2] the withering scorn he poured on 'Pagett M.P.',[3] and his confident faith in a God who had 'smote for us a pathway to the ends of all the Earth'.[4] Polemicists and philosophers in England and America gave intellectual support to the new ethos. Social Darwinists justified the politics of Power in

---

[1] William Watson, 'Our Eastern Treasure' (Apr 1885), in *The Poems of William Watson*, vol. ii, p. 42.

[2] Rudyard Kipling, 'England's Answer', in *Sixty Poems* (1939), p. 24.

[3] Kipling, 'Pagett M.P.', in ibid. p. 77.

[4] Kipling, 'A Song of the English' (1893), in ibid. p. 11.

terms of the 'survival of the fittest';[1] Frederick Greenwood
preached a 'New Machiavellism';[2] the ennobling effects of war
were lauded by a host of minor prophets;[3] peace was painted
as a weakness and an aberration.[4] Even theologians joined in.
One of them brought Darwin and the doctrine of the Crucifixion
together to bear upon the problem, and was able by means of
them to justify, and indeed to rhapsodise over, imperialism, war,
aggression, suffering and death in battle.[5] On every level of the
literary scene, from the popular newspaper to the philosophical
treatise, were found such expressions – and many of them – of
what might be termed 'intellectual jingoism'.

Few of them were typical of anyone but their authors. Nor
were their practical implications as serious as many feared. Yet
they illustrate in some degree the new dimension which had
accrued to imperialism: a dimension which was regarded by
Radicals with bewilderment and apprehension because it was
'reactionary' and, at the same time, 'irrational'.

II. ECONOMIC IMPERIALISM

The second great problem which Radicals saw as 'new' to the
imperialism of the nineties was its mercenary character. The

---

[1] Richard Hofstadter, *Social Darwinism in American Thought*; and see
especially Karl Pearson, *National Life from the Standpoint of Science*.

[2] Frederick Greenwood, 'Sentiment in Politics' in *Cosmopolis*, Nov 1896,
pp. 340–54, and 'Machiavelli in Modern Politics', ibid. Aug 1897, pp. 307–22.
See also T. E. Kebbel, 'England at War', in *C19th*, Mar 1898, p. 339.

[3] See Sidney Low, 'Should Europe Disarm?' in *C19th*, Oct 1898, p. 521;
and 'The Future of the Great Armies', ibid. Sept 1899, p. 383. And cf.
John Ruskin, *The Crown of Wild Olives* (1901 ed.), pp. 115–71.

[4] e.g. Edward Dicey, 'After the Present War', in *C19th*, Nov 1899, pp.
693–707.

[5] Rev. W. W. Peyton, 'The Crucifixion and the War in the Creation', in
C.R., Oct 1900, pp. 518–31, and Dec 1900, pp. 835–57. Cf. the verse by
Dr Alexander, Archbishop of Armagh:

> And as I note how nobly natures form
>   Under the war's red rain, I deem it true,
> That He who made the earthquake and the storm,
>   Perchance made battles too!

Jameson Raid of December 1895 pointed a clear and unmistakable connexion between empire and finance. But the signs had been there, and known about, some time before.

Much of the discussion in the following chapters will be concerned with the origins and development of the 'economic' or 'surplus capital' theory of imperialism: that argument which attributed imperial expansion to the pressure for new markets and fields for investment, and attributed this pressure in turn to capitalist over-production at home. It will be as well to make clear at the outset that the novelty of this theory as it was formulated at the turn of the century did not lie in its mere attribution of imperialism to economic factors, nor even in its assertion that 'over-production' was the root cause. Neither of these things was revealed for the first time by J. A. Hobson in 1900; they had been common knowledge both to Radicals and to imperialists for years. The chief difference was that the 'surplus capital' theory, before 1900, was an argument in *support* of imperialism rather than against it.

The 'economic theory' was a kind of syllogism. Over-production led to pressure for new markets, pressure for new markets led to imperial expansion, therefore the cause of imperialism was over-production. The second stage of the argument was, in another form, simply the assertion that imperial adventures were motivated by traders and capitalists, and in this form it was familiar to all anti-imperialist Radicals. The events of the 1880s and 1890s made such a conclusion unavoidable. The Egyptian campaign of 1882 was, quite openly, undertaken in the interests of bondholders, and Radicals condemned it as such.[1] Even more revealing was the situation in tropical and southern Africa. Here colonies were administered, and their boundaries pushed forward, by commercial companies chartered by the Crown: the British South Africa Company in Rhodesia, the East African Company in Uganda, the Niger Company in the west. The capital–empire correlation could hardly be made more obvious.

The 1890s saw chartered companies growing in public and

[1] See, for example, *C.H.B.E.*, iii 151; and Frederic Harrison, *Autobiographic Memoirs*, vol. ii, pp. 123–6.

official estimation,[1] and Radicals expressed alarm at this trend. Criticism of the government of colonial territories by such companies had a long history in Free Trade ideology, dating back at least as far as Adam Smith's denunciation of them in 1776 as 'always more or less inconvenient to the countries in which they are established, and destructive to those who have the misfortune to fall under their government'.[2] Smith's chief objection to them was that they found it more conducive to their interests to discourage cultivation, and so keep prices high, than to promote it. The same argument could be applied as well to the companies of the 1880s and 1890s, as the *Economist* in 1891 demonstrated:

> Sovereign companies are probably the worst possible agencies for developing a new country. Instead of their object being to open up territory for settlement it is to close it. They want to make good dividends for themselves, not to see the ordinary emigrant flourishing.[3]

This was the classical Free Trade case against monopolistic enterprises; but there were other factors in the contemporary African situation which were even more disturbing. The South African Company, it seemed, was not even a healthy proposition in its own right. The *Investors' Review* in 1894 arraigned it on a charge of 'swindling' its shareholders; the very financial basis of the enterprise, it claimed, was unsound.[4] And beyond this there were moral and political considerations to be taken into account. The same journal spoke of the injustice that had been done to 'many a tribe of blacks' in 'robbing' them of their lands.[5] The *Economist* expressed concern that such companies as the B.S.A.C., possessing power without responsibility, might provoke friction

---

[1] See R. Koebner, 'The Concept of Economic Imperialism', in *E.H.R.*, vol. ii, no. 1 (1949), p. 12.

[2] Adam Smith, *Wealth of Nations* (Everyman ed.), ii 137; and cf. ibid. ii 73: 'Of all the expedients that can well be contrived to stunt the natural growth of a new colony, that of an exclusive company is undoubtedly the most effectual.'

[3] *The Economist*, 9 May 1891, pp. 591–2.

[4] [A. J. Wilson], 'Rhodesian Finance, or a New Story of a Golden "Fleece" ', in *Investors' Review*, Mar–Apr 1894, pp. 167–73 and 228–35.

[5] Ibid. p. 173, and Feb 1896, p. 90.

with European nations in Africa.[1] Lugard's attack on Mwanga in Uganda in 1892 seemed to prove its point,[2] and the Jameson Raid provided yet further confirmation.[3] Throughout 1896 and 1897 the *Economist* conducted a protracted campaign against monopoly company rule in general and Rhodes in particular. It demanded the suspension of Rhodes's directorship, an inquiry into the Company's affairs, and the publication of its list of shareholders. The history of the B.S.A.C., it claimed, was 'the most effective object lesson which could be imagined as to the danger in our day of mixing up pecuniary adventure and politics'.[4] And the danger was still present. 'No-one who watches events', it said as early as April 1896,

> can doubt that a powerful group in the Transvaal, supported by great financial interests in London, desire that the British Government should be compelled to solve all questions in South Africa by a resort to force. . . . If we are compelled to fight let us fight, but let us not be dragged involuntarily into the fight through the ignorant suspiciousness of the Boers, and the perverseness of that English group which, having been betrayed by its greed into an amazing blunder, now seeks to cover up all evidence and arrest all inquiry by forcing on a war.

If amity and unity in South Africa were defeated, the *Economist* concluded, 'it will be by the unreasonable impatience, not of patriots, but of men who at heart are moved only by the hope of great percentages'.[5] The same lesson was drawn in all other Radical quarters. The *New Age* commented after the Raid that 'Our final moral must be this: that the real ruler and the real enemy of mankind today is the international capitalist power.'[6] The capitalist nature of imperialism, and its dangers, were clearly apparent.

Apply it generally to all contemporary colonial expansion, and one had here an 'economic theory'. Find its prime moti-

---

[1] *The Economist*, 9 May 1891, pp. 591–2.
[2] Ibid. 4 June and 8 Oct 1892.   [3] Ibid. 4 Jan 1896 *et passim*.
[4] Ibid. 4 July 1896.
[5] Ibid. 25 Apr 1896.   [6] *The New Age*, 9 Jan 1896, p. 232.

vation in the industrial situation of the time, and there was born, in a crude form, the 'surplus capital' argument. This half of the syllogism was as familiar in the last decades of the century as the other. In 1890 the socialist William Morris stated it thus:

> in the last age of civilisation men had got into a vicious circle in the matter of production of wares. They had reached a wonderful facility of production, and in order to make the most of that facility they had gradually created (or allowed to grow, rather) a most elaborate system of buying and selling, which has been called the World-Market; and that World-Market, once set a-going, forced them to go on making more and more of these wares, whether they needed them or not. . . .
>
> The appetite of the World-Market grew with what it fed on: the countries within the ring of 'civilisation' (that is, organised misery) were glutted with the abortions of the market, and force and fraud were used unsparingly to 'open up' countries *outside* that pale. . . . When the civilised World-Market coveted a country not yet in its clutches, some transparent pretext was found – the suppression of a slavery different from, and not so cruel as that of commerce; the pushing of a religion no longer believed in by its promoters; the 'rescue' of some desperado or homicidal madman whose misdeeds had got him into trouble amongst the natives of the 'barbarous' country. . . .[1]

Among English socialists Morris was the first to relate imperialism so closely to over-production. But the idea was not his. He was only repeating the common view of the imperialists themselves.

For years it had been the unblushing assertion of capitalists and traders, accepted and implemented by governments, that the 'flag' should be used in the service of commerce.[2] Both had persistently stressed the necessity of finding new markets for British manufactures and new fields for investment. To those in the middle of the nineteenth century who were anxious about

---

[1] William Morris, *News From Nowhere* (1890), in *Selected Writings and Designs* (ed. Asa Briggs), pp. 263–5.

[2] Pitt is quoted by Lord Cromer (*Political and Literary Essays*, p. 11) as saying that 'British policy is British trade'. And cf. above, p. 24.

the 'falling tendency of profits', foreign investment and colonisation had seemed to offer them salvation. Gibbon Wakefield,
arguing that 'the economic difficulties of England in the thirties
and forties arose out of over-population and over-supply of
capital', had proposed to 'remedy both evils by sending men and
capital to the colonies'.[1] Governments were aware of the pressure
for foreign markets, and used the political and diplomatic power
at their disposal to extend the area of British commerce.[2] During
the Free Trade era this could usually be done 'informally', but
occasionally when peaceful means failed force was used to gain
entry into closed markets.[3] However it was done, it was the
accepted view that one of the functions of the Foreign Office
was to provide outlets for British manufactures.

The industrial depression of the 1880s led many manufacturers
to re-emphasise the pressing need for new markets. In 1885,
Sheffield and Birmingham industrialists told a Commission of
Inquiry into the Depression that colonial markets must be
opened up to satisfy this need.[4] Already Joseph Chamberlain
appeared to be responsive to their demands, and ready to direct
them into imperial channels. In the eighties he began to give
great emphasis to the commercial value of the Empire, and to
stress in particular the vested interest which the working classes
held in it, from the point of view of employment and their
standards of living:

> Is there any man in his senses who believes that the crowded
> population of these islands could exist for a single day if it
> were to cut adrift from us the great dependencies, which now
> look to us for protection and assistance, and which are the
> natural outlets for our trade? [1884]

A great part of our population is dependent at the present

[1] W. H. B. Court, 'The Communist Doctrines of Empire', in W. K.
Hancock, *Survey of British Commonwealth Affairs*, vol. ii, pt. 1, p. 295.
Paul Leroy-Beaulieu made similar claims before the French Government
in 1874. See Henri Brunschwig, *French Colonialism 1871–1914*, p. 27.
[2] See Gallagher and Robinson, 'The Imperialism of Free Trade', *E.H.R.*
[3] Ibid.
[4] Quoted in Victor Bérard, *L'Angleterre et l'Impérialisme*, pp. 75–80.

time upon the interchange of commodities with our colonial fellow-subjects. [1888][1]

To the London Chamber of Commerce in May 1888 he advocated the extension of the Empire in Africa. Trade was vital to our interests, and trade followed the flag.[2]

While such commercial pressures could be satisfied in an 'informal' diplomatic way, and while those who upheld the importance of imperial trade did so within the limits of the existing Empire, Cobdenite principles – though shaken by the appeals for 'warlike establishments or large armaments for the purpose of encouraging our trade in distant parts of the world'[3] – were not seriously threatened by aggressive or protectionist policies. During the 1890s, however, German economic growth and commercial competition, together with the new competitive and exclusive form which European imperialism was taking in Africa, presented new dangers to free-traders. Despite a recovery in British trade, there was in the mid nineties a strong under-current of anxiety about Britain's ability to compete successfully with protectionist nations, of which E. E. Williams's *Made in Germany* (1896) was a symptom. In March 1896 Chamberlain outlined his scheme for a British 'Imperial Zollverein',[4] and a debate ensued which resurrected the Free Trade controversies of the 1840s.[5] Imperialism was once again linked with mercantilism. It was even more clearly linked with over-production and un-employment. Cecil Rhodes was reported as saying in 1895:

> In order to save the forty million inhabitants of the United Kingdom from a bloody civil war, our colonial statesmen must acquire new lands for settling the surplus population of

[1] Quoted in W. Scovell Adams, *Edwardian Heritage*, pp. 66 ff.

[2] W. L. Strauss, *Joseph Chamberlain and the Theory of Imperialism*, ch. iv.

[3] Cobden, 1850, quoted in J. A. Hobson, 'Free Trade and Foreign Policy', in *C.R.*, Aug 1898, p. 168.

[4] Canada Club Dinner, 25 Mar 1896.

[5] Protectionist articles in the reviews include Arnold-Forster in *C19th*, Feb 1896; Sir Frederick Young, ibid. July 1896; Sidney Low, ibid. Aug 1896; Sir Julius Vogel, ibid. Mar 1897; and Percy Hurd in *C.R.*, Aug 1897. *The Economist* came out in strong opposition to an imperial customs union (1 Feb, 28 Mar, 6 and 13 June 1896).

this country, to provide new markets for the goods produced in the factories and mines. The Empire as I have always said is a bread and butter question. If you want to avoid civil war, you must become imperialists.[1]

And in November 1896 Chamberlain re-emphasised the commercial motives behind international politics. Commerce was 'the greatest of all political interests';

All the great offices of state are occupied with commercial affairs. The Foreign Office and the Colonial Office are chiefly engaged in finding new markets and defending old ones. The War Office and the Admiralty are mostly occupied in preparations for the defence of those markets and for the protection of our commerce.

To this end he recommended to the country a policy of 'the development of our imperial estates'.[2] The commercial motivation of imperialism – whether or not it was the true motivation – had been pointed simply and clearly by the arch-imperialist himself.

It was one of the main *justifications* for imperialism, not a criticism of it. Commercial expansion of this kind had a number of unpleasant features: its protectionist implications, the irresponsibility of its chartered agents. Its opponents could attack these. But they would make no kind of impression merely by pointing to its roots in 'over-production'. Over-production was its excuse. What anti-imperialists had to do was, somehow, to *counter* the 'economic theory' offered by the imperialists themselves.

William Morris did it by pouring scorn on the industrialism which had produced this situation. His remedy was to go back on the industrial revolution, to lower production by producing quality in place of quantity.[3] English Marxian socialists, as we shall see, could afford to take a similar line against the 'system'.[4] But those Liberals who were committed to *laissez-faire* could

[1] Quoted in John Strachey, *The End of Empire*, p. 146.
[2] Chamberlain to Birmingham Chamber of Commerce, 13 Nov 1896 (*A.R.*).
[3] William Morris, *News from Nowhere*, p. 267.
[4] See below, pp. 98–104.

hardly be expected to abuse their own idols so casually. If they accepted that there was over-production, then they must either accept the solution offered by the imperialists, or provide an alternative. This was the economic problem presented by the imperialism of the 1890s.

III. TROPICAL DEVELOPMENT

Beneath the surface of the controversy over 'imperialism' there was a third unresolved problem, perhaps the most perplexing and important of them all. For the 'New Imperialism' was not only a phenomenon affecting England, generating enthusiasm or concern according to how one assessed its implications for the home country: though to read the propaganda of the time it might have seemed such. It affected tropical countries too – the point is obvious, yet it was often forgotten in the debates of the 1890s – and at this time it affected Africa most of all. It raised fundamental questions about the morality and the methods of African 'development' or 'exploitation', about the native African's part in all this, the relations between what Sydney Olivier was to call 'white capital and coloured labour': and this in a form more acute than ever before, because of the new interest which European industry was taking in Africa's natural products. The problem was put most clearly by an imperialist, Benjamin Kidd, in the mid nineties, and can best be stated in his own terms. Kidd was aware, as he put it, that 'In any forecast of the future of our civilisation, one of the most important of the questions presenting themselves for consideration, is that of the future relationship of the European peoples to what are called the lower races.' [1] It was a question that could not be ignored, because it was both inevitable and right that European nations should want to exploit Africa's resources. It was inevitable because the greater 'energy, enterprise and social efficiency' of the northern races were 'part of the cosmic order of things',[2] and because over-production and over-population at home would drive them to 'seek new outlooks for

[1] Benjamin Kidd, *Social Evolution*, p. 303.   [2] Ibid. p. 317.

their activities' and 'turn their attention to the great natural field of enterprise which remains in the development of the tropics'.[1] It was right because it was 'inexpedient' to allow 'a great extent of territory in the richest region of the globe – that comprised within the tropics – to remain undeveloped, with its resources running largely to waste under the management of races of low social efficiency.'[2] The tropics, therefore, 'must be administered from the temperate regions'.[3] How should it be done? Europeans could not colonise the tropics and exploit its resources by their own labour.[4] The coloured races could not be trusted to develop those resources on their own, or to govern themselves with any degree of efficiency.[5] Nor was it either possible or permissible to drive them into forced labour,[6] to regard the tropics merely as 'an estate to be worked for gain'.[7]

> We come, therefore, to a clearly defined position. If we have to meet the fact that by force of circumstances the tropics *must* be developed, and if the evidence is equally emphatic that such a development can only take place under the influence of the white man, we are confronted with a larger issue than any mere question of commercial policy or of national selfishness. The tropics in such circumstances can only be governed as a trust for civilisation, and with a full sense of the responsibility which such a trust involves.[8]

Radicals need not go along with all the stages of Kidd's argument. Yet the doctrines it implied – of 'social efficiency', free labour and 'trusteeship' – had to be considered by them. For Europe *was* administering Africa. The interests of natives and of 'civilisation' were coming into conflict. The choice between leaving the native alone, forcing him to work and something in between was a real and urgent one. And the natives' welfare, and how it was best to be secured, were questions which had remained unresolved since the 1850s.

[1] Benjamin Kidd, *The Control of the Tropics*, p. 19.
[2] *Social Evolution*, p. 316.
[3] Ibid. p. 317.   [4] Ibid. p. 316; and *Control of the Tropics*, p. 48.
[5] *Social Evolution*, pp. 316–17; and *Control of the Tropics*, pp. 51–2.
[6] *Social Evolution*, p. 316.   [7] *Control of the Tropics*, p. 49.   [8] Ibid. p. 53.

C

The cynical solution to the 'native question', of course, was
their extinction, naturally rather than forcibly, in the face of a
superior civilisation. This was what was happening in the New
Hebrides: 'The cause of the extinction is the old one, *i.e.*, the
incapacity of the native race ... to change from their old habits
and ways of thought, and to adopt and adapt the European habits
and ways of thought which must prevail in the struggle for
existence.' [1] To a great extent it had happened already in Australasia and North America, and Sir Charles Dilke – by no means
anti-humanitarian – regarded it as 'not only a law of nature, but a
blessing to mankind'.[2] The process there seemed inevitable (until
the anthropologists thought of ways to prevent it).[3] But, whatever the situation in America and the Pacific, for Africa this kind
of 'final solution' was clearly out of the question. African Negroes
did not die off in the same way as Amerindians and aborigines;
they were, said Mary Kingsley, 'a great world race – a race not
passing off the stage of human affairs, but one that has an immense amount of history before it.' [4] They would proliferate,
and white men would have to work with them and through them.
The question was, how?

The natives were not without their champions. The Anti-
Slavery Society and the Aborigines Protection Society had
carried through to the 1890s the humanitarian concern for native
rights which had inspired their founders in the 1830s, and in
approximately the same form. Proud of their country's 'imperial
destiny', they preached its moderation by Christian charity and
justice. Thomas Hodgkin said in 1896:

> It was the mission of the Anglo-Saxon race to penetrate into
> every part of the world, and to help in the great work of
> civilisation. Wherever its representatives went, the national

[1] The High Commissioner for the Western Pacific, in a Report on the
New Hebrides issued as a supplement to P.P. (1907), lvi (Cd. 3288), p. 75,
para. 35.
[2] Dilke, *Greater Britain* (8th ed., 1885), p. 88; and cf. ibid. p. 223: 'The
Anglo-Saxon is the only extirpating race on earth.'
[3] See W. H. R. Rivers, *Essays on the Depopulation of Melanesia*; and
below, p. 325, fn. 2.
[4] Mary Kingsley, *The Story of West Africa*, ch. x.

conscience should go also.... Native races were like
children; they must be protected against the superior brain
power of the races which had reached maturity.[1]

So Britain was right to spread civilisation among the savages;
the humanitarians must ensure only that she did not take unfair
advantage of her strength.

In practice this meant first of all wiping out slavery and the
slave trade (although there were not many parts of the world
where overt slavery was still practised, and the *Anti-Slavery
Reporter* found it difficult in the 1890s to find material to fill its
pages outside of Pemba and Zanzibar). It also meant protecting
the native from the evils of liquor: for this purpose a 'Native
Races and Liquor Traffic United Committee' was set up in
1887.[2] Thirdly, 'punitive expeditions' against ill-armed African
malcontents must be vigorously opposed – this was the special
concern of Henry Fox Bourne, secretary of the A.P.S.[3] And
finally, it meant securing for native races under European rule
'the due observance of justice and the protection of their rights':[4]
this was the chief aim of the A.P.S. It was more fully elaborated by
Fox Bourne in 1900. The native, he said, had three fundamental
rights: a right to his land, to the free practice of his own customs
and the maintenance of his own institutions, and to an equal share
in 'all the beneficial arrangements' introduced into his country
by the white man. None of these rights could be taken from him
by force. His lands and their products should not be appropriated
without his legitimate and intelligent consent. He should not be
forced to work except 'under voluntary contracts fairly entered
into'. And his 'barbaric institutions' should be suppressed
only by means of 'reasonable persuasion'. In sum, the general
aim of the colonising power should be less the 'material ad-

[1] *The Aborigines' Friend* (journal of the A.P.S.), July 1896; and cf.
H. R. Fox Bourne, *The Story of Our Colonies*.

[2] K. K. D. Nworah, 'Humanitarian Pressure-Groups and British Attitudes
to West Africa, 1895–1915', p. 151.

[3] See two pamphlets by Fox Bourne, *Expéditions de Représailles ... en
Afrique*, and *'Civilisation' by War*.

[4] Fox Bourne, *The Aborigines Protection Society: Its Aims and
Methods*.

vantage' of the white man than the 'moral advantage' of those he ruled.[1]

This gave the humanitarian societies a firm basis from which they could seek to temper the worst abuses of European colonisation. They protested as loudly as anyone against Matabele wars, Congo atrocities, Arab slave-traders, West African liquor-merchants, suppression of Bechuana rebels, forced labour in gold and diamond mines, Sudan massacres, Boer maltreatment of Kaffirs, and the rest. They published pamphlets, organised meetings, inaugurated parliamentary debates, and wrote long letters of protest to the Colonial Office. For all parts of British Africa they were the most active and dedicated 'friends of the aborigine'.[2]

This was all well and good, and much needed in the 1890s. As Alfred Pease pointed out in 1899,

> The constant and rapid extension of European control over uncivilised races in Africa and elsewhere, generally brought about by disastrous wars, and attended by neglect and abuse of the responsibilities thus incurred, render the work of the Aborigines Protection Society ... far greater than ... in 1837.[3]

Their arguments were somewhat antiquated, still drawn from the old reformism of the 1830s; but they were not thereby obsolete – men could not be reminded too often of the 'human rights' of their fellows in Africa. Yet they lacked a certain sophistication and clear relevance to the 'new' conditions of the later period. Thomas Hodgkin's 'children' metaphor, for example, was well meant, but not very exact. Children share the culture of their parents or guardians; they are not as a rule brought up in traditions alien to their own. With Africa it was not a simple case of 'immaturity'. Hodgkin's words betrayed a unilinearism as rigid as the anthropologists', and from this sprang an over-simple view of the problems of African government common to most

[1] Fox Bourne, *The Claims of Uncivilised Races.*
[2] See *The Aborigines' Friend* and the *Anti-Slavery Reporter, passim.*
[3] *The Aborigines' Friend,* Nov 1899. Pease became President of the A.P.S. in 1899.

of his colleagues at 'Exeter Hall'. They saw clearly the dangers which derived from the meeting of white and black in Africa, its harmful implications for the African: but they saw the conflict only in terms of the weak versus the strong, the mature versus the immature. Evil in Africa arose out of this, out of the white man's using his superior knowledge and power to defraud the unlettered and ill-armed Negro. So their policies were directed almost exclusively against *wilful* oppression. Words like 'fraud', 'theft' and 'murder' are prominent in the humanitarians' writings and speeches.[1] The implication was that the imperialists' motives had only to be purified for their activities to benefit the African. Simple justice – the kind of justice acceptable in England – would suffice; for the rest, 'The negro races nearly always welcome British rule, and cheerfully submit to it when it is just.'[2] Imperial expansion in tropical countries was a great and glorious thing so long as it was conducted in conformity to the processes of English law, and with respect for the equal rights of all men, created (as the motto of the A.P.S. put it) *ab uno sanguine*.

But the situation in Africa was more complicated than this. Wilful wickedness was still the most frequent cause of oppression there. But what of those who claimed to be doing the African good by teaching him, against his will, of the sanctity of labour, or by developing his country's resources with his reluctant assistance? or those who, like Benjamin Kidd, denied the right of primitive tribes selfishly to leave those resources to waste? and who pointed to the impossibility in some parts of Africa of obtaining sufficient labour to develop them without compulsion? Such arguments may have been hypocritical, but they had a semblance of philanthropy. They must at least be considered by anyone who had the interests of the African at heart. And what of those people in another quarter who were casting doubt on the beneficence even of clearly selfless colonialism – those who regarded the good intentions of 'civilisers' as hardly less injurious than the wickedness of the exploiters? There were some

---

[1] See, for example, Fox Bourne's *The Claims of Uncivilised Races*.
[2] Annual Report of the A.P.S. for 1895, published in *The Aborigines' Friend*, July 1896.

(they will be treated in a later chapter)[1] who disputed the universal validity of European civilised standards, and who considered that even those Western customs which were freely appropriated by the native might do him harm. The African, they said, was in no position to judge his own best interest; he might, for example, alienate his land, legally and with a full understanding of what he was doing, yet regret it afterwards; or he might abjure freely his 'barbarous customs', attracted by the superficial glitter of what the white man had to offer, and find himself rootless and unhappy thereafter. Even within the Aborigines Protection Society one or two had begun to think of these things at the very end of the century; the Bishop of London, for example, who felt that in dealing with native races 'our object should be, not to make them like ourselves, but to help them to work out their own destiny'.[2] Such considerations dictated a far more sophisticated approach to native questions than the humanitarians could offer. The complexities of African land-law, the demands of economic development in the tropics, and the problems of acculturation all had to be studied in considerable detail before it could be discovered what the true interests of Africa's indigenous population were. It might be that after such a study the humanitarians' policies would be found still to be valid; but if so it would be for different reasons. Exeter Hall's defence of 'human rights' was not necessarily out of date in the 1890s, but it seemed to be, because it had not yet come to terms with the economic and social problems posed by the New Imperialism and the scramble for Africa. So in the 1890s and 1900s, says a recent study, its influence waned.[3] The tactics of the A.P.S.

[1] See below, Ch. 5; and cf. above, pp. 26–33.
[2] The Bishop of London (Creighton) quoted in the Annual Report of the A.P.S. for 1900 (*Aborigines' Friend*, Apr 1901). Cf. also Creighton's speech at the Annual General Meeting of the A.P.S., 1 Mar 1900 (in ibid., loc. cit). The 'great interest of the future', he said, was to raise 'these black races by a continuous process to a level that, however different from ours, might be almost equal with our own'; and also Fox Bourne, *The Claims of Uncivilised Races*: 'when the utmost has been done, it must not be expected that the highest civilisation of the black will be in all respects equal to, still less identical with, the highest civilisation of the whites'.
[3] Nworah, 'Humanitarian Pressure-Groups', pp. 182–3, 188–95, 659–60.

reflected an attitude both intellectually and psychologically unprepared for the problems of the new empire. Almost barren of new ideas, which demanded a thorough grasp of economic principles, Exeter Hall continued to harp on the early Christian ideals. Justice, humanity and charity still struggled with slavery and intemperance as in the traditional order.[1]

The humanitarians went some way towards curbing the excesses of the New Imperialism; but they failed to provide a viable solution to the ideological crisis it had provoked.

These three problems of jingoism, capitalism and tropical development – all of them put most plainly by the other side – together constituted the imperial challenge to the Left in the nineties. It remains to be seen how the various Radical groups reacted to it. Our starting-point is the Jameson Raid of 1895, which raised in a dramatic fashion all these problems: an unprovoked invasion, as Radicals saw it, of a friendly country, undertaken for mercenary ends, cheered on by a jingo Press, and backed by an enterprise whose recent native policies were now to be subjected to public scrutiny.

[1] Ibid. p. 658.

CHAPTER THREE

Liberals and the Empire

THE Liberal Party constituted the main opposition group to the 'imperialist' Unionist Government of the late 1890s. If there was criticism of the New Imperialism and its manifestations, then it should be sought here first of all. What kind of stand did Liberals take on questions of colonial policy, and on the broader issue of 'imperialism'?

From the beginning they appeared bewildered by it. The New Imperialism was, it seemed, outside the range of their experience, and certainly outside their range of competence. They were forced to discuss it, but without ever being sure or agreed about what it was. Imperialists themselves gave conflicting definitions which merely added to the Liberal confusion. To imperialists this mattered little: a policy which was being implemented by a government in power did not need to be spelt out; it was defined by what it was, by its practical manifestations, and the interpretation of that policy could safely be left to its adherents (so long as they agreed to what their leaders were doing) to discuss among themselves. But the policy of a party out of office had to be translated into words, because they had nothing concrete to point to when words failed them. This task the Liberal Party found overwhelmingly difficult. Their opponents had chosen the battlefield and the weapons, and Liberals were familiar with neither. Their discomfort was manifested in the colonial debates of the nineties.

I. THE LIBERAL RESPONSE

Many imperial issues they preferred to ignore. Egypt was an exception. The Sudan campaign of 1896–8, culminating in the recapture of Khartoum and the 'revenging' of Gordon, provoked among them a lively interest, a resurrection of the old Egyptian controversy between 'evacuationists' and 'retentionists', and a strong moralistic offensive led by John Morley against the 'atrocities' of Omdurman.[1] But this was a special case. The Uganda Railway, with its implications *vis-à-vis* the 'forward' policy in Africa, stimulated very little opposition or even interest among the bulk of the Liberal Party, outside a few Little Englander Radicals.[2] The Ashanti Wars met with even less criticism,[3] and in a general debate on West Africa in February 1898 only twenty-seven voted against the Government.[4] The transfer of the administration of Nigeria from the Royal Niger Company to the Colonial Office in 1899 provoked a few grumbling protests about the amount of compensation paid to the Company, and expressions of regret that Britain had ever had anything at all to do with the country, but nothing from the Liberal side on the more vital questions involved.[5] And when Sir Charles Dilke raised the Congo question in the House of Commons in April 1897, and used it to point a more general moral concerning the treatment of native races under the rule of monopoly companies, the resulting debate was desultory and inconclusive.[6] Dilke was the only member of the Liberal Party (and he was suspected for his 'imperialist' tendencies) who took any great interest in native problems; and to him the parliamentary position was very unsatisfactory. 'I am not sure', he wrote in the autumn of 1896, 'that we Radicals sufficiently attacked the policy of the Sudan and Matabele wars.'[7] In fact they had, so far as was possible, ignored colonial issues.

[1] See the Commons debates of 16 and 20 Mar, 5 June 1896, and 5 Feb 1897.
[2] See H. of C., 2 July 1896, 3 Mar 1898, 27 Feb 1899, and 22 Feb, 30 Apr, 7 and 14 May 1900.
[3] See H. of C., 12 Mar 1896, and 18–19 Mar 1901.
[4] See H. of C., 24 Feb 1898.   [5] See H. of C., 3, 19, 26 and 27 July 1899.
[6] See H. of C., 2 Apr 1897.   [7] *P.R.*, Oct 1896, p. 60.

C2

But certain questions they could not avoid. Those events which had made headline news called for full-scale discussions in Parliament. The military campaign which culminated in the Fashoda crisis of 1898 was one of them. It had stimulated in the country a bout of jingoism more powerful than anything since Crimea. Contemporaries drew attention to the new national temper. From one side of the political fence Sidney Low noted that 'the last few months have forced foreign politics into unavoidable prominence, and have compelled all Englishmen to think of the external relations of the Empire and its means of defence against aggression'.[1] From the other side, Wilfrid Scawen Blunt put it more strongly. 'The whole country,' he wrote in his *Diaries*, 'if one may judge from the press, has gone mad with the lust of fighting glory, and there is no moral sense left in England to which to appeal. It is hideous but unmistakeable.'[2] In this atmosphere the Liberals were compelled to discuss the issue of 'imperialism': and in a series of speeches in the country the leaders of the Party gave their views on the broad political question of the moment. But it did them no good. The Liberal debate was characterised by a surface unanimity: but this unanimity was due only to the abstract and general way in which they treated the problem. All Liberals agreed in deprecating what they variously called 'false', 'insane' or 'bastard' imperialism; yet Unionists would concur in this also. They failed to define much more closely what they meant, and so the debate had very little meaning.[3] And things were happening within the Party which destroyed any chance of real agreement. Sir William Vernon

---

[1] *C19th*, Jan 1899, p. 14.

[2] Wilfrid Scawen Blunt, *My Diaries*, vol. i, p. 365. And cf. *The Times*, 15 Nov 1898: 'It is interesting to observe how the growth of the Imperial sentiment has for the moment submerged party passions and party interests. A good many speeches have lately been delivered on political platforms, but in all the same note has been struck by Liberals and Radicals as well as by Unionists.'

[3] See the speeches of Asquith at Birmingham 16 Dec 1898 and Louth 16 Jan 1899; Morley at Brechin 17 and 19 Jan 1899; Grey at Oxford 25 Feb 1899; Harcourt at Nantyglo 31 May 1899; and Campbell-Bannerman at the National Liberal Federation Meeting, Hull, 21 Mar, and the City Liberal Club 30 June 1899.

A PROTEST IN THE PARLIAMENT HOUSE.

Honest John (*M-rl-y*). "NAY, FRIEND BALFOUR, OUR POCKETS ARE CLOSED TO THIS ACCURSED MAN-OF-ARMS! SUCH UNSEEMLY GLORY WILL BRING OUR LITTLE LAND TO SHAME. VERILY, IT BRINGETH TO MIND THE WORST DAYS OF THE MEN WELLINGTON AND NELSON!"

Three leading Liberal anti-imperialists – Henry Labouchere, John Morley, and C. P. Scott – by E. T. Reed of Punch, 31 May 1899

Harcourt and John Morley resigned from the Liberal front bench in December 1898, and their resignation was interpreted by many – by Harcourt and Morley themselves, by Arthur Balfour, by the *Manchester Guardian* and other newspapers, and by Blunt[1] – as having been provoked by the imperialism of their party's right wing. This wing resented the charges which the two dissentients levelled against them – 'I must repudiate ... his [Morley's] suggestion that all nous autres are wallowing in the mud of Jingoism,' wrote Asquith[2] – but nevertheless the Party was clearly divided on the issue of imperialism, and Lord Rosebery was to underline the division in the spring of 1899. The Liberal Party, he told the City Liberal Club, must be 'reconstituted in one form or another' to return to 'the old Liberal spirit which existed before the split of 1886'. And,

> If the old Liberal party as it was before 1886 is to be revived again, or any new party is to be founded on its severance, this factor, at any rate, must be prominent to the minds of those who construct or revive – the factor of the larger patriotism that I have called imperialism.[3]

The imperialism of the imperialist Liberals – and Rosebery was not alone in his views – was apparently very different from that of the rest of the Party. The division, and the implications which the ex-leader had pointed, could not be ignored.

Fashoda raised the general issue, and Liberals could not agree on that. Events in South Africa raised more particular issues, and ones more vital to the interests of African colonies. Here there was greater unanimity and stronger conviction, and out of it grew the beginnings of a new critical approach to imperial questions.

The Jameson Raid of December 1895, and more especially its subsequent developments – the publication in April 1896 of cypher telegrams revealing the complicity of Rhodes, Beit and

---

[1] See Balfour's speech at Keighley 20 Dec 1898; Blunt, op. cit. i 380; and *M.G.*, 14 Dec 1898, leader, p. 5.

[2] Asquith to Campbell-Bannerman, 18 Jan 1899; C.B.P., B.M. Add. MS. 41210, f. 161.

[3] Rosebery, speech to City Liberal Club, 5 May 1899 (*A.R.*).

Harris of the British South Africa Company, and the suppression by the Company in May of the Matabele rebellion – raised two imperial questions of great practical importance. Should the government of 'lower races' be entrusted to a commercial company, a company which in this instance had shown itself to be irresponsible? Secondly, what were the implications of the obvious and tangible connexion between capitalism and imperialism which had been sharply pointed by the telegrams? The two questions were interconnected; the suspicion of mercenary motives raised anew doubts as to the ability of chartered companies to fulfil an imperial trust. On these points, surely, the Liberals could come to some agreement and work out a positive and electorally attractive policy.

The material was here for a powerful attack on the New Imperialism. For, whatever one's feelings about patriotic imperialism, this 'stock-jobbing' type was another matter. It was sordid, selfish and materialistic. And the opponents of the Raid in Parliament did not overlook it. The lesson that money and government should not be mixed was made to appear so axiomatic that even a Unionist, H. O. Arnold-Forster, could repeat it. Such companies as the B.S.A.C., he said in February 1898, were 'mixing up totally dissimilar things – things not only dissimilar, but which ought on every principle of ethics and good sense to be eternally dissociated – the right to govern men and the desire to make money'.[1] Campbell-Bannerman spoke of the dangers of entrusting 'the administration of a great territory to a trading company – or rather not to a trading company, but to a speculative financial company – with administrative powers'.[2] And from the Radical wing of the Liberal Party Labouchere considered this aspect of the question to be so vital that he could offer to support Chamberlain 'tooth and nail' in everything else if only he would 'put an end to Chartered Cies, and this one in particular'.[3]

[1] H. of C., 13 Feb 1896; 4 P.D. 37, c. 290. Cf. John Ellis in the same debate: 'there ought to be no mixing of commercial objects and political duties' (ibid. c. 363).

[2] H. of C., 26 July 1897; 4 P.D. 51, c. 1162.

[3] Labouchere to Dilke, Jan 1896 (Dilke Papers, B.M. Add. MS. 43892, f. 211).

The Radicals took up the anti-capitalist line with enthusiasm. Labouchere talked of 'shady financiers' carrying on a 'gambling establishment' under the Union Jack; Rhodes had 'used his position to promote his personal sordid interests';[1] and he pressed these charges – ineffectively – on the Committee of Inquiry into the Raid.[2] Leonard Courtney – a dissentient Unionist – made the same accusation: he could, he said, 'feel little sympathy with claims for political rights when tainted with share-rigging'.[3] And from the Liberal front bench Harcourt delivered this broadside against the cypher telegrams: 'It is a sordid and squalid picture of stock-jobbing Imperialism. . . . The very lingo is the language of the company promoter. . . .'[4]

The same theme was pursued during the South African War. The leaders of the Liberal Party felt constrained to leave it well alone: whatever they thought of the theory that the War was 'a scandalous plot of money-seekers using the British Government as a catspaw', as Campbell-Bannerman wrote to Bryce in November 1899, they could not use it; and Bryce replied: 'tho' the capitalists do count for a good deal, and there has been a lot of the old policy of Rhodes, Flora Shaw, Moberly Bell & Joe, still one has no evidence to produce'.[5] But other Members of Parliament were less scrupulous, and for many of them their anti-imperialist case was built around the hypothesis of a 'capitalist conspiracy'. By far the greater part of that case was concerned with the diplomacy which led to the War; with demonstrating that there was no *casus belli* and that the Boers had been provoked into issuing their ultimatum by Chamberlain and Milner;[6] or with the effects of the War. But, once they had argued this, the question of motives was raised. If the War was unjustified from

[1] H. of C., 8 May 1896; 4 P.D. 40, c. 952.

[2] P.P. (1897), ix, paras. 7307, 7666 ff.

[3] G. P. Gooch, *Life of Lord Courtney*, p. 334.

[4] H. of C., 8 May 1896; 4 P.D. 40, c. 889.

[5] Campbell-Bannerman to Bryce, 10 Nov, and Bryce to Campbell-Bannerman, 11 Nov 1899; C.B.P., B.M. Add. MS. 41211, ff. 61, 63.

[6] The best statements of the case against Chamberlain's diplomacy are found in James Bryce's introduction to the 3rd ed. of his *Impressions of South Africa*; and in G. P. Gooch's pamphlet, *The War and its Causes*.

the point of view of national security or honour, and detrimental to the true interests of Britain and the Empire, as they maintained, then why had it been provoked? It did not require much ingenuity, after the Jameson Raid had made an economic interpretation of events in South Africa inescapable, to find the answer among the capitalists of the Rand and their 'parasites' on the Stock Exchange; and the despatches which J. A. Hobson sent to the *Manchester Guardian* from Johannesburg in 1899, together with his later books and articles, filled in the details of a sinister tale of gold-lust and intrigue.[1] Among Members of Parliament the Irish Nationalists consistently took this line,[2] and they were supported in it by Broadhurst and Burns for Labour,[3] and Labouchere, Lloyd George, C. P. Scott, Bryn Roberts, Francis Channing and A. B. Markham among the Radicals.[4] And the anti-War organisations (the South African Conciliation Committee, the Transvaal Committee, the Stop-the-War Committee and the League against Aggression and Militarism)[5] joined in the anti-capitalist chorus. F. Reginald Statham, for the Transvaal Committee, traced the history of the 'capitalist conspiracy' back to the Kimberley diamond mines:

> Take note of the enormous power of the influences at work, look at the interests that became involved, and you will better understand the necessity of grappling at the present moment with the conspiracy ... that aims at enriching a small band of speculators at the cost of the British Empire.[6]

From South Africa F. W. Reitz described the 'Capitalistic Jingoism' which had made the War:

[1] See below, Ch. 6, Sect. v.

[2] John Dillon (Mayo) was the first M.P. to make this point, on the opening day of the session of Dec 1899 (4 P.D. 77, cc. 94 ff.).

[3] See below, pp. 127 ff.

[4] See the speeches in Parliament of Labouchere, 25 Oct 1899; Bryn Roberts, 27 Oct 1899 and 2 Feb 1900; and A. B. Markham, 20 Mar 1902. Also Spence Watson, Lloyd George and Channing to the National Liberal Federation, 27 Mar 1900; and Morley at Forfar 24 Jan 1900 and at the Oxford Palmerston Club, June 1900 (*A.R.*).

[5] See J. S. Galbraith, 'The Pamphlet Campaign on the Boer War', *J.M.H.*, vol. xxiv, no. 2 (June 1952), p. 119.

[6] F. R. Statham, *South Africa and the Transvaal.*

an alliance between Capitalism, with its great material influence, but barren of any one single exalted idea or principle on the one hand, and Jingoism, sterile, empty, soulless,
but with a rich stock-in-trade of bombastic ideas and
principles, prompted by the most selfish aspirations, on the
other hand.[1]

An anarcho-communist, Morrison Davidson, designated the
regiments fighting in South Africa as the 'shameless jannissaries
of the unconvicted thieves of the London Stock Exchange';[2] and
from the other end of the Radical spectrum Francis Hirst, the
man who in 1897 had tried to steer Liberalism back on to its
'traditional' path,[3] wrote:

We see a fight for gold-fields introduced by gambling.
Kaffirs as well as consols fluctuate with every change in its
fortune.... You have quotations before and after a
skirmish, failures and fortunes after a defeat, failures and
fortunes after a victory. Long Tom's discharges reverberate
in every synagogue of England and America.[4]

These are only a few examples. The Boer War stimulated a flood
of propaganda against 'capitalist imperialism' never equalled in
England subsequently. The arguments bore a great similarity, as
we shall see, to J. A. Hobson's: the 'conspiracy' was not only a
capitalist conspiracy but an international-Jewish-financial one;
it worked through the Press, which it controlled, and the South
African League, which it had taken over; and one of its main
aims was to enforce native labour on the Rand.

Yet despite the virulence of the attack (albeit from a minority),
and despite the attention which the New Imperialism in general
and the War in particular focused on Africa and imperial problems, little came out of it in the way of a policy towards the
colonies and the peoples of the Empire. Any concern which

[1] F. W. Reitz, A Century of Wrong, p. 42.
[2] M. Davidson, Africa for the Afrikanders: Why I am a Pro-Boer.
[3] See F. W. Hirst et al., Oxford Essays in Liberalism.
[4] F. W. Hirst, G. Murray and J. L. Hammond, Liberalism and the Empire,
p. 44.

Radicals in Parliament showed for the natives of South Africa was generally half-hearted and ignorant. In the controversies over the Jameson Raid, it was left to the Aborigines Protection Society to emphasise the implications of chartered-company rule for the welfare of natives. Thomas Bayley at their Annual General Meeting in 1897 'objected to semi-imperial powers being conferred upon Chartered Companies, which, as in South Africa, imposed a system of forced labour that was not distinguishable from slavery'; the solution was for the Crown to 'assume direct responsibility for the good government of our African colonies'.[1] But no such interest was shown in Parliament, where the Radicals were too occupied with the 'stock-jobbers' and with exposing their sordid motives. During the Boer War it was the same. The native question was seldom prominent in the minds of many on either side. F. Edmund Garrett, a former editor of the *Cape Times*, noticed that 'Liberals who have taken up "Afrikanderdom" have lost interest in the native populations'.[2] There were a few instances of a disinterested concern for the African; but this was rare.

When the native question played any part at all in the debates on the War, it was usually merely as a weapon for either side in the controversy over the justice of the War. Mrs. Leonard Courtney regarded the very raising of the issue as a hypocritical attempt to distract attention from this more important question:

No I will not read a paper on the 'treatment of the Native Races in S. Africa' at the Christian Conference.

While we are sinning so deeply in S. Africa it seems to me to be mere hypocrisy to be condemning other peoples sins.[3]

What irritated Mrs Courtney was the common plea of government supporters, that the War was being fought on behalf of the natives. As a Conservative put it at the end of 1900: 'We are now fighting the last great slave war – that is to say, we white men trying to save the blacks.'[4] Similar sentiments, expressed

[1] *The Aborigines' Friend*, May 1897.   [2] *C.R.*, Aug 1900, p. 171.
[3] Mrs Courtney to Brooke Lambert, 16 Nov 1900 (copy); Courtney Papers, vol. 7, f. 104 (L.S.E.).
[4] J. E. Gordon in Commons, 6 Dec 1900; 4 P.D. 88, c. 100.

more moderately, were heard too from Salisbury and Chamberlain.[1] One or two writers drew parallels with the American Civil War.[2] The Boer had shown himself unfit to govern native races. He was

> fighting for an independence which he has abused, and struggling for a freedom to carry on a native policy that is far worse than the slavery once practised in the Southern States of America. The cause of the Boers is *inherently* unholy and unjust, and is fundamentally opposed to all true progress and civilisation. . . . Our cause is righteous and true. . . . The British Empire is fighting a holy war for the cause of freedom and justice to the native races of South Africa.[3]

Contributions to the discussion from South Africa itself, bitterly complaining of the way emancipation had been effected in the 1830s, only served to confirm this 'missionary view'.[4] The African native would seem to be on the side of the British.

This necessarily rendered the raising of the native question a hazardous risk for pro-Boers. But there was an answer to the missionary view – the charge of hypocrisy. 'That the Dutch in South Africa have treated the blacks as the English in other colonies have treated the aborigines is probably true . . . ,' wrote W. T. Stead, 'but it does not do for the pot to call the kettle black.'[5] The British were as culpable, or more so. Davitt in the House of Commons, citing the Matabele Wars as an example, quoted 'from a weekly paper':

> O Lord, Thou knowest our anguish sore
> When blacks are butchered by the Boer!

[1] Salisbury in Lords, 17 Oct 1899, 4 P.D. 77, c. 22; and Chamberlain in Commons, 19 Oct 1899, 4 P.D. 77, cc. 271–2.

[2] Spencer Wilkinson, 'The War in South Africa and the American Civil War', in *C.R.*, June 1900; James Green, *Causes of the War in South Africa, from the American Lawyer's Standpoint*; Rev. Dr Wirgman, 'The Boers and the Native Question', in *C19th*, Apr 1900, p. 600. The Radical retort was to cite another American parallel, namely, 1776.

[3] Wirgman in *C19th*, Apr 1900, pp. 600, 602.

[4] See Reitz, *A Century of Wrong*, pp. 5–9; and F. S. Tatham, 'A Voice from Natal', in *C19th*, June 1900, pp. 883–5.

[5] W. T. Stead, Introduction to Reitz, op. cit. p. xiv.

'Tis our prerogative of yore
To slaughter niggers;
Only to make them love Thee more
We pull our triggers.[1]

Not only was there no evidence that the natives in the Transvaal
would fare better under a change of government: there was
every reason to believe, said Radicals, that they would be worse
off. Far from this being 'the last slave war', it was a war to
reintroduce slavery. Indeed, wrote Dilke to Dr Cust of the
Anti-Slavery Society, 'the Rand Jews have already got slavery,
and our Government must repeal the laws they have. Reading
together the Pass Law & the coloured labour clause, which you
will find was the end of the latest Gold Law, we have slavery by
law.[2] 'That', said Lloyd George in the Commons, 'is what our
brave troops are shedding their blood for; they are dying to
restore slavery under the British flag.'[3] Gilbert Murray gave the
use of the word 'slavery' the seal of approval of classical scholarship:

> 'my whole argument is that the legal status of slavery has
> little to do with the question; the essential object of both the
> ancient slave-system and these diverse modern makeshifts
> is a world-wide division of labour among breeds of men, the
> inferior work going to the inferior races, the higher work to
> the higher and more highly-paid races. The ancient employer
> did not specially want legal slaves; he wanted cheap alien
> labour, and that could only be had in the form of slaves.
> The modern employer can, as a rule, get his cheap alien
> labour by processes less wasteful, less shocking to outside
> opinion, and less disastrously cruel. But the essence of the
> demand is the same, and the essence of the thing supplied is
> the same.[4]

And the Aborigines Protection Society, holding no brief for

[1] Quoted in H. of C., 20 Oct 1899; 4 P.D. 77, c. 440.
[2] Dilke to Cust, 18 Dec 1900 (copy); Dilke Papers, B.M. Add. MS. 43916,
f. 257.
[3] H. of C., 6 Feb 1900; 4 P.D. 78, c. 762.
[4] Hirst, Murray and Hammond, *Liberalism and the Empire*, p. 147.

either side in the main controversy,[1] came out in support of the view that, however badly the Boers treated the natives, capitalists would treat them worse.[2] The argument was given weight and substance by the pamphlets issued by the Society's secretary, H. R. Fox Bourne, closely argued and packed with detailed evidence. The Outlanders, he said, wanted only 'power to use the natives in any way that pleases them for their own profit'.[3] The sole remedy for both Boer and capitalist exploitation was 'such interference by the Crown, in the exercise of powers undoubtedly possessed by it, and in fulfilment of duties clearly devolving upon it, as the present upheaval renders both opportune and urgent'; and he went on to formulate a 'Suggested Charter for the South African Natives' to ensure their liberty and elevation.[4]

Fox Bourne's indictment of the capitalists was taken up and used by the anti-War M.P.s. But his constructive proposals were not considered so immediately important. There was a short debate on native labour in South Africa in August 1901, when Dilke and Harcourt launched a strong attack on the Pass Laws ('the principles of these laws', said Dilke, 'were vile; they were specially directed against coloured people on the mere ground of colour').[5] But the general attitude was one of apathy towards the labour problem. All the natives wanted, said Labouchere, was 'a bottle of brandy to get drunk and a gun to shoot his neighbour': and we should do nothing to make him otherwise.[6] The same

---

[1] The A.P.S. Annual Report of 1899 denied any obligation to commit itself on the war issue, and in 1901 it expressed resentment at the fact that it had been blamed by partisans of both sides for not doing so (*Transactions* of the A.P.S., Annual Reports, 1899 and 1901).

[2] See 'Natives in South Africa', in *The Aborigines' Friend*, Nov 1899; Sir W. B. Gurdon (Chairman) at A.P.S. Annual General Meeting, 26 Mar 1901 (*Transactions*), etc.

[3] H. R. Fox Bourne, *Blacks and Whites in South Africa*.

[4] H. R. Fox Bourne, *The Native Question in South Africa*.

[5] H. of C., 6 Aug 1901, 4 P.D. 98, c. 1484; and cf. Harcourt, ibid. cc. 1454 ff. See also galley-proofs of an article by Dilke on 'The Treatment of Native Races', in Dilke Papers, B.M. Add. Ms. 43645, ff. 175-7.

[6] H. of C., 6 Aug 1901; 4 P.D. 98, c. 1521.

indifference was shown in the infrequent and badly attended debates on other African affairs. Occasionally there was a plea for 'sympathy' with native habits and customs,[1] and Thomas Lough and C. P. Scott in a debate on the Ashanti War made notable statements in favour of indirect rule through chiefs.[2] But more often than not the African native was used only as an excuse for an attack on capitalists,[3] or a protest against expansion in general.[4] The same trend is seen later in the debates on Chinese labour. When in 1906 and 1909 came the really vital debates on the future of South Africa, and native rights were seen to be one of the most important issues at stake, it was not the old pro-Boer Radicals (or such of them as remained in Parliament) who stood out as the most important opponents of the 'colour-bar', but the 'imperialist' Liberals Dilke and Josiah Wedgwood and the Labourites MacDonald, Barnes and Keir Hardie.[5]

All along, the Harcourts and Laboucheres had displayed only a superficial concern for native races. If the native provided a stick with which to beat imperialists and capitalists, then they took up his cause. If not, then the solution to all problems imperial was to leave well alone. They had little more to offer.

This was as far as the Liberal counter-attack against the Unionists' 'imperialism' went. The Party never seemed to come to terms with the new situation, which was characterised in Africa by a policy they did not understand, and in England by a popular

[1] e.g. Buxton in H. of C., 18 Mar 1901; 4 P.D. 91, c. 345.

[2] Lough, H. of C., 18 Mar 1901 (4 P.D. 91, cc. 337 ff.): 'these people. . . were struggling for an idea, namely, that the overlord of the country should be allowed to be the means of communication between them and us. What was wrong with that? Why should we not accept that system of Government under which the people were willing to live?' The argument is put in such a way as to ally it with the old Liberal principle of 'National rights' or 'Home Rule'. Lough regards the Ashanti revolt over the Golden Stool as a constitutional struggle of much the same kind as the Armenian and Bulgarian revolts. See also C. P. Scott in H. of C., 19 Mar 1901; 4 P.D. 91, cc. 427 ff.

[3] e.g. Labouchere in H. of C., 22 Feb 1900; 4 P.D. 79, cc. 893 ff.

[4] e.g. Burns in H. of C., 22 Feb 1900 (4 P.D. 79, cc. 873–4): 'We have to recognise this fact, that in foreign expansion we are biting off more than we can chew, swallowing more than we can digest.'

[5] See below, pp. 299–307.

enthusiasm – 'a decade of delirium ... a bad dream, with the strum of the banjo sounding through it a sort of mirthless, demoniac laugh' [1] – which left them cold. They gave no kind of lead to their followers. 'The people stand by passive, unconsulted, uninstructed, puzzled, doubtful; they are halting between two centuries and two opinions.' [2] They gave the impression – a misleading impression – that imperialism was carrying all before it. On the one side there was this imperialism, with its un-blushing self-assertiveness and its mass-emotional appeal; on the other a notoriously divided Liberal Party, liable to break into fragments at the very mention of the word empire, its leaders soft-pedaling and saying nothing on vital imperial issues, and with a left wing criticising as loudly as the circumstances per-mitted, but rarely offering anything constructive or really relevant to the Empire as it existed. The Party seemed, in the words of the *Annual Register*, 'for the time imperially impossible'.[3]

II. POLITICAL EXIGENCIES

The reasons for this flaccidity lie partly in the exigencies of the party situation. At the beginning of their period of opposition the Liberals found themselves in a bad position from which to criticise the Government's imperial policy. When in office im-perial questions had proved a constant source of embarrassment to them. The 'Home Rule' split of 1886 had been (said Rosebery) 'far more on what I call foreign and imperial questions, so far as I know, than on the Irish question'.[4] The shedding of the Liberal–Unionist wing did not resolve their differences. The Gladstone–Rosebery Ministry of 1892–5 had been deeply divided over such questions as Armenia and Nicaragua, the Anglo-Belgian Treaty of 1894 over the Nile, the Grey Declaration

[1] A. G. Gardiner, *Prophets, Priests and Kings* (1908), pp. 293, 295.
[2] F. W. Hirst, in Hirst, Murray and Hammond, op. cit. p. 2.
[3] *A.R.*, 1900, p. 204.
[4] Rosebery at City Liberal Club, 19 July 1901 (*The Times*, 20 July). This interpretation is confirmed by David Hoskin, 'The Genesis and Significance of the 1886 "Home Rule" Split in the Liberal Party'.

AN <u>ALMOST</u> EXTINCT SPECIES!

["The remains of a prehistoric animal were dug up close to the City Liberal Club a few days ago."
Daily Paper.]

WAS IT THE OSAPLESADŌNT (PHILANTHROPOD MAJUBATHERIUM) OR SHELL-LESS DISARMADILLO !?

E. T. Reed's representation of the Liberal Little Englander, in Punch 19 September 1900

of March 1895 and the issue of Uganda.[1] The quarrel between Harcourt and Rosebery which had so sapped the energy of that ministry was both a personal one and a conflict of ideas, and the ideological aspect centred on the question of imperialism. The electoral defeat of 1895 widened these divisions. From the beginning of 1896 the Liberal leadership was unable to agree on a consistent attitude to adopt towards imperial issues, and it was in the interests of unity that the Party should try to avoid such questions. All the time it was distracted by sectional disputes among its members: attempts by the Left to set up a 'Radical Committee' in opposition to the front bench;[2] resignations from its leaders;[3] and the quarrels and intrigues which accompanied the Boer War. There was a considerable degree of bad feeling in the Party, and suspicion among its members as to the motives of their leaders. Sir Ughtred Kay-Shuttleworth wrote of ' "deals" with the front bench opposite',[4] and the conduct of Harcourt on the Committee of Enquiry into the Jameson Raid, in consenting to a report which the *Westminster Gazette* called 'a scandal of the first order',[5] stimulated rumours which continued well into the Boer War that he had been bribed in one form or another by Rhodes.[6] Such disputes not only made impossible any agreement on imperial questions; they also distracted attention from them. While Radicals were so occupied with the 'Hawkesley Telegrams'

[1] See P. Stansky, *Ambitions and Strategies*, pp. 5–15, 106–25.

[2] e.g. in Apr 1896 a 'Radical Group' was organised by Dilke, Labouchere and eleven others (Dilke Papers, B.M. Add. Ms. 43915, ff. 240–1); and in Nov a further attempt was made to set up a 'Radical Executive Committee' (*A.R.*).

[3] Rosebery resigned from the leadership 9 Oct 1896, Morley and Harcourt from the front bench in Dec 1898.

[4] Kay-Shuttleworth to Campbell-Bannerman, 17 Dec 1898; C.B.P., B.M. Add. MS. 41221, f. 3.

[5] *Westminster Gazette* (Liberal), 14 July 1897.

[6] See Stansky, op. cit. pp. 234–52; and 'Quaesitor' in *C.R.*, July 1897. The *Spectator*, Aug–Oct 1901, charged the Liberal leaders with having been (more or less) bribed by a gift of £5,000 which Rhodes had made a few years earlier to the Party funds, on certain conditions (e.g., that the Party would not evacuate Egypt). There is much agitated correspondence about this in the Campbell-Bannerman and Viscount Gladstone papers (B.M. Add. MSS. 41216, 41219, 41222, 41236, 45987, *passim*).

and Harcourt's failure to insist on their revelation, they missed that aspect of the Jameson Raid which was the most important from the point of view of African colonial policy (and for which the Inquiry had been set up in the first place)[1] – the general question of administration by chartered company. Despite the publication of Sir Richard Martin's Report in July 1897, which confirmed the charge that compulsory labour was being enforced under the B.S.A.C. in Matabeleland,[2] the Company was allowed to continue (with a new constitution but still under Rhodes) in its efforts to involve the British Government in hostilities with the Boers and to enforce native labour on the Rand (or so it appeared to Radicals after the outbreak of war). And the Radicals had done little to prevent this.

Whether or not its leaders had been 'bribed' (and the charge was ill-founded), the Party had been compromised and its left wing hoodwinked. It was difficult to criticise the principle of the Uganda Railway in view of the fact that it was a Liberal government which had first sanctioned it, and Harcourt who had announced the Uganda Protectorate to the Commons in 1894.[3] It was difficult to condemn Fashoda after the Grey Declaration. Harcourt was unwilling to condemn Milner 'on account of my obligations to him in my financial measures'[4] (presumably the help which Milner as Chairman of the Board of Inland Revenue had given to him in framing his 1894 Budget).[5] And the position of the Liberal Party vis-à-vis South Africa was not made easier by their failings on the Jameson Raid Committee.

It was during the South African War that the 'imperial

[1] The original motion for the appointment of the Committee (moved by Chamberlain, 30 July 1896) had omitted all reference to the Raid, and recommended the inquiry only to deal with 'the administration of the B.S.A.C., and to report what alterations are desirable in the government of the territories under the control of the Company' (4 P.D. 43, c. 1057).

[2] Published in the *Daily Chronicle*, 17 July 1897; issued later as P.P. (1897), lxii.

[3] Stansky, op. cit. p. 121.

[4] Harcourt to Campbell-Bannerman, 20 Nov 1900; C.B.P., B.M. Add. MS. 41219, f. 151.

[5] A. G. Gardiner, *The Life of Sir William Harcourt*, vol. ii, p. 175. Harcourt recommended Milner for a K.C.B. in 1895.

impossibility' of the Party was revealed in all its nakedness. The
Party had a policy on the War; until the end of 1900 it was
criticism of Chamberlain's diplomacy, thereafter the theme of
'conciliation'. On the basis of this policy it managed to maintain
a very imperfect unity: there was still one Liberal Party in May

THE SOUTH AFRICAN BOOMERANG.

SIR W. H——T
and
SIR H. C——L B——N   } *"Oh, do be careful with that boomerang;*
it might fly back and hurt us.*"*

The Liberal dilemma, 1897; Labouchere, Harcourt and
Campbell-Bannerman (by F. Carruthers Gould in the
Westminster Gazette, *23 July)*

1902. But on the issue of imperialism, which was inseparable
from the War (or so the imperialists claimed), they had no
policy; and even on the War there were occasions when the
Party was painfully divided.[1] Such a situation was predictable
from what had gone before. But the circumstances of October
1899 aggravated the Liberals' difficulties. Two things prevented

[1] e.g. on 25 July 1900, in a division on an amendment moved by Sir
Wilfred Lawson against Chamberlain, 40 Liberals voted with the Govt.,
31 against, and 35 (including Campbell-Bannerman) abstained. 4 P.D. 86,
cc. 1164 ff.

the Party from being more outspoken than it might otherwise have been; the dilemma in which the War itself placed 'patriotic' Liberals; and the activities of the Roseberyites on the imperialist wing of the Party.

The dilemma of the Liberal Party in the autumn of 1899 is illustrated in the personal dilemma of its leader. Campbell-Bannerman, whose position on imperialism was ambiguous when he was elected leader in January,[1] had little sympathy either with the South African policy of the Government or with the various policies and emotions which together went under the name of 'imperialism'. He protested more than once that he was 'a Liberal and also an Imperialist enough for any decent man',[2] but his imperialism, which he never closely defined, was weaker than most. In public he sat tight on his middle-of-the-road fence; but in his private letters he admitted to a considerable sympathy with his anti-War colleagues. 'I am very much in harmony with your views', he wrote to Channing soon after the beginning of the War, 'although I am not at liberty to speak out quite so freely.' [3] The War he regarded as a 'sordid quarrel',[4] and the responsibility he placed squarely on the shoulders of 'Rhodes, Joe, & Milner'.[5] Chamberlain was 'the very embodiment of all that is bad in policy and spirit; of all that will wreck and ruin our country',[6] and Milner – 'the real arch-offender' [7] – he railed against continually. 'What a petulant, weak undignified tone there is about the High Commissioner!' he wrote to Bryce; 'and this whimpering petulance is characteristic of narrow-minded obstinacy

---

[1] In February 1899 *Reynolds's Newspaper* could call Campbell-Bannerman 'The Jingo and Old Liberal Leader' (5 Feb, p. 1).

[2] Campbell-Bannerman to Buxton, 21 Nov 1900; J. A. Spender, *The Life of the Right Hon. Sir Henry Campbell-Bannerman*, vol. i, p. 308.

[3] Campbell-Bannerman to Channing, 10 Nov 1899; C.B.P., B.M. Add. MS. 41213, f. 20.

[4] Campbell-Bannerman to Buxton, 31 Oct 1899; Spender, op. cit. i 253.

[5] Campbell-Bannerman to his cousin, Jas Campbell, 9 Feb 1900; C.B.P., B.M. Add. MS. 41246, f. 77.

[6] Campbell-Bannerman to Bryce, 26 Jan 1903; Spender, op. cit. ii 87.

[7] Campbell-Bannerman to Jas Campbell, 19 Nov 1899; C.B.P., B.M. Add. MS. 41246, f. 25.

[*sic*]'.[1] He distrusted the methods and motives of these men: 'they have nobbled the entire press. . . . How many shares in Rand mines have all these editors and pressmen got given to them?'[2] He was repelled, in an old-fashioned Liberal-moralistic way, by jingo 'flag-waving' and imperialistic 'Cock-a-doodle-do',[3] and by the depraved national temper which these years manifested: 'But oh! the degraded, apathetic, sport-loving, empty-headed, vulgar lot that our countrymen have become.'[4] When Rosebery affirmed later that Campbell-Bannerman's private sympathies had always been with the anti-War faction,[5] he was broadly correct. He said little about the Empire specifically. But by temperament he was the stuff that anti-imperialists were made of.

Yet during the war years he kept these opinions usually to himself, and many of his 'moderate' colleagues did the same.[6] Their position was a difficult one, and they had every reason to lie low until the storm had blown over. Jingoism was too strong, it seemed, to be reasoned with. As an irrational emotion it made all discussion on rational grounds irrelevant and unnecessary. Even if this were not so, if there were no popular war-fever, the

[1] Campbell-Bannerman to Bryce, 25 Dec 1899; C.B.P., B.M. Add. MS. 41211, f. 83.

[2] Campbell-Bannerman to Jas Campbell, 9 Feb 1900; C.B.P., B.M. Add. MS. 41246, f. 77.

[3] Campbell-Bannerman to Buxton, 31 Oct 1899; Spender, op. cit. i 254.

[4] Campbell-Bannerman to Bryce, 29 Dec 1903; C.B.P., B.M. Add. MS. 41211, f. 260.

[5] Marquess of Crewe, *Lord Rosebery*, pp. 573–4; R. R. James, *Rosebery*, p. 434.

[6] How many of his 'moderate' colleagues shared his feelings it is difficult to say. On the Radical wing of the Party there were about thirty who voted consistently for unambiguously anti-War amendments. Of the rest, Sir Edward Grey claimed that four-fifths of the Party were 'Liberal Imperialists' (Grey to Campbell-Bannerman, 17 Nov 1900; C.B.P., B.M. Add. MS. 41218, f. 8); while an officer of the National Reform Union estimated at the same time that '4/5ths of the party are . . . strongly against the war' (Arthur Symonds to Campbell-Bannerman, 8 Jan 1901; C.B.P., B.M. Add. MS. 41236, f. 81). Campbell-Bannerman himself considered that there were more anti-War men than appeared from the division-lists, for 'a lot of our people have not the pluck of a flea, and funk the newspaper abuse' (Campbell-Bannerman to Campbell, 9 Feb 1900; C.B.P., B.M. Add. MS. 41246, f. 77).

very fact that Britain was at war would place the problem outside the bounds of reason. Arguments which are valid in peace-time become subject to more overriding considerations when the normal relationships between men and nations are disrupted by the call to arms. Even the indisputable rationality of free trade, said Adam Smith, was superseded by considerations of national security: 'defence is of more importance than opulence'. Hence when Kruger issued his ultimatum to the British Government many Liberals felt that a new situation had been created, and with it a new order of priorities. 'For the moment', said the Liberal *Westminster Gazette*,

> the Boer ultimatum has salved uneasy consciences and rendered the discussion of alternative courses futile. Liberals, no more than Conservatives, need quarrel among themselves about what might have been. The momentary duty is to support the Government in making the inevitable expedition as prompt and effective as possible.[1]

The justice of the War could be debated later; the most pressing need was to vote supplies and ensure a British victory. Whatever their view of Chamberlain's actions before the ultimatum – and most of them, on both wings of the Party, had agreed in deploring the provocative tone of his diplomacy[2] – the Empire was now being attacked and most Liberals felt that they could not impede the military measures necessary for its defence. Once they had admitted this necessity any criticism was hampered. It was difficult, for example, to advocate a more generous peace settlement than the Government was prepared to consider without being accused of encouraging the Boer guerillas to hold out until the Unionist government fell (although from the beginning of 1901 the Liberals took this risk, and incurred such accusations).[3] There could, it appeared to some, be no 'patriotic' criticism of a

---

[1] *Westminster Gazette*, 12 Oct 1899. Cf, Rosebery's letter to *The Times*, 11 Oct; Fowler quoted in Spender op. cit. i 248; and (even) Labouchere in H. of C., 25 Oct 1899; 4 P.D. 77, c. 634.

[2] Even Rosebery had his doubts. See James, op. cit. pp. 410–11.

[3] Cf. Mr Harold Wilson on television 28 Feb 1966 (reported in *The Times*, 29 Feb), making a similar point about the Rhodesia crisis.

war policy, unless it were on grounds of military incompetence; and when Dilke suggested an amendment on these lines in December 1899[1] Campbell-Bannerman saw that this would merely be to 'run away with the question' on a 'side issue'.[2] To censure the Government for 'want of preparedness' before the War (as Dilke wished) was to admit that there was a need for military preparation, and this implication the Opposition wished to avoid.

There was another obstacle to criticism. However easily Liberals could see and point out that the British Government was in the wrong in South Africa, it was difficult for them to infer from this that the Transvaal was in the right. There were a few Radicals who were genuinely 'pro-Boer', who upheld every one of Kruger's diplomatic moves and regarded the Transvaal as a model of good government.[3] But there were many more who were exasperated by 'the stupid obstinacy of the Boers',[4] by the way that Kruger had 'played the game of our war party with provoking pertinacity'.[5] And the assertion of Herbert Paul before the War, that 'No Liberal can possibly sympathise with the policy of the Boer Government. . . . It is too like what they have been opposing all their lives at home',[6] contained much truth. At best an anti-War Liberal could only weigh two wrongs against one another, and find one more wrong than the other.

These difficulties, arising from the war situation, were real. Campbell-Bannerman gave vent to his frustration in a letter to John Ellis: 'the public are not in the humour for party speeches;

[1] Dilke to Herbert Gladstone, 27 Dec 1899; H.G.P., B.M. Add. MS. 46057, ff. 248–9.

[2] Campbell-Bannerman to Bryce, 14 Jan 1900; C.B.P., B.M. Add. MS. 41211, f. 86 (Spender, op. cit. i 270).

[3] Most prominent among these was Dr G. B. Clark, M.P. for Caithness 1885–1900, and ex-Consul-General for the S. African Republic.

[4] Bryce to Campbell-Bannerman, 6 Oct 1899; C.B.P., B.M. Add. MS. 41211, f. 50.

[5] H. Gladstone to Bryce, 7 Oct 1899; in C.B.P., B.M. Add. MS. 41211, f. 52.

[6] C.R., July 1899. Cf. F. Edmund Garrett in C.R., Oct 1899: 'an English Radical must become a Jingo'; and A. R. Carmen in C.R., Jan 1900.

nor can one let oneself go as one would like'.[1] Every other imperial issue was subordinated to the South African one; and on South Africa the Liberal leaders could not 'let themselves go'.

Yet within the Liberal Party there lay another and more serious enervating factor: the fear of a new Liberal split, and the spectre of Lord Rosebery. Behind Campbell-Bannerman's political actions between 1899 and 1902 these considerations played an all-important part. That the threatened defection of 'Liberal Imperialists' did not transpire was due chiefly to Campbell-Bannerman's skilful management of the Party and the indecisive and enigmatic conduct of Rosebery himself. But the threat was a serious one. In May 1899 Rosebery had given a hint of nefarious designs;[2] and throughout the War he kept stepping into the limelight (it was always limelight where he stepped) to provoke and tantalise an expectant public with speeches of the most perfect eloquence and the most imperfect clarity.

'I venture to think', he told his audience in Bath in October 1899,' – I may be wrong, – in ten years time perhaps you will remember my prophecy, – I believe the party of Liberal Imperialism is destined to control the destinies of this country.' [3] In July 1901 he averred that the Liberal divisions were 'based on a sincere fundamental and incurable antagonism of principle with regard to the Empire at large'; the two sections of the Party could no longer 'row in the same boat', and Liberals should begin again with a 'clean slate as regards those cumbersome programmes with which you were overloaded in the past'.[4] Six months later, at Chesterfield, he again advised the Party to wipe its 'slate' clean of the 'fly-blown phylacteries of obsolete policies', and to fill it with the 'new sentiment of Imperialism' and the philosophy

[1] Campbell-Bannerman to Ellis, 1 Nov 1899; C.B.P., B.M. Add. MS. 41214, f. 62.
[2] See above, p. 60.
[3] Rosebery at Bath, 26 Oct 1899; quoted in Crewe, Lord Rosebery, ii 562.
[4] Rosebery, letter to City Liberal Club, 17 July 1901; quoted in Gooch, Life of Lord Courtney, pp. 425–6.

of 'Efficiency'.[1] His general meaning seemed clear: a new party of Liberal Imperialism. But his own position was not. 'For the present at any rate, I must proceed alone. I must plough my furrow alone. That is my fate, agreeable or the reverse; but before I get to the end of that furrow it is possible that I may find myself not alone.'[2]

Such ambiguity made Campbell-Bannerman's position difficult. Rosebery's speeches were followed on each occasion by a frenzied activity of textual analysis by him and his colleagues in their correspondence with one another. While Rosebery remained imprecise in his utterances and silent and aloof between them, they could never be sure of his real views or intentions. Could he be accommodated in a moderate party-line? Where did he stand in relation to other Liberal Imperialists? How could Campbell-Bannerman get through his speeches 'without any open or even controversial reference to R.'?[3] Did he want to come back into the Party, and if so on what terms?

If Rosebery wanted to form a new party, he had a strong following in the Commons, with Fowler, Grey, Haldane and Asquith at their head, and an unknown number on the backbenches. R. W. Perks, M.P. for Louth, was doing his best to organise this dissentient group. In October 1900 an 'Imperial Liberal Council' called upon the Party to 'clearly and permanently distinguish Liberals in whose policy with regard to Imperial questions patriotic voters may justly repose confidence from those whose opinions naturally disqualify them from controlling the action of the Imperial Parliament of a world-wide community of nations'.[4] But as yet Rosebery would have nothing directly to do with this section. In the first months of 1902, however, he announced his 'definite separation' from Campbell-Bannerman,[5]

[1] Rosebery at Chesterfield, 16 Dec 1901; Crewe, op. cit. ii 571–2; and James, op. cit. pp. 430–1.
[2] Rosebery, speech to City Liberal Club, 19 July 1901. Crewe op. cit. ii 569–70; James, op. cit. p. 426.
[3] Campbell-Bannerman to H. Gladstone, 4 Nov. 1899; H.G.P., B.M. Add. MS. 45987, f. 35.
[4] Resolution passed by the I.L.C., 19 Oct 1900 (A.R.).
[5] Rosebery, letter to The Times, 21 Feb 1902.

and threw in his hand with the Liberal Imperialists. A 'Liberal League' was founded with Rosebery as its president and Asquith, Fowler and Grey vice-presidents.[1] The seeds seemed to have been planted of a rival organisation to the Liberal Party.

These were the surface manifestations of the Liberal Imperialist movement. Behind the scenes there was even more cause for alarm. Deputations visited Campbell-Bannerman to ask – with every pretension of innocence – when he was going to step down for Rosebery.[2] Grey threatened to withdraw his allegiance in November 1900.[3] Munro-Ferguson resigned from his position as Scottish Whip soon after the Khaki election, on account of his imperialist views.[4] And, most distressingly of all, the Party's Chief Whip, Herbert Gladstone, suddenly turned proselyte at the same time, urging nothing less than the complete abandonment of the Liberal line on South Africa in order to appease Rosebery.[5] To Campbell-Bannerman the Party seemed to be crumbling about him, and he saw 'Perksite intriguers' behind every tree.

The Liberal leader was in an unenviable position. He could not but be conscious of the fact that many of his followers regarded him as a caretaker, looking after the Party until such time as Rosebery returned to the helm. And the latter appeared to have all the aces – if he only chose to play them. As an ex-prime minister and a man who commanded devoted, if bewildered, respect in the country his position was a strong one – far stronger, if ever he wished to declare himself as a rival, than that of the Liberals' relatively unknown, apparently pedestrian and certainly third-choice leader. Among his supporters there appeared to be a general willingness to follow his lead should he decide to break

[1] Other members included Haldane, Perks, Munro-Ferguson, Josiah Wedgwood and Cecil Harmsworth (James, op. cit. pp. 438–9).

[2] e.g. see Campbell-Bannerman to (?) Grey, 22 Nov 1900; C.B.P., B.M. Add. MS. 41218, f. 29.

[3] See C.B.P., B.M. Add. MS. 41218, ff. 8, 17, 24.

[4] See C.B.P., B.M. Add. MS. 41222, *passim*; and H.G.P., B.M. Add. MS. 46058, *passim*.

[5] H. Gladstone to Campbell-Bannerman, 5 Nov 1900; C.B.P., B.M. Add. MS. 41216, ff. 31–40. See also ibid. MSS. 41211, ff. 129, 136; 41214, ff. 89–91; 41222, f. 33; 41224, ff. 134, 140; Ripon Papers, B.M. Add. MS. 43517, f. 157; and H.G.P., B.M. Add. MS. 45987, ff. 137–43.

D

completely with his old party and strike out in some new direction. This kind of development had been foreshadowed for some years. Morley wrote to Francis Hirst in 1897 that 'The spirit of the times is not at the moment very favourable to us. Party creeds are vague and shifting. Considerable changes are, quietly and unseen, overtaking the parliamentary systems.'[1] The 'Decay of Party Government'[2] was the subject of constant speculation. And there appeared to be strong ideological foundations for the formation of a *new* party, which would abandon Manchester parochialism, pacifism and *laissez-faire*, and base itself firmly upon the new ideology of 'imperialism and social reform' which was being compiled for it by young Liberal politicians like Herbert Samuel[3] and Fabian 'permeators' like Sidney Webb.[4]

In these circumstances the path Campbell-Bannerman had to tread was narrow and tortuous. He had to try to strengthen his own position as leader while leaving a door open for Rosebery to re-enter, if he so wished. And at the same time he saw that 'the same old humming & hahing sort of speech wld. not do',[5] he must take a 'decided line' and avoid antagonising Harcourt and the other implacable enemies of Rosebery. If he failed to play his cards right, there existed the nucleus of an alternative party with an established leader willing (it was thought) to take over. No one was sure how much support such a party could command, or whether Rosebery intended to take advantage of the situation. It was dangerous to try to test this unknown factor by open provocation, in case it stimulated Rosebery to return to politics and, perhaps, form a 'centre' or 'National' party of right-wing Liberals and left-wing Unionists.[6] In this event the anti-War Radicals would be stranded in an impotent minority on the left wing. The risk was a great one, and more dangerous to the Radicals than to the imperialists. Hence their comparative loyalty

---

[1] Quoted in F. W. Hirst, *In the Golden Days*, pp. 159–60.
[2] The title of an article by Frederick Greenwood in *C.R.*, Sept 1896.
[3] See Herbert Samuel, *Liberalism*.   [4] See below, Ch. 4, Sect. II.
[5] Campbell-Bannerman to H. Gladstone, 4 Nov 1899; H.G.P., B.M. Add. MS. 45987, f. 35.
[6] See Sidney Low, 'The Liberal Collapse: A Case for Coalition', in *C19th*, Jan 1899, pp. 10–19.

to their leader: 'I have no complaint to make', he wrote in February 1901, 'of the way I have been met even by the extremest men – Lloyd George, H. J. Wilson, C. P. Scott, Channing, Pirie, etc.' [1] The imperialist wing, on the other hand, could be more self-confident. The only thing holding it back was Rosebery's hesitation. Apart from this they appeared to have everything in their favour.

Such considerations rendered the Liberal opposition to the War misleadingly inarticulate. They also served to blur the issue *vis-à-vis* the relationship between the War and 'imperialism'. Moderates were on much safer ground if they restricted their criticism to the merits of the case, and avoided the wider question. It was the Liberal Imperialists who wanted to make 'imperialism' the point of contention between the two wings, and this is perhaps chiefly why Campbell-Bannerman scarcely mentioned the word in his private correspondence. He was irritated when Rosebery brought it up in October 1899:

I confess that all these philosophic and historic students with whom we have to deal are beyond my modest range. I do not see where the lofty principles of Imperialism come in to this somewhat sordid quarrel. Those who do not approve of the war must regard it with dislike; those who approve of it have all along repudiated the notion of our wanting to grab anything.[2] If it was necessary it was a great calamity: if it was not necessary it is a stupid and dangerous blunder. But where there can be any ground for Cock-a-doodle-do I fail to see.[3]

By saying nothing in public which was incompatible with the broader views of the 'Perksites',[4] Campbell-Bannerman gave the

[1] Campbell-Bannerman to Ripon, 16 Feb 1901; Ripon Papers, B.M. Add. MS. 43517, f. 188.

[2] See Salisbury's speech at Mansion House, 9 Nov 1899: 'We seek no goldfields, we seek no territory' (*A.R.*).

[3] Campbell-Bannerman to Buxton, 31 Oct 1899; Spender, *Life of Campbell-Bannerman*, i 253–4.

[4] See Campbell-Bannerman's speech at Birmingham, 24 Nov 1899, partly printed in Spender, op. cit. i 257–8: perfectly orthodox and moderately 'imperialist'.

latter less excuse to break away from the Party on the grounds of a fundamental divergence of opinion. He avoided the thrusts of the imperialists by feinting. The result was that the Liberal Party managed to survive the War without giving an authoritative statement on the 'question of the hour', without ever pronouncing officially on 'imperialism'.

III. PEACE, RETRENCHMENT, REFORM AND IMPERIALISM

Yet when all these political considerations have been taken into account, the fact remains that within the Liberal Party – even under the surface – there was a dearth of ideas about the Empire or colonial reform. Campbell-Bannerman disliked the general tenor of Chamberlainite imperialism, but his attitude even in private was negative and unspecific. The same applies to those to the left of him – apart from Dilke and, perhaps, Bryce. The reasons for this go beyond the dilemmas of the political situation.

Their failure was an ideological one. In the vague body of theories and attitudes which made up the Liberal 'tradition',[1] there was no guidance for a Radical placed in a situation such as the late nineteenth century presented, an imperial situation. Cobdenite Liberalism assumed a world of independent nations, of domestic and foreign policy only, and even this policy was to be minimal. It said nothing about colonial policy, about the rule of subject races. If Liberals had read John Stuart Mill on India, instead of Cobden on foreign affairs, they might have found something worth saying about Africa. Dilke *did* read Mill, and indeed corresponded with him in 1869,[2] and his real concern for native races and the economic and cultural problems involved in the government of tropical colonies contrasts markedly with the attitude of his colleagues. These men, the Radical anti-imperialist section of an otherwise apathetic and distracted Liberal Party,

[1] See above, Ch. 1, Sec. II.
[2] See J. S. Mill to Dilke, 9 Feb 1869; Dilke Papers, B.M. Add. MS. 43897, f. 1; printed in Elliot, *Letters of J. S. Mill*, ii 187–90.

went instead to a newer tradition, and chiefly to the slogans of
'peace, retrenchment and reform', and on this foundation they built
a consistent, but singularly unhelpful, anti-imperialist philosophy.

Labouchere, for example, concentrated his attack on imperialism almost exclusively along two lines: a scathing denunciation
of the selfish motives behind African policy, and the application
of the 'non-intervention' principle in its extreme form. Did
Chamberlain, he asked in reference to the Ashanti expedition,
'recognise this duty of establishing the *Pax Britannica* – which
he took to mean laying hold of the thing for ourselves . . . only
. . . when we could get something for ourselves – when it was
only a weak Power we interfered with . . . ?' [1] Professions of
altruism were only the cover for a policy of 'grab': the real
reason for these military expeditions was that the Government
coveted goldfields, or the Nile Valley, or a Cape–Cairo railway.
Hence his attacks on the Rand capitalists after the Jameson Raid:
their selfish motives offended his moral susceptibilities. For those
in Africa most seriously affected by a policy of 'capitalistic
imperialism' he professed sympathy but displayed little understanding. He would not admit that the situation created by
European penetration in Africa imposed on Britain any responsibility towards the natives. His approach was the unrealistic one of
laissez-faire. The Sudanese, he said, preferred the Khedive's
bad government to our good government,[2] and he agreed with
them. 'His sympathies were with the men to whom the country
belonged, and who were struggling against a foreign invasion.' [3]
Mwanga's rebellion in Buganda in 1899 he saw in the same light.
'The Ugandese have patriotism which we think is confined to
Englishmen. They like their independence, they have a Government – it may be a bad Government, but they want it. They want
to be Ugandese.' [4] And there was no point in helping native
races. Labouchere had very little respect for the African. The
Sudanese were 'some of the most unmitigated scoundrels on the

[1] Labouchere in H. of C., 12 Mar 1896; 4 P.D. 38, cc. 829–30.
[2] Labouchere in H. of C., 20 Mar 1896; 4 P.D. 38, c. 1490.
[3] Labouchere in H. of C., 16 Mar 1896; 4 P.D. 38, c. 1033.
[4] Labouchere in H. of C., 27 Feb 1899; 4 P.D. 67, c. 726.

face of the globe';[1] and the Ugandese 'without exception the very laziest of that laziest race in the whole world, the African negro'.[2] We should leave them alone to drink and fight and eat bananas as they wanted.[3] In December 1900 he showed a more constructive approach, in advocating the setting up of 'Labour Bureaus' in the Transvaal to prevent forced labour.[4] But in general his alternative to the abuse of the imperial trust was no imperial trust at all.

Sir William Harcourt represented another school of thought: the 'retrenchment' school of Cobden and Goldwin Smith. The cost of African adventures was higher than their commercial benefit, no trade was to be expected from 'waterless deserts', and so (reported Wilfrid Scawen Blunt) Harcourt intended at the beginning of 1899 to 'bring forward the whole anti-imperial case on grounds of economy'.[5] This seemed to be his only objection to imperial expansion. His son quoted him as saying in 1892 that 'even Jingoism is tolerable when it is done "on the cheap" ' – by chartered companies;[6] and in a speech of November 1897 he affirmed that 'He was as willing as anybody that there should be reasonable extensions of empire, but he liked to see some advantages from the process.' [7] This betrayed a somewhat one-sided vision. But the cost of the Government's policy was central to the Radicals' case. It constituted a great part of Labouchere's opposition to the Uganda Railway, of Morley's objection to the 'forward' policy in Chitral,[8] and of Harcourt's against the Dongola advance. Money was being wasted in Africa which could more profitably be used at home. 'Talk of spheres of interest!' ejaculated Labouchere in 1900; 'I would rather see the money spent on spheres of population in England.' [9]

[1] Ibid. c. 725.   [2] Labouchere in H. of C., 30 Apr 1900; 4 P.D. 82, c. 302.
[3] Ibid. loc. cit.
[4] Labouchere in H. of C., 13 Dec 1900, 4 P.D. 88, c. 755; and see Labouchere to Campbell-Bannerman, 12 Jan 1901, C.B.P., B.M. Add. MS. 41222, f. 48.
[5] Blunt, *Diaries*, i 382 (4 Jan 1899).   [6] Gardiner, *Life of Harcourt*, ii 199.
[7] Harcourt, speech at Kirkcaldy, 26 Nov 1897 (*A.R.*).
[8] Morley, speech at Arbroath, 28 Sept 1897 (ibid).
[9] Labouchere in H. of C., 7 May 1900; 4 P.D. 82, c. 923.

From another quarter came concern for the international implications of a forward policy. Critics of the Government were worried by the possibility that Britain would be weakened in Europe by having her military forces locked up in such places as Egypt.[1] The danger was heightened by the provocation of boundary disputes with France on the borders of Nigeria and the Sudan. And Courtney and Morley were particularly agitated by the effect which the occupation of Egypt was having on Britain's *moral* influence in the world. In part collaboration with Morley,[2] Courtney wrote to the *Times* in October 1896:

> Lord Rosebery is afflicted by the Armenian horrors. We have a right to interfere; but we are distrusted if not detested by every European Power, and we are weak with our swollen Empire.... Is there no way of setting ourselves right with the rest of civilised Europe, of proving our sincerity by act as well as word? We might surrender Cyprus. ... But the real key to the situation is Egypt. We must exchange our exclusive control for an international settlement. This transfer has been rendered infinitely more difficult by recent operations in the Sudan; but unless and until it is done we cannot claim the trust of other Powers, we cannot resent their sneers at our sincerity.[3]

Morley and Courtney looked to Britain to provide moral leadership for the world; and imperialism was destroying all chance of this.

The Radicals' case against African colonies was, perhaps, a strong one, but it tended towards parochialism. And their solution was over-simple: 'Abandon your colonies and none of these complications – native wars, extravagance, foreign hostility – will arise.' In the 1890s this attitude was unrealistic. It was like trying to go back on the Fall.

This was the argument against the *Empire*. The Radicals' objections to that more ambiguous and disputable phenomenon called

---

[1] e.g. Courtney in H. of C., 16 Mar 1896; 4 P.D. 38, cc. 1052–6.
[2] See Courtney Papers, vol. 6, f. 60.
[3] Quoted in Gooch, *Life of Courtney*, pp. 336–7.

imperialism were cast in the same mould. Whatever imperialism is or was, whether it is a fact or an idea, a policy or an emotion, need not concern us here. So long as it is used, and so long as its use carries with it the implications of a moral judgment, the word will always have emotional under- and over-tones which may obscure its meaning. This is not the place to try to disentangle (even if it were possible) all the various policies, doctrines and feelings which have accrued to it. But a word about what the *Radicals* meant by 'imperialism', when they spoke of it and attacked it, if it tells us little about imperialism, will tell us much about the Radicals.

For the 'imperialism' which the Radicals protested most against was not so much a policy as a *state of mind*, which they broadly termed 'jingoism'. Jingoism did not merely mean 'mafficking' and flag-waving, although these were its most blatant manifestations; it was a way of thinking and a crude philosophy of political action. On the one hand it was a perverted patriotism, composed of national conceit, whose intellectual foundations were the various doctrines of Anglo-Saxon 'manifest destiny' and race-pride, and whose chief characteristic was an 'engrossing arrogance' [1] content to be ignorant of, and unsympathetic towards, foreign nations, intolerant and unreasonable. On the other hand it was the worship of power and force, [2] the glorification of war, again with an intellectual basis in Social Darwinism and the other various forms of fatalism, [3] but more popularly expressed (it was alleged) in that sentence of Baden-Powell's which the anti-imperialists were so fond of quoting: 'Football is a good game, but better than it, better than any other game, is that of man-hunting.' [4] With the worship of force were found those doctrines of international politics which went under

[1] Courtney to L. S. Amery, 30 Nov 1899; Courtney Papers, vol. 7, f. 49.
[2] See Hirst, Murray and Hammond, *Liberalism and the Empire*, p. vi.
[3] On fatalism see Hirst, Murray and Hammond, op. cit. pp. 161–3.
[4] R. R. S. Baden-Powell, *Aids to Scouting for NCOs and Men*, p. 124; quoted in J. A. Hobson, *Imperialism: a Study*, p. 214, and by G. P. Gooch in C. F. G. Masterman *et al.*, *The Heart of the Empire*, p. 318, among others.

*Liberal personifications of imperialism: F. Carruthers Gould's
caricatures, in the* Westminster Gazette

1. 'The Music Hall Jingo'; 2. 'The Throgmorton-street Patriot'; 3. 'General
Blazer'; 4. 'The Yellow Press Journalist'; 5. 'A Mafficker mafficking';
6. 'The Kimberley Frog' – Rhodes. (*Westminster Gazette* 15, 23, 27 and 29
December 1899, 12 March and 26 May 1900.)

the name of 'Might is Right', or 'Machiavellism', or *Realpolitik*;[1] and they were buoyed up by a literature of 'hooliganism' [2] and a national temper of 'vulgarity' and materialism.[3] These were the things which revolted humanitarian Liberals: the atrocities of Omdurman and the injustice of the Boer War, yes; but more than these the popular temper which made them possible and applauded them. To them 'imperialism' was not merely, or even chiefly, a colonial policy; it was a national psychology, and everything in England that was vulgar, aggressive and retrograde, all the various defects which men diagnosed in the national character – materialism, gambling, apathy, amorality – were attributed by anti-imperialists to imperialism.

It was the *domestic* manifestations of 'imperialism', therefore, which enraged the Radicals. This was the burden of Jerome K. Jerome's complaint against the South African capitalists, which he communicated to his prospective Liberal candidate, Herbert Samuel, in 1900 (under the mistaken impression that the latter would sympathise with his views):

> Liberty of thought is to be denounced as treachery – to cosmopolitan stockjobbers and their lackeys, who have come to regard England as their own property. The British Flag is to be their 'Commercial asset'. Our peasants are to be drilled into an armed horde and their blood spent on mere financial exploits for the sole benefit of the rich. And those who prefer the cause of England, her fair name and her

[1] See Gooch, ibid. p. 312.
[2] See Robert Buchanan's essay on Kipling, 'The Voice of "The Hooligan" ', in *C.R.*, Dec 1900; J. M. Robertson, *Patriotism and the Empire*, pp. 52–5 (Kipling, Henley and Co., he says, 'stand for the type of the Barbarian Sentimentalist'); and Dr Emil Reich, *Imperialism*, pp. 29, 67, 92 f., 95 ff., 117 (Reich claims that imperialism and art are incompatible, although he does not infer from this that imperialism is wrong).
[3] See Blunt, *Diaries*, i 391–2, where he quotes Herbert Spencer on 'the militarism and brutalities of the day, the idealisation of football and all games of force, the rehabilitation of Napoleon and all other war-making scoundrels . . .'. See also Sir Edward Russell to Campbell-Bannerman (C.B.P., B.M. Add. MS. 41235, f. 95) on imperialist speeches 'infected with a very immoral and degenerate vulgarity'; and Frederic Harrison, 'Imperial Manners', in *Memories and Thoughts*, p. 125.

prosperity, to the success of the gold mines on the Rand, are denounced by the German Jew Press as unpatriotic![1]

The anti-imperialism was there, but it was directed more against jingoism at home than imperialism in Africa. And this was characteristic. In part, of course, it was a natural petulant reaction against the intolerance and mass hysteria which had broken up the Radicals' meetings and forced upon them the indignities of the Khaki election. They were irritated by people who would not listen in a calm, cool manner to their arguments. But it also went deeper. Jingoism not only made their life difficult, it undermined their hopes and ideals. Robert Buchanan, in an essay on Kipling, voiced the Liberals' despair. English society, he said,

> has drifted little by little, and day by day, away from those humanitarian traditions which appeared to open up to men, in the time of my own boyhood, the prospect of a new Heaven and a new Earth ... repudiating the Enthusiasm of Humanity altogether and exchanging it for the worship of physical force and commercial success in any and every form ... a Hooligan Imperialism.[2]

Doctrines of fatalism, the politics of cynical aggression, and the national temper of arrogance and intolerance went against the principle on which the most optimistic hopes of the Liberals rested: that of rational morality in international affairs. Imperialism denied that such a principle was viable as a basis for action. Lord Salisbury told the Primrose League in May 1900 that 'he recognised distinctly the unfriendliness of other nations, and bade his hearers remember that we had nowhere to look for support but to ourselves';[3] and this kind of political 'realism', translated into practical policy, destroyed the Liberals' nobler ambitions for international peace and concord through co-operation, understanding and a rational assessment of national

---

[1] Jerome K. Jerome to Herbert Samuel, 25 Sept 1900; Lord Samuel Papers (H.L.R.O.), box marked 'General Political Correspondence 1896–1902'.
[2] R. Buchanan in *C.R.*, Dec 1900, pp. 775–6.
[3] 9 May 1900 (*A.R.*).

self-interest. 'If the Chauvinistic and Jingo parties become predominant in the various nations of Europe,' they predicted,

security and progress will become constantly more difficult, commerce will decline, our manufacturing supremacy will disappear, and 'inevitable' wars, with their inevitable accompaniments of suffering and poverty, will become the staple food of politics.[1]

Hence the most fervent *cri de cœur* of the anti-imperialist Liberal is his protest against the irrationality and amorality of jingoism, and his appeal to the rule of morality in international affairs. William Lecky's *Map of Life*, published in October 1899, while acknowledging the moral dilemmas which inevitably faced statesmen, asserted unequivocally that 'Nothing is more calamitous than the divorce of politics from morals.'[2] Yet recent political events, he said, and in particular Chamberlain's defence of Rhodes's honour in 1897, had shown a regrettable lapse from this principle.[3] The Bishop of Hereford[4] – the most 'progressive' of the bench of bishops – sadly noted that, after 2,000 years of Christianity, they still did not apply the Sermon on the Mount to international politics.[5] And – leaving aside the pacifists, whose blanket rejection of all war puts them outside the bounds of more sophisticated argument[6] – this was the chief complaint of the Liberal left wing. 'The important point', wrote G. P. Gooch, 'is that the existence and authority of the moral standard should be recognised in public as it has long been recognised in private relations.'[7] And the authors of *Liberalism and the Empire* pleaded to their countrymen to turn from 'the false excess of patriotism' which now gripped them and to return to the principles of

the older school of English Liberals, who judge of national honour by more or less the same standards as they apply to

[1] Hirst, Murray and Hammond, *Liberalism and the Empire*, p. xiii.
[2] William Lecky, *The Map of Life*, p. 194.
[3] Ibid. pp. 185–97.   [4] John Percival.   [5] *C19th*, Aug 1900, pp. 226 ff.
[6] For a Quaker view of the S. African War, see Joseph J. Green, *War: Is It or Is It Not Consistent With Christianity?* A pacifist approach was taken in Parliament by Sir Wilfred Lawson (esp. H. of C., 7 Feb 1900) and Keir Hardie (H. of C., 7 Dec 1900).
[7] G. P. Gooch, 'Imperialism', in Masterman *et al.*, *Heart of the Empire*, p. 331.

private honour; who believe in international morality and in the co-operation of nations for mutual help; who, if they are to dream at all, will dream not of Armageddons and Empires, but of progress and freedom, and the ultimate fraternity of mankind.[1]

This 'dream' – the dream of Cobden[2] – was being shattered by imperialism. In 1917 John Morley remembered the thirty years before the nineties as 'an animated, hopeful, interesting, and on the whole ... a happy generation ... it was a generation of intrepid effort forward'.[3] Among Liberal idealists there had been dissatisfaction at the way things were, and yet a confidence in the future; for 'peace, retrenchment and reform' were reasonable aims, and man was reasonable, and as more reasonable men came to control their own destinies the politics of the 'interests' – war, waste and reaction – would, gradually but permanently, be revealed for what they were. Progress had seemed, to the most hopeful of them, to be assured, for it rested on simple common-sense and depended only on enlightenment and education. To these same Liberals in the nineties, inheriting from Bright their pacifism and from Gladstone their moralism, the New Imperialism, and especially its popular 'democratic' aspect, threatened not only the peace of the world, but progress and social reform also. For 'jingoism' meant that men were consciously acting against their own interests, and if progress were not achieved through the enlightened self-interest of the majority it would not be achieved at all.

Hence when Radicals talked about 'imperialism', they were referring more to a phenomenon in England than to a policy in the colonies. To the anti-imperialists in Parliament, the real debates about 'imperialism' were not those on Africa or India, but those on, for example, the army and navy estimates. Their definition of the word was wide enough to include colonial policy, but too wide to allow many of them to devote very much time to it. Consequently the Empire was neglected.

[1] Hirst, Murray and Hammond, op. cit. p. xiii. J. L. Hammond's essay in the same volume is chiefly concerned with this moral point (pp. 158–211).
[2] See Cobden, quoted above, pp. 14–15.
[3] John Morley, *Recollections*, vol. i, p. 26.

The Liberal Party was more 'anti-imperialist' than appeared from the parliamentary division-lists of the late nineties. Had it not been enervated by the political dilemmas presented by the Boer War – by its need to maintain some kind of unity despite its internal divisions, and by the special difficulties which the war situation brought to the discussion of imperialism – then it might have spoken up more articulately. But if it *had* spoken up, how would it have conducted its offensive? The approach of its left wing provides the only clue to this hypothetical question. The Radical anti-imperialists fell back on arguments which, however right they may have been in principle, gave little help to those who recognised that (albeit regrettably) Britain had an empire, and who wanted to reform it. Several years later John Holt, the West African merchant, said of the Asquith government, 'Their Liberalism is a parochial one, and has only to do with local affairs.' [1] This was not true of all Liberals, but it was true, in 1900, of the anti-imperialists among them. They were so anti-imperialist, in fact, that they did not want to know about empire. They had been against it all along, and if the country had gone against their advice and got itself a larger tropical empire, they were not going to tell it how to run it. To cut their losses and say something constructive about its administration would seem to be to compromise with their principles. This approach was perhaps the most consistent of all anti-imperialisms, but once Britain had sinned in Africa, and there was no going back on that sin in the way Labouchere would have liked, something more needed to be said about how to bring some good out of it: how best to fulfil the trust which the country had assumed. Such a policy could not come from these Radicals. To be an imperial reformer, it seemed, one had to be an imperialist of sorts, and it was among those men who were less rigid in their anti-imperialism, while still condemning the 'new' or 'capitalist' imperialism, that those ideas were born which could be used to modify and alleviate the effect of the imperialism of the nineties.

[1] John Holt to E. D. Morel, 13 July 1910; E.D.M.P. (L.S.E.), box F8.

CHAPTER FOUR

Labour and the Empire

I. APATHY AND ANTI-IMPERIALISM, 1895–9

IT was unreasonable, perhaps, to expect from the Liberal Party a strong critical line on an imperial situation which, after all, had been partly of its own making. As Unionists never tired of pointing out, the colonial record of Gladstone's third and fourth administrations was not entirely free from stain, even though his intentions might have been pure; and many Radicals felt themselves compromised by their party's past actions. But Labour's hands were clean. As yet in the 1890s a long way from political power, they had had no chance to share any of the direct responsibility for the territorial acquisitions of the past decade. Here was a parliamentary group whose independence and welcome freedom from an embarrassing past might help it to provide the kind of criticism which was conspicuously lacking among the main opposition party.

Yet what is their record with regard to the tropical empire in these years? Modern opinion appears to be sharply divided on the question. Labour has been dubbed 'imperialist' by one group of critics, and 'Little Englander' by another; John Strachey writes confidently of the 'anti-imperialist tradition of the Labour movement',[1] while Miss Hannah Arendt talks of its 'complicity' in imperialist programmes,[2] and an American historian of its 'acquiescence'.[3] Each of these views is supported by ample and genuine evidence. Yet they cannot both be correct. Either Labour

---

[1] J. Strachey, *The End of Empire*, pp. 215–16.

[2] H. Arendt, *The Origins of Totalitarianism* (2nd ed.), p. 151.

[3] Tingfu F. Tsiang, *Labour and Empire*, p. 95. This work is based almost exclusively upon a study of parliamentary debates.

was imperialist or she was anti-imperialist; or – which is far more likely – her attitude was more complex and equivocal than either of these judgments implies.

One difficulty is that 'Labour' is almost as ambiguous a term as 'imperialism'. In the late nineteenth century it could be used to cover a multitude of people, parties, interests and ideologies, whose only claim to be treated as a single category was sometimes that they quarrelled about the same issues. Certainly there was little agreement among them with regard to the Empire. The Social-Democratic Federation differed markedly in its attitude from the Independent Labour Party, and the I.L.P. from the T.U.C. or the Fabian Society: and none of them was completely in tune with that larger, more amorphous body called 'working-class opinion' (represented more faithfully, perhaps, by the Tories and Liberals whom many of the enfranchised workers elected to Parliament, or by the crowds in the London streets on Mafeking night). The Labour movement at this time was not only dispersed and disunited; as a political force it was not yet strong enough for there to be discerned within it even a main stem of Labour opinion.

On one level there seemed to be nothing but an apathy and unconcern akin to that of the Liberals. On the Labour benches in Parliament, and in the official deliberations of such bodies as the T.U.C. and the Independent Labour Party, men wanted nothing to do with the Empire. In the House of Commons they tried as far as they could to ignore it. John Burns spoke in the debate on Africa inaugurated by Dilke in April 1897, but only to praise the British record in tropical Africa to the detriment of other imperial powers;[1] Henry Broadhurst in April 1899 criticised the Government's action in sending troops to South Africa,[2] and spoke on Zanzibar slavery in August of the same year[3] – but this was the sum total of Labour's contribution to colonial debates. On none of the 'burning issues' of empire – the Ashanti and Sudan expeditions, Uganda, even the Jameson Raid – did any

[1] H. of C., 2 Apr 1897; 4 P.D. 48, cc. 447–9.
[2] H. of C., 24 Apr 1899; 4 P.D. 70, cc. 493–4.
[3] H. of C., 3 Aug 1899; 4 P.D. 75, cc. 1356–7.

Labour M.P. say a word in Parliament between 1895 and October 1899. This silence extended to the War Office debates. When Labour Members spoke on military and naval estimates, it was never to criticise expenditure – in March 1899 W. C. Steadman expressly dissociated himself from such action[1] – but only to secure better working conditions for soldiers and sailors.[2] Similarly, only once was Africa ever mentioned at the Trades Union Congress (in September 1898 when a resolution protesting against forced labour in South Africa and Rhodesia was passed without discussion);[3] and the annual conferences of the I.L.P., while manifesting a certain interest in such issues as conscription and war,[4] made virtually no effort to discuss the colonies.[5]

This was the position in Parliament, in the I.L.P. and the T.U.C. Yet behind the scenes this reticence about the Empire was by no means reflected in the Labour Press or among doctrinaire socialists on the left wing of the movement. On this level Labour was as concerned about imperial expansion as anyone, loud and uncompromising in its opposition to imperialism and unanimous in attributing it, in true socialist fashion, to capitalism or capitalists.

Those who followed Marx had a firm precedent for attacking imperial ventures. The letters he had written to the *New York Daily Tribune* in the 1850s, arraigning British rule in India, gave them their lead.[6] Marx himself cannot be said to have provided

---

[1] H. of C., 16 Mar 1899; 4 P.D. 68, c. 1034: 'It is not my intention . . . to criticise the action of HMG in reference to our Navy, because although a man of peace myself, I believe the most practical way of ensuring peace is to have a strong Navy, much stronger than any other European Power has. . . .'

[2] e.g., see ibid., and the contributions of John Burns to army debates.

[3] T.U.C. *Annual Report*, 1898.

[4] At the 1896 I.L.P. Conference a resolution was passed deprecating war scares; and in 1898 a resolution attacking conscription – especially when it was designed to 'extend the Empire or to develop trade' (I.L.P. *Annual Reports*, 1896 and 1898).

[5] The 'wholesale massacres' in the Sudan were mentioned in the Report presented to the 1897 I.L.P. Conference (I.L.P. *Annual Report*, 1897).

[6] See K. Marx and F. Engels, *On Colonialism*, pp. 24–207.

them with a fully worked-out 'economic theory' of imperialism: E. M. Winslow has described the confusion of this aspect of his thought:

> Definite conclusions regarding any positive place for Marx in the theory of imperialism . . . are not easy to state. We are thrown off the track at the outset by his tendency to dismiss colonial expansion and exploitation as a pre-capitalist phenomenon. . . . Even . . . where he speaks of foreign trade, and even appears to emphasise its necessity, it was distinctly a side-issue. . . . His portrayal of the capitalist world as a closed system . . . could certainly be taken as evidence that he would not have held capitalism responsible for imperialism in the sense that the latter was absolutely necessary. . . .[1]

Yet *Das Kapital* had asserted clearly the doctrine of 'periodical overproduction of wealth in its capitalistic and self-contradictory form',[2] which gave them the clue, and we have seen already how capitalists themselves were proposing to solve this problem of 'over-production' imperially.[3] William Morris had made the obvious inference in 1890,[4] and as soon as the rest of the socialist movement could come to take an interest in foreign and imperial affairs, then the line they should take would almost suggest itself.

In Germany Kautsky claimed the credit for formulating the 'economic theory' in 1898.[5] Yet in England the Social-Democratic Federation had been familiar with it some years before. The S.-D.F. presented a striking contrast to parliamentary Labour at this time. Its members called themselves Marxists, and they seemed more responsive than other socialists to Marx's plea

[1] E. M. Winslow, *The Pattern of Imperialism*, p. 146. See also his article on 'Marxian, Liberal, and Sociological Theories of Imperialism', in *J.P.E.*, vol. 39, no. 6 (Dec 1931), pp. 717–18; and W. H. B. Court in Hancock, *British Commonwealth Affairs*, ii 1, p. 297.

[2] K. Marx and F. Engels, *Capital*, iii, 15, 2, quoted in R. Freedman (ed.), *Marx on Economics* (1961), p. 172.

[3] See above, pp. 44–5.

[4] See above, p. 44.

[5] Winslow, 'Theories of Imperialism', *J.P.E.*, p. 719.

that they should 'master themselves the mysteries of international politics'.[1] Henry Mayers Hyndman took up this plea, and in the pages of *Justice* – the organ of the S.-D.F. – tried to persuade the socialists of the nineties not to 'confine themselves to the boundaries of a narrow municipalism' but to read and learn about foreign politics, and to do all they could to try to influence them.[2] He himself took in hand the task of educating them in the 'mysteries' of secret diplomacy and colonial rivalries.[3] Aiding him in this was the Marxist philosopher and publicist Ernest Belfort Bax,[4] and it was Bax who dealt more specifically with imperial affairs. In a series of articles in *Justice* he pointed the moral of 'imperialism' for the working classes. Capitalism, he said, was breaking down under its own weight. That was an article of Marxist faith. Consequently socialists were looking forward to its early demise. But they had forgotten Marx's warning – that 'no social formation can be superseded until it has exhausted all the forms under which it can possibly maintain its existence'.[5] Imperialism was the latest expedient by means of which the capitalist system was seeking to prolong its own life and delay the inevitable advent of communism:

> the system of the exploitation of labour by the monopoly of the means of production has reached a stage at which it cannot control the means of exchange. The home markets of every country are exhausted, and the foreign

[1] Marx, address delivered at the inaugural meeting of the Working Men's International Association, 28 Sept 1864; printed in Marx and Engels, *Selected Works*, vol. 1, p. 384.

[2] *Justice*, 20 June 1896, p. 6; and 15 June 1895, p. 4.

[3] Hyndman contributed numerous articles to *Justice* on foreign affairs. See n. 2 above; and *Justice*, 3 Feb 1894, 8 Feb 1896 and 26 Feb 1898.

[4] Ernest Belfort Bax (1854–1926), for a short time editor of *Justice*; wrote many works of philosophy and history, as well as one or two collections of political essays; travelled widely in Germany (his second wife was German) and in contact with the German socialist movement; collaborated closely with William Morris, whose own theory of imperialism, similar to Bax's is cited above (p. 44). A strong opponent of the Boer War, but supported Britain in the First World War; and an anti-feminist. See the short biography of him in pamphlet form by Robert Arch, *Ernest Belfort Bax, Thinker and Pioneer* and Bax's own *Reminiscences and Reflexions*.

[5] *Justice*, 20 May 1899, p. 4.

markets hitherto open are becoming rapidly exhausted too.

So capitalists were looking further afield.

> What the governing classes and their catspaws, the philanthropists, really want is to open-up markets into which to shoot the shoddy products of their factories, and to acquire fresh fields and pastures new wherein to start fresh profit-grinding operations.
> ... the one hope of prolonging the existence of the present capitalist system lies in the opening-up of new territories to commercial and industrial enterprise, in other words, in the extension of the world market and the acquirement of fresh sources of cheap labour.[1]

The relevance of imperialism to socialism was, therefore, obvious. It was retarding the revolution.

> It is high time that the socialist working classes became thoroughly alive to the fact that ... every new market opened up is an obstacle in the way of their own emancipation ... it is a thing of vital importance to the early realisation of Socialism to stem the tide of annexation and colonial expansion without delay.[2]

This was the Marxist line, and it impelled the British 'Social-Democrats' to take more notice of imperial affairs than a 'narrow municipalism' would have allowed. Manifestoes were regularly issued by the Federation in the late nineties protesting against specific manifestations of 'capitalist imperialism',[3] and *Justice* kept a vigilant watch on events in Africa and India.[4] The same

[1] Ibid. 1 May 1896, pp. 7–8.
[2] Ibid. 16 June 1894, p. 4. One practical method Bax suggested of 'stemming the tide' was for socialists to help in 'the organisation of native resistance in drilling, and in teaching the effective use of firearms'. *Justice*, 1 May 1896, p. 8; and cf. ibid. 16 June 1894, p. 4.
[3] Reported in *Justice*: e.g. 4 July 1896 (Matabele), and 8 July 1899 (S. Africa). In 1897 the S.-D.F. organised an agitation against British rule in India.
[4] Ibid. *passim.* Hyndman and R. B. Cunninghame Graham were especially prolific on African and Indian matters.

line was adopted by the International Socialist Congress of 1900, meeting in Paris:[1]

> Le développement du capitalisme et du machinisme amène à l'expansion coloniale; on a besoin de marchés nouveaux, pour l'évolution du capitalisme et du commerce; cela est inévitable et fatal, car sans cela le monde serait acculé à une révolution prochaine. . . .[2]

The theory was less sophisticated than the one J. A. Hobson was to develop a little later: it confined its attention to commercial capitalism (not financial), and it was never worked out by Bax in any great detail. But it did provide, at least, the basis for a neo-Marxist anti-imperial ideology.

The extreme left wing was not alone in taking a firm stand on imperial questions. The three chief Labour weeklies – Robert Blatchford's *Clarion*, Keir Hardie's *Labour Leader* and W. M. Thompson's *Reynolds's Newspaper*[3] – all kept their readers well informed about foreign affairs and left them in no doubt as to what they considered the proper socialist attitude towards the Empire. This attitude was not so doctrinaire as Bax's: it had the appearance of being more empirically deducted than the Marxian

[1] The 1896 London Congress does not appear to have mentioned the subject of imperialism, although in May Bax expressed an intention to submit a resolution on the subject (*Justice*, 1 May 1896, p. 8). At that Congress, however, a resolution was passed declaring the cause of the *war* to be 'the capitalist mode of production'; but the discussion of this motion did not concern itself with this diagnosis of war, only with its prevention. See *Justice*, 1 Aug 1896, p. 4.

[2] *Compte rendu sténographique non officiel de la version française du cinquième Congrès Socialiste International, tenu à Paris du 23 au 27 septembre 1900* (Paris, 1901), p. 172 (speech by van Kol of Holland). van Kol's use of the word *inévitable* is a little misleading, in view of the importance Lenin was later to attach to the issue of whether imperialism was a policy *chosen* by capitalists or an inevitable concomitant of the system (see below, p. 214). A little later on he speaks of the U.S.A. as having 'choisi, pour éviter le socialisme, pour éviter la Révolution menaçante, l'impérialisme . . .' (ibid.). The resolution passed by the Congress is couched in the same terms; see ibid. p. 175.

[3] *Reynolds's* should perhaps technically be described as a Democratic Republican paper, but it combined this policy with strong and consistent support for the Labour, Trade Union and Co-operative movements.

A "CAPITAL" IDEA.

S. A. Co. Dragoon: "Ha! ha! They may hang Jameson; but they won't touch us!"

PATRIOTISM!

Showing how the South African Lion "honours" the British Flag.

The Clarion's commentary on the Jameson Raid, 11 January and 1 February 1896

line, and certainly it concentrated less on the 'theory' of capitalist imperialism than on its specific and tangible manifestations in Africa. Nevertheless, the lessons it drew were the same. In South Africa a small republic of peasants was being besieged by a band of 'the most unscrupulous financiers the world has ever seen';[1] the Press was controlled by them (the 'hired myrmidons', said the *Clarion*, 'of parvenu Hebrew diamond-thieves'),[2] native mine-workers were being exploited by them, and the Matabele and Mashona robbed by them – all in the interests of bigger profits. This line was pursued relentlessly from 1896 onwards, while Labour M.P.s sat silent in the House of Commons.[3] It was not confined to South Africa, but built up into a general case to cover the whole of the Empire. The socialist, wrote a contributor to the *Leader* in 1897, knew that imperialism 'simply means NEW MARKETS, and nothing more; that the whole bombastic business is just a glorification of commercialism'.

These pioneers, of whose heroism we have heard so much, we know them for the advance agents of a shoddy commercialism opening a way with their bayonets and paving it with dead bodies, for the shoddy goods of British capitalists to follow. Trade follows the flag, and trade is production for profit, that sharks and financiers and sweaters of all degrees may flourish, and Labour gets sixpence an hour or less,

---

[1] *Labour Leader*, 23 Apr 1898, p. 130. [2] *Clarion*, 21 Mar 1896, p. 93.
[3] *Reynolds's* suffered a temporary lapse from Labour orthodoxy in Jan 1896, when it was for a time persuaded by evidence coming from S. Africa after the Jameson Raid that 'our fellow-countrymen and women in Johannesburg ... were threatened by the Boers with an immediate attack. ... Dr Jameson, however imprudent, will become one of our national heroes' (12 Jan, p. 1). Yet within a few months the paper had seen the error of its ways (see ibid. 19 Apr, 3 and 17 May), and in Aug explained its aberration thus: 'There was a time when the first news of the raid reached this country, and when as yet the real facts of the case had been successfully concealed, when it was possible for a Democrat to feel considerable sympathy with the undertaking. ... It was a pretty tale for a few days.' But then 'It was made clearer and clearer ... that the whole affair was a coolly and carefully-planned Stock Exchange gambling transaction. This "heroism" was merely an attempted "deal" on the part of one or two millionaires, German Jews, and their "pals" ... sordid and squalid' (ibid. 2 Aug 1896, p. 4). From then on *Reynolds's* was uncompromising in its hostility to S. African capitalists.

with intervals of nothing an hour. That is what the glorification of the flag means.[1]

By this argument, the popular talk of Britain's 'civilising mission' and the like stood condemned as a mere pretence, the hypocrisy of a 'plundering, piratical, murderous, gospel-spreading race' which was trying to dignify its policy of 'rapine, slaughter, and conquest by pious snuffles of self-righteousness'.[2] At the centre of the imperial web lay 'the swollen, ugly, bloated spider body of the capitalist financier'. It was 'his empire and his flag';[3] and so it was in his interests, and his interests only, that Britain was 'exterminating' native races in the Sudan, Uganda, Nigeria and the Gold Coast.[4] In October 1898 Alex Thompson of the *Clarion* took this line of argument one stage further, when he used J. A. Hobson's 'surplus capital' explanation of imperialism (although his source was not Hobson but the American writer Charles Conant):[5]

There you have the real reason of the world's murderous turbulence. It is the excessive accumulation of capital, and the insatiable greed of capital for profitable investment, that causes the bloody and ruthless scramble now threatening to set all Europe by the ears. . . .[6]

The *Labour Leader*'s argument was not quite so sophisticated; but all three papers concurred in putting the blame on 'Stock Exchange sharps and the Fat Men of Commerce.'[7] There was no prevarication here, no disagreement in the Labour Press about the hidden forces underlying colonial expansion.

[1] 'F. H.' on 'Liberalism and Imperialism', in *Labour Leader*, 17 July 1897, p. 234.
[2] *Clarion*, 4 Dec 1897, p. 388. Cf. the *Labour Leader*, 4 Apr 1896, p. 115.
[3] *Labour Leader*, 17 July 1897, p. 234.
[4] See *Reynolds's*, 14 June 1896; the *Labour Leader*, 29 Oct 1898, 17 June 1899 (Sudan), 4 Mar 1899 (Uganda), 22 July 1899 (Nigeria), 18 Jan, 25 Jan and 4 Apr 1896 (Gold Coast); and the *Clarion*, 8 Apr 1899 (Sudan) and 26 Feb 1898 (Nigeria).
[5] See below, p. 194 fn. 3. Thompson quotes extensively from Conant, but without mentioning him by name.
[6] *Clarion*, 1 Oct 1898, p. 316.
[7] Ibid. 9 Apr 1898, p. 113.

This being so, why was Labour so reticent in the House of Commons? The arguments were there for Labour M.P.s to draw on. Why then, at the height of the late-nineteenth-century 'forward' movement in Africa, did they make so little use of them? One thing is clear, and that is that it was not so much a question of their conscious and positive 'acquiescence' in imperial schemes as of a certain negligence and lack of initiative. Labour M.P.s did little explicitly to support the policy of the Government; indeed, when they voted at all on colonial matters they voted against it.[1] The same applies to delegates at Labour conferences. Their sin, if it was one, was the sin of omission: of not clearly speaking out against imperialism when the opportunity arose – of declining to tread where Liberals feared to. We have to account, then, not for their imperialism but for their apathy. The reason for this becomes a little clearer when we consider the *nature* of their 'Labourism'.

All told, about a dozen men in Parliament between 1895 and 1900 were commonly termed 'Labour members'.[2] Yet none of these had been elected under the auspices either of the I.L.P. or of the S.-D.F., and all of them fitted more comfortably into the category of 'Lib-Labs' than anything else. Of the I.L.P. candidates who had stood in 1895, Keir Hardie, for example, one of the leading advocates of an anti-imperialist line in the pages of the *Labour Leader*, had been defeated at West Ham in that year, and was not in Parliament to assume the leadership of Labour's assault on the Government's African policy until after the election of 1900. Other defeated I.L.P. candidates included S. G. Hobson and Ramsay MacDonald, either of whom might have spoken up on foreign affairs had they been in Parliament; and William Randal Cremer, formerly a trade unionist M.P. who was also a prominent internationalist, was narrowly beaten at the hustings in 1895.

Those who did manage to get into Parliament, usually by

---

[1] An account of how Labour M.P.s voted on such questions before 1900 is given in Tsiang, *Labour and Empire*, pp. 32–54 (India) and 64–75 (Africa).

[2] See G. D. H. Cole, *British Working-Class Politics 1832–1914*, pp. 147–150, on the election of 1895; and, for a list of Labour M.P.s and candidates, pp. 270–5.

arrangement with the Liberals, were not so much 'socialist' as 'Labour'. The distinction is an important one. It was a difference less of ideology than of function. A socialist was returned to Parliament to promote a general social and political policy, a trade union or miners' M.P. to forward the demands of his constituents. The two things were not, of course, incompatible; but the latter tended in practice to limit a member's field of activity more than the former. What Belfort Bax said of the ordinary rank-and-file socialist was even more true of the trade unionist M.P.: because foreign politics lay outside his 'habitual sphere of interest', he had 'never given himself the trouble to think out the logical outcome of his position as regards international relations'.[1] Not only this, but there was a feeling that, even if they *had* thought about foreign affairs, it was not their business to pronounce on them. They were in Parliament to represent the interests of the working man, and their intervention in debates should be confined to issues which affected directly those who had elected them. Such an attitude was never, it is true, admitted in Parliament. But outside it was occasionally put forward as an apologia for neutrality. When the South African question was raised at the Trades Union Congress of September 1899, W. E. Clery, one of the delegates, protested on these grounds against the introduction of such 'party questions' into their deliberations. 'They as working men', he said, 'should aim at benefiting the conditions of working men, their labour, and their wages, and not make themselves a stalking horse for political topics.'[2] From a very different quarter Bernard Shaw voiced the same kind of opinion when he called the Transvaal affair 'a non-Socialist point of policy'.[3] For trade unionists this might appear a viable proposition; for socialists like Shaw it was shortly seen to be impossible. It was a useful rationalisation of Labour's natural preference for social over imperial questions, but they could not ignore the Empire indefinitely. We shall see that

[1] E. Belfort Bax, 'Socialism and Foreign Politics', in *Justice*, 15 Feb 1896, p. 6.
[2] T.U.C. *Annual Report*, 1899. Cf. Laidler of Newcastle at the 1901 Conference and Davies at the Apr 1902 Conference of the I.L.P. (I.L.P. *Annual Reports*); also S. G. Hobson quoted on p. 124 below.
[3] G. B. Shaw to E. R. Pease, 30 Oct 1899 (Fabian Soc. MSS.).

events were soon to demonstrate that the Labour movement would have to take some official account of imperialism – if only because its rank and file could not be trusted to avoid it. By 1899 the plea of Clery and Shaw to keep South African politics out of socialism had become impracticable.

Clery and Shaw might have known it was impracticable, and certainly their protest has the appearance less of an abstract statement of principle than of an alarmed reaction to the dissension they saw being sown among the Labour movement by the South African issue. This dissension was not so acute as first appeared, and it grew less serious as time went on. But it was nonetheless another factor making for official prevarication in the months surrounding the Boer ultimatum. To those who feared for the unity and solidity of the young stripling Labour movement, there was the evidence of the 'yellow press' and the music-halls for the popularity of the new mood of jingoism. There were the oft-repeated claims of the Chamberlainites, difficult to disprove, that the working-classes were behind the Government.[1] There was the more tangible evidence of the war-time Trades Union Congresses, displaying a disturbing dubiety towards the socialist case: in 1900 the T.U.C. passed an anti-War resolution only by a small majority, and in 1901 their refusal to debate a similar motion was interpreted by the Government Press as indicative of pro-War sentiment.[2] And there were symptoms too of a disquieting temper among certain Labour leaders who, if they had been true to the European socialist tradition of internationalism and fraternity, should have been firmly on the side of the anti-imperialists. John Burns, for example, in November 1898 had given a speech at Battersea which seemed redolent of the jingoism of the time.[3] Joseph Havelock Wilson, a prominent

---

[1] e.g. see Chamberlain in H. of C., 19 Oct 1899; 4 P.D. 77, c. 254 ff.

[2] Annual Reports of T.U.C. for 1900 and 1901; and see W. J. Davis, *The British T.U.C.: History and Recollections*, vol. ii.

[3] See *The Times*, 14 Nov 1898; and William Kent, *John Burns, Labour's Lost Leader*, p. 88 (Burns was speaking about Fashoda). He also gave a speech soon after the Jameson Raid which called on the Government to send 15,000 troops to the Transvaal to 'clear things up'; this the *Labour Leader* for 11 Jan 1896 condemned as 'foolish talk' (p. 12).

trade unionist M.P., voted consistently for the Government on the War.[1] And among socialist newspapers Blatchford's *Clarion*, despite its unequivocal denunciation of imperial expansion as a product of the economic system it had pledged itself to eradicate, and despite its gospel that under socialism there would be no colonialism and no war, could not bring itself to adopt what seemed to be the obvious conclusion from all this. In February 1898 it had felt constrained to warn its readers that the ideal solution to imperial problems was not – with the world as it was – the simple and hasty one its strictures on imperialism implied.

> Give us Socialism, and we need not in the least excite ourselves about new markets in China. But we have not got Socialism, and our cotton operatives will find it painful to be out of work. . . . We are for peace, and we are for Socialism, and we are against the 'extension of the Empire', and the 'opening up of foreign markets'; but we want to be fair, even to the Tories, and we do not propose to sink our ships till we are in sight of land; nor to burn our furs in the Arctic seas, because at some remote period of time we hope to reach a genial climate where muslin and fans are your only wear.[2]

In October 1899 Blatchford went one better and came out in favour of the War.

> I cannot go with those Socialists whose sympathies are with the enemy. My whole heart is with the British troops. . . . Until the war is over I am for the Government.[3]

> I believe that the real cause of the present war is the ignorance and the bumptiousness of the Boers . . . these uncultivated bullies.[4]

However unrepresentative this view was of the official Labour leadership, there could be no certainty that Blatchford did not

[1] See his speech in H. of C., 6 Feb 1900 (4 P.D. 78, cc. 798–800): 'I do believe in upholding the integrity of the British Empire. I am a British patriot above all things.' Wilson was M.P. for Middlesbrough; he had founded the National Amalgamated Sailors' and Firemen's Union in 1887.

[2] *Clarion*, 12 Feb 1898, p. 52 (unsigned leader); and cf. ibid. 7 Jan 1899, p. 4 (by Alex M. Thompson).

[3] Ibid. 21 Oct 1899, p. 332 (by Blatchford).

[4] Ibid. 28 Oct 1899, p. 337 (by Blatchford).

mirror perfectly accurately the opinion of the electorate. And the position appeared worse in 1900, when a section of the socialist intelligentsia – the Fabians – came over to his side.

II. THE FABIANS

Before 1900 the Fabian Society had seldom shown any concern over, or even knowledge of, the wider world outside the bounds of the municipal corporations and the parish councils which were its own special provinces. All its energies were directed towards the achievement of social reform, on a parochial level. On one occasion it made a pronouncement on international affairs, and then it took the orthodox pacifist line of deploring large armies, attributing wars to the machinations of capitalists and condemning 'filibusters acting as the agents of Chartered Companies';[1] but in general it restricted its activities exclusively to the domestic scene. Soon after the outbreak of the South African War, however, it found itself compelled to make up its mind, unambiguously, on the issue of imperialism; and the position it eventually took up was (as Walter Crane pointed out) not 'in accord with the opinion of other Socialist bodies'.[2] However much its leaders protested that their imperialism was not that of the Tories, to everybody else, socialists and non-socialists alike, the Fabian Society in 1900 had gone jingo. The story of the

[1] Fabian Tract no. 70, *Resolutions of the Fabian Society* (1896), sect. viii. In July 1897 the economist W. J. Ashley wrote to a member of the Society urging on it the adoption of 'a socialist-imperialist policy' (Ashley to Graham Wallas, 22 July 1897, in Wallas Papers, box 1). Nothing came of this at the time. In Dec 1898 W. A. S. Hewins – Director of the L.S.E. and later a leading protectionist propagandist – gave a lecture to the Society in which he propounded a doctrine of 'imperial efficiency' similar to the Fabians' later creed. Hubert Bland followed it with a strongly argued defence of Britain's colonial expansion 'on the grounds that if she did not make use of her opportunities in this direction other countries would oust her; and that England was the only country fit to pioneer the blessings of civilisation'. All this was reported in the *Labour Leader*, 10 Dec 1898, p. 407. But, again, none of it found its way into official Fabian publications, or into the discussions of the executive committee.

[2] Crane to Guy Bentley, 11 Feb 1900 (copy), in Fabian Soc. MSS.

events which led up to this commitment has been told many times before.[1] Briefly, the facts are these. Despite a strong current of feeling in the Society that they should avoid making any *ex cathedra* pronouncement on the 'question of the hour', Sydney Olivier (a strange animal – socialist and colonial administrator) and S. G. Hobson in October 1899 pressed the executive committee for 'a debate and declaration by resolution of the view of the Society on the war'.[2] Accordingly a members' meeting was held in December, at which an anti-War resolution moved by S. G. Hobson was met by an amendment of Bernard Shaw which made no judgment as to the justice of the War, but called, in the event of victory, for the nationalisation of the Transvaal mines.[3] Shaw's amendment was negatived, but a vote on Hobson's resolution was forestalled by the passing of 'the previous question'.[4] Hobson's reaction to this was to demand a Society referendum on the subject:[5] and Ramsay MacDonald prepared for the committee a draft questionnaire asking members to state (1) whether they wished the Society to make a pronouncement, and (2) whether such a pronouncement should condemn the War as 'the result of Capitalism', or alternatively demand (as Shaw had done) the nationalisation of the Rand mines.[6] As finally submitted to members the referendum omitted the second question and asked merely for a decision on the desirability of some – unspecified – pronouncement on the War, and the result was a majority against it.[7] Shaw meanwhile was trying to persuade the

[1] The fullest account is given in A. M. McBriar, *Fabian Socialism and English Politics 1884–1918*, pp. 119 ff. See also G. D. H. Cole, *A History of Socialist Thought*, vol. iii, pt. i, pp. 190 ff.; Margaret Cole, *The Story of Fabian Socialism*, pp. 95 ff.; Edward Pease, *A History of the Fabian Society*, pp. 128 ff.; S. G. Hobson, *Pilgrim to the Left*, pp. 63 ff.; B. Semmel, *Imperialism and Social Reform*, pp. 67 ff.; and E. J. Hobsbawm, 'Fabianism and the Fabians, 1884–1914', pp. 134 ff.

[2] Olivier to Pease, 14 Oct 1899, inserted in Executive Committee Minutes for 20 Oct 1899 (Fabian Soc. MSS.).

[3] Both resolutions are printed in full in McBriar, op. cit. pp. 121–2.

[4] Minutes of Fabian Society Meetings, 8 Dec 1899 (Fabian Soc. MSS.).

[5] Fabian Society Executive Committee Minutes, 15 Dec 1899 (ibid.).

[6] Ibid. 12 Jan 1900.

[7] Ibid. 23 Feb 1900. The figures were: Ayes 217, Noes 259.

Society that 'a Fabian is necessarily an Imperialist',[1] and a link
was beginning to be forged, surreptitiously, between the Webbs
and Lord Rosebery.[2] While this was going on, thirteen members,
including MacDonald, resigned from the Society.[3] Then came
news of the impending general election, and the committee –
newly constituted after the resignations[4] – decided after all to
issue a manifesto, to be drafted by Shaw, whose 'imperialist'
sympathies were, by this time, notorious.[5] The result was
Fabianism and the Empire, published shortly before the election:
a perversely unorthodox document (as was only to be expected
from Shaw), but generally taken to be imperialist and pro-War.
From this point there was no return. The Fabian Society – more
particularly the Webbs – became deeply embroiled with the
Roseberyite section of the Liberal Party. A *Nineteenth Century*
article by Sidney Webb in September 1901 announced that he
was putting his money on Rosebery to inspire a 'virile', collectivist, imperialist opposition party to his liking:[6] which delighted
Haldane, Asquith and Rosebery himself.[7] *Facilis descensus
Averno*: and by 1904, with the publication of *Fabianism and
the Fiscal Question*,[8] of which Graham Wallas complained that
'All the turns of phrase and all the underlying assumptions

[1] Lecture delivered on 23 Feb 1900; see *Fabian News*, Mar 1900; and cf.
a lecture by Shaw reported in the *Daily Chronicle*, 4 Mar 1900.

[2] See, for example, Beatrice Webb, *Our Partnership*, p. 198.

[3] Fabian Society Executive Committee Minutes, 20 Apr 1900 (Fabian Soc.
MSS.). See Pease in Margaret Cole (ed.), *The Webbs and their Work*, p. 24:
'Somebody said that the Boer War was a great evil, but there was one
compensation: for us it got rid of MacDonald'.

[4] Minutes of Fabian Society Meetings, 27 Apr 1900. The *Daily Chronicle*,
in a cutting inserted into these Minutes, reported the elections for the new
committee as the 'victory of the Imperialists'.

[5] Fabian Society Executive Committee Minutes, 27 Apr 1900 (Fabian
Soc. MSS.).

[6] Sidney Webb, 'Lord Rosebery's Escape from Houndsditch', in *C19th*,
Sept 1901, pp. 366–86 (republished two months later as Fabian Tract no.
108).

[7] Rosebery to Beatrice Webb, 3 Sept 1901 (Passfield Papers, L.S.E.,
II.4.b, item 23a, f. 72a); and Haldane to Sidney Webb, 5 Sept 1901 (ibid.
II.4.b, item 25, ff. 76–9). On Fabian relations with the Liberal Imperialists,
see Semmel, op. cit. pp. 72–82.

[8] Fabian Tract no. 116.

are Protectionist',[1] the Society seemed condemned to perdition.

The Fabians had declared in favour of imperialism: but the reasoning on which they based this decision was very much more devious than the uncomplicated patriotism of some of their harness-companions. When *Fabianism and the Empire* was published, feeling about the South African War ran so high in England that opinions tended to become polarised about the extremes of 'imperialism' and 'anti-imperialism', 'patriot' and 'pro-Boer'. More subtly defined categories in between were lost to view, and the Fabian brand of imperialism was forced into a popular category in which it had no true place. For the Fabians' beliefs were a long way removed from those of (for example) Chamberlain, Kipling or Milner. In a way it was only by their own insistence that they were placed on the imperialist side of the fence. Yet by many of the popular patriotic yardsticks of the time they were on the other side, the side of J. A. Hobson and the pro-Boers.

Their sympathies were never with the jingoes. Beatrice Webb's diaries reveal a strong distaste on her part for the events which led up to the South African War:[2] for the 'sordid' Jameson Raid,[3] the 'hysterical loyalty' she found in London in 1897,[4] and the 'muddy intrigues and capitalist pressure' which had provoked the conflict.[5] Nowhere did she give any sign of approval for the British Government's policies. When war was declared, she wrote in despair of the 'unsavoury' actions of 'our own people in the Transvaal':

> an underbred business, from the Raid to the South African Committee of Enquiry, from the hushing up of this Enquiry

---

[1] Wallas to Pease, 21 Jan 1904 (Fabian Soc. MSS.). Wallas resigned from the Society in protest against the tract.

[2] There are three sources for Beatrice Webb's diaries covering this period: (*a*) the original manuscript version in the Passfield Papers; (*b*) a later copy typed by Beatrice Webb and her secretary, in the Passfield Papers; and (*c*) excerpts printed in Beatrice Webb, *Our Partnership*. These will be referred to respectively as '*MS. Diary*', '*TS. Diary*' and '*O.P.*'. There are discrepancies between all three, and the original versions will be cited whenever these discrepancies affect the meaning.

[3] B. Webb, *TS. Diary*, vol. 16, p. 82 (23 Feb 1897).

[4] B. Webb, *O.P.*, p. 140 (25 June 1897).   [5] Ibid. p. 194.

and the whitewashing of Rhodes, to the flashy despatches of Milner, and the vulgarly provocative talk of Chamberlain bringing us face to face with war with that little remnant of 17th century puritanism – the Transvaal Republic. I have been mortified. . . .[1]

Sidney, she reported, shared her views. 'First and foremost, I know he loathes the war; he thinks the whole episode of the Rand and the Chamberlain negotiations a disgrace to this country. . . .'[2] And he was opposed all along to tariffs.[3] Bernard Shaw was more impressed by protectionist arguments,[4] and persuaded of the inevitability and (in a Social Darwinist kind of way) of the justice of the South African War.[5] But even he found a great deal to criticise in the British Empire as it was being managed at the time, and his scathing exposé of certain aspects of British rule in Egypt, which he incorporated into his Preface to *John Bull's Other Island*, was as strongly worded as any anti-imperialist propaganda of that period:

> if her Empire means ruling the world as Denshawai has been ruled in 1906 – and that, I am afraid, is what the Empire does mean to the main body of our aristocratic-military caste and to our Jingo plutocrats – then there can be no more sacred and urgent political duty on earth than the disruption, defeat, and suppression of the Empire. . . .[6]

[1] B. Webb, *MS. Diary*, vol. 20 (10 Oct 1899).
[2] B. Webb, *O.P.*, p. 218 (9 July 1901); and cf. ibid. p. 190 (Dec 1899); *MS. Diary* vol. 20 (10 Oct 1899); Sidney to Beatrice, 13 Dec 1899 (Passfield Papers, 11.3.i., item 31).
[3] See B. Webb, *O.P.*, pp. 266–7, 272; Hewins to Sidney Webb, 1 June 1903 (Passfield Papers, 11.4.b. item 99, ff. 221–6); and Shaw to B. Webb, 28 June 1903 (ibid. 11.4.b. item 103, f. 223).
[4] '. . . being a Socialist, I am a Protectionist right down to my boots' (Shaw to Burns, 11 Sept 1903, in Burns Papers, B.M. Add. MS. 46287, f. 327). To Webb he wrote in the same month: 'I am going to speak in Glasgow on the 2nd. Oct. on "Is Free Trade Alive or Dead" & am going to answer Dead with terrific emphasis' (Passfield Papers, 11.4.b. item 116, f. 267, marginal note); and cf. Shaw to Webb, 29 Sept 1903 (ibid. 11.4.b. item 117, f. 275).
[5] See below, p. 116.
[6] George Bernard Shaw, *John Bull's Other Island*, p. lvi.

E

Here there was nothing to give comfort to Conservative or Liberal imperialists; and *Fabianism and the Empire*, the Society's official declaration of its colonial policy, was no less critical of their record in South Africa, condemning as powerfully as J. A. Hobson or the *Clarion* the influence exerted over imperial counsels by 'the passions of the newspaper correspondents' and the 'cosmopolitan capitalists' of the Rand.[1] The Boer states, it advised, must be formally incorporated into the British Empire; but they should be allowed to fly their own flag; the rights of native races – including African labour on the Rand – should be safeguarded by the imperial authority; and the mines should be taxed to pay for the new administration (and, if possible, nationalised) to demonstrate that annexation was not designed merely to 'secure private property for European speculators at the public expense'.[2] None of these measures was contemplated, or ever effected, by the Government.

So the Fabians were far from being mere sycophants of the Conservatives. Their imperialism had its own distinctive flavour, and the Empire they wanted to see was very different from the Empire the Tories were creating. It was to be 'socialistic', in the sense in which the Fabians understood socialism. Shaw's manifesto described their aim as 'the effective social organisation of the whole Empire' – the mother country as well as the colonies – 'and its rescue from the strife of classes and private interests'.[3] This meant first of all the more efficient utilisation of imperial resources – employing the consular service, for example, to help British commerce,[4] replacing free enterprise by state enterprise in Africa,[5] and (surprisingly and a little disturbingly) reconstituting the Army on the basis of compulsory part-time military service for all.[6] 'Efficiency', in fact, became the special slogan of the Fabians at this time, and it was taken up by men like Lord Rosebery who were looking for a watchword which would provoke among the

---

[1] *Fabianism and the Empire*, pp. 4, 24.   [2] Ibid. pp. 30–1, 35–7.
[3] Ibid. p. 6.   [4] Ibid. pp. 7–13.
[5] Ibid. pp. 8, 24, 30–1. Beatrice Webb's objection to the Jameson Raid seems to have been mainly on the ground that it was 'Private enterprise'; see *MS. Diary*, 5 Jan 1896.
[6] *Fabianism and the Empire*, pp. 38–44.

general public a more enthusiastic response than the old Liberal
ideals (at a time when the marked inefficiency of the Army in
South Africa seemed to be making that public receptive to it), but
which would at the same time distinguish them from Conservative imperialists. Yet this was not the whole sum of the Fabians'
desires. As well as being efficient, the Empire must be humane; the
imperial administration should be beneficial to the interests of
those alien races under its sway. Shaw's chapter on India advocated a number of practical reforms in this direction, stopping
short of self-government through parliamentary institutions, but
consistent throughout with the orthodox Liberal 'progressive'
line.[1] For South Africa he suggested measures designed to protect
native races against exploitation,[2] and for China a 'labour code'.[3]
There was no question here of colonial exploitation; or even, he
tried to suggest, of imperial dominion. The Empire of the
Fabians' dreams was not the Empire of ruler and ruled, of white
overlords and coloured subjects, but what Shaw called a 'partnership' between the races,[4] and what Sidney Webb was later to
term a 'Commonwealth': 'I want Laurier & Botha & Redmond &
the Hindoo leader whoever he is, *each* to push his own nationality
within the British Commonwealth. . . .'[5] The Fabian plan for the
Empire was never (until, perhaps, the publication of *Fabian
Colonial Essays* in 1945) worked out in detail. But, as far as it
went, it was largely in accord with those ideas which a later
age would call enlightened and progressive.

And yet the Fabians – not inaccurately – called themselves
imperialists. They accepted the Empire; they accepted, moreover,
that the Empire and its extension were good and necessary.
Shaw's object in *Fabianism and the Empire* was not only to show
that the Empire needed reforming – in the same way that a
doctor might prescribe a sedative to alleviate the worst effects of a

---

[1] Ibid. pp. 17–21.
[2] Ibid. pp. 22, 37. Beatrice Webb claimed (wrongly) that Shaw was the
only person who 'ever mentioned the claim of the native population' in
South Africa (*O.P.*, pp. 191–2).
[3] *Fabianism and the Empire*, p. 51.
[4] Ibid. p. 21 (referring to India).
[5] Sidney Webb to Graham Wallas, 23 July 1908 (Wallas Papers, L.S.E.).

disease; but to demonstrate that a reformed Empire was a desirable thing, and certainly better than no Empire at all. He was concerned with the justice of imperialism, as well as the form it should take. But his own moral attitude towards empire was never one of wholly enthusiastic commendation. In the first place, it had in it a strong streak of fatalism. 'The partition of the greater part of the globe...', he wrote, 'is, as a matter of fact that must be faced, approvingly or deplorably, now only a question of time'.[1] To H. M. Hyndman he wrote that: 'I am a pure natural-history student, and feel no more indignation against Rockefeller or Rhodes than I do against a dog following a fox.' [2] This was not a moral judgment, but a resigned acceptance of the inevitable, of a natural process he later compared to 'the extinction of the stagecoach by the locomotive'.[3] Empires had come to stay and to grow bigger, and we must be realistic and acknowledge it. And when Shaw used more utilitarian arguments to defend empire, it was in terms very similar to Benjamin Kidd's, and to those we shall find J. A. Hobson using. Hobson admitted that the old Liberal 'rights of nationality' argument was no longer applicable to the world-society of the late nineteenth century, and that considerations of 'international social utility' could, theoretically, justify the imperial annexation of a backward country.[4] Shaw (and Webb) said the same:

> The notion that a nation has a right to do what it pleases with its own territory, without reference to the interests of the rest of the world, is no more tenable from the international socialist point of view – that is, the point of view of the 20th century – than the notion that a landlord has a right to do

[1] *Fabianism and the Empire*, p. 3.

[2] Shaw to Hyndman, n. d. (Apr 1900), copy, in Shaw Papers, B.M. Add. MS. 50538, f. 127.

[3] Shaw to Burns, 11 Sept 1903; Burns Papers, B.M. Add. MS. 46287, f. 327. See also Sydney Olivier to Shaw, n.d. (1899), in Shaw Papers, B.M. Add. MS. 50543, f. 123: 'When you argued, the other evening, that the Boers are a seventeenth century people, and your supporter that they are peasant proprietors, and Maccrosty that their industrial organisation is condemned by the evolutional theories of the F[abian] S[ociety] you all set my teeth on edge....'

[4] See below, pp. 180–1 and 230–1.

what he likes with his estate without reference to the interests of his neighbours.[1]

Atomistic nationalism, said Webb, was as dead as *laissez-faire* individualism; 'we have become a new people',[2] with a wider and more socialistic conception of world-society. Hobson's basic position was the same, right down to his rejection of Liberalism and his belief in a 'New Age'. The difference between them was really very slight; but for Hobson it was crucial. Shaw admitted that 'theoretically' the development of those resources which were not being used for the benefit of the world should be 'internationalised, not British-Imperialised'; but he maintained that until 'World Federation' was achieved, 'responsible Imperial federations' could provide a viable substitute.[3] It was on this last point that Hobson disagreed with him, for he could not bring himself to trust, as Shaw appeared to do, in the altruism and freedom from selfish motives of any single great power whose intervention was not clearly directed and supervised by an international mandatory authority.[4] The question at issue was whether the British Empire – bad as it was – could be made into an agency for good; whether it could be reformed sufficiently to provide the means to an end upon which they both agreed. Hobson, obsessed by the corruption of the Empire and the difficulties in the way of reform, said no; Shaw claimed there was little alternative. They had to accept the Empire as the only means by which a system of international relations based upon a 'socialistic' or 'organic' conception of the world economy could be achieved. It was only this slender distinction – a difference more of emphasis than of opinion – which divided the Fabian 'imperialist' from the Hobsonian 'anti-imperialist'.

Sidney Webb was slower to commit himself on the issue than Shaw. He did not lack experience of imperial affairs: from 1881 to 1891 he had worked at the Colonial Office; he had toured

---

[1] *Fabianism and the Empire*, pp. 44–5. Cf. S. Webb, 'Lord Rosebery's Escape', *C19th*, p. 371.

[2] Ibid. p. 368.   [3] *Fabianism and the Empire*, p. 24.

[4] See J. A. Hobson, 'Socialistic Imperialism', in *I.J.E.*, vol. xii (1901), pp. 44–58.

Australia, New Zealand and Canada as recently as 1898;[1] and he numbered among his friends and colleagues such 'imperially minded' men as Haldane, Dilke and Sydney Olivier. But none of these things seems to have aroused in him any real interest in the Empire (except in socialist movements within the white dominions), and even after the South African War had been in progress for nearly two years he refused to make any judgment on it, protesting (when his wife tried to persuade him at least to read the relevant Blue Books) that 'it is not my show'.[2] If anything, he was sentimentally a pro-Boer.[3] Beatrice herself was more inclined to support Chamberlain; 'he has convictions and he expresses them honestly and forcibly – qualities at present rare in the political world'.[4] (Here her attitude was perhaps coloured to some extent by a brief love-affair she had had with Joseph Chamberlain in the 1880s, and on which her private diaries for the years 1899–1902 dwelt with a somewhat morbid intensity.)[5] But

[1] Letters from the Webbs in Canada and Australasia appear in the Passfield Papers, II.4.a.

[2] B. Webb, *O.P.*, p. 218.

[3] See above, p. 113.   [4] B. Webb, *O.P.*, p. 191.

[5] This affair has recently been chronicled by Mr Peter Fraser in his *Joseph Chamberlain* (1966), ch. 5, and has been treated in more detail by Kitty Muggeridge and Ruth Adam, *Beatrice Webb: A Life* (1967); but no one has yet treated her emotional resurrection of it in 1899–1902. The entries in her manuscript diary for 15 June and 10 Oct 1899; 22 May, 4 July, 19 Oct and 16 Nov 1900; 1 Jan, 22 Mar, 24 Apr, 1 Oct and 9 Dec 1901; and 15 Feb 1902, are especially revealing. It is difficult to know how much weight to attach to them, as they were written while Beatrice Webb's physical health was poor and her mental health considerably depressed. She herself later wrote that one of her bad habits was the 'dramatising of relationships' (*TS. Diary*, vol. 20, p. 38), and much of what she wrote about her 'passionate attachment' to Chamberlain appears to have been exaggerated retrospection. But if these entries are not entirely reliable as a guide to what happened in the 1880s, they throw a little light on her mood in 1900. The burden of them is that Beatrice met Chamberlain in 1883 ('He had energy & personal magnetism – in a word *masculine force* – to an almost superlative degree'), and instantly fell in love with him ('he absorbed the whole sexual emotion of my nature'). Chamberlain reciprocated, but later (she said) rejected her; and a few years afterwards she decided to marry Sidney ('In this relationship, I had, at any rate, the complete intellectual sympathy & the identity of moral aim which had been totally lacking in the other: & the fact that neither my physical passions nor my social ambitions were stimulated by the relationship seemed

neither of them wanted to involve themselves in the controversy, and it was only under considerable pressure from Shaw[1] that Sidney publicly committed himself, in September 1901, to the latter's view. When he did so, it was not by reason of a genuine imperialist sympathy on his part, so much as the belief, inculcated by Shaw, that by 'plunging in with Rosebery' he would give himself 'the best chance of moulding home policy'.[2]

This is the real key to the Fabians' position. Shaw's exposition of their imperialism demonstrates that even for him it was not an article of positive faith, but rather a second-best solution made inevitable by political circumstances. He was scarcely enthusiastic over it, and other Fabians were even less so. To them imperialism was a tool, a means to an end, and the end was still those measures of social reform which had all along been their only real concern. In the furtherance of their domestic programme they should make use of whatever political forces appeared most powerful and malleable; and in 1900 imperialism, as preached by Rosebery, seemed to them to be the only possible agency by which their schemes could be realised. So the Fabian cuckoo laid his socialist egg in the Liberal Imperialist nest. This was 'permeation'.

The Fabian debate of 1899, culminating in the resignations of April the next year, was at bottom not about the War or the Empire, but about the function and methods of the Society. Hubert Bland wrote to Edward Pease in October 1899:

> It looks as though you and I and the remnant of the old gang ... would have to make one more big fight to secure the society's usefulness in the future, a usefulness which will be entirely crippled if we throw ourselves dead athwart the

---

in itself an element of stability and restfulness. Then again my pity was appealed to: I felt that his passion for me & his need for me were so overpowering that his life & work might be wrecked if I withdrew myself ...'). But now, in 1900, she occasionally regretted that she had not been able to marry Chamberlain, and she retained for him a somewhat reluctant admiration. A case, perhaps, of *cherchez l'homme*.

[1] See Shaw to Beatrice, 24 July 1901; and Shaw to Sidney, 26 July 1901 (Passfield Papers, 11.4.b., items 22, 23).

[2] B. Webb, *O.P.*, p. 220.

Imperialist, or any other, strong stream or tendency. As we cannot break up those streams, but only be broken up by them, we should try in our humble, but sometimes quite effective, way, to direct them.[1]

This was the hub of the 'imperialist' Fabians' argument, and it convinced Webb. Whatever he thought of the merits of the imperialist case, other factors made it imperative that he do nothing to go against this 'strong stream or tendency'. Like Shaw, he appears to have had an exaggerated respect for the powerful forces which he saw dominating politics – like the growth of empire sentiment and the disruption of the Liberal Party – and to have felt, perhaps more than Shaw, a sense of impotence in their midst.[2] On their own the Fabians could never be directly effective in politics. 'We can never hope to get hold of the "man in the street",' wrote Beatrice; 'we are "too damned intellectual".' [3] They had to rely on others to put their proposals into practice, and who could do this in 1900? The Conservatives' hostility to social reform ruled them out of court. The Liberal Party was out of touch with the twentieth century; by clinging to an outworn individualism, 'administrative nihilism' and atomistic nationalism it was sounding its own death-knell.[4] The Labour parties had spoilt any chance they had once had of replacing it by siding with the Liberals on foreign policy: 'They out-morleyed Mr Morley in their utterances on the burning topic of the day; and now the Independent Labour Party is as hopelessly out of the running as the Gladstonian Party.' [5] Fabians could not alter the broad tendency of politics: they could only hope to divert it a

---

[1] Bland to Pease, 17 Oct 1899 (Fabian Soc. MSS., box 1). Yet he was not merely an opportunist; Bland's imperialism was the most pronounced of all the Fabians': see above, p. 109, fn. 1. In Apr 1900 he contributed a pro-War article to the *Clarion* (7 Apr, pp. 105–6).

[2] His consciousness of the limitations of political action is further illustrated by his attitude towards Kenya while Colonial Secretary in the second Labour Government (1929–31). See Sir Drummond Shiels in M. Cole (ed.), *The Webbs and their Work*, p. 207.

[3] B. Webb, *O.P.*, p. 202.

[4] S. Webb, 'Lord Rosebery's Escape', *C19th*, pp. 366–71.

[5] Ibid. p. 374.

little.[1] They were presented with a choice between Gladstonian Liberalism and imperialism, and because the fundamental tenets of their philosophy were hostile to *laissez-faire* and individualism they had to come down on the other side. If they wanted collectivism, then they must support the only party which both stood a chance of coming to power and was not irrevocably committed to *laissez-faire*.[2]

> We have no illusions about the Liberal Imperialists. We think that neither Rosebery nor Asquith mean to declare themselves in favour of our measure of collectivism. But they hold no views that are inconsistent with it – have nothing to offer but a refusal to take up the distinctive side of the old Liberalism. The time will come when, if they are to be a political force, they will have to 'fill up' the political worker with some positive convictions. Then, we think, for the needful minimum of nourishment they will fall back on us and not on the other section.[3]

And so, in the hope of influencing Rosebery if and when he came to power, the Webbs followed Shaw's advice and declared their allegiance to him. In exchange for a 'measure of collectivism', they offered a measure of imperialism. With their view of the political situation, and their social priorities, the bargain was a fair one.

Whether they gained by it in the long run is doubtful. Certainly subsequent developments show them to have been a little short-sighted. Beatrice Webb's sister Kate, the wife of Leonard

[1] Shaw, writing to H. M. Hyndman about the S. African War, defended his apparent alliance with the Rand capitalists in this way: 'as Mammon can be developed into a Socialist power . . . my sympathies are with Mammon' (Shaw to Hyndman, n.d. (Apr 1900), copy; Shaw Papers, B.M. Add. MS. 50538, ff. 132–4).

[2] In this connexion there is an interesting sequence of letters from W. A. S. Hewins, Director of the L.S.E. from 1895 and the economist behind Chamberlain's tariff reform campaign, to the Webbs in 1903 trying to persuade them that their collectivism and antipathy to Liberal individualism necessarily involved their allegiance to the cause of tariff reform (Passfield Papers, 11.4.b, ff. 217, 221, 230a, 231, 295, 299). See also Hewins, *Apologia of an Imperialist*, ch. 1, which describes how he saw the collectivist's choice as a straight one between Manchesterism and imperialism.

[3] B. Webb, *O.P.*, p. 224.

Courtney, thought at the time that they had put their money on the wrong horse: 'Leonard does not believe you will catch that bird [Rosebery] effectively at all . . .';[1] and Shaw was soon to realise how right she was. 'The utter emptiness of the Rosebery campaign is very exasperating. I am beginning to think that we shall have to go revolutionary after all & try to bring off a Labour-Collectivist Opposition. . . .'[2] Their assessment of contemporary political trends was shown by the 1906 election, and by what happened afterwards, to have been grossly inaccurate. Labour was not 'out of the running'; the pro-Boers were not implacably hostile to social action (as Lloyd George was to demonstrate); and the tide of imperialism was by no means so strong or so permanent as it had appeared to them in 1900. But the real failure of the Fabians, from a socialist point of view, lay in their parochialism, of which their imperialism was, paradoxically, a symptom. They were imperialists because they did not think foreign affairs mattered to them; hence they were able to barter their support over the South African War to the highest bidder. If by becoming imperialists they could more easily promote their social programme, then they would do so. They failed to realise that domestic reform to a large extent depended on foreign policy; that a great international crisis could ruin the social work of generations. Hence in 1914 they appeared pathetically impotent. 'Under the red glow of the war sky, molten with passion and destructive of thought, the Webbs look rather forlorn and strangely small.'[3] In this respect J. A. Hobson's wider vision

[1] Kate Courtney to B. Webb, 12 Sept 1901; Passfield Papers, 11.4.b., f. 80.

[2] Shaw to the Webbs, 24 Mar 1902, ibid. 11.4.b., f. 105; and see B. Webb, *O.P.*, p. 232: 'Having done our little best to stimulate the "Limps" into some kind of conviction, and having most assuredly failed, we now return to our own work.'

[3] Mary Agnes Hamilton, *Sidney and Beatrice Webb*, p. 219. Cf. Leonard Woolf's comment in 1949: 'The problem of imperialism, international relations, and war and peace cannot very easily be stated in terms of the structure and functions of institutions or reduced to mere questions of organisation. They have been the major causes of disorder, misery, and evil in the world for the last hundred years and they have made the orderly and civilised life for which the Webbs worked so devoutly impossible.' (*The Webbs and their Work*, p. 261.)

rendered him more far-seeing, if no more effective, than the Webbs; with the same broad aim of social reform, he nevertheless concentrated his attention, after 1900, on international policy,[1] recognising as the Fabians failed to do that the two things could not be put in separate compartments. In 1923 the Webbs at last accepted his conclusions.[2] But in 1900 their opportunistic methodological philosophy stood in the way of any such insight.

It was this way of thinking which cut the Fabians adrift from the Labour movement. Their views were deduced from a set of considerations which had little intrinsically to do with empire, but more to do with imperial*ism* and imperial*ists*; they were influenced less by a consideration of the merits of the imperial case – on this they agreed, more or less, with Hobson – than by a calculation of its popularity and utility. Factors which were extraneous to the Empire *per se* determined their position: but these factors were sufficient to deprive the Labour parties of what might otherwise have become a useful academy for the working-out of a new philosophy of empire. With the Fabians on the other side of the fence, Labour had now to look to others for its anti-imperialist ideology.

III. THE SOUTH AFRICAN WAR AND CAPITALIST EXPLOITATION

It says much for the Labour movement's devotion to principle – and even more, perhaps, for the indifference with which the Fabians were regarded by their less intellectual colleagues – that they did look elsewhere, and courted a temporary unpopularity by clearly and consistently opposing the Boer War. They had never appeared troubled by the Fabians' ideological dilemmas, nor did they share the latter's doubts as to the effectiveness of a

---

[1] See below, pp. 235 ff.
[2] See S. and B. Webb, *The Decay of Capitalist Civilisation*, pp. 147–58; and cf. a similar change of heart on the part of Shaw, in *The Intelligent Woman's Guide to Socialism and Capitalism*, vol. 1, pp. 150–7.

party swimming against the tide. The only thing holding them back was their reticence; and the War put an end to that. Once war was declared, there was no longer any question of ignoring it as some of them had tried before to ignore the Sudan and the Jameson Raid. He had once heard it said, wrote S. G. Hobson in December 1899, that socialists should not concern themselves with such issues as South Africa, that their business lay nearer at home; but now,

> I am glad to say that it is not necessary to urge this point . . . because practically everyone concedes the contention that our Socialism does compel us to take note of and to define our position towards this movement of expansion. . . .[1]

The War did not bring imperial matters to the notice of Labour for the first time – we have seen how for some years their Press had been fully cognizant of what was going on in Africa – but it compelled them to speak out more openly than they had before, to bring to the parliamentary surface their detestation of 'capitalistic imperialism' in South Africa and elsewhere.

Labour M.P.s, in fact, were in the van of the pro-Boer agitation of 1899–1902. They were unanimous against the War with one single exception, Havelock Wilson; and *his* influence, claimed Keir Hardie, 'either in trade union or political affairs, is *nil*'.[2] There were different degrees of opposition amongst them. Some, like Burns and Hardie, early made known their intention to 'support any Amendment that challenges, denounces or condemns the war',[3] and these men seized every possible opportunity to vote against supplies for its prosecution. Others felt qualms about the responsibility of such action. The War, said Frederick Maddison, was 'unnecessary' and 'wicked', but now it had started it was inevitable that superior British strength would prevail, and so, to prevent its prolongation, it was 'to the interests

[1] S. G. Hobson, 'Imperialism: A Socialist View', in the *Labour Leader*, 16 Dec 1899, p. 396.
[2] *Keir Hardie's Speeches and Writings*, p. 97.
[3] Burns in the H. of C., 6 Feb 1900; 4 P.D. 78, c. 788.

of the Boers that the force you send should be overwhelming'.[1] Such men abstained when the House divided on Army Estimates. Yet Burns and Maddison differed only over the remedy they proposed for the War – not in their analysis of its causes, or in their hatred of its injustice. In these things they were at one, and Keir Hardie was right when he contended that, 'With very few exceptions, the Movement is solid against the war and for peace.' [2] Behind him were the S.-D.F., the I.L.P., a great part of the T.U.C. and the newly founded Labour Representation Committee,[3] all but one of the Labour M.P.s, and the whole Labour Press, with the exception of the *Clarion* – and even the *Clarion* contained more anti-War matter than Blatchfordian jingoism.[4]

The virulence of the Labour attack was unrivalled. John Burns – despite the 'imperialist' lapses of his past – took on the leadership of the parliamentary offensive with enthusiasm,[5] until Keir Hardie assumed his mantle in December 1900. Some idea of the tone of the latter's rhetoric can be gauged from this excerpt from an article on Cecil Rhodes:

> Mr Rhodes is a confirmed drunkard – a dipsomaniac, in the language of social and conventional diplomacy. During his visit to this country after the Jameson Raid, he had to be constantly watched by his friends, so that he might be fit for the duties of the hour. That his friends were not always successful is well known. So Mr Rhodes makes merry in Kimberley; champagne flows copiously, and the special

[1] Maddison in H. of C., 20 Oct 1899, 4 P.D. 77, cc. 399–400. Cf. Broadhurst in H. of C., 15 Feb 1900: 'I am not prepared to refuse the demands of the Government now. A great conflagration has been started and the only thing to be done is to extinguish it as soon as possible.' (4 P.D. 79, c. 162).

[2] *Labour Leader*, 6 Jan 1900, p. 4.

[3] See I.L.P. and L.R.C. reports for 1899–1902.

[4] During the War the *Clarion* carried contributions by such prominent 'pro-Boers' as Burns, Morrison Davidson and J. A. Hobson. Its assistant editor, Alex Thompson, was against the War and said so in its pages: see especially his article on 'The Imperialism of Commerce', in the *Clarion*, 13 Jan 1900, p. 12.

[5] See especially 4 P.D. 78, cc. 781–97 (6 Feb 1900); and Burns's Diaries (Burns Papers, B.M. Add. MSS. 46317–20), where he records the occasions when he gave public speeches on the War.

refrigerating plant keeps the nectar of the diamond gods deliciously cool. There is occasion for merry-making. British soldiers and statesmen are at length playing Mr Rhodes' game to its final. The music of the guns and the groans of the dying and the dull, dead, cold weight of sorrow at the heart of tender women, whose loved ones are cold and stiff in death, are all to him so many indications of his coming triumph. When the settlement comes he and the hungry pack who yelp at his heels will line their pockets with thousands wrung from the sweat and blood of Briton and Boer and Uitlander.[1]

No punches were pulled here; more than the Radical pro-Boers, the Labour leaders sought to drive home their case by resorting to personal calumny and emotive oratory.

Yet in other ways they followed the Liberal-Radicals closely. We find the same 'Peace, Retrenchment, Reform' line running through their speeches on imperial expansion, especially those of Burns;[2] and on South Africa the arguments they used were the same – the legalistic case against British 'suzerainty',[3] the indictment of a provocative diplomacy,[4] the resentment against jingo hooliganism[5] and newspaper misrepresentation,[6] and scepticism as to the genuineness of the Uitlander grievances.[7] They attacked Milner[8] and 'methods of barbarism'[9] in much the same

---

[1] *Keir Hardie's Speeches and Writings*, p. 97. Rhodes's latest biographers call the stories of his intemperance 'complete fabrications, perhaps due to his habit of sipping many drinks one after another and leaving them all unfinished' (J. G. Lockhart and C. M. Woodhouse, *Rhodes*, pp. 211–12).

[2] e.g., see Burns in 4 P.D. 116, cc. 518–22 (Uganda), and ibid. 130, c. 1043 (Somaliland). See also I.L.P. reports, Apr 1900 *et passim*.

[3] e.g. Burns in H. of C., 6 Feb 1900; 4 P.D. 78, cc. 788–90.

[4] e.g. ibid. loc. cit.

[5] e.g. Maddison in H. of C., 29 Mar 1900, ibid. 81, c. 691; Broadhurst in H. of C., 6 Dec 1900, ibid. 88, c. 149; and Burns in H. of C., 7 Dec 1900, ibid. 88, c. 291.

[6] e.g. Burns in H. of C., 6 Feb 1900; ibid. 78, c. 785.

[7] e.g. ibid. 78, cc. 791–2.

[8] e.g. Broadhurst in H. of C., 12 Dec 1900; ibid. 88, c. 640.

[9] e.g. Broadhurst in H. of C., 6 Dec 1900, ibid. 88, cc. 146–7; Hardie in H. of C., 7 Dec 1900, ibid. 88, c. 302; and Hardie in H. of C., 17 July 1901, ibid. 97, c. 755.

terms as the Liberals. They were just as pessimistic over the effect of the War on foreign opinion[1] and on the prospects of racial concord in South Africa.[2] And their impugnment of the Rand capitalists was the same, only stronger.[3]

The bulk of Labour's case was concerned with proving the 'capitalist' origin of the South African War, as was that of many of the Liberal pro-Boers. The arguments they used against the Rand mine-owners and Park Lane financiers were closely similar, yet for Labour M.P.s they assumed a far more central importance, and for obvious reasons. Whereas Radicals did not necessarily object to capitalism *per se*, but only to its enlistment of war and conquest as an unfair aid to the natural growth of commerce, Labour had always assailed the capitalist for what he was and the economic and social system he upheld. So when capitalists were revealed to them at the centre of the conspiratorial web in Johannesburg, they avidly seized on this as further confirmation of all their socialistic theories and prejudices. If an evil wanted accounting for, the rule was *cherchez le capitaliste*: and once they had found him in South Africa there was no need to look further.

From the very first war-time session of Parliament, therefore, the anti-capitalist argument took pride of place in nearly every speech against the War by a Labour M.P.[4] The fullest exposition of it in the Commons was given by Burns in February 1900: the War, he declared, was being fought not for the franchise, but

[1] e.g. Burns in H. of C., 7 Dec 1900, ibid. 88, cc. 284–5; and Cremer in H. of C., 11 Dec 1900, ibid. 88, c. 578.

[2] e.g. Burns in H. of C., 7 Dec 1900, ibid. 88, c. 288; Hardie in H. of C., 7 Dec 1900, ibid. 88, cc. 298–9; Hardie in H. of C., 26 Feb 1901, ibid. 89, cc. 1276–7; and Hardie in H. of C., 31 July 1901, ibid. 98, c. 736.

[3] In connexion with the similarity between Radical and Labour attitudes to the S. African problems, it is significant that in 1900 a 'National Democratic League' was launched, whose purpose was to unite the two groups on the basis of their agreement on this issue. See Cole, *History of Socialist Thought*, III i 195.

[4] Broadhurst was the first Labour M.P. to put forward the 'capitalist conspiracy' theory in the Commons, on 25 Oct 1899: 'We believe the force came from the South African League, the Chartered Company, and their rich friends...' (4 P.D. 77, c. 672).

'in the interest of gold and diamonds in South Africa'. It had been 'engineered' by a 'financial gang', led by Rhodes and Beit and their friends – 'mostly Jews, who if they got the vote would sell it'. These men had 'captured' the Rhodesian Press, and by means of it had managed to inflame popular opinion in England and persuade the man in the street that he was fighting for rights and principles which were, in fact, spurious.

> This demand for the franchise in South Africa is a bogus demand, and a fraudulent pretext of the financiers to cover ulterior designs, to buy up and use the votes of industrial nomads to increase their commercial power, to lower the social standard of the miners, to lower wages and to increase hours.

The capitalist could never change his spots. In South Africa, as in Europe, all he wanted was cheap plentiful labour in the interests of bigger profits: the depression of white skilled labour and the imposition of 'slavery conditions' on natives and Asiatics. This was the whole answer. 'Wherever we go in this matter we see the same thing. Wherever we examine there is the financial Jew operating, directing, inspiring the agencies that have led to this war.' [1] The War, wrote Keir Hardie, was

> a Capitalists' war, begotten by Capitalists' money, lied into being by a perjured mercenary Capitalist press, and fathered by unscrupulous politicians, themselves the merest tools of the Capitalists.... As Socialists, our sympathies are bound to be with the Boers.[2]

There was the argument, and a familiar enough one it was. We need not go far to discover its source. Once a Labour man's interest in South African affairs had been aroused, all he had to do was to look through his back-numbers of *Reynolds's Newspaper*, *Justice*, the *Labour Leader* and the *Clarion*, or at the reports in *Hansard* of the debates on the Jameson Raid, and there was the image of the 'cosmopolitan financier', lovingly depicted with money-bags in one hand and a Union Jack in the other, grinning

---

[1] Burns in H. of C., 6 Feb 1900; 4 P.D. 78, cc. 785–96.
[2] Hardie in *Labour Leader*, 6 Jan 1900, p. 4.

up at him. Or, if somehow he had missed all the controversy about South Africa which had gone before, others were there to hammer the point home to him during the war years in the Labour Press. The *Leader*, for example, besides innumerable editorials and features by Keir Hardie and other prominent socialists about 'capitalistic imperialism' and related subjects,[1] gave considerable publicity to the books and articles of J. A. Hobson – quoting from them extensively in leading articles,[2] reproducing them in full from other journals,[3] or strongly urging 'those who can afford it' to go out and buy them.[4] Even the *Clarion*, despite its contrary editorial line, printed a pro-Boer article by him.[5] The arguments used by Hardie and Burns in their speeches and writings generally kept very close even to the details of Hobson's argument, and there is one piece of evidence – albeit inconclusive – which suggests that Burns may have been directly and personally influenced by the latter. Only eleven days before his long – and very Hobsonian – Commons speech against the War in February 1900, he wrote in his diary: 'Talbot House. Cadbury Crook Mackarness Hobson on war. Had a long chat with Hobson on general position and the Imperialism of today.' [6] Even if this entry does not refer to J. A. Hobson (it may refer to his Fabian namesake S. G.), there can be little doubt that the Labour leaders made use of the evidence he presented to put the final touches to an argument which had been, in broad outline, familiar to them since 1896.

Hobson's argument will be discussed in detail in the following chapters. It was both wider in its application, and more complex

[1] e.g. S. G. Hobson, 'Imperialism: a Socialist View', in *Labour Leader*, 16 Dec 1899; and Hardie, 'The War in South Africa – the Outcome of Capitalism in Politics', ibid. 31 Mar 1900. Nearly every war-time issue of *Reynolds's Newspaper* contained at least one leading article attacking the 'Anglo–Jewish Financial Party' on the Rand.

[2] e.g. *Labour Leader*, 23 Dec 1899, pp. 404–5.

[3] e.g. ibid. 30 Dec 1899, pp. 412–13.   [4] Ibid. 20 Jan 1900, p. 19.

[5] Hobson, 'The Settlement in South Africa', in the *Clarion*, 31 Mar 1900; and cf. A. M. Thompson's long and favourable review of Hobson's *War in South Africa* in ibid. 17 Mar 1900.

[6] John Burns, Diary, 25 Jan 1900; Burns Papers, B.M. Add. MS. 46318, f. 5.

philosophically, than those parts of it which Labour M.P.s took
and used to strengthen their indictment of the South African
War. Their whole emphasis was different. Although at this time
he was preoccupied with the specific manifestation of 'capitalistic imperialism' in South Africa, Hobson had insisted that this
was really only a symptom of a much more general phenomenon,
and one whose origins, essentially, lay in England rather than in
Africa. The 'tap-root' of imperialism was underconsumption at
home, and hence its remedy, too, lay in economic reconstruction
at home. Labour M.P.s, or those among them who were socialists, might have been expected to find this analysis of the economic
system congenial to them. Yet in Parliament they ignored Hobson's broader thesis and concentrated exclusively on the South
African end of the capitalist/imperialist process. The brunt of
their attack fell not on the European industrialists and financiers
who were seeking (according to Hobson) fresh markets for
their surplus manufactures and new fields for the investment of
surplus capital, but on the Rand mine-owners who wanted cheap
labour.[1] They concentrated on that one aspect of his theory
which lay closest to their hearts: the issue of capitalist exploitation
of labour.

The emphasis on 'exploitation' was the natural corollary of
that strong tradition within the Labour movement, of apathy
towards all issues which did not lie within its terms of reference
as a strictly functional organisation. To many trade unionists and
others before 1899 the Empire had not been a question of working-
class politics because it did not seem directly relevant to 'the
conditions of working-men, their labour, and their wages'.
Others, as we have seen, had always rejected this restricted view
of the function of the Labour movement, and insisted on a
'socialist' solution being applied to foreign and colonial politics

[1] Alex Thompson in the *Clarion* displayed a greater awareness of the
problems that Hobson was wrestling with. See the *Clarion*, 7 Jan 1899, p. 4:
'If we were all Socialists – if all the workers of Europe were Socialists, and
if the governments were Socialist governments, the difficulties would disappear; for if all the elements of profit were eliminated from the scramble,
all rivalries and hatreds would immediately cease. . . . But in the meantime,
what? . . .'

as well as to industrial problems. In a way the history of the development of the movement's attitude towards empire in the 1890s can be seen as a running conflict between these two different ways of looking at Labour's function: between the internationalist socialism of the S.-D.F. and the more parochial 'Labour' approach of the trade unions and the Fabians. In 1899 a kind of compromise was reached between them. The parliamentary representatives of the movement found a slogan which would combine socialist anti-imperialist doctrine with the more practical and hard-headed approach of the parochial Labourite. The 'exploitation' argument was part of the general doctrine of empire worked out by Bax, Hobson and others; but it was pointed in such a way as to emphasise the immediate relevance of imperialism to the situation and interests of the working classes. The argument of Bax and the Marxists, that imperialism affected them because it was delay-ing the realisation of their Utopia, meant little to men who were more concerned with the day-to-day problems of industrial organisation than with the millennium. 'Exploitation' gave them something more tangible, more immediately recognisable, to work on.

So just as, when Labour M.P.s discussed domestic industrial matters, it was the 'exploitation' theme which rang out most strongly and clearly, so in the debates on South Africa it was the exploitation by voracious mine-owners of black and white labour which elicited their deepest interest and sympathy. They appear to have identified themselves with the man in South Africa who was being 'depressed' in the same way as their constituents were in England. So they made his grievances their own special con-cern. Keir Hardie spoke in Parliament on most aspects of the South African question; but, he said, 'a subject in which naturally he had a more direct interest' was that of native labour.[1] Hence Labour M.P.s, while following the lead of the Radicals on other imperial issues, on this question were usually found taking the initiative themselves. During the latter half of the War they seized on any piece of information which seemed to lend weight to the 'exploitation' charge, and plied the Government with

[1] Hardie in H. of C., 13 Dec 1900; 4 P.D. 88. c. 758.

questions and accusations about the mine-owners' schemes for 'forcing' the natives into the mines.[1] 'It is', said Burns, 'a matter of considerable importance to labour. . . .'[2] The official attitude of the I.L.P. and the L.R.C. was the same. The former passed a number of resolutions to the effect that the War had been undertaken in order 'to enable a gang of inter-national speculators to enslave coloured men and reduce to starvation-point the wages of white men in South Africa'[3] – again with the emphasis on exploitation – and the L.R.C. adopted an identical position at its first Annual Conference in February 1901.[4] The leadership of the T.U.C., less happy about the solidarity of its rank and file, went further out of its way to point the relevance of South Africa to the interests of trade unionists. Not only did the War highlight an industrial situation there similar to that in England (this was continually reiterated), it would also bring 'great suffering and irreparable injury to the workpeople of both countries'[5] by diverting the people's attention away from social reform and the Government's failures in this field, by increasing the tax burden and by diminishing the opportunities for white *émigré* employment in South Africa.[6] In fact the whole affair, claimed one leading delegate, was part of an international capitalist plot to 'hold the workers of all countries in universal, social, and economic servitude'.[7]

[1] See Hardie in 4 P.D. 88, cc. 541 and 758; ibid. 97, c. 756; ibid. 98, cc. 1165, 1167; and Burns, ibid. 94, cc. 1027–8.

[2] Burns in H. of C., 23 May 1901; 4 P.D. 94, c. 1028.

[3] Report presented to the 9th Annual Conference of the I.L.P., Leicester, 8 Apr 1901; I.L.P. *Annual Reports*.

[4] L.R.C. *Annual Report*, 1901. The resolution adopted on this occasion was moved by the I.L.P. delegates; it condemned 'the corrupt agitation of the Transvaal mineowners, having as its object the acquisition of monopolies and a cheap supply of coloured and European labour'. It was passed unanimously.

[5] T.U.C. *Annual Report*, 1899 (resolution moved by W. C. Steadman).

[6] T.U.C. *Annual Reports*, 1899–1901, *passim*, especially the resolution moved by J. Ward at the 1901 Congress. *Reynolds's Newspaper* mentioned another way in which the War might affect the workers – the danger of conscription (12 Nov 1899, p. 1).

[7] T.U.C. *Annual Report*, 1902 (Ward). One exception to the general attitude of concern for the conditions of native mine-workers in S. Africa

Given this emphasis on 'exploitation', the greater part of Labour's line of reasoning, until 1906, followed naturally on. The Boer War debate defined both the extent and the limits of Labour's attitude towards empire until that date. It aroused in their parliamentary representatives a moderate degree of interest in imperial affairs, which had been absent before: but to a great extent it restricted that interest to the problems surrounding colonial labour. This is why, after the end of the War, it was South Africa which still held their strongest attention, for it was here that the capital/labour issue stood out in clearest relief. Between May 1902 (the signing of the Vereeniging treaty) and December 1905 Labour M.P.s made 17 speeches and put 31 questions in the Commons on colonial affairs. Twelve of these speeches and 26 of the questions were about South Africa, and nearly all of them on labour – white, native or Asiatic. The debates on Chinese labour were just a continuation of those on the War. Broadhurst charged the Government with 'sitting there at the bidding of the goldmine owners of Johannesburg to do their behest and rake the world through to provide them with cheap labour';[1] they were the dupes, said Burns, of 'Mr Phillips, Mr Beit, and other patriots who sang "God Save the King" in broken English, and wanted an interpreter for the top notes' [2] – pawns in the hands of rapacious capitalists who, because they refused to pay whites and natives enough to attract them to the mines, were now seeking to enslave Chinese. And so it went on, Labour against the capitalist exploiters. It was more difficult to apply this line of argument to the tropical African Empire, where the Colonial Office exercised a firmer control over private enterprise. In Uganda the offender was the Foreign Office, not the capitalist, and John Burns had to blame the incompetence of that department when he wished to draw attention to the unsatisfactory condition of native workmen

is an article by 'Kopjes' in the *Labour Leader*, 20 Aug 1898, p. 278, which contrasts their lot with that of their counterparts in the East End of London, to the latter's detriment. 'It is true that in some instances the native gets ill-treated ... but taking it all in all he lives a more wholesome, happier, and healthier life than the wage-slave of Europe.'

[1] Broadhurst in H. of C., 16 Feb 1904; 4 P.D. 129, c. 1575.
[2] Burns in H. of C., 17 Feb 1904; 4 P.D. 130, c. 95.

there.[1] But Broadhurst tried his best to point the 'anti-capitalist' moral in the case of the Ashanti War (undertaken to deprive King Prempeh of his symbol of authority, the 'Golden Stool'):

> It was noticeable of late years that the loadstone which called the Government to relieve oppression was generally found in the gold mines, and here it was again. When this Government professed to go to the relief of human beings it would be found, if it were looked into a little further, that speculators were near the scene of the action. . . . We should have heard nothing about the stool if it had been a wooden one.[2]

But here the connexion was a little more tenuous, and Labour on less firm ground than in South Africa.

In broad terms, therefore, Labour M.P.s confined their attention to one small aspect of the thesis which had been worked out by Hobson a few years before. They owed much to his indictment of South African capitalism, and enthusiastically seized on its implications *vis-à-vis* the exploitation of labour. They did not, however, take it very much further, never at any time in the Commons repeating the 'surplus capital' argument *in toto*, and seldom discussing in any great depth the problems of tropical administration to which, as we shall see, Hobson and Ramsay MacDonald devoted much of their attention.

The former was left to a few individual socialists and others in England to take up and use, and to those representatives of the international socialist movement who met in Paris in September 1900 – 'on a besoin de marchés nouveaux, pour l'évolution du capitalisme . . . '.[3] English Labour made no such fundamental analysis. Similarly, when it came to the 'native question' only a few men on the fringes of the movement ever looked beyond the 'exploitation' idea and tried to come to terms with the real difficulties involved in the government of subject races. John

---

[1] See Burns in H. of C., 22 Feb 1900 (4 P.D. 79, cc. 872–4); 30 Apr 1900 (ibid. 82, cc. 331–3); 14 May 1900 (ibid. 83, cc. 122–5); 9 Dec 1902 (ibid. 116, cc. 518–22); and 11 Dec 1902 (ibid. 116, cc. 952–8).

[2] Broadhurst in H. of C., 19 Mar 1901; 4 P.D. 91, c. 446.

[3] See above, p. 101.

Burns (loosely termed a 'Labour Member' and one of the leaders of Labour's opposition to the Boer War, yet regarded by many of his colleagues as a turncoat and never a member of any Parliamentary Labour Party) did make some effort to define Britain's responsibilities towards native races.[1] He was quite clear that she was doing wrong in trying in Africa to interfere with indigenous religious and social customs;[2] but he did not seem to be certain whether anything should be put in its place. At one moment he was lauding the British record in Africa as the 'one bright spot' on that continent, exhorting the Government to 'do everything in her power to save the natives from the baneful influence of drink',[3] and suggesting that Africa should be 'civilized and Imperialised, in the best sense of the word' by the British;[4] the next moment he was resurrecting the old Liberal anti-imperialist line:

> If they were going to carry out philanthropic humanitarianism where it was most needed, there were women in London and in the slums of other cities who might be rescued from a calling which they pursued for economic reasons.[5]

Yet Burns did emphasise, as few others did, the need for colonial administrators to have knowledge of, and sympathy for, the peoples they were governing;[6] and on one occasion he formulated a colonial doctrine very close to that of E. D. Morel:

[1] Burns had worked as an engineer for Goldie in Nigeria in the early 1880s.

[2] On interference with native customs, see Burns on Somaliland, H. of C., 19 Mar 1901 (4 P.D. 91, c. 507): '. . . just as in proportion as they used force to destroy native habits and customs they were damaging trade, weakening their prestige, and accentuating permanently the very thing they hoped to remove'; and 25 Feb 1904 (4 P.D. 130, c. 1042): '. . . it was not our business to go to the four corners of the earth adjusting religious differences between Buddhist passive resisters and High Churchmen there'. And on Uganda, 9 Dec 1902 (4 P.D. 116, c. 519): 'They would superimpose upon these people certain habits and customs that would more than counterbalance some of the supposed advantages of civilisation.'

[3] Burns in H. of C., 2 Apr 1897; 4 P.D. 48, c. 449.

[4] Burns in H. of C., 9 Dec 1902; 4 P.D. 116, c. 518.

[5] Burns in H. of C., 11 Dec 1902; 4 P.D. 116, c. 957.

[6] e.g. Burns in H. of C., 22 Feb 1900; 4 P.D. 79, c. 872, etc.

'He believed in Imperialism of the old-fashioned type – the establishment of coast trading stations and commerce extended by winning the confidence of natives by fair dealing.' [1] This way of thinking, insignificant at the time, was nevertheless a little more constructive than anything any other Labour M.P. had yet offered, and it anticipated a future line of speculation whose influence on Labour colonial policy was to be far more notable. This line – a positive policy designed to be implemented in the existing Empire – was being worked out by others; but already it was beginning to permeate the Independent Labour Party. At the I.L.P. Conference of 1900 the delegate for the City of London moved a resolution against imperialism which, among other things, called on the Government to 'withdraw the iron and unnatural dominance of our western political ideas, and allow the development of native forms of rule'.[2] In the next month a pamphlet was published by the same branch of the Party asserting that a country like Britain had responsibilities 'to the world', but that it was not part of that responsibility to 'teach' civilisation to alien races. Civilisation, it maintained, was a growth; it was determined by

> the religion, the history, the circumstances of a people. . . . You cannot carry it about with you. . . . A western civilisation cannot be imposed on an Eastern, or a Temperate upon a Tropical, people. We can no more send our civilisation to central Africa than we can send our climate there.[3]

This policy – a policy of 'Indirect Rule' – and the 'anthropological' way of thinking which gave it philosophical support, were a new departure for Labour.

But while Labour had only a dozen men in Parliament, most of these 'trade unionist' M.P.s, and while Ramsay MacDonald was

[1] Burns in H. of C., 11 Dec 1902; 4 P.D. 116, c. 958. On Morel, see below, Ch. 8.

[2] I.L.P. *Annual Report*, Apr 1900.

[3] *Imperialism: Its Meaning and Its Tendency*, published by the City Branch of the I.L.P., May 1900, p. 7. In view of the very close similarity of many of the views contained in this pamphlet to the writings of Ramsay MacDonald (discussed below, pp. 185–9), it is worth noting that MacDonald had joined the I.L.P. in 1894.

still not among them, then it made very little showing on the parliamentary surface. Despite the Fabians, Labour *was* anti-imperialist, and after 1899 she did press home, hard, the attack on 'capitalist imperialism'. Yet seldom at this time did she do more than repeat what Liberals had said before, or alternatively play simple variations on her own special 'exploitation of labour' theme. It was clear and unequivocal, so far as it went, but it did not go far towards working out what might be called a 'policy' towards the Empire, in particular towards those colonies where the exploiting capitalist did not appear quite so ostentatious as in South Africa. Labour M.P.s were too independent, perhaps, to bother with such things or to think they needed to bother with them. A 'party' had to have a colonial policy, because it was formed, generally, with the intention one day of forming an alternative government. But an 'independent Labour' M.P. – as most of them were – was in Parliament not to form a government but to represent the interests of labour – of his constituents – to the government in power. This functional conception of their position may go some way towards explaining the Labourites' attitude to the Empire. Before 1899 the 'interests of labour' seemed to exclude everything beyond the strictly domestic scene; after 1899 South Africa was brought into the picture, because it could not very well be left out: but only that aspect of South Africa which was made to appear immediately relevant to their own constituents. From 1906, when the new Labour Party won 30 seats (to be augmented a little later by the adhesion of a number of independent trade unionists to its ranks), the right conditions existed for a socialist colonial policy. The Empire could then become a field for constructive policy-making, instead of a mere object-lesson in 'exploitation'.

CHAPTER FIVE

'The New Knowledge'

THROUGHOUT the 1890s a number of Liberals and socialists – more, perhaps, than is sometimes assumed – had refused to join the imperialist bandwagon, and had sharply criticised some of its less savoury characteristics. But their criticism only rarely rose higher than mere polemic, and even then fought shy of offering constructive alternatives. It seemed as though imperialism was not accounted for in Radicals' schemes for the improvement of mankind, an unknown and unexpected obstruction which their theorists and philosophers had failed to foresee or provide any explanation for. Consequently its tangible effects on Africa, and the deeper issues these involved, aroused little or no response among them.

The traditional depositaries of Britain's colonial conscience – the missionary societies and Exeter Hall – were more fully cognizant of what was happening in Africa. They appeared less bewildered and distracted by the 'imperialist' controversy which raged about them, because their own policies were rooted in something specific and concrete – the cause of the African and the amelioration of his conditions; and they could base their protest on a firm tradition of humanitarian and Christian ideas. Nevertheless, Exeter Hall was very much less effective than it had been in the past, and its failure could, in part, be attributed to the same factor which had so enervated the Liberals – ideological anachronism. Whether its attitudes were in themselves right or wrong – and it is no part of our purpose to cast judgment on them – they appeared, in the 1890s, unsuited to the 'new' Empire, its pressures and necessities.

Yet Exeter Hall and the Liberal and Labour parties were not

at this time the only sources of imperial criticism. Outside them, other Radical groups were, more quietly, making their own contributions to progressive thinking about empire. In the context of one of them John Atkinson Hobson, in company with Ramsay MacDonald and one or two others, was to construct a whole new imperial philosophy which appeared, at the time, to be more in keeping with the conditions of the age. Another group centred around Edmund Dene Morel and a Liverpool trading interest, and was concerned more specifically with the guiding principles behind tropical government in Africa. The following chapters will be devoted to a description and analysis of the colonial ideologies of these two groups of men. We shall find that they were consistent with each other, if not identical; and the similarities between them arose, in part, from Hobson's and Morel's common receptiveness to certain new ideas and attitudes which the speculation of the late nineteenth century, over a broad field, had thrown up. As a prelude to our main discussion, therefore, we must here make a diversion away from matters purely imperial, and briefly survey a few of these ideas. Some of them might seem at first sight to have little relevance to questions of empire. Nevertheless, they furnished Hobson and Morel, as we shall discover, with a quarry of new and pertinent concepts, by means of which they were enabled to break away from the trappings of nineteenth-century thought and give to their imperial theory an edge of originality.

For many Radicals in the country the failures of the Liberal Party in the 1880s and 1890s had been symptomatic of a deeper political malady. There was a widespread feeling that times had changed, that there was a new and sinister spirit in public affairs which Liberalism was unfitted to combat. It went further than 'imperialism'. Free Trade had been given half a century to fulfil the promises of its keenest advocates, yet what Cobden and Bright had dreamed of had not come to pass. Industrialists were complaining about unfair competition, some alarmists were predicting trade depression, and the pacifist hopes of the Cobdenites were being rudely shattered by the wars, militarism, rising armaments and *Realpolitik* of the late nineteenth century. Again, the 'Condition of England Question' was coming once more to the front of the stage, in the guise of the 'Social Problem', brought to the attention of humanitarians by socialism, the work of the Salvation Army,[1] industrial disputes organised in a newly articulate way, and the researches of Charles Booth. Liberalism – even the more compromising Liberalism of the Factory Acts – seemed to have failed here too. And democracy itself appeared to have failed. The simple dichotomy between the forces of good – the people, progress, freedom, reason – on the one hand, and bad – the privileged interests and reaction – on the other seemed no longer to be valid. Reason was no longer seen to reside in the majority. Democracy (and most people considered that they had democracy)[2] was not enough: something sinister still resided beneath the surface, the 'interests' still controlled policy.

Whether or not this situation really was different from the past, many Radicals outside the Liberal Party in the 1890s believed that they were living in an age of transition. To them, the failure of Liberalism was an ideological one. Its 'traditional' policies were irrelevant to the new times, and the result was an ideological vacuum on the left. This did not matter so long as there was no broad, tangible and positive political policy to fill its place. The Liberal Party could hobble along, as it had before, from day to day by means of *ad hoc* progressive solutions to *ad hoc* problems, even if inconsistency were the result. The critics, who offered little that was attractive to the people, could be ignored. But the danger came when a new policy, apparently hostile to Liberalism, threatened to fill this vacuum: to provide not only a new antagonist to 'progress' but a new alternative as well. Chamberlain's Birmingham-Radical Imperialism did this.

[1] See General Booth, *In Darkest England and the Way Out* (1890), about the Social Problem, but inspired by Stanley's *In Darkest Africa*, and offering a colonial solution.

[2] e.g. J. H. Bridges in the *Positivist Review*, Oct 1898, p. 164: 'Democracy came, rather sooner than Bright expected, with Disraeli's Reform Act of 1867.' Bridges is making the same point, that whereas the Cobdenites had claimed that democracy would bring with it a rational policy (see above, p. 11), events had proved them wrong.

Appealing both to 'progressive' and Tory sentiments, the New Imperialism forced those who still believed the Left should be Liberal nevertheless to reconsider the roots of their political beliefs, and to make out a more convincing case for a libertarian ideology.

The results were multiform: on the one hand socialism in a variety of guises, revolutionary or social-democratic, utopian or Fabian. On the other, discontented Liberals set themselves to reform their creed, and called it 'The New Liberalism', a term which embraced at the same time such divergent doctrines as Herbert Samuel's Roseberyite Liberal Imperialism and L. T. Hobhouse's Liberal Socialism. And outside party boundaries new weapons were being forged by another, more informal group we shall call the 'New Radicals', in response to the same challenge: the failure of the Party of progress to cope with the 'new' situation.

Liberalism, said the New Radicals, was a child of its time, the product of the knowledge and assumptions of the early nineteenth century. That was why it was inadequate in the nineties. Its successor must take into account all the changes and developments which had intervened, and with their help build an ideology more suited to the new age. And the New Radicals, free from party allegiances, could afford to be eclectic.

Within the realm of political philosophy they could go for their ideas to two main alternatives to Liberalism. There was Hegelian idealism, which T. H. Green and Bernard Bosanquet, in different ways, sought to make palatable to English audiences. Secondly, there was socialism. Each of these alternatives seemed (despite whatever dialectic they used to deny it) to emphasise the State at the expense of the individual, which made liberal-minded progressives wary of them: but, nevertheless, socialism in particular provided – between the mild 'creeping' socialism of Harcourt's 1894 budget and the more revolutionary ideas of Marx and Engels – a wealth of theory and a variety of approaches which could be harnessed to non-socialist political speculation. On the one hand, economic analysis could be employed as a method for explaining politics. Liberal hostility to the 'interests' was easily adapted to a theory which explained social problems in terms of 'class'.

Perhaps political democracy did not work because there was no economic democracy: in economics might lie the explanation for social regression. On the other hand, on the level of solutions rather than analysis, a form of socialism could be welded into the fabric of Liberalism to ensure the social justice which Liberals sought. This was Hobhouse's answer to the problem of the inequalities between capital and labour.[1] Individual freedom could be perfected by means of social restraint.

For those who were dissatisfied with things as they were, economics was clearly at the root of the problem. For many it went deeper than the mere question of imbalance between the propertied and the property-less. The very foundation of Victorian euphoria had been 'political economy'. The happy assumption of the more dogmatic *laissez-faire* Liberal that non-interference and trade would produce both domestic and international peace and prosperity was based upon an economic system which was bound up so intimately with morality as to give it the force of a creed. There was a natural law which dictated that supply and demand were in a perfect state of equilibrium, with supply creating its own demand. The creation of an effective demand, therefore, was no problem, and economic growth depended not on this but on the accumulation of capital. Unlimited saving was safe because in a free economy it could not affect the natural law of markets, and it was virtuous because it provided the capital necessary for prosperity. Social evils could not be attributed to the system; man should better himself by his 'individual action, economy, and self-denial; by better habits, rather than by greater rights'.[2] Such a creed, in its pure form, made solutions to social and economic problems simple: 'thrift', 'self-help' and Say's Law. It made impossible any attempt to reform society by modifying the economic system.

Early in the nineteenth century Sismondi and Malthus had provided an alternative view of economics, which could be used as the basis for a social critique which did not leave the economic system inviolate. In short, they questioned Say's Law, and asserted the feasibility of a disequilibrium between supply and

[1] L. T. Hobhouse, *Liberalism*.   [2] Samuel Smiles, *Self-Help* (1879 ed.), p. 2.

demand, or underconsumption. Throughout the nineteenth century (said Lord Keynes) this idea lived 'furtively, below the surface'.[1] But others were worried about the profitability of investment. 'Although it was conceived differently by different writers, the "natural tendency of profits to fall" hung like a nightmare over the speculations of the classical economists.' [2] From very different vantage-points Marx and Engels (in the third volume of *Capital* and in *Theories of Surplus Value*)[3] analysed the 'falling rate of profits', and John Stuart Mill predicted a 'boundary' to the expansion of capital.[4]

Doubts as to the inviolability of the economic system opened up a whole new field of investigation for those concerned with the social problem. Most of the more radical and revolutionary schemes of social reform rested on new economic creeds. Marxism was based on a critique of capitalism. Henry George's *Progress and Poverty* (1880) attributed social injustice to private property in land, and his scheme for reform rested on the simple but drastic expedient of the 'single tax'. Nearer home John Ruskin, when he turned from aesthetics to social reform in 1860, founded his recommendations upon an attempt to infuse into the 'dismal science' some warmth and humanity: 'There is no wealth but life. Life, including all its powers of love, of joy, and of admiration.'[5] And at about the same time Frederic Harrison was saying the same thing in more mundane language:

> The economist may be able to judge to what degree in a particular society competition is a dominant motive; where it is, where it is not paramount; how far it is interwoven with social institutions; what in each case is its relative importance as compared with other influences – provided he

[1] Keynes, quoted in E. M. Winslow, *The Pattern of Imperialism*, p. 77. See also E. E. Nemmers, *Hobson and Underconsumption*, ch. i; and M. P. Schneider, 'Underconsumption and Imperialism', ch. i. Other early underconsumptionists included Rodbertus, Shaftesbury, Berkeley, Chalmers.

[2] W. H. B. Court in Hancock, *British Commonwealth Affairs*, ii 1, p. 295.

[3] Freedman, *Marx on Economics*, pp. 97 ff.

[4] *Principles of Political Economy*, p. 731.

[5] J. Ruskin, *Unto This Last*, in 1905 Library ed. of his *Works*, vol. xvii, p. 105; and see below, p. 171.

has analysed society as well as industry, and has traced the manifold ramifications of human activity – provided he be a politician and a moralist as well as an economist, but scarcely otherwise.[1]

All of them were trying to make political economy once again a matter of *choice*.

This tentative revision of political and economic assumptions furnished a foundation for new Radical doctrines and ideologies; and it could be augmented by developments in other branches of knowledge. 'Political philosophy', said Sir Ernest Barker,

> not only advances of itself, and through its own acquisition of new, or restatement of old, philosophic conceptions; it also advances through the contributions of other studies, which can either supply analogies to guide its method or new facts to increase its content.[2]

Darwinist biology had already been applied to politics (against the advice of Darwin himself)[3] by such men as William Graham Sumner and John Fiske in America, and Frederick Greenwood, Karl Pearson and Benjamin Kidd in England. In the hands of these writers it was used to put a blanket of fatalistic approval over political force. Herbert Spencer, from whom the Americans learnt their Social Darwinism,[4] also seemed to point this moral in his first book, *Social Statics* (1850). But other lessons could be drawn from biology and from Spencer which were more Liberal. One could accept the broad evolutionary hypothesis, yet deny the appropriateness for the history of mankind of the strict analogy with animal selection. Man differed from other forms of life in his power of reasoning; unlike the lower animals, he could choose which path of progress he would follow, and control his environment accordingly – and this factor might, to some extent,

---

[1] Frederic Harrison, 'The Limits of Political Economy' (1865), in *National and Social Problems*, p. 283.

[2] Sir Ernest Barker, *Political Thought from Spencer to Today*, p. 12.

[3] Richard Hofstadter, *Social Darwinism in American Thought* (1955 ed.), pp. 91–2.

[4] Ibid. ch. ii.

modify the evolutionary process in its higher stages. Such a doctrine freed political thought from the confinement of Sumnerian determinism; it allowed men to call themselves evolutionists, yet still discuss politics in terms of ethics, in terms of what *should* be and not what must be.

So evolution could be reconciled with a belief in the efficacy of rational free-will. Yet biology, as it was represented by Spencer, also carried a warning against too naïve an acceptance of this kind of rationalism, against what Graham Wallas called 'the intellectualist assumption' – 'that every human action is the result of an intellectual process, by which a man first thinks of some end which he desires, and then calculates the means by which that end can be attained'.[1] For those who could detect it, the 'organic' analogy which Spencer took from biology and applied to society might suggest a very different approach to political institutions.[2] Society was an 'organism' in that its parts were mutually dependent. No institution, therefore, could be understood merely as a rationally conceived means to a single and specific end. More was needed to explain social and political phenomena than an account of the wishes or interests of individuals; they should be seen in terms of the functions they fulfilled in relation to the whole complex fabric of society. The seeds were here of the 'sociological' method of a later age, of Durkheim and the functionalists. In England sociology could never have the fundamental impact which it was to have on continental thought, for English social scientists were still tied to the intellectualist tradition which, for Lord Annan, renders their political speculation so infertile.[3] If Spencer accepted the irrationalist implications of his 'organic' analogy for his own time, yet he believed that such considerations would soon become irrelevant, that man would shortly evolve into a creature capable of organising his social environment by rational criteria.[4] Nevertheless, extra-rational factors had to be

[1] Graham Wallas, *Human Nature in Politics* (1962 ed.), p. 45.
[2] See J. W. Burrow, *Evolution and Society*, pp. 190 ff.
[3] N. G. Annan, *The Curious Strength of Positivism in English Political Thought*, pp. 16–21.
[4] Burrow, op. cit. pp. 222–3.

F

taken into account, even by an 'intellectualist'. If they did not explain all, they explained a great deal; they were obstructions on the road to rational progress, and must be revealed – and hence (it was hoped) destroyed – if the rationalist millennium was to be brought closer. Sociology and social psychology would not displace political moralism, but they might at least elucidate some of the evidence upon which political moralists could work.

Anthropology and ethnology had enjoyed a longer history than sociology as recognised and respectable disciplines. We have seen already how anthropological theory only served to confirm the old ethnocentric ideas of the Victorians, how its evolutionary bias detracted from scientific objectivity.[1] In the 1920s Bronislaw Malinowski was to castigate it for its neglect of social institutions, studied in their own right, in favour of the quaint and the curious, the sensationalist and the antiquarian;[2] and the writings of the 1880s and 1890s bear out Malinowski's charges. The Anthropological Institute's *Journal* carried much in the way of useful analysis of common customs and institutions – but contributed always by colonial officials, missionaries or soldiers.[3] The 'experts' confined their attention to more esoteric topics – craniology, prehistoric remains, folk-lore and sexual practices – or else to the working out, *a priori*, of grand evolutionary schemes.[4] As yet the anthropologist could shed little new light on social and political science; nor was his discipline particularly relevant to

[1] See above, pp. 29–30.
[2] B. Malinowski, 'Ethnology and the Study of Society', in *Economica*, vol. ii (1922), pp. 217–18; 'Practical Anthropology', in *Africa*, vol. ii (1929), pp. 22–38; 'The Rationalization of Anthropology and Administration', in *Africa*, vol. iii (1930), pp. 406–9.
[3] e.g. Rev. Godfrey Dale on the Bondei Country, *J.A.I.*, vol. 25 (1895), pp. 181–239; Col. Sir Thomas Holdich on the tribes of the North-West Frontier, ibid. vol. 29 (1899), pp. 1–9; Lieut.-Col. J. R. L. MacDonald on Juba, ibid. vol. 29 (1899), pp. 226–47.
[4] *J.A.I.*, *passim*. As illustration, see the contents of *Man* for Apr 1903 (vol. 3): 1. 'Pre-Phoenician Writing in Crete'; 2. 'Note on the Paleolithic Graves of Savernake Forest, Wiltshire'; 3. 'Cornelius Magrath, the Irish Giant'; and 4. 'A Tunisian Ghost-House'.

those practical questions of colonial administration which came with empire. Throughout the 1890s the Anthropological Institute tried to persuade governments of the value of its work for those set in authority over alien races, in an effort to secure for the British Empire a 'Bureau of Ethnology' on the lines of the Smithsonian Institute in America;[1] but to no avail.[2] While their interests were so recondite and their methods so unhelpful, they could expect little response. Indeed, the chief purpose behind their agitation appeared to be not to assist in the work of colonial government but to obtain official financial backing for projected researches, on esoteric lines, among subject races which might soon become too 'civilised' to hold any further interest for them.[3] They were not so much anthropologists in the modern sense of the term as 'curio-hunters' or historians of man.

Yet there were hints of a more edifying approach. If the anthropologists themselves were barren of original ideas, this was because of the evolutionary straitjacket they had inherited from the middle of the century, and the preconceptions that went with it. Take away these restricting factors, and there lay underneath a body of half-formed doctrines and suggestions which might, if properly handled, turn anthropology in new directions, point it towards the relativism of a Herskovits or the functionalism of a Malinowski. What was needed was a man who would

[1] *J.A.I.*, vol. 20 (1890), p. 358; vol. 22 (1892), p. 381; vol. 23 (1893), p. 416; vol. 24 (1894), pp. 467–8; vol. 26 (1896), pp. 427–8; vol. 27 (1897), p. 554; vol. 28 (1898), p. 321. The American Bureau of Ethnology was set up in 1879, and financed by Congress, in order to study the customs, laws and philology of the American Indians. See the *First Annual Report of the Bureau of Ethnology*, New York, 1880, p. xiv.

[2] The practical utilisation of anthropology in colonial administration was not entirely unknown in the late nineteenth century. A number of distinguished colonial civil servants were members of the Anthropological Institute; S. African governments had undertaken official inquiries into native laws and customs since the 1850s; and in 1885 Sir Herbert Risley had been appointed to conduct a survey of customs, castes and occupations in Bengal. See Daryll Forde, 'Applied Anthropology in Government: British Africa', in Kroeber, *Anthropology Today*, pp. 843–7; and (on Risley) *J.A.I.*, vol. 20 (1890), pp. 235–63, and *Man*, vol. 10 (1910), pp. 163–4, and vol. 12 (1912), pp. 1–4.

[3] See *J.A.I.*, vol. 24 (1894), pp. 467–8, and vol. 28 (1898), p. 321.

extricate himself from the prevailing climate of opinion, assert his scientific independence, and then take up those anthropological threads which in the past had been overlooked in the contemporary passion for reducing social phenomena to unity and order.

The interest and practical value of empirical investigation into social institutions was not unknown in the later nineteenth century; it was deliberately ignored in favour of more academic and philosophical pursuits. Like most of his colleagues, Sir Edward Tylor was chiefly concerned to construct 'a philosophy of primeval history'; but he also wrote of his science:

> It is wonderful to contrast some missionary journals with Max Müller's Essays, and to set the unappreciating hatred and ridicule that is lavished by narrow hostile zeal on Brahmanism, Buddhism, Zoroastrism, beside the catholic sympathy with which deep and wide knowledge can survey those ancient and noble phases of man's religious consciousness; nor, because the religions of savage tribes may be rude and primitive compared with the great Asiatic systems, do they lie too low for interest and even for respect. The question really lies between understanding and misunderstanding them. Few who will give their minds to master the general principles of savage religion will ever again think it ridiculous, or the knowledge of it superfluous to the rest of mankind. Far from its beliefs and practices being a rubbish-heap of miscellaneous folly, they are consistent and logical in so high a degree as to begin, as soon as even roughly classified, to display the principles of their formation and development; and these principles prove to be essentially rational, though working in a mental condition of intense and inveterate ignorance.[1]

Knowledge gave birth to sympathy, and it was only a short step from this to a real empiricism, a study of alien customs for themselves, unhampered by *a priori* philosophies or prejudices.

[1] E. B. Tylor, *Primitive Culture* (3rd ed., 1891), vol. i, pp. 22–3, 25; and cf. Sir John Lubbock, *The Origin of Civilisation and the Primitive Condition of Man* (2nd ed., 1870), pp. 1–3; and J. W. Powell, 'From Barbarism to Civilization', in *American Anthropologist*, vol. i (1888), pp. 99–103.

For those who were willing to take this step, existing anthropological doctrine provided the foundations for a new approach. The evolutionist preoccupation of the nineteenth century had, in one way, devalued alien cultures by treating them as inferior, as primitive stages in a uniform pattern of progress; but in another way it had contributed towards an understanding and toleration of them. It had at least destroyed the notion that strange customs and institutions were pointless aberrations, illogical and perverted, and had demonstrated instead their value and suitability for the cultures – or stages of culture – of which they were part.[1] Tylor's plea for religious toleration is an example. If unilinearism were abandoned, and Western Europe deposed from the top of the evolutionary scale, then this sympathetic analysis of alien customs would remain. Herbert Spencer's 'organic' sociology, asserting the interdependence of social institutions, could have the same effect.[2] And the 'diffusionist' hypothesis – maintaining that cultural similarities between different races arose, not from independent invention, but from definite historical contact – might, by undermining the theory of the 'psychic unity of mankind', destroy one of the pillars supporting unilinear evolutionism.[3] All these factors made for functionalism and relativism. Cast away the evolutionist framework which was distracting and distorting the work of the anthropologists, and the way was clear for others to consider alien institutions *per se*, and for the social functions they fulfilled.

Already in the 1890s, but outside the anthropological establishment, one person had made the vital break with evolutionism. Mary Kingsley's sole justification for her anthropological studies was that they enabled her and others to reach a full and

[1] Burrow, *Evolution and Society*, p. 218.

[2] See above, p. 145. Sir Henry Maine also has been credited with a degree of functionalism: see Lowie, *History of Ethnological Theory*, p. 53.

[3] See Lowie, op. cit. pp. 72 *et passim*. Lowie points out, however (pp. 27–9), that a diffusionist could be an evolutionist too. See also D. F. Pocock, *Social Anthropology* (1961); and, for a contemporary view of the 'diffusionist – independent invention' controversy, Otis Tufton Mason, 'Similarities in Culture', in the *American Anthropologist*, vol. viii (1895), pp. 101–17.

sympathetic understanding of the African mind.[1] She never concerned herself with general theories and academic hypotheses, but only with what she saw herself on the West Coast of Africa – native society in its entirety and for its own sake. In many ways she was the first English *social* anthropologist, and as such she exerted a considerable influence on the colonial thinking of many of the men we shall be discussing in the following chapters.

Mary Kingsley's greatest asset was her unorthodoxy, which manifested itself in almost everything she did – not least in the masculine energy and courage she displayed in exploring alone, between 1893 and 1895, some of the least salubrious regions of West Africa. It extended also to the views of native African culture she propounded on her return. Here the contrast with the anthropology of the schools, of her academic friends, is striking. Mary Kingsley was as bound by prejudices and preconceptions as any other ethnologist in the nineteenth century: something will be said of this in a later chapter. But her preconceptions were not the conventional ones, and this accounted for the freshness and fertility of her ideas. In the first place, her *methods* differed from those of the professionals. They built theories, and then tested them by the facts – the experimental method. She went to the facts first, and saw what came out of them. In 1897 she wrote to a friend: 'Those white men who make a theory first & then go hunting travellers tales for facts to support the same may say what they please of the pleasure of the process – give me the pleasure of getting a great mass of facts & watching them. . . .'[2] Both methods were 'scientific', but hers was more empirical. It led her into areas of anthropological investigation which until then had been ignored because they seemed to have no bearing on the general scheme of things, and out of it came ideas and suggestions which were far closer to those of the 1920s than to the anthropology of her own time.

[1] For a more detailed description of Mary Kingsley's career, see below, pp. 240 ff.
[2] Mary Kingsley to Mrs Alice Stopford Green, 22 Mar 1897; A.S.G.P., N.L.I., Dublin.

She looked at African society from the inside, to find out how it worked, and saw that its different features could not be treated in isolation; that law and religion, for example, were interrelated and interdependent. This was a step in the direction of functionalism, and she pointed the functionalist's moral: 'that this intimate connection is the reason of the great difficulty of destroying African native customs as they are called'.[1] The style was hardly polished, but the point had not been put so clearly before.

Still more unorthodox – and, to many of her contemporaries, shocking and heretical – was the peculiar form of cultural relativism she preached. Mary Kingsley was not bound, like the humanitarian or the professional anthropologist, to regard the African and European as alike, actually or potentially; as equals or as close cousins at different stages of development. She was not looking for similarities or for evolutionary consistency. She was free to examine what she saw in Africa without any regard for philosophical necessities: and this she did. It made her an inegalitarian, even a racist, but a sympathetic one. Ethnologists, she said, would have to 'throw their origin of the human race back and divide it into three or five stems, instead of one'[2] – abandon the unilinear hypothesis and return to the old, discredited doctrine of polygenesis. For the Negro was a different type of man from the European, another branch of the evolutionary tree; he was 'no more an undeveloped white man than a rabbit is an undeveloped hare',[3] but, on the contrary, 'a strong type of humanity with virtues and vices arranged in his character in a different way to that of the European character'.[4] He was a distinct species: and he was a lower one – not merely lower in the evolutionary scale, but an inferior breed. She was quite categorical about this. 'I own,' she said, that 'I regard not only the African, but all coloured races, as inferior – inferior in kind not in degree – to the

[1] 'African Religion and Law' (Hibbert Lecture, 1897), printed in the *National Review*, vol. xxx (Sept 1897), p. 138; and in the 2nd ed. of *West African Studies* (1901), p. 413.
[2] Mary Kingsley to Matthew Nathan, 28 Aug 1899, quoted in Stephen Gwynn, *The Life of Mary Kingsley*, p. 229.
[3] *Travels in West Africa*, p. 659.
[4] Quoted in Gwynn, op. cit., p. 235.

white races'.[1] Her favourite simile was that of the distinction between the sexes: 'A great woman, mentally or physically, will excel an indifferent man, but no woman ever equalled a really great man.'[2] As evidence of the African's inferiority she instanced – as white supremacists have done before and after her – his apparent failure to produce by his own unaided efforts scientific or artistic achievements to compare with those of Europe: '... remember that, unless under white direction, the African has never made an even fourteenth-rate piece of cloth or pottery, or a machine, tool, picture, sculpture, and that he has never even risen to the level of picture-writing'.[3] The railway engine, she said, was to her 'the manifestation of the superiority of my race'.[4]

To this extent she was as racially arrogant as the evolutionists, or more so; but it was the relativistic implications of her polygenesism which were most significant, both to her and to her disciples. The African was 'inferior', but she would not allow that this inferiority was altogether to be despised. It did not imply real intellectual incapacity, or the inability of the Negro races to advance further.[5] The African had not produced the steam-engine, but this was because he used his intellect along different lines from the European: he was less materialistic in his thinking.

The African mind naturally approaches all things from a spiritual point of view. Low down in culture or high up, his mind works along the line that things happen because of the action of spirit upon spirit; it is an effort for him to think in terms of matter. ... This steady sticking to the material side of things, I think, has given our race its dominion over matter; the want of it has caused the African to be notably behind us in this. ... The African regards spirit and matter as undivided in kind, matter being only the extreme low form of spirit.[6]

[1] *Travels in West Africa*, p. 669.
[2] 'The Development of Dodos', in the *National Review*, Mar 1896, p. 71; and cf. Gwynn, op. cit. p. 146: 'The African is a female nation'.
[3] *Travels in West Africa*, p. 670. [4] *West African Studies*, p. 330.
[5] *Travels in West Africa*, p. 679.
[6] *West African Studies*, p. 330; and cf. 'African Religion and Law', *National Review*, p. 124.

This she had deduced from her study of what she termed 'fetish'. In less guarded moments she called it 'superstition'. But the conclusions she drew from it were the same. It merited the most careful study and sympathy. And it compelled the wise administrator to recognise that civilisation was (in her metaphor) a range of mountains, and that the Negro should be encouraged to climb his own peak rather than be dragged up that of the white races.[1]

Sympathetic knowledge and the recognition of impermeable cultural distinctions: these were the principles upon which a just and viable colonial government should be founded. The native must be studied in his own environment, and legislation affecting him adapted to his own customs. An analogy she used is worth quoting at length:

> If civilised man starts to build a house, a bridge, or an engine, he does not content himself with having a good design alone, and say, 'Oh, all matter is the same, it's an affair of vortex rings, or hydrogen in a certain state, or the pace of atoms,' or whatsoever may be the prevalent view of the constitution of matter at the time, but on the contrary, he acquaints himself with the practical qualifications and properties of the materials he is going to use, he notes their differences, and it is largely from this part of his knowledge that he succeeds in his endeavour. Yet when civilised man starts in as an 'Architect of Fate, working in the Walls of Time', in the matter of building up a Civilisation out of uncivilised man, he does not seem to care to trouble himself about the nature of his material. He relies on the beauty and virtue of his design, and says, 'Oh, there is no difference in human beings beyond that of degree – or education.' This may or may not be as true and useful as the pace-of-atoms way of regarding matter, but it does not give you that practical knowledge required for good craftsmanship. . . .[2]

They should try to civilise the African, but not Europeanise him. West African civilisation in its present stage was a low form of

[1] *Travels in West Africa*, p. 680.
[2] 'Liquor Traffic with West Africa', in the *Fortnightly Review*, 1 Apr 1898, p. 544.

African civilisation; and even in its highest form it would be 'inferior' to that of the West. The fatal mistake, however, was to assume – and to act on the assumption – that it was a lower form of *Western* culture. Empirical investigation had convinced her that it was different, and always would be. The European's duty to the African, therefore, was to help him develop on his own lines. This meant Indirect Rule.

Here for the first time was an 'applied anthropology'. Many of the assumptions on which it was based were dubious, and it was over-conservative, perhaps, in its cautious and respectful preservationism. Yet Mary Kingsley's books provided, as the professionals had not done as yet, an anthropology clearly and vitally relevant to the problems of colonial administration, and suggestive of provocatively original solutions. Very soon the professionals themselves, a little falteringly, were to follow her example. Sidney Hartland in 1900 advocated Indirect Rule in front of the anthropological section of the British Association – though he was speaking of preserving native civil and criminal law, and not the wider aspects of African culture.[1] In the same year the members of the Anthropological Institute presented a petition to the Colonial Secretary pleading the necessity of setting up an inquiry into South African native customs. The contact with civilisation, they said,

> tends to break up their organisation, to destroy their customs, and to set them free from many of the old moral restraints without imposing new ones, and generally to render them difficult of management by a European Government; . . . this tendency is greatly accelerated where, as too frequently happens, the Government does not take special pains to ascertain the customs and institutions of the natives, and to make regulations for them carefully considered in the light of such information. . . .
> . . . while some of such customs and institutions are of a

[1] Paper read to the British Association, 10 Sept 1900, and reported in *Anthropological Reviews and Miscellanea* (*J.A.I.*), 1900, pp. 22–4; and see also his article in *Man*, 1902, pp. 34–6. Mary Kingsley had been elected a member of the Anthropological Institute in June 1898; see *Anthropological Reviews and Miscellanea*, 1900, pp. 7–9.

character not to be tolerated by a civilised government, careful enquiry is necessary before deciding on any legislation, so as to ascertain the precise meaning and consequences of the customs it may be proposed to abolish or to modify. . . .[1]

Chamberlain would have none of this.[2] But at least the professional anthropologists had begun to crawl a little way out of their academic shells.

For those who looked disapprovingly at things about them, particularly at contemporary imperialism and the conduct of colonial policy, and who at the same time were willing to make a radical reappraisal of common ideas and assumptions, these new developments in the social, political, economic, biological and anthropological sciences provided some of the tools with which to do it. Together they added up to something far short of a rival *Weltanschauung* to the Victorians'; they were too diffuse and tentative – a few discordant notes scattered about the score which might jar a little on the ear, but which had not yet been brought together to make an alternative melody. Yet to any Radical who was attuned to them, they could at least suggest modifications to the body of ideas on which he drew to combat those policies and doctrines he disagreed with; they might reshape and sharpen the Liberal protest without displacing it entirely. It was from such a synthesis of old and new, a patchwork of traditional doctrines with novel concepts stitched in somewhat intrusively and incongruously, that there arose the colonial ideologies of Hobson and Morel.

[1] Memorial addressed by the Anthropological Institute and the Folk-Lore Society to the Colonial Secretary, 1900, printed in *Man*, 1903, p. 71.
[2] Letter from the C.O., 28 Oct 1902, printed in *Man*, 1903, p. 74. See also *Folk-Lore* (Transactions of the Folk-Lore Society), 1901, p. 11.

CHAPTER SIX

The New Radicals

I. THE ETHICAL MOVEMENT AND THE RAINBOW CIRCLE

It was J. A. Hobson[1] who felt most acutely the deficiencies of the old Radical approach to empire. With the help of the 'new knowledge' described in the last chapter he tried to make good these deficiencies, to supply the Left with an imperial ideology which was as critical of colonial policy as Labouchere's or Hardie's, but at the same time in keeping with the new conditions, as he saw them, of the 1890s. This he did in the context of a political movement quite apart from the main stream of Radicalism.

The existence of this movement is hardly noticed today. It is too easy to look back on the amorphous state of Radical politics in the 1890s and early 1900s with the hindsight of the inter-war period, and to see in it only the shapes of a declining (though temporarily revived) Liberal Party and a rising Labour Party. The error in such a view is not only that it assumes too great a political continuity before and after the First World War, and in so doing underestimates the strength of the pre-war Liberal Party, but also that it neglects certain other left-wing groupings which at the time seemed to have as good a chance as Labour of filling the ideological vacuum left by the Liberals. Only socialists

[1] John Atkinson Hobson, born in Derby 6 July 1858, educated at Derby Grammar School and Lincoln College, Oxford. From 1880 to 1887, a schoolmaster (classics) in Exeter; University extension lecturer for the Oxford and London Boards 1887–97. The rest of his life was spent lecturing and writing, chiefly on economics. Died 1 Apr 1940. His autobiography, *Confessions of an Economic Heretic*, was published in 1938; like John Stuart Mill's it is reticent about his life but illuminating on his intellectual development. The fullest description of his life appears in the *Derbyshire Advertiser* (founded by his father) for 5 Apr 1940.

believed that Labour was the party of the future. This possibility
was always in the minds of other Radicals, but many of them
feared that a new Labour–Conservative orientation would only
exacerbate the class-conflict, and so fail to provide a really
democratic solution. Outside, or on the fringes of the Liberal and
Labour parties a number of writers and politicians were working
to try to achieve a Radical party upon a more broadly democratic basis, a 'Lib-Lab' alliance representing democrats of all
social classes. Hobson was one of these. His ideas were formed
in the context of an extra-partisan group of friends, organised
loosely in a religious sect, 'the Ethical Society', and a progressivist
discussion-group, 'the Rainbow Circle'. Each of these societies
saw itself as a kind of *avant-courier* of the New Radicalism,
regenerating the Left and planting, perhaps, the seeds of a new
progressive party. In this they failed; but indirectly they made a
significant impact on progressive thought. It was while they
were members of one or both of these groups, and through the
vehicles for the expression and discussion of Radical views which
they provided, that such men as Hobson, Ramsay MacDonald,
J. M. Robertson and William Clarke formulated their attitudes
to empire. The new 'anti-imperialist' ideology of the turn of
the century came chiefly not from the Labour or Liberal parties,
but from this intellectual 'Lib-Lab' group in the middle.

The two organisations were very different from one another –
united only by one or two leading members they had in common, and by their self-conscious freedom from the shackles of
conventional thought. The first of them, the Ethical movement,
was primarily a secularist 'religious' society, whose chief function
appears to have been to satisfy the cravings of late-Victorian
agnostics for the trappings of conventional religion by providing
for them formal chapel-like Sunday meetings in which readings
from the various humanist gospels (Voltaire, Tom Paine) were
interspersed with the singing of secular 'anthems'. Besides this
its activities were wide and varied. There were nine Ethical
institutions in London, and a few in other parts of the country.
Each was sturdily independent of the others, even after a number
of them had come together to form the 'Ethical Union' in 1896.

Ramsay MacDonald, for example, had joined the East London Society in 1898; this society soon proved too 'intellectual' for the working people of Bow and Bromley, and could only revive the flagging enthusiasm of its members by becoming scarcely distinguishable from a Labour Church. The South Place Society, where Hobson was a leading figure, was descended by many devious routes from the Philadelphians of the 1790s, took on the varying creeds of its successive ministers and refused to join the Ethical Union. But in general the Ethical societies all performed the social function of providing for intellectually inclined humanists a forum for discussion, Sunday schools for their children, and organised forms of such healthy spiritual and physical exercise as chamber-concerts and rambling excursions for their leisure hours.[1]

But the Ethical movement also had a gospel to preach, which had political implications. It was similar in many ways to that of Positivism, the leading representative of secularist thought in the later nineteenth century, one or two of whose adherents we have met already. Richard Congreve, who in 1857 had owned to a respect for alien civilisations unusual for his time,[2] and Frederic Harrison, preaching the subjection of economics to morality,[3] were both members of the 'Church of Humanity', and these two attitudes fairly represented the Positivist approach to politics. Harrison expressed its 'Aims and Ideals' thus:

The problem before Positivism is threefold. . . . It seeks to transfer religion from a supernatural to a scientific basis, from a theological to a human creed; to substitute in philosophy a relative anthropo-centric synthesis for an absolute, cosmical analysis; to subordinate politics, both national and international, to morality and religion.[4]

---

[1] See Gustav Spiller, *The Ethical Movement in Great Britain, a Documentary History* (1934); [Anon.], *A Short History of the South Place Ethical Society*; F. J. G[ould], 'The English Ethical Societies', in *The Reformer*, 15 Oct 1897, pp. 223–4; the *Constitution and Reports* of the Ethical Union, *passim*; and F. H. Swinny in the *Positivist Review*, Oct 1894, pp. 185–8.
[2] See above, pp. 27–8.   [3] See above, pp. 143–4.
[4] Frederic Harrison, 'Aims and Ideals' (1901), in *The Creed of a Layman*, p. 255. There is an excellent summary of the Positivist philosophy by John Morley in the *Encyclopaedia Britannica* (14th ed., 1929) under 'Comte'.

It was very much a political creed, and in its application to imperial questions its point of view was clearly defined by its basic tenets. Their relativistic anthropocentrism made Positivists sceptical of the 'civilising mission' of the West; native races, they said, should be encouraged to develop their own indigenous cultures and not have Europe's forced upon them.[1] Their moralism put them strongly against an Empire of power or 'grab'.[2] This kind of outlook was shared by the Ethical movement. Where the latter differed from Positivism – and this made it more attractive to men like Hobson and MacDonald – was in its greater doctrinal laxity. Positivism was encumbered by various paraphernalia which made it appear, to outsiders, faintly ridiculous – veneration for a 'Great Being', the synthetic philosophy of Comte, ancestor-worship, the Positivist calendar; it also held to certain points of faith which were uncongenial to many Ethicists: opposition to socialism, and to pacifism, woman suffrage and internationalism. The Ethicists were free from such dogmas, far more 'agnostic', politically, than the Church of Humanity.[3]

Their own creed revolved around the much more vaguely defined 'general principle' that 'the Good Life has a supreme claim upon all men and women, and can and should be pursued independently of theological sanctions'.[4] Opinion as to what constituted the Good Life might reasonably differ among members,[5] but all could agree that ethics, however defined, should be supreme over all things. It should govern social and political as well as individual relations, for mankind was 'interdependent'

[1] See E. S. Beesly, 'The Western Treatment of Backward Races', in the *Positivist Review*, Sept 1896, pp. 176–82. Positivists quite naturally refused to acknowledge Christianity as the norm of civilisation. In reply to a pro-missionary article in the *Spectator*, Beesly wrote sarcastically in 1899: 'By "reasonable creed" it means that creed which has for its central doctrine that Jesus had no male parent' (*Positivist Review*, Mar 1899, p. 56).

[2] *Positivist Review, passim*. Throughout its history the *Review* was strongly and consistently Little Englander on every imperial topic.

[3] F. S. Marvin, in the *Positivist Review*, Nov 1898 (pp. 187–91), criticised the vagueness of the Ethicists' ultimate ideal.

[4] Gould, loc. cit. p. 223.

[5] H. J. Bridges, *et al.*, *The Ethical Movement, Its Principles and Aims*, p. 2.

and no branch of its activities could be treated apart from all the others. Commerce, for example, should not be regarded as 'exempt from the more searching dictates of the moral law', 'divorced from the conscious service of humanity, and pursued merely for the financial and social advantages of its devotees,' for it had social ramifications, and must be conducted in such a way as to further 'the general good'. Those 'sinister interests of groups and classes' which conflicted with the general good must be eliminated from national life.[1] And, since 'the task of perfecting the individual' could only be achieved 'in and through the perfecting of human society', Ethicists should concern themselves with politics, 'declare their attitude towards the great social problems of the time', and work to remove economic disabilities, abolish slums and 'sweating', and so on.[2] On the international scene, too, the supremacy of moral considerations must be emphasised.[3] In other words religion and politics could not be put in separate compartments, individual virtue regarded as something to be striven for independently of social perfection. Men should not be told to shun politics as something 'worldly' and seek only the salvation of their individual souls. The good of the individual was dependent upon the good of society, and both depended in turn on the permeation of rational morality through all aspects of life.

This way of thinking made the Ethical societies as much a political movement as a 'religious' one. It also predisposed their politics towards a broad form of socialism.[4] One exception was the London branch, which Hobson had joined in the late 1880s;

[1] Ibid. pp. 27–30.
[2] Ibid. pp. 79–80, and *Manifesto of the First Congress of the International Ethical Union* (1896), p. 2.
[3] Bridges, op. cit. p. 30; and see *Manifesto of the First Congress*, p. 4.
[4] See Bridges, op. cit. pp. 83–5, where the authors suggest for discussion a number of practical reforms: minimum wage, unemployment insurance, education, female suffrage, an international law-court, etc.; and a solution to the much-discussed eugenic problem: 'A wise alertness to promote the future fitness of the race should be fostered, and young men and women should be educated to the idea of applying a high physical, intellectual and moral standard in the selection of marriage-partners; while certain people should be advised to abstain from parenthood altogether.'

it counted among its leaders such men as Bernard Bosanquet, R. B. Haldane, J. H. Muirhead and J. R. Seeley, and Hobson fitted ill into this company. The London society was, he said, 'excellent in its assertion of free discussion'; but it was also 'committed so strongly to the stress on individual moral character, as the basis of social progress, as to make it the enemy of that political-economic democracy which I was coming to regard as the chief instrument of social progress and justice'.[1] The South Place Society was less rigid, and in 1897 Hobson transferred his allegiance here. Its emphasis was on 'the promotion of human welfare, in harmony with advancing knowledge',[2] this welfare conceived in the broadest ethical terms. 'Progress, to be permanent, must proceed, as far as possible, simultaneously in the material, intellectual, moral, aesthetic and social [spheres].' [3] This was far more congenial to Hobson, and his connexion with South Place, which lasted over forty years, furnished him with a platform for the expression of his views, a stimulus for 'clarifying my thought and enlarging my range of interests in matters of social conduct',[4] and the society of like-minded people.

More specifically, the Society arranged for him and his colleagues lectures and debates on a variety of topics, but with a strong predilection for social and political questions. From early on the Empire figured prominently at their meetings.[5] In 1895 there began a series of seventy lectures with 'the object of affording trustworthy information concerning the various colonies,

[1] Hobson, *Confessions of an Economic Heretic*, p. 56. Hobson was on the committee or sub-committees of the Society from 1891 to 1895. See the *Annual Reports* of the London Ethical Society, *passim*.

[2] *Report of the Committee of the South Place Ethical Society*, 1896.

[3] *South Place Magazine*, vol. i (1896), p. 103.

[4] Hobson, *Confessions*, p. 57.

[5] Among early lectures on colonial problems announced in the *South Place Magazine* were: 'Philosophy in its national developments, in race and civilisation', by Professor W. A. Knight, 3 Nov 1895 (see below, p. 182); lectures by Mary Kingsley in Oct 1897 and on 9 Jan 1898; W. S. Sebright Green on 'Colonisation, and our relations towards subject races', 9 Feb 1898; Mrs Bradlaugh Bonner on 'The forward policy in India', 23 Feb 1898; and the Rev. A. Caldecott on 'The treatment of native races by Europeans', 5 June 1897.

settlements and countries scattered over the world which go to form the whole known as "the British Empire" ';[1] they were delivered by experts (one of whom was Mary Kingsley), and published in 1900 in four volumes by Kegan Paul. Other lectures were occasionally printed in the Society's monthly magazine, or in a slightly less esoteric but shorter-lived journal, *The Reformer*.[2] More important was a new weekly paper which the Ethical movement inaugurated early in 1898, edited by the minister of South Place, Stanton Coit, and called *The Ethical World*.[3] This journal boasted a more distinguished list of occasional contributors than its somewhat exclusive nature might suggest. Among them were James Bryce, William Clarke, S. G. Hobson, H. M. Hyndman and George Bernard Shaw.[4] For eleven months after April 1899 (much of which time he was in South Africa) Hobson shared the editorship with Coit; and he and other prominent members of the Ethical movement – in particular Ramsay MacDonald, G. H. Perris and J. M. Robertson[5] – made the

[1] W. Sheowring (ed.), *The British Empire Series*, vol. ii, *British Africa*, Preface.

[2] The *Reformer* ran from 1897 to 1904. It was edited by Charles Bradlaugh's daughter, Mrs Hypatia Bradlaugh Bonner, and it appears to have had as its main purpose Mrs Bonner's own private crusade to vindicate her father's career. Most of the articles are about him, or about the favourite topics of the free-love and nut-cutlet type of *fin de siècle* progressive: vivisection, vaccination, free thought, flogging, women's rights and vegetarianism. There are one or two articles, however, about imperialism. Among its regular contributors were J. M. Robertson and the 'democratic poet' Edward Carpenter; Hobson also contributed one or two papers.

[3] Later it was subtitled, significantly, 'an organ of DEMOCRACY in RELIGION, EDUCATION, ART, INDUSTRY and POLITICS', and later renamed *Democracy*.

[4] Others were Edward Bernstein, Edward Carpenter, Mrs Leonard Courtney, G. P. Gooch, Bruce Glasier, Keir Hardie, H. W. Massingham, Olive Schreiner and Herbert Spencer.

[5] Ramsay MacDonald: see Lord Elton, *The Life of J. Ramsay MacDonald*. He was active in the Ethical movement between 1898 and 1902, once taking the chair at an annual meeting of the Ethical Union, and contributing to a collection of essays published in 1900 on *Ethical Democracy*. He wrote frequently for the *Ethical World*, usually on 'labour' or 'democracy', but also, in Nov 1898, on imperialism (see below, pp. 185 ff.).

G. H. Perris: at this time he was on the editorial staff of the *Speaker*. He wrote a number of anti-imperialist articles for the *Ethical World*, e.g. 'Imperial Profligates' (19 Mar 1898), 'Mr Salter's "Abstraction" ' (10 Dec

Ethical World the platform for the first published statements of their views on political, social and imperial questions. Stanton Coit had ambitious hopes for the paper. He saw it as a means of regenerating the Radical Left, and of organising it into a new political party preaching the ideals of 'Ethical Democracy', to replace the Liberal and Labour parties.[1] 'Is there no possibility', he asked Ramsay MacDonald in 1899, 'that the I.L.P. would change its name to "The Democratic Party" and introduce some new ethical elements, into its principles and programme?'[2] This, of course, was not to be; but Coit's plea illustrates the political preoccupation of his movement. It provided in the *Ethical World* and at its weekly meetings a platform for the discussion, on ethical lines, of social and political issues, and for the cross-fertilisation of ideas; and the aim of all this was the resuscitation of a dying Radicalism.

The function of the 'Rainbow Circle' was the same. It had been founded in 1893 as a political discussion group consisting of about twenty writers and politicians, representing all shades of opinion from socialism to liberal-imperialism. Ramsay MacDonald was its secretary, Hobson was a member, and others

1898), and 'Imperialism – and the Alternative' (11 Mar 1899). See also his book, *Blood and Gold in South Africa*.

J. M. Robertson: later Liberal M.P. for Tyneside and Parliamentary Secretary to the Board of Trade, the author of many books on a variety of literary and political subjects. See his *Patriotism and the Empire*, and *Wrecking the Empire*. He contributed to the *Ethical World* on the particular and philosophical aspects of empire. A 'rationalist', both in the sense of agnostic and of believer in reform through reason (see *Patriotism and the Empire*, pp. 136–7 and 202–3); this rationalism tallied closely with Hobson's (below, pp. 172–3), though his political views were closer to orthodox Liberalism.

[1] See Stanton Coit to MacDonald, 2 Apr 1898 (MacDonald Papers); and a report in the *Labour Leader*, 6 Dec 1899, of a speech by Coit to the West Kensington Ethical Society, which quotes him as saying that there was need for 'another political party as distinct from the Liberal and Conservative parties', a party 'based upon the necessity for the organic unity of an ideal society'.

[2] Coit to MacDonald, 1 Dec 1899 (MacDonald Papers). See also a letter from Coit to MacDonald, 16 Apr 1900 (ibid.): 'a new party – "The Democratic Party" – must be formed now, into which men like Hobson would throw themselves. . . . Would you not join me in urging week after week in the Ethical World that a new party should be formed . . . ?'

included Herbert Burrows, William Clarke, G. P. Gooch, Sydney Olivier, Russell Rea, William Pember Reeves, J. M. Robertson, Herbert Samuel and Charles Trevelyan. Despite their diversity these men professed a single aim, adumbrated in a notice distributed amongst them in August 1894: their discussions, it said, would be so directed and concentrated as to

> provide a rational and comprehensive view of political and social progress, leading up to a consistent body of political and economic doctrine which could be ultimately formulated in a programme of action, and in that form provide a rallying point for social reformers, so much needed in the present chaotic state of opinion.

To this end the Circle would discuss 'the reasons why the old Philosophic Radicalism and the Manchester School of Economics can no longer furnish a ground of action in the political sphere'; how the transition was to be effected from this to the 'New Radicalism'; and finally ' the bases, ethical, economic and political, of the newer politics, together with the practical applications and inferences arising therefrom in the actual problems before us at the present time'.[1] Like Stanton Coit and his Ethicists, therefore, the members of the Rainbow Circle saw themselves as the intellectual spearhead of a new progressive politics, providing it with an ideology suited to the demands of the age.

To propagate this ideology the Rainbow Circle – again like the Ethical movement – ran its own journal. The plans for it were first mooted in February 1895. 'Generally,' wrote Ramsay MacDonald,

> the idea would be to afford to the progressive movement in all its aspects – political, ethical, literary, &c. – a medium of expression such as the Whig movement had in the Edin-

---

[1] Copy in the Samuel Papers, A10, f. 1 (H.L.R.O.). It was signed by Burrows, Clarke, Hobson, J. Murray MacDonald, Ramsay MacDonald and Richard Stapley. The same circular gives notice of a discussion arranged for 7 Nov, to be opened by Hobson, on 'The Economic Deficiency of the Old Radicalism'.

burgh Review, and the later Radical and Positivist movements found in the original Fortnightly.[1]

The *Progressive Review* came out in October the next year, edited by William Clarke;[2] its object, said Lord Samuel, was 'to propagate those doctrines which were held in common' by the Circle.[3] The venture was ill-starred from the beginning. Anti-imperialists and Liberal Imperialists could not, it seemed, live peaceably together in print. Clarke wrote to MacDonald:

The real crux of politics is not going to be Socialism & anti-Socialism, but Jingoism and anti-Jingoism. It is well for the directors to know that Hobson & I take strong views on this, & that we are dead against Jingoism in every form (in the form of a huge navy & of an aggressive policy), & that we should make the P.R. anti-Jingo. . . .[4]

He saw this intention being thwarted by a 'pestilent mischievous clique', led by Herbert Samuel, out to 'promote a bastard Liberalism & a lot of imperialist bosh in which I do not believe';[5] Hobson, he said, was behind him in resisting the demands of these men.[6] Such differences of outlook could not prevent the *Review* from coming out, or from taking a decidedly anti-imperialist position. But it lasted for only twelve months. The discord in which it was born was exacerbated by an acrimonious personal quarrel between Clarke and MacDonald, who was

[1] Private circular to the members of the Rainbow Circle, signed by MacDonald, 27 Feb 1895, in the Samuel Papers, A10, f. 2.

[2] William Clarke (1852–1901), a member of the Fabian executive and contributor to *Fabian Essays* (1889), on the staff of the *Daily Chronicle*, 1890–9. Suffered from insomnia, which probably contributed to his ill-temper. Died of diabetes while touring Europe with Hobson and Herbert Burrows. See H. Burrows and J. A. Hobson (ed.), *William Clarke, A Collection of his Writings*, which contains a short biographical sketch of Clarke.

[3] Lord Samuel, *Memoirs*, p. 24.

[4] Clarke to MacDonald, n.d. (1896), in MacDonald Papers.

[5] Clarke to MacDonald, 2 Feb 1896; MacDonald Papers.

[6] See Clarke to MacDonald, 16 Feb 1896 (MacDonald Papers): 'Hobson had a long talk with me at the NLC on Friday, & told me, what I was not surprised to hear, that he did not intend to have his own copy for P.R. cut about by a young inexperienced man like Samuel, nor could he join a review in which the erroneous & belated views of the Fabian gang Webb & Wallas were going to form a feature.'

editorial assistant and secretary to the *Review*. The quarrel
reached breaking-point in July 1897, and two months later the
journal ceased publication.[1] But in its short life it made a significant contribution to the New Radicalism, and a vital contribution
to its imperial ideology. Clarke was the active editor, assisted by
Hobson, Charles Trevelyan, Richard Stapley and MacDonald;[2]
and these men established from the first an editorial policy which
was consistent, distinctive and pregnant for the future.

This policy was summarised in the *Review*'s first number. The
progressive forces which were enthusiastic and active in the

[1] Something is said of the circumstances surrounding the death of the
Review in John Bowle, *Viscount Samuel; a Biography*, pp. 34–6; and there
are one or two relevant letters in the MacDonald Papers. Clarke, it appears,
became exasperated by MacDonald's 'frequent & prolonged absences from
London & your absorption in so many things when you are here' (Clarke to
MacDonald, n.d.; MacDonald Papers); and when the latter decided to visit
the United States in 1897 Clarke demanded his resignation. He wanted
someone as secretary, he wrote to Samuel, *'who is on the spot every day & will
do his work* & who does not run away for weeks at a time on lecturing
engagements and wire-pulling' (Clarke to Samuel, 12 July 1897; Samuel
Papers, A10, f. 10). Samuel, on behalf of the directors, wrote to MacDonald
asking for his resignation: 'The Directors have to deal with this position:
the chief editor of the Review and the Secretary of the Company are not
working harmoniously together, and their relations do not appear likely to
improve; the Secretary proposes to go abroad for three months, at a time
when the second editor [Hobson] is ill, and at a time when the position of
the Review renders initiative indispensable' (Samuel to MacDonald, copy,
6 July 1897; Samuel Papers, A10, f. 8). MacDonald refused to resign immediately (MacDonald to Samuel, 15 July 1897; Samuel Papers, A10, f. 17).
But sales were bad, the editors were unable to find good writers (Clarke to
MacDonald, n.d.; MacDonald Papers), Clarke had lost faith in the future of
the enterprise, and the capital was nearly exhausted (Richard Stapley to
Samuel, 18 July 1897; Samuel Papers, A10, f. 20). So Samuel – 'since Hobson
is unable to help, Clarke is lukewarm and MacDonald impossible' – decided
to discontinue the *Review* (Samuel to Stapley, 19 July 1897; copy, Samuel
Papers, A10, f. 23).
[2] In a letter to MacDonald, 16 Feb 1896 (MacDonald Papers), Clarke
divided the work between Hobson, who was to take economics, MacDonald
(the reviews) and himself 'to deal with politics political philosophy &c.'
Whether this still stood in October is uncertain. Most editorial articles were
anonymous, because 'each article will not so much represent the opinions of a
writer as the ideas of a school' (circular from MacDonald, Aug 1896;
Samuel Papers, A10, f. 5). One or two can definitely be attributed to Clarke,
but the others are of dubious authorship.

country, it said, were nonetheless 'paralysed' by their disagreements and diversity. They had to be united, given 'solidarity of structure, singleness of aim, economy of force [and] consistency of action' before they could adequately deal with 'that huge unformed monster, "the Social Question" '. So the *Progressive Review* must aspire to 'a re-formation and re-statement of the principles of Progress' in terms which could be applied in a progressive policy and party. No such policy or party existed then. The Conservative Party was unsuited to the task of social reconstruction, and the Liberal Party 'has wellnigh done the work which it was fitted to accomplish by its traditional principles and its composition . . . in its present condition it is utterly powerless to undertake the new work which now confronts it'. A new Radical ideology was needed, and 'a strenuous social policy' which would 'apply clear rational principles of political and economic theory, with proper regard to the conditions of historical development'. Such a policy must abjure the old individualism of the Liberals. It must give to the State a larger part

> in ordering the life of the future, not confining its activities to the defence of individuals against certain forms of positive and palpable aggression, but contributing direct aid and support to individuals in their struggle towards a higher physical and moral life.

They must expose the 'pernicious fallacy' that there was 'an antithesis between the State and the Individual', and show how the State should properly check abuses of private enterprise and monopoly. So their main emphasis would be on social questions; but foreign affairs would not be neglected, and the *Review* would seek to show how England should 'establish for herself some right and abiding principles of international intercourse and some just policy for the adaptation of the outwardly conflicting claims of racial development throughout the world'. In sum, the *Progressive Review* would put to its readers 'this present urgent need for a rally of the forces of progress upon the newer and higher ground which the 19th century has disclosed'.[1]

[1] 'Introductory' article in the *P.R.*, i, pp. 1–9 (by William Clarke).

Both the Ethical movement and the Rainbow Circle, therefore, were concerned to do the same thing: to replace an inadequate Liberalism with something more suited to the conditions of a 'new age' – to the problems, social and international, which it posed, and to the new knowledge which the past century had accumulated. They were trying to bring a New Radical order out of ideological chaos. And for both groups of men the way to this New Radical order lay in the same direction: in a discarding of the old atomistic view of society, and a recognition of the social implications of men's actions.

II. HOBSON AND THE SOCIAL PROBLEM

In the context of this amorphous body of progressivist unorthodoxy Hobson and (to a lesser extent) MacDonald, Clarke and J. M. Robertson worked out their ideology of empire. It sprang from the social philosophy of the New Radicals, which was to be expounded most clearly by Hobson himself in the 1890s. Although it may seem to be wandering rather far from the subject of imperialism, it is worth examining this social philosophy in a little more detail, in order to arrive at a better comprehension of the New Radicals' imperial theory. Hobson was a writer who above all aimed for consistency, and his thinking on the subject of empire was a natural concomitant of his thinking about 'the Social Problem'.

One area where the two things impinged was his view of 'saving'. Hobson's 'heresy' of underconsumption is notorious for its contribution to the 'surplus capital' theory of imperialism. It was, indeed, a vital part of his anti-imperial ideology, and the element of his thought most destructive of contemporary political and economic assumptions. He had first expounded it in 1889 in *The Physiology of Industry*, written in collaboration with A. F. Mummery, the businessman and mountaineer who first persuaded him of the 'fallacy of saving'.[1] Saving, they said, was the prime cause of poverty, unemployment and trade depression; by subtracting money which otherwise would find its way into the hands

[1] Hobson, *Confessions*, p. 30.

of consumers it had the effect of reducing consumption, and so stimulating over-production. Such a doctrine, as we have seen, was not original;[1] but it seemed to be going against all current social and economic dogma. 'In appearing to question the virtue of unlimited thrift,' wrote Hobson later, 'I had committed the unpardonable sin.' He had offended against 'the new science built up in the nineteenth century for the explanation, the defence, and the glorification of the era of capitalism'.[2] In *The Physiology* he wrote that

> We contradict the generally accepted dogmas that the saving of the individual must always and necessarily enrich the community, that the individual seeking his own advantage necessarily works for that of the community, and that wages can only rise at the expense of profit, or profit at the expense of wages, or both at the expense of rent.[3]

At the time, the doctrine of underconsumption had little effect on anyone's thought but Hobson's own; but it was commended fifty years later by Lord Keynes as marking 'in a sense, an epoch in economic thought'.[4] From the point of view of the history of economic theory *The Physiology* was important as in some small way a precursor of the Keynesian revolution.[5] From the point

---

[1] See above, pp. 40–8. Hobson later acknowledged this himself; see *The Problem of the Unemployed*, p. ix; *Confessions*, p. 31; and his *John Ruskin, Social Reformer*, p. 121, where he credits Ruskin with having detected the 'fallacy of saving'. J. M. Robertson had also at that time written, but not yet published, an essay which reached the same conclusion by a different path; see his *The Fallacy of Saving*.

[2] Hobson, *Confessions*, pp. 31–2. His heresy, he claimed, led the London Extension Board to forbid him to teach political economy, and the Charity Organisation Society, a stronghold of opposition to social intervention, to withdraw an invitation to him to lecture (ibid. loc. cit.). Later he claimed that he had wished to imply no 'disparagement of individual thrift'; other under-consumptionists had, he said, gone too far in this direction by their 'failure to grasp the true relations between individual and social saving' (*The Problem of the Unemployed*, p. x).

[3] Hobson, *The Physiology of Industry*, pp. iv–vii.

[4] J. M. Keynes, *The General Theory of Employment, Interest and Money*, pp. 364–5.

[5] M. P. Schneider, 'Underconsumption and Imperialism', pp. 24–38. Hobson's elder brother, the economist E. W. Hobson, taught Keynes at Cambridge (*D.N.B., 1931–40*, p. 434).

of view of imperial theory, its significance lies in the conclusions which Hobson himself drew from it. Underconsumption provided the essential basis upon which what is known as the 'economic theory of imperialism' could be built; and further, its wider implications *vis-à-vis* social economics suggested to him the general lines on which a new social philosophy, which itself touched the question of empire at another point, should proceed.

Hobson's 'underconsumptionism' is familiar to historians and economists, and much written about. Less familiar, because less influential, is his broader social theory; yet to Hobson this was at least as important, if not more so. Men's reputations are seldom what they would wish them to be, and the ideas to which Hobson himself gave most emphasis are now 'interrèd with his bones' – perhaps rightly, for they betrayed a certain naïvety in his own time and seem to have little relevance to ours. But they lay at the back of his imperial thinking and that of his New Radical colleagues, and are worth exhuming, therefore, for the light they shed on it. In some ways they are more significant than the somewhat narrow economic doctrine with which Hobson's name is almost exclusively associated.

Hobson is called an economist. Yet G. D. H. Cole wrote of him on the occasion of his centenary:

> I prefer to think of him chiefly, as he thought of himself, as the champion of a comprehensive study of the conditions of human welfare embracing all the social studies, within which economics and other specialist subjects were really no more than subordinate and closely interrelated branches.[1]

Economics, in fact, was never Hobson's exclusive or even his main concern. In a way it was the very reverse. His 'economics' was a kind of anti-economics, an endeavour to dethrone political economy from its privileged position above the law. As a good Ethicist he wanted to bring to its study a consideration of factors which had, in the past, stood outside the more rigidly defined field of economics; to 'humanise' it and bring it under the control of political morality, instead of allowing it, as the classical

[1] *New Statesman*, 5 July 1958, p. 12.

economists had done, to operate above or be identified with the moral law. This is why it is ironical that, by his influence on Lenin, he should have contributed towards the elaboration of a system of economic determinism. For Hobson, man must control economics, not vice versa.

At present economics seemed to lie outside man's control, and the liberty it was allowed was patently obstructing social morality. Whatever the classical economists said, the free play of economic forces was not furthering social progress, but rather retarding it – witness the Social Problem. There was a flaw in the economic system. Partly it was 'saving', which was preventing the circulation of sufficient capital to maintain the equilibrium between supply and demand which Say's Law had posited:[1] but the fault went deeper than this. The trouble was, said Hobson, that the real scope of economic science had been misunderstood. It had been divorced from the service of humanity.

From John Ruskin he learnt 'the necessity of going behind the current monetary estimates of wealth, cost, and utility, to reach the body of human benefits and satisfactions which give them real meaning'.[2] Until then economics had 'deliberately and systematically degraded the true and formerly accepted meaning of such terms as "wealth", "value", and "profit" by putting them to the narrow service of business mentality'.[3] It rated, for example, £1,000 of 'poisonous gin destined for export to West Africa' as equivalent in value to '£1000 worth of bread which will support the lives of many English families';[4] of course it was, in terms of money, but not in terms of real social 'value'. Ruskin considered this monetary assessment to be immoral and irrational, and he redefined 'wealth' according to higher criteria: 'A truly valuable or availing thing is that which leads to life with its whole strength.'[5] Hobson followed him. In a monograph on Ruskin published in

---

[1] In *Problems of Poverty* and *The Problem of the Unemployed* Hobson sought, on the data supplied by Charles Booth, to 'establish underconsumption as the direct economic cause' of the Social Problem (*The Problem of the Unemployed*, p. viii).
[2] Hobson, *Confessions*, p. 42.   [3] Ibid. p. 39.
[4] Hobson, Introduction to Ruskin, *Unto This Last* (1907 ed.), pp. 12–13.
[5] Ruskin, *Unto This Last* (1905 Library ed.), p. 84.

1898 he maintained that 'the true "value" of a thing is neither the price paid for it nor the amount of present satisfaction it yields to the consumer, but the intrinsic service it is capable of yielding by its right use'.[1] 'The deeper significance of *Unto This Last*', he wrote later, 'consists in the enforcement of a consistent and rational definition of Wealth and a serviceable standard of Value.' [2] It would not do to assess Wealth in narrow quantitative terms. It must be measured against some *ethical* standard.[3]

Ruskin and Hobson both exaggerated the rigidity of their opponents' position, just as Hobson had underestimated the strength of 'underconsumptionism' in Britain. The great reforming legislation of the 1840s was itself nothing if not a retreat from the 'quantitative' methods of the classical economists, back to the 'welfare-ism' of a previous age. The change in outlook had come then; the debates on Fielden's Bill of 1846, says G. M. Young, 'mark at once the waning of the economics of pure calculation and the growth of that pre-occupation with the quality of life which is dominant in the next decade'.[4] We have already come across several such examples of historical misconception on the part of Radicals, of too great an emphasis put upon stated dogmas, and we shall find more. But the important point is that Hobson had been brought up to believe that economics was inviolable and the pursuit of 'wealth' universally beneficial, and now Ruskin had come to tell him that this was not so. The implications of this for Hobson were profound. The belief that there was no need to regulate the economic system, because it worked better on its own, was discredited. Economics could now come within the scope of *policy*. And that policy should recognise the primacy of social and moral values over impersonal economic ones.

A new lease of life had been given to human reason. For Hobson was always an 'intellectualist' in the old pattern;[5] all his

---

[1] Hobson, *John Ruskin, Social Reformer*, p. 79.
[2] Hobson, Introduction to *Unto This Last*, p. 11.
[3] Hobson, *John Ruskin*, pp. 78–9.
[4] G. M. Young, *Victorian England; Portrait of an Age*, p. 54.
[5] See above, p. 145.

hopes for progress and social reform rested on his belief in men's ability to consider their own rational interests and act upon them, to use their reason to adapt their society to the new conditions of the machine age.[1] If economics had lain outside the area of human volition, then it would mean that the Social Problem was impermeable and rational progress unattainable. Now he had found a way over this hurdle. Economic laws were no longer inviolable, so man could once more consciously apply his reason to the controlling of his environment. This happy intellectualist faith was to remain with him throughout his career. The events of the twenty years which culminated in the First World War discouraged his hopes, and made him sometimes overstate the potency of irrational phenomena and so appear fatalistic. But as late as 1931 he could still hold aloft his somewhat tattered banner: 'Man is not a very reasonable animal, but (barring such temporary outbursts as the Great War), he becomes continuously more reasonable.'[2] Despite the Boer War, the First World War and the rise of Fascism, he remained an optimistic rationalist, pitting himself (as he saw it) against the irrational factors which threatened progress, and never allowing himself to accept their inevitability.

Ruskin had helped him here, and also in another way. It was he, said Hobson, who had first pointed the way to a science of sociology, 'by insisting upon the organic integrity and unity of all human activities, and the organic nature of the co-operation of the social units, and finally by furnishing a social ideal of reasonable humanity'.[3] Here, perhaps, he was reading more into Ruskin than Ruskin himself had intended; he owed more to Herbert Spencer for his 'sociological' ideas.[4] And these ideas were not really 'sociological' in the modern sense of the word: if they had been then they would have proved more difficult to square with his 'intellectualism'. What he derived from Ruskin was an illustration of the necessity for abandoning the old individualism, and for

[1] See Hobson, *The Evolution of Modern Capitalism*, p. 351.
[2] Hobson, 'The State as an Organ of Rationalisation', in the *Political Quarterly*, vol. ii, no. 1 (1931), p. 34.
[3] Hobson, *John Ruskin*, p. 89.   [4] See Hobson, *Confessions*, p. 24.

formulating a political philosophy upon a more 'social' basis. This philosophy, for Hobson, relied on two related concepts, both drawn from the new biology: 'organism' and 'evolution'. The use of these words was dangerous; to the neo-Hegelians and the Social Darwinists they denoted an illiberal and manifestly irrational political philosophy. And Hobson's use of them – not merely as analogies but as precise definitions – reads like Bernard Bosanquet:

> The individual feeling, his will, his ends and interests, are not entirely merged in or sacrificed to the public feeling, will and ends, but over a certain area they are fused and identified, and the common social life thus formed has conscious interests and ends of its own which are not merely instruments in forwarding the progress of the separate individual lives, but are directed primarily to secure the survival and psychical progress of the community regarded as a conscious whole.[1]

But in so far as it affected his practical recommendations, the point he was trying to make with this somewhat alarming 'organic' analogy was, simply, that all individual actions had a social import; that arrangements between individuals should not be made merely with the good of the individuals directly concerned in mind, but the social good of the whole community of which they were members. It was his way of reconciling the State and the Individual.[2]

In the same way he liberalised his 'evolutionary' concept by making it 'rational'. This is illustrated in the last chapter of his *Evolution of Modern Capitalism*, a tentative prophecy of things to come. For the Social Darwinists social evolution was an extra-rational process, but Hobson managed to find a place within it for the exercise of human reason. Social evolution, he said, would be expedited when society learned to 'bring its conscious will to bear upon the work of constructing new social and industrial forms to fit the new economic conditions', and so render in-

[1] Hobson, 'A Restatement of Democracy', in *C.R.*, Feb 1902, pp. 265–6.
[2] See Hobson, *The Social Problem: Life and Work*, p. 219.

dustrial progress 'subordinate to larger human ends'.[1] Evolution was the process whereby the 'struggle for survival' in the industrial field – competitive capitalism – was replaced by industrial co-operation, so that individual enterprise, repressed on this lower level, was free to devote itself to higher things.

> If ... we regard human life as comprising an infinite number of activities of different sorts, operating upon different planes of competition and educating different human 'fitnesses', we shall understand how the particular phase of industrial evolution we are considering is related to the wider philosophic view of life. All progress, from primitive savagedom to modern civilisation, will then appear as consisting in the progressive socialisation of the lower functions, the stoppage of lower forms of competition and of the education of the more brutal qualities, in order that a larger and larger proportion of individual activity may be engaged in the exercise of higher functions, the practice of competition upon higher planes, and the education of higher forms of fitness.[2]

The reconciliation which Hobson had effected between the 'new knowledge' and its implications on the one hand, and the old rationalistic liberalism to which he was still firmly attached on the other, was not altogether satisfactory. Most of the time he appeared merely to be using 'sociological' and evolutionary concepts for an intellectualist end, shoring up the crumbling defences of democratic liberalism with any materials that came to hand, and this in a somewhat unsophisticated manner. His 'organic' analogy, for example, led him very close to a 'functionalist' view of society; from it he might have drawn the same moral as Mary Kingsley – that social customs, especially primitive customs, had far-reaching ramifications, and should not be tampered with, therefore, in isolation. But Hobson was not interested in anthropology; his organic concept was intended to furnish a code of social action and not an excuse for conserving the *status quo*; and in any case his rationalistic evolutionism to a great extent nullified the effects of his 'sociology'. For him, the

[1] Hobson, *The Evolution of Modern Capitalism*, pp. 351–2.   [2] Ibid. p. 364.

social interdependence of mankind was not irrational or purely customary; or if it were, then its irrational aspects would soon be shed. The functionalists tended to regard these irrational features of society as organically essential to its health; Hobson would have agreed more with Sir Edward Tylor in dismissing them as 'survivals' from an earlier age. If he pleaded for the preservation of primitive cultures, it would be for other reasons than the 'sociological' one. He was still too much of an 'intellectualist'. Nevertheless, Hobson's emancipation from customary ways of thinking was greater than that of most of his Radical contemporaries. He had taken some account, at least, of considerations which had been given no place before in orthodox Liberal doctrine – 'the newer and higher ground which the 19th century has disclosed'; and this went some way towards justifying his and his colleagues' contention that they had superseded traditional Radicalism, were more relevant to the times. The New Radicals were able to look anew at contemporary political controversies and to take up an independent position on them. This position would be grounded in two broad and general doctrines which the philosophies of the Ethical movement and the Rainbow Circle had at their centre: that moral considerations should outweigh considerations of necessity, and that individual good should not be pursued independently of social good. More specifically, Hobson had reduced these doctrines to a more definite form, in preaching the ideal of a fully integrated society acting according to the criterion of an ethically and rationally conceived standard of 'social utility'. In the intellectually congenial surroundings of South Place he was to develop this theme and, under the pressure of events, apply it to the problem of empire.

III. THE ETHICS OF EMPIRE: HOBSON AND MACDONALD

We are in a position now to trace the development of Hobson's imperial thinking from its genesis in the social philosophy of his early works to the fully fledged theory of empire contained in

Imperialism: a Study. This thinking had two aspects. First, Hobson was concerned to elucidate the reasons and motives behind contemporary expansion. This was the 'economic theory'. Secondly, he examined the morality and justice of imperialism, irrespective of its capitalist origins. This was his ethical theory. It is less well known than the other facet of his ideology, yet in its way it was just as significant. It was developed in the pages of the *Progressive Review* and the *Ethical World* between 1897 and 1899.

In August 1897 an article appeared in the *Progressive Review* entitled 'Ethics of Empire'. It was signed simply 'Nemo'; but in view of the fact that the ideas expressed in it and the methods of reasoning employed are identical to Hobson's, it can with some confidence be regarded as his first contribution to the discussion of these problems. In November the next year the *Ethical World* carried three articles by Ramsay MacDonald on 'Ethics and Empire', and a paper by Hobson on 'Expansion in the Light of Sociology'. Finally, Hobson contributed four further articles to the same journal in July 1899 entitled 'Issues of Empire'. Together these papers form the bridge between Hobson's social ideology and the ideas he put forward in the second part of *Imperialism*; and between MacDonald's early liaison with the Ethicists and his later writings on empire. Hobson's *Ethical World* paper of November 1898 shows the transition most clearly. It was originally one of a series of lectures he delivered to the London branch of the Christian Social Union, and later (1901) published under the title *The Social Problem: Life and Work*. Taking these lectures as a whole, we can see how his ideas about empire sprang directly and naturally from his broader philosophy.

In *The Social Problem* the argument went like this. Hobson began by reiterating his case against 'political economy', and in particular against the classical economists' assumption that an 'unseen hand' ensured that the free play of enlightened self-interest would automatically redound to the good of the community.[1] It did not; and the reason he gave was Ruskin's: 'A science which still takes money as its standard of value, and

---

[1] Hobson, *The Social Problem*, bk. 1, ch. iii, pp. 17–32.

G

regards man as a means of making money, is, in the nature of the case, incapable of facing the deep and complex human problems which compose the Social Question.'[1] The old political economy was unsocial, inhuman and quantitative in its method, and so it ignored the 'higher needs' of man in society. Yet this did not mean that there was no possibility of elaborating a political economy on a scientific basis. It could be done, as soon as the 'New Political Economy' looked to (the new) organic and evolutionary science for its inspiration. Utilitarianism need not be abandoned as its yardstick, so long as it was qualitative (and therefore, Hobson admitted, partly subjective),[2] and recognised the laws of organic interaction. This would reveal a new 'natural law'. So the New Political Economy should not be content with 'what is', but must look instead to 'what OUGHT to be'.[3] Secondly, it must recognise the essential interaction and interdependence of different parts of the social mechanism. And thirdly, it must take into account qualitative distinctions between different kinds of good.[4] This for Hobson added up to the 'standard of value' which he had called 'social utility'.[5] By this criterion policies and actions should be judged. It was at once ethical, 'organic' and qualitative. Translated into practical terms, 'social utility' was very near to 'efficiency' in meaning: its antonym was 'waste' and, were it not for Hobson's later clarification of the ethical standards he wished to apply,[6] it could be confused with the very different doctrines of 'efficiency' promulgated by the Fabians and Lord Rosebery.[7] To Hobson, however, 'social utility' was neither illiberal nor, in essence, anti-individualistic. Once accept the social nature of man and the organic nature of society, and a 'reconcilement' could be achieved between the apparently antithetical claims of the individual and society by combining

[1] Ibid. p. 38.
[2] Ibid. p. 39, and pp. 280–8, where Hobson deals with the problem of the subjectivity of men's judgments of qualitative values: not altogether satisfactorily, for he assumed that differing assessments of 'the good' could be overcome by education.
[3] Ibid. ch. vi.   [4] Ibid. ch. vii.   [5] Ibid. p. 39 *et passim*.
[6] Hobson, 'Socialistic Imperialism', in *I.J.E.*, vol. xii (1901), pp. 44 ff.
[7] See above, pp. 114–17.

collectivism and individualism. 'The right ordering of work and
life of an individual member of society ... will be determined by
harmonious adjustment of the needs and capacities of his individual nature, and those of his social nature as interpreted and
directed by the needs of society.'[1] This was not a compromise
between conflicting interests; 'There are no conflicting claims.'[2]
It was a 'genuine harmony'.[3]

The bearing of all this on the problem of imperialism was
pointed in Chapter XIX, 'The Economy of National Life'.[4] Here
Hobson applied the doctrine of Social Utility to the wider
'society' of nations. On the level of world-society, nations were
the equivalent of individuals in smaller societies. Therefore, if
Manchester individualism had to go, so must the Manchester
criterion of judgment for international affairs – that is, the Gladstonian respect for the rights of nationalities. Just as individual
claims were not pre-eminent on a national level, so national
claims could not be pre-eminent on a supra-national level.

The simple solution of the Manchester School, therefore, was
inadequate; and on the other hand the fatalistic solution of those
who preached 'Manifest Destiny' or the 'Survival of the Fittest'
were repugnant because they denied the potency of reason in
human affairs.[5] The *Progressive Review* put the point clearly in
1897. We must, it said, dismiss such negativistic conceptions, 'and
plainly face the issue as one involving the duty of a nation to
make a rational choice of its career, guided by some conception
of an end or ideal'.[6]

There were two ways in which imperialism might be justified
on rational grounds. The first was that a country needed territory
'in which to adequately realise its national end'. This argument
could not be countered with any confidence. There were risks
involved in expansion which might enfeeble national life; and
'intensive' rather than 'extensive' cultivation might be a wiser

[1] Hobson, *Social Problem*, p. 224.   [2] Ibid. p. 223.
[3] Ibid. p. 219.
[4] Ibid. pp. 272–9. (This chapter first appeared in the *Ethical World*,
19 Nov 1898.)
[5] *Ethical World*, 1 and 8 July 1899.   [6] *P.R.*, ii, pp. 448–50.

policy.[1] But these considerations were 'purely hypothetical: there is nothing to prevent a nation growing big and great at the same time'.[2] The second justification was the appeal to a 'wider standard of human utility': the claim of an imperial power to be contributing to the civilisation of the world. Sometimes this claim sounded like the old Manchester 'enlightened self-interest' plea; 'the ethical philosophy of laissez-faire upon a grand scale'.[3] It no longer sufficed for a nation to be its own judge. 'The mere *ipse dixit* of a nation which professes a mission to annex some portion of the globe, and to break it in for the civilisation of Christendom, will have little weight in any rational consideration of a world economy.'[4] But on the other hand there was, in the case of sparsely populated territories, 'a *primâ facie* and obvious gain in their settlement by a nation of civilised progressive habits'.[5] No countenance could be given to the view that a population always had an absolute right over the territory it occupied. According to the doctrine of Social Utility,

> If a land capable of yielding a large supply of food is held by a nation too feeble or ignorant to utilise its powers, their occupation is not defensible against the needs of humanity. No one made the land, occupation is entirely a question of time and degree, and international morality will confirm the decree, 'the land to those who can use it', and in theory, at any rate, must go further, and affirm the principle, 'the land to those who can best use it.'[6]

And Hobson put it more bluntly in the *Ethical World*: 'A rigid conservation of existing territorial boundaries is neither histori-

---

[1] *Social Problem*, pp. 277–8. In the *Ethical World*, 22 July 1899 (pp. 450–451), Hobson tried to define a little more closely the limits of a 'socially sufficient' Empire. Using again the analogy of intensive *versus* extensive cultivation, he concluded that, although it was difficult to decide what was 'for a given nation a truly economic area of empire', the evidence pointed to the British Empire's having exceeded this limit. She was too diverse environmentally, racially and administratively, and this diversity would undermine her permanence. Cf. Gustave Le Bon, *Psychology of Peoples*, p. 137: 'Great Empires, embracing diverse peoples, have always been condemned to an ephemeral existence.'

[2] *P.R*, ii, pp. 450–1.   [3] Ibid. p. 451.
[4] *Social Problem*, p. 274.   [5] *P.R.*, ii, p. 452.   [6] Ibid. p. 452.

cally feasible nor desirable. The utilisation of the natural resources of each portion of the globe should be assigned to the
people which can most effectively undertake it' [1] – precisely what
the imperialist, Benjamin Kidd, had asserted in 1894.[2]

But while conceding the theoretical right of an 'efficient' nation
to override the territorial claims of a backward people, Hobson,
unlike Kidd, saw difficulties in the way of its practical implementation. First, mere capacity for conquest did not attest efficiency
for 'civilising' or even 'developing' purposes. Military efficiency
did not necessarily imply industrial efficiency.[3] Secondly, the
conflicting claims of nations to be furthering the progress of
'cosmic utility' could not be decided impartially; 'there exists no
court before which the case can be tried'.[4] Our judgment in
South Africa was that of an interested party;

> We claim to replace a lower by a higher civilisation: who is
> to determine whether the slow-going civilisation of the
> Transvaal Boer is really lower or less profitable for the world
> in the long run than a more rapid development of the country
> for mining speculation by Englishmen and German Jews?[5]

And thirdly, the appeal to a 'higher' standard of civilisation
assumed a uniform scale of civilised values to be applied universally. This was fallacious:

> this notion is utterly at variance both with the 'theory of
> evolution' and with the facts of history.... The wide
> variants of natural environment and race, reacting con-
> stantly one upon the other, oblige us to conceive civil-
> isation as 'multiform' ... deeply marked characters of
> historic race, physical and psychical ... tend to express
> themselves firmly and constantly in widely divergent types
> of civilisation.[6]

This 'cultural relativism' of Hobson's was unusual in the
1890s, but it was not original. We have seen how it arose naturally

[1] *Social Problem*, p. 274.   [2] See above, p. 49.
[3] *Social Problem*, p. 274; and cf. 'Socialistic Imperialism', *I.J.E.*, pp.
44–58.
[4] *P.R.*, ii, p. 454.
[5] Ibid. p. 454. Cf. Richard Congreve in 1857: see above, p. 28, fn. 2.
[6] *Social Problem*, p. 275.

from the Positivist philosophy of Richard Congreve and Frederic Harrison, from the 'anthropocentrism' which Comte's sociology implied.[1] The same doctrine was promulgated to a meeting of the South Place Ethical Society in November 1895 by the Professor of Moral Philosophy at the University of St Andrews, William Knight:

> It was a mistake to try to europeanise the Indian, to asiaticise the African, to americanise the Polynesian. What was needed was the removal of every hindrance in the way of the freest national and racial development. All normal individual growth and all healthy national development began from within, and extended outwards. It was not possible to import it from without; although occasionally there might be a healthy graft on the old stem, with a view to richer and fuller development.... In all cases the development of indigenous qualities and characteristics, their elevation and refinement, was the end to be striven after....[2]

And more fresh in the minds of Ethicists were the lectures delivered to them by Mary Kingsley in October 1897 and January 1898, putting the same point: that the 'civilisation' of native races should be preceded by empirical study and encouragement of their own indigenous cultures.[3] Hobson must have been familiar with these arguments from his own attendance at South Place. The authority he cited in *The Social Problem*, however, was none of these, but the French sociologist Gustave Le Bon.

Le Bon's *Psychology of Peoples* demonstrated, he said, that races could only absorb some characteristics of alien civilisations, and these only very gradually.[4] The lesson was plain. A nation

[1] See above, pp. 27–8 and 159.

[2] *South Place Magazine*, vol. i (1895), p. 76. Knight's lecture was entitled 'Philosophy in its National Developments, and Race in Civilisation'.

[3] Published in Sheowring, *British Empire Series*, ii 377.

[4] *Social Problem*, p. 276. Hobson's acceptance of some of Le Bon's chief conclusions (both here and in *The Psychology of Jingoism*) was only made with considerable reservations. Le Bon saw men in the irrefrangible grip of heredity and unconscious psychological forces (*Les Lois psychologiques de l'Evolution des peuples*, 1891; *Psychologie des Foules*, 1895). Hobson saw and

could not implant the essential features of its civilisation on another within a few generations. And if civilisations were multiform, it could not be said that one civilisation was better than another, only that it was different.[1] The fallacy was a dangerous one. In India, for example, although 'taking a commercial, or even a short-range humanitarian, application of the standard of utility, the case for British rule is indisputably strong',[2] from a wider and deeper viewpoint our influence had been less beneficial. We had failed to 'civilise and elevate India'. We had done nothing to enable her peoples to 'realise their higher possibilities in the arts of political and moral self-government'.[3] By coercion we had made her society artificial. And even our pacifying influence had been an unwonted interference with India's natural development.

That terrible internecine struggle of nationalities, which it is our boast to have repressed, may it not have been the natural war of types nearing a crisis from which some powerful, persistent race-type would have emerged, capable of developing a civilisation conformable to the physical and moral conditions of the environment, with political institutions, industrial and religious life, which were the normal slow growth of seeds of national character, and not the exotic products of an alien civilisation implanted and sustained by

---

accepted that these forces were powerful, perhaps dominant; and this demonstrated how wrong it was (he said) to assume that, for instance, a black man could be given white civilisation. But he accompanied Le Bon no further: because civilisations were different, it did not follow (as Le Bon said) that they were mutually antagonistic; because men were moved by irrational forces, it did not mean that they would never be amenable to reason. All it meant, for Hobson, was that psychology and sociology must be taken into account in social and political action, and not ignored; and that different psychological mentalities must be sympathised with and allowed for. Cf. *Social Problem*, ch. xvii. How far apart the two writers diverged is demonstrated in Le Bon's *Bases scientifiques d'une philosophie d'histoire* (1931), which condemns democracy and internationalism, and praises Mussolini and aggressive nationalism. Hitler is supposed to have learnt from him (see Werner Maser in *Der Spiegel*, no. 33 (1966), p. 57).
[1] *Social Problem*, p. 276; cf. *P.R.*, ii, p. 454.
[2] *P.R.*, ii, p. 455.   [3] Ibid. p. 456.

force, and doomed to perish if ever its artificial supports are weakened or withdrawn?[1]

A culture indigenous to a people was, therefore, *per se* preferable to one imposed from outside. All our claims to be 'civilising lower races' fell before this fact. We were destroying what was good in India, and replacing it with a superficial veneer. And this process was having grave repercussions upon our own 'capacity of inward growth'. We were parasites on India, and 'parasitism is a disease which means untimely death'.[2] Our moral influence in the world was impaired by our 'selfish, greedy past'. Our trade did not benefit, for 'the specious allegation ... that trade follows the flag, is crushingly refuted by the test of commercial statistics'.[3] And expansion was diverting attention from social reform – as was the intention of the European ruling classes:

> No one who intelligently watches the rulers of Russia, Germany, and Italy can possibly deny that the most powerful motive in their present policy is to divert the stream of holy discontent with social conditions into distant channels of foreign enterprise

so that their 'class dominance' would be preserved. In continental nations this policy was pursued 'with brutal frankness of design'; in England it was 'thinly veiled by a serviceable admixture of other commercial, political, and philanthropic motives'.[4]

These were the main lines of the ethical side of Hobson's imperial theory. Moral reason could and should be applied to international affairs. Social Utility could, in theory, justify imperial expansion. But in practice it was difficult to uphold a claim made on such grounds. There was no international 'court' which could adjudicate between 'social efficiency' and interest. Western civilisation was not necessarily the best form of civilisation for all peoples, and it could not be grafted on to alien cultures. And, lastly, imperialism was too often the enemy of reform and the tool of reaction.

[1] Ibid. p. 458. [2] Ibid. p. 459.
[3] Ibid. p. 461. [4] Ibid. p. 460; and cf. Hobson, *The Crisis of Liberalism*.

MONARCHY v. REPUBLIC.

ENGLAND FORCES WAR.

THE BOER ULTIMATUM.

ORANGE FREE STATE PROCLAIMS WAR.

CAPITALISTS' CAMPAIGN.

£7,000,000 ALREADY SPENT.

THE PRICE OF BREAD TO RISE.

CHAMBERLAIN'S VICTIMS.

70,000 BRITISH FIGHT 20,000 BOERS.

THIEVES' KITCHEN REJOICES.

WHAT ABOUT TOMMY ATKINS?

" Was ever any freak of Imperialism so grotesque as that of going to war in order to force a friendly Power to turn loyal subjects of our Queen—our own fellow citizens—into aliens and Republicans? And this is called the consolidating of the Empire and the maintenance of our Imperial predominance! The British Empire is to be strengthened by dubbing the admit male citizens of a stubborn and warlike Republic, which we declare has been for years past both unfriendly and dangerous."—FREDERIC HARRISON.

THREE EASY STEPS DOWN-HILL.

We've Jingoes. How they love the flag!
    And here's a Jingo song:
"That flag is right in any fight,
    Our country, right or wrong."

We've partisans. They're lower still,
    And here's the party song:
"When at the polls you have no souls,
    Our party, right or wrong."

We've boodlers. Down another step,
    And here's the boodler's song:
"We take no bluff, we want the stuff,
    Our pockets, right or wrong."

England having forced the Transvaal to declare war on behalf of the foreign capitalists— no Transvaal workman took part in the Outlanders' agitation—it was natural that the Thieves' Kitchen in the City of London, that is the great gambling den, known as the Stock Exchange, should celebrate the event by rejoicings after the manner of a class whose business it is to ruin investors to make themselves rich.

Meanwhile the first instalment of the Butcher's Bill has been presented to the British taxpayer. It amounts to about £7,000,000. A few days hence, the class Government will be asking for about

in this Republic, and finally, by your Note of September 25, 1899, broke off all friendly correspondence on the subject and intimated that they must now proceed to formulate their own proposals for a final settlement, and this Government can only see in the above intimation from Her Majesty's Government a new violation of the Convention of London, 1884, which does not reserve to Her Majesty's Government the right to a unilateral settlement of a question which is exclusively a domestic one for this Government and has already been regulated by it.

NO BRITISH PROPOSALS MADE.

" On account of the strained situation and the consequent serious loss in, and interruption of, trade in general which the correspondence respecting the franchise and representation in this Republic carried in its train, Her Majesty's Government have recently pressed for an early settlement and finally pressed, by your intervention, for an answer within forty-eight hours (subsequently somewhat modified) to your Note of September 12, replied to by the Note of this Government of September 15, and your Note of September 25, 1899, and thereafter further friendly negotiations broke off and this Government received the intimation that the proposal for a final settlement would shortly be made, but although this promise was once more repeated no proposal has up to now reached this Government.

INDEPENDENCE OF THE REPUBLIC THREATENED.

" Even while friendly correspondence was still going on an increase of troops on a large scale was introduced by Her Majesty's Government and stationed in the neighbourhood of the borders of this Republic. Having regard to occurrences in the history of this Republic which it is unnecessary here to call to mind this Government felt obliged to regard this military force in the neighbourhood of its borders as a threat against the independence of the South African Republic, since it was aware of no circumstances which could justify the presence of such military force in South Africa and in the neighbourhood of its borders. In answer to an inquiry with respect thereto addressed to His Excellency

A succinct summary of the Radical case against the Boer War:
composite headline in Reynolds's Newspaper, *15 October 1899*

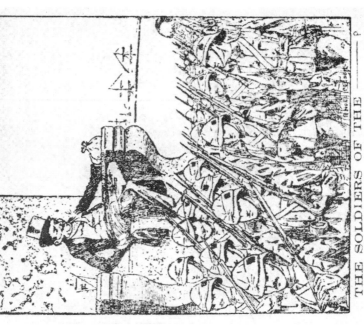

The capitalist power behind the throne (Labour Leader, *6 March 1897 and 17 March 1900*)

Top left:
  Ramsay MacDonald

Top right:
  John Atkinson Hobson

Left:
  William Clarke

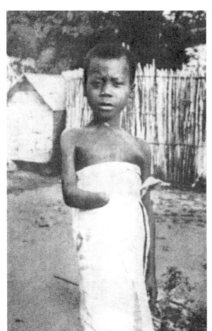

E. D. Morel's campaign against the Congo Free State relied greatly for its effect on 'atrocity pictures': these examples are taken from King Leopold's Rule in Africa, *1904*

The resemblance between these views and those which Ramsay MacDonald published ten years later in *Labour and The Empire* (1907)[1] is striking. The latter took a more positive and practical approach to imperial problems (as befits a politician), and he discussed aspects which Hobson never touched: but the broad line of argument was the same. And yet the similarity is not remarkable; for the imperial thinking of both men had a common source. MacDonald had been on terms of close friendship with Hobson since the mid nineties.[2] The two of them had worked together on the abortive *Progressive Review*, and they were both members of the Rainbow Circle and of the Ethical movement. And although MacDonald was more firmly committed to socialism than Hobson (he had joined the S.-D.F. in Bristol in 1885, and was a member of the Fabian executive from 1894 to 1900),[3] part of his allegiance went to this other, New Radical group. It was under the aegis of this group that he first formulated his views on empire. Probably he owed them to Hobson. But, however this may be, in a series of articles for the *Ethical World* in 1898[4] and later in a paper published in the *International Journal of Ethics* in July 1901,[5] he took an ethical view similar to Hobson's.

He shared with Hobson the opinion that imperialism was not, *per se*, necessarily an evil; but the reason he gave was not 'social efficiency'.

> So far as the underlying spirit of Imperialism is a frank acceptance of national duty exercised beyond the nation's political frontiers, so far as it is a claim that a righteous nation is by its nature restless to embark upon crusades of righteousness wherever the world appeals for help, the spirit of Imperialism cannot be condemned. Morality is

---

[1] See also his *What I Saw in South Africa*, ch. v; and *The Awakening of India*, Pt. iii, ch. vi.

[2] Hobson, *Confessions*, p. 51. They were still corresponding in 1926. Hobson's daughter, Mrs Scott, testifies to their friendship.

[3] Elton's *Life of MacDonald*.

[4] *Ethical World*, 5, 12, 19 Nov 1898, pp. 707–8, 725–6, 742–3.

[5] J. R. MacDonald, 'The Propaganda of Civilisation', in *I.J.E.*, vol. xi, no. 4 (1901), pp. 455–68.

G2

universal. . . . I want to make it clear that however successful designing men may be in prostituting the high purposes of the nations to their own ends, or however imperfectly the nations themselves interpret their ideals in their political policies, the compulsion to expand and to assume world responsibility is worthy at its origin.[1]

So there might be a *moral* case for imperialism. A case which was based on the claim of a country to need more territory for its own commercial development or its own security was weak; the commercial value of colonies was, he said, 'much less than panic-stricken merchants would lead us to believe', and strategically 'much territory increases the number of vulnerable points and the risks of international conflicts'.[2] A nation's own interests would not appear to be served by its adopting an imperial policy. But the more altruistic justification of empire, the argument based on a nation's 'duty to the world', could not be dismissed so easily. 'We must not lightly dismiss this claim which every vital people makes, that it is the chosen instrument for the advancement of good in the world.' It had 'very objectionable features'. But, said MacDonald, the 'range of moral responsibility' now was wider than it had been in, for example, classical Athens. 'An America heedless of Cuban misery, or a Britain unmoved by Armenian tortures, would be a monster.' We had to concede now that, 'under certain circumstances, an Imperial policy is justifiable'.[3]

But like Hobson, MacDonald saw practical difficulties in the way of implementing this principle, difficulties which had, in the main, been ignored by the imperial powers. Contact with coloured races tended to undermine the democratic spirit of the imperial nation both at home and in the colonies. 'The democracy of Britain is beginning to assume more and more the functions and the mental state of the Indian official; of the South African nigger-driver. . . . The events in Africa of the last year or two have brought sentiment in this country nearer and nearer to a lynching potentiality.'[4] Secondly, the appeal to philanthropy was

---

[1] Ibid. pp. 456, 458.
[3] Ibid. loc. cit.
[2] *Ethical World*, 5 Nov 1898.
[4] *Ethical World*, 19 Nov 1898.

too often a mask for more sinister designs. 'The fact is, civilisation is largely the excuse of imperialism. ... Empire follows the course of gold reefs rather than the shadows of human degradation.' [1] Thirdly (again repeating Hobson), 'the different civilising value of nations can not be assessed by any impartial and expert assessor', territorial acquisition was left to 'haphazard chance'.[2] And fourthly, there was the more profound obstacle put in the way of 'civilisation' by racial and national differences.

MacDonald echoed Hobson in his insistence upon the relativity of civilised standards.

> Civilisation is not expressed by the reading of the Bible, the drinking of Rum, and the weaving of cotton, for there are other civilisations besides that of the West. When we have developed the sense of ascertaining, as open-minded inquirers, how far civilisation differs with climate and other circumstances, and how far its habits must vary with different peoples – how far, for instance, English civilisation can no more be carried to India by Englishmen and lived up to there by them than they can carry ice in their luggage – we cannot pretend to be a great civilising agency.[3]

He elaborated on this theme in 1901. The civilisation of a people was not 'a veneer',[4] but 'an organic and disconnectable part of its existence'.[5] 'The lowest barbarian has his civilisation. He may be a child, but he is a child with a social inheritance. He is not a thing to bend at will.' [6] Not only were there different civilisations; each of them had something in it that was good –, ... every civilisation has some political, social or ethical excellence which in that respect may place it superior to the propagandist's civilisation itself'.[7] The Indian 'patriarchal system of common-sense equity' was in many ways more compassionate than our 'mechanical justice';[8] and the 'true liberty' fostered by tribal social organisations in Africa was superior to the 'disorganisation of individualism', based on personal property, with which we were trying to replace it.[9] Morality demanded that such institutions be preserved;

[1] *Ethical World*, 5 Nov 1898.   [2] Ibid. loc. cit.   [3] Ibid. loc. cit.
[4] 'The Propaganda of Civilisation', *I.J.E.*, p. 458.   [5] Ibid. p. 459.
[6] Ibid. p. 459.   [7] Ibid. pp. 459–60.   [8] Ibid. p. 461.   [9] Ibid. p. 462.

and necessity dictated that the alternative policy was bound to be abortive.

> Civilisation cannot be transplanted; it may be tended and pruned, but nothing more. Hence it is that the very last function which a civilising agent should seize is the governing and administrative function of a foreign State, for there he is dealing with the organised life of the people, the product of their religion, their superstition, their history, their mental state, and their natural condition. . . . Imperialism as an agent of civilisation is incapable, ruthless, ill-fitted for its work.[1]

If the 'propagandist of civilisation', therefore, was to benefit native races, 'his influence must be directed not *de novo* but on lines already determined by tribal experience'.[2]

> When we start our search for the best means to fulfil our duty in the world, with the idea in mind that the peoples of low civilisation are children, we may happily be led to consider educational methods. The first essential of a sound education is, not that you have to make the child, but that you have to assist it to grow. The educationalist does not begin to operate on a featureless nothing, but on something which offers him resistance if led in certain directions and encouragement if led in others. So with the propaganda of civilisation. To abolish any native method, saving perhaps some of the most revolting customs like cannibalism – is a mistake. The care of the educator should be to rationalise all native methods on the lines of the development which those methods have followed already.[3]

Yet even such a policy would be only the lesser of two evils. We could benefit the world more, he said, by setting a worthy domestic example. 'In the long run, we can do more for Africa by civilising the East End of London than by putting an end for ever to the iniquities of the Khalifa in the Soudan.' [4]

[1] *Ethical World*, 5 Nov 1898.
[2] 'The Propaganda of Civilisation', *I.J.E.*, p. 459.
[3] Ibid. p. 466. Like Hobson (*Imperialism*, pp. 258–9; see below, p. 234), MacDonald cites Basutoland as an example of enlightened native policy.
[4] Ibid. p. 468.

MacDonald was as deeply aware of the pitfalls in the way of a
beneficent colonial policy as Hobson. But he did not stop there.
His practical political sense told him that an ostrich-like moralistic
attitude was unrealistic, that a constructive policy could not
be built upon such an abstract view. 'The question of Empire
cannot be decided on first principles, so far as this country is
concerned. We have a history, and it is an Imperial one.' It was
too difficult to 're-write history, to undo evil . . . we have gone so
far in our Imperial history that we can hardly look back. We can
be guided in our future work; we cannot re-cut and re-carve the
past.' ¹ They could not abandon India while she could not defend
herself; but they *could* encourage 'a native Indian civilisation' and
reform their Indian Government. They could not prevent the
parcelling-out of the world among the civilising powers – 'why
not face it?' – but they could mitigate its more evil effects, which
stemmed from *uncertainty* as to the frontiers of spheres of influence, by working to put inter-colonial boundaries on an un-
disputed legal footing.² And, above all, they should 'rule our
Empire wisely', 'take more interest in its welfare'. 'Our supreme
duty to our Empire is to provide able rulers for it. . . . We have
not done that nearly so well as we might.' ³

By the end of 1898, therefore, in the context of the Ethical and
Progressive movements, Hobson and MacDonald had worked out
a coherent philosophical attitude towards empire. In rejecting
Manchesterism and the doctrine of non-intervention, they found
themselves impelled to admit the possible theoretical justification
of imperialism; Hobson on grounds of international social effi-
cency, MacDonald on grounds of international moral responsibility. But both of them were quick to point out the ethical problems which a practical imperial policy involved: the danger of
abuse, the absence of any means of impartial arbitration between
nations, and, in particular, the complex difficulties produced by
the 'multiform' character of civilisation. Hobson appeared to be

¹ *Ethical World*, 12 Nov 1898.
² Ibid. loc. cit.
³ *Ethical World*, 19 Nov 1898.

overwhelmed by these problems, and the critical, condemnatory side of his thought is uppermost in 1898, as it is four years later in *Imperialism: a Study*. MacDonald, however, was willing to compromise with the fate which had given Britain an empire. His Hobsonian ethical approach did not deter him from putting forward a constructive and realistic alternative to the New Imperialism. *Labour and the Empire* (1907) combined (with the injection of a little more specific socialism) moral criticism with practical politics, and so adapted the philosophy of Hobson to the needs of a political party which anticipated, one day, having to govern an empire.

IV. THE ECONOMIC THEORY

Until the late 1890s, Hobson's main concern had been to provide the broad basis for a rational analysis of social, economic and political phenomena: for a scientific sociology, upon which alone the measures that would ensure social progress could safely rest.[1] His treatment of specific problems – industrial organisation, unemployment, poverty, imperialism – he tried to link closely with this wider conception, basing his judgments firmly on rational criteria derived from a standard of 'social utility' which was 'organic', ethical and qualitative. He was to become better known, however, as the originator of a theory by which to explain certain political phenomena, which was somewhat cruder yet more comprehensive than he intended. Apart from *The Evolution of Modern Capitalism*, *Imperialism* is the only one of his many works still in print, and chapter VI of that book – 'The Economic Taproot of Imperialism' – is, one suspects, the only part widely read. In the context of the whole of Hobson's thought, the economic interpretation of imperialism must be seen as an attempt to describe the economic obstacles in the way of rationalistic social reform: a survey of the forces of reaction. But through the eyes of Lenin it has been interpreted as an analysis of an inevitable economic process, to be overcome only by means of the seeds of

[1] See Hobson, *Social Problem*, Ch xvii, esp. p. 262.

destruction contained within itself. That Hobson himself shared
no such deterministic view is shown in the last chapter of *The
Evolution of Modern Capitalism*.[1] The force with which he propounded his economic analysis of imperialism, however, rendered
it vulnerable (even in 1902) to the charge of materialism.

What are the roots of this 'economic interpretation'?

We have seen how 'capitalist imperialism', in the shape of
chartered companies, had come under Radical fire early in the
1890s; and that the attribution of imperialism to over-production
and pressure for new markets had first been suggested by the
imperialists themselves, as a *justification* for expansion.[2] This
latter consideration made it difficult for Liberals to use over-
production as an *indictment* of imperialism. In the face of capitalist
demands, it seemed that they either had to deny that expansion
was made necessary by over-production, and so abandon the
'economic interpretation' in this form; or to accept that there were
surplus manufactures being produced, and hence cast doubt on
the beneficence of that industrial system they were so proud of.
Socialists could, and did, take this latter line; *laissez-faire* Liberals
could not.

There was a third solution to the dilemma, and that was to
attribute imperialism not to the capitalist system *per se*, but to its
abuse. By this argument, capitalists were responsible for colonial
expansion, but 'over-production' was only their excuse. Their real
motives were less commendable, more selfish and sinister. This
was the line taken by those who attacked chartered companies in
Africa, either because they were monopolistic and therefore, in
Cobdenite terms, profitable only to a minority of capitalists; or
because they were run by men who were not members of the
British industrial community at all – the 'international capitalist
power'. Those who argued in this way had to show, first of all,
that capitalists were intriguing to harness government policy to
their own selfish ends; and secondly, that their claim to be providing necessary outlets for surplus manufactures was a pretence.

Between November 1896 and June 1897 William Clarke set out
to do the first of these things in the pages of the *Progressive*

---

[1] See above, p. 175.   [2] See above, Ch. 2, sect. II.

Review. In the course of demonstrating that imperialism was anti-pathetic to democracy, he attributed to financiers the imperialist policies of the 1890s.[1] Increased armaments, protectionist tariffs, expansion in Africa and Asia, and social reaction in all its forms were the products of that 'excess of nationalism' which was called jingoism. Jingoism was 'stimulated' by 'the general romantic movement in literature' and by 'the extreme statement of the organic conception of society in political philosophy'; but it was 'artfully worked on in every country on behalf of sinister interests which have nothing to do with any normal or healthy national feeling'. Capitalism, although potentially 'one of the leading factors in breaking down nationalities',[2] had, through its control of the Press, 'stimulated Jingoism more than any other cause'.[3] Consequently foreign policy was controlled not by the people, but by the autocrats of Germany, Austria and Russia, 'with unknown financiers behind them'.[4]

> For the force which is ruler today is . . . a force directed by a vast international money-power, which uses governments as its pawns on the world's chess-board, and which is able to hide its moves from the eyes of the uninitiated. If we must look for the underlying causes of the policy of the German Kaiser, we must fix our eyes on the bankers of Berlin. . . . The present English ministry is, to no small extent, a collecting agency for millionaires.[5]

Their power had until recently been confined to Europe; but now they were opening up Africa in search of gold. 'The exploita-

---

[1] 'The Liberal Leadership', *P.R.*, i, pp. 97–110; 'The Genesis of Jingoism', *P.R.*, i, pp. 397–406; 'Is Democracy a Reality?', *P.R.*, ii, pp. 20–9; and 'The Reign of Force', *P.R.*, ii, pp. 211–18. All these articles were published anonymously. 'The Genesis of Jingoism', however, was published again under Clarke's name in H. Burrows and J. A. Hobson (ed.), *William Clarke, A Collection of His Writings*. The others were probably written by Clarke, perhaps after editorial consultation.

[2] See below, p. 218.

[3] *P.R.*, i, pp. 400–6 (by Clarke – see note 1 above).

[4] *P.R.*, ii, p. 26.

[5] *P.R.*, ii, p. 216. Cf. Clarke to Mrs Courtney, 5 July 1899 (Courtney Papers, vol. 7, f. 10): '. . . we are launched on an ocean of international capitalism which knows no laws of right & justice'.

tion of the globe is the aim of the money-power, for that power cannot live except by fresh conquests.' [1]

Here was the conspiracy revealed (with a hint, perhaps, of its over-productionist roots: 'it cannot live except by fresh conquests'). Others were engaged in demonstrating that colonies were not a necessary outlet for surplus goods, and in this way: by showing that the markets they were supposed to provide were barren and insignificant.[2] The Increased Armaments Protest Committee, whose secretary was the Ethicist G. H. Perris and whose executive included William Clarke, issued soon after its formation in 1896 a pamphlet specifically replying to the capitalist-imperialist challenge:

> more important than all the other bogeys with which the Jingo Imperialists have frightened, or the pretences with which they have cajoled, us into a 'spirited foreign policy', is the bogey of 'Our Trade in Danger', and the pretence that 'Trade follows the Flag'.[3]

The pamphlet printed statistics to show

> That the total of British Trade has not by any means advanced in proportion or direction with the area and population of the Empire, that in brief, trade does *not* follow the flag...
> That by far the greatest proportion of our trade always has been and still is, not with our colonies, but with foreign countries...
> That the proportion, and in some important cases the amount, of colonial trade is not increasing; and that recent

---

[1] *P.R.*, ii, p. 217.

[2] Frederic Harrison in 1882 had sought to do it in another way, by trying to persuade the working classes that 'These new markets which our great merchants are ever seeking to "open up" only derange the labour market at home, bringing violent gambling in the employment of capital, to be followed by gluts, reaction, and slack trade upon an over-stocked market and an over-stimulated labour population' (quoted in Harrison, *National and Social Problems*, p. 191). In other words, new markets only made the over-production situation worse.

[3] *Empire, Trade and Armaments. An Exposure*, published by the Increased Armaments Protest Committee, 1896, p. 16.

acquisitions which have involved so heavy a political and financial burden, have only infinitesimally increased that trade . . .[1]

and so on. The whole thing was a myth, perpetuated in order to beguile the 'labouring and trading classes' into backing a policy which could only harm their real interests.

The same argument, that trade did not follow the flag, was repeated by Lord Farrer in the pacifist journal *Concord* at the beginning of 1898.[2] This was the prelude to a controversy over the economics of foreign trade which was to rage in the intellectual monthlies throughout the following year, and which was the occasion of the first full statement by Hobson of the 'surplus capital' theory of imperialism.[3]

Like the pamphlet of 1896, this statement came as a *reply* to those men who were putting the commercial argument for expansion from the other side. More specifically, it was a reaction to an immediate threat that this argument might be translated into a practical and dangerous policy.

For at the beginning of 1898 the question of empire and foreign trade was made more urgent and concrete by events in China.

[1] Ibid. p. 17.

[2] *Concord*, Jan 1898, p. 3. Cf. his later article in the *C.R.*, Dec 1898, pp. 810–35.

[3] Hobson himself (*John Ruskin*, pp. 323–5) attributed to Ruskin the detection of 'the distinctly financial origin of modern wars'. He quotes *Fors Clavigera*, letter vii: 'And the guilty thieves of Europe, the real sources of all deadly war in it, are the Capitalists.' But it is clear that both Ruskin and Hobson are referring here to usury rather than to industrial capitalism.

Many writers have neglected Hobson's *C.R.* article of Aug 1898 and assumed that ch. vi of *Imperialism* was the first statement of the economic theory of imperialism. William L. Langer (*Foreign Affairs*, Oct 1935, pp. 102–19) on this assumption wrongly suggested that Hobson 'took over the idea from' Charles Conant, whose article *advocating* imperialism as a means of disposing of surplus capital did not appear (in the *North American Review*) until Sept 1898. Other critics have assumed that the theory arose out of the S. African War. Three writers, M. P. Schneider ('Underconsumption and Imperialism'), and Koebner and Schmidt (*Imperialism*), have correctly attributed its origins to the year 1898, although without explaining the political events which stimulated it.

In November 1897 the Kaiser had seized Kiaochow, and in March of the next year Russia occupied Port Arthur. The British Government faced the dilemma of having to decide between her official policy of abstaining from the 'scramble for China', or demanding some 'territorial or cartographic consolation' [1] there. Balfour had affirmed in January that 'our interests in China are not territorial; they are commercial';[2] but to many the two things were identical. In its commercial aspect the debate over China took the form of a discussion about annexations and free trade, and there were three different points of view. The Liberal opposition attacked the lease by Britain of Wei-hai-wei from China, and favoured the policy of non-intervention in the hope that, despite foreign annexations, the 'Open Door' would be maintained. There was some agitation to persuade the Government to annex, or at least proclaim 'spheres of influence' in, China in order to compensate for loss of trade to Germany and Russia.[3] And between the two extremes there was the position taken up by Hicks-Beach in January: 'We did not regard China as a place for conquest or acquisition,' he said, but 'the Government were absolutely determined, at whatever cost, even – and he wished to speak plainly – if necessary at the cost of war that the door should not be shut'.[4]

It was the old free-trade dilemma once again; a variation on the theme: was 'Free Trade in one country' feasible?

Hicks-Beach appeared to be advocating the protection of free trade by force. To Hobson this was a contradiction in terms. In the August number of the *Contemporary Review* he sought to dispel the illusion that the Open Door policy was in the interests of free trade, and to reinstate the pacifist and internationalist sides of Cobdenism. His starting-point was the foreign policy of the Unionist Government, supported by many Liberals;

[1] Salisbury, Dec 1897, quoted in J. A. S. Grenville, *Lord Salisbury and Foreign Policy*, p. 143.
[2] Ibid. loc. cit.
[3] e.g. 'Our Future Empire in the East', by 'The Author of "1920" ', in the *C.R.*, Aug 1898, pp. 153 ff.
[4] Grenville, op. cit. p. 143; and see the H. of C. debates of 1 Mar and 29 Apr 1898.

particularly in 'the case of China, which is most in evidence'.[1] 'The "Free Trade" pretensions of the open markets policy', he wrote, 'will not bear the slightest scrutiny.'

The working principle it avowedly involves is the supposition that England must be prepared to 'fight for markets', not only for the retention of our colonial possessions, but for new markets and the acquisition of fresh territory, or, at any rate, for the exercise of such influence over weaker nations as shall prevent them from giving to other nations trading advantages denied to us.[2]

The old school of Liberals would not have tolerated this. For Cobden, free trade had a 'larger meaning'. More than a commercial policy, it was 'a phase of social evolution by which, on the one hand, militarism is displaced by industrialism, and, on the other hand, political limits of nationalism yield place to an effective internationalism based upon identity of commercial interests'.[3] To use force in the interests of commerce was 'a direct repudiation both of the logic and the utility of Free Trade'.[4]

Why then had Cobdenism been 'overridden'? Because, said Hobson, of 'three deeply rooted assumptions': that markets 'could only be secured by increased armaments and an extension of the area of empire'; that it was 'sound economy' to 'undergo these risks and these expenses' in order to find markets; and that 'England requires continual expansion of foreign trade'.[5] These were the arguments that were being put forward by the advocates of a forceful commercial policy:

We need investments for British capital, outlets for our superfluous labour and enterprise, markets with 'inferior' races for the disposal of our increasing manufactures. Such a policy admittedly involves risk and expense; but we possess the ships, the men, and the money, and the policy 'pays'.[6]

[1] Hobson, 'Free Trade and Foreign Policy', in the *C.R.*, Aug 1898, p. 169.
[2] Ibid. p. 167.
[3] Ibid. p. 168. Cf. Hobson, *Richard Cobden, the International Man.*
[4] Hobson, 'Free Trade and Foreign Policy', *C.R.*, p. 167.
[5] Ibid. p. 169.   [6] Ibid. p. 171.

But each of these three assumptions was false. The benefits of trade were not to be secured by force. If other countries secured monopolies or set up tariff barriers against us, these could never exclude us from real indirect benefits.[1] Secondly, to seize territories by force in order, professedly, to ensure markets was both bad business - for the cost of the necessary armaments was always greater than the increase in trade – and demonstrably useless. In the last twenty years trade had not followed the flag.[2] Thirdly (and here Hobson went beyond Cobden) it was not true that 'our national prosperity demands a constant expansion of external markets'. Foreign trade was less important than home trade. Home trade was 'a more solid and substantial basis of industrial prosperity', it was 'less amenable to fluctuations arising from commercial and political policies over which we can exercise no control', and its benefits were 'double instead of single, the full advantage which both parties obtain from exchange being kept within the nation'. There was 'an immense potential market' for commodities among our own people; and this market should increase proportionately to the number of goods manufactured. 'With each increase of production is created a corresponding power of consumption.' This market should suffice.[3]

This being so, Hobson asked, why was there pressure for external markets? For he was not going to let the economic system off scot free. In good Cobdenite–Liberal fashion he had denied the necessity for markets forcibly acquired, but this did not mean that the system would work smoothly without them, finding its own natural outlets in obedience to Say's Law. There *was* pressure for markets which was not being satisfied. The home

[1] Ibid. pp. 169–71. Cf. Sir Henry Birchenough (Chairman of B.S.A.C.) in *C19th*, June 1897, who had also claimed that foreign annexations, even with tariff barriers, did not injure trade.

[2] Hobson, 'Free Trade and Foreign Policy', *C.R.*, pp. 171–6.

[3] Ibid. pp. 176–7. As early as 1894 the Positivist E. S. Beesly had made a similar assertion: that 'all the foreign markets in the world are not worth as much, even from the material point of view, as the home market furnished by a well-paid, prosperous working class' (*Positivist Review*, Feb 1894, pp. 41–2). It does not follow from this, of course, that all foreign markets were dispensable – the point Hobson was urging.

market, he had affirmed, *should* suffice: but it did not. Why not?
For his answer he turned back to his old underconsumptionist
heresy:

> Though a potential market exists within the United Kingdom
> for all the 'goods' that are produced by the nation, there is
> not an 'effective' demand, because those who have the power
> to demand commodities for consumption have not the desire,
> since their material needs are amply satisfied, while those
> who have the desire have not the power.[1]

The upper and middle classes, not wanting themselves to con-
sume, and not finding a sufficient home market among the under-
paid workers, 'are compelled to struggle with the classes of other
nations in the same predicament for foreign markets, which
seem to them limited in extent at any given time'. Hence the
'large surplus of our national income which, being needed neither
for home consumption nor for capital in home industries, seeks
foreign investments'.[2] And this, he suggested, was the power
behind foreign expansion.

> It is possible, indeed, that the growing pressure of the need
> for foreign investments must be regarded as the most potent
> and direct influence in our foreign policy. Our surplus pro-
> ducts, which the working classes cannot buy and the
> wealthier classes do not wish to buy, must find customers
> among foreign nations, and, since those who sell them do
> not even desire to consume their equivalent in existing
> foreign goods, they must lie in foreign countries as loans or
> other permanent investments. . . . Thus, in the first resort, it
> is the excessive purchasing power of the well-to-do classes
> which, by requiring foreign investments, forces the opening
> up of foreign markets, and uses the public purse for the
> purposes of private profit-making.[3]

The first cause of imperialism therefore was surplus capital,
accumulated because of domestic underconsumption, which was
the result of maldistribution of wealth: and the solution could
only be the radical one of a 'juster and more equal distribution of

[1] Ibid. pp. 177–8.
[2] Hobson, 'Free Trade and Foreign Policy', *C.R.*, p. 178.   [3] Ibid. p. 178.

wealth'.[1] The alternative lay between reactionary imperialism, and social reform.

Hobson's suggested explanation for the phenomenon of imperialism, and his solution, were passed over or ignored at the time. After all, people were not unfamiliar with the charge that imperialism was 'mercenary' and 'stock-jobbing', and Hobson's view of the Social Problem could be disregarded as either eccentric or revolutionary. The discussion which followed in the monthly reviews concerned itself with the question which was regarded at the time as the most pressing one, and to which Hobson had devoted the greater part of his article: the problem of whether 'trade followed the flag'.

Each stage of the 'economic theory of imperialism' had, however, been clearly worked out in the last few pages of this article. It was to be given a dramatic and tangible illustration – and also a new emphasis – by the events of the following year, restated just before the Boer War by Hobson's fellow rationalist J. M. Robertson,[2] and enlarged and elaborated in *Imperialism: a Study*. But the Boer War merely confirmed Hobson in the opinion he had formed in 1898. The origin of his 'economic theory' lies, not in South Africa, but in the China crisis of 1898, in which imperialism had been 'stripped bare of all motives and methods save those of distinctly commercial origin'.[3] It was formulated under the pressure of an assault on free trade, made more acute by the threat of a partition of China; it was suggested, in the first place, by the demands of businessmen for markets for their surplus products and fields for their surplus investments, and by the explicit statement of the Colonial Secretary that the motive behind imperial policy was the expansion of commerce; and it was incorporated into a seemingly coherent, all-embracing economic ideology by Hobson's concern with the Social Problem and his underconsumptionist 'heresy'.

[1] Ibid. pp. 178–9.   [2] Robertson, *Patriotism and Empire*, pp. 162–201.
[3] Hobson, *Imperialism*, p. 328.

V. SOUTH AFRICA, THE CONSPIRACY THEORY

In the summer of 1899 Hobson was sent to South Africa as the special correspondent there of the *Manchester Guardian*.[1] For the first time he came into direct contact with some of those politico-economic forces which he had described in a speculative fashion the year before; and the result was that the emphasis of his thinking changed. His despatches to the paper during the autumn, and the covering letters he wrote to its editor C. P. Scott, reveal the development of a new commitment not to an 'economic' theory of imperialism, for he was committed to this before, but to a 'conspiracy' theory which was, in 1901, to be grafted on to that economic theory to give it a different, more sinister complexion.

His earliest despatches to the *Manchester Guardian* - written in August and appearing in the paper in September[2] - took the orthodox Liberal anti-War line: condemnation of the High Commissioner ('I regard Milner as bent on war,' he wrote to Scott),[3] denial of the so-called 'Afrikander conspiracy' and of the 'suzerainty' claim,[4] sympathy with the Boers' suspicions of British intentions,[5] and the assertion that the Uitlander grievances - though to some extent justified ('There is evidently much ground for charges of corruption and maladministration')[6] - were nevertheless grossly exaggerated. These all related to the rights and wrongs of the situation; but Hobson was also much

---

[1] It was L. T. Hobhouse, then a leader-writer on the *M.G.*, who persuaded Scott to send Hobson out (Hobson, *Confessions*, p. 60). Hobson's contract with the paper was drawn up in July: he was to be paid at the rate of £300 p.a., plus expenses, and in addition £100 was paid him 'to cover certain lectures and literary engagements I must cancel and for "moral and intellectual" damages connected with the postponement of two books which are now in the press and for which it is really important for me to secure an early publication' (Hobson to Scott, 15 July, and Scott to Hobson 16 July 1899; Hobson–Scott correspondence, *Guardian* archives).

[2] Hobson's short news-cables appeared in Aug and Sept; the first long despatch appeared 4 Sept. The bulk of these latter were published as a book in Mar 1900 under the title *The War in South Africa: Its Causes and Effects* (pt. i).

[3] Hobson to Scott, Cape Town, n.d.; and cf. *M.G.*, 9 Sept 1899.

[4] *M.G.*, 3, 7, 8 Nov 1899 (*The War in South Africa*, pp. 99–118).

[5] *The War in South Africa*, pp. 146–54.   [6] Hobson to Scott, 2 Sept 1899.

interested in the causes of the quarrel, and he set himself to try to untangle the complex of motives that lay underneath.

What led him to the view that it was a 'conspiracy' on the part of the Rand capitalists was a trip to Johannesburg which he made at the end of August. Earlier he had been convinced that 'This outrage business' – the more extreme accusations which the 'jingo' party were making against the Boers – was 'wholly fabricated', 'simply one act in the press conspiracy';[1] but where the conspiracy originated he was uncertain. From Johannesburg he wrote on 27 August: 'There is no great Uitlander movement, the League is an unimportant factor excepting for "press" purposes, the Uitlander Council has men of influence on it, but I think the whole business has been worked up by a small number of men.'[2] By the same mail he sent a despatch to the *Guardian* describing the strong capitalist, and in particular the Jewish, factor in the town.[3] But he was unwilling as yet to draw any more striking conclusion. In his letter to Scott he continued: 'I doubt how far it is to be regarded as a capitalist agitation, there is a good deal of evidence to show that the big capitalists of the Rand are indifferent or simulate indifference. This however is a matter for probing.'[4] So he probed; and a week later he had made up his mind. From the Rand Club in Johannesburg – 'the palatial headquarters of the "helots"' – he wrote to Scott on 2 September:

> I am convinced that the Government under a free admission of Uitlanders will be as corrupt as this one. The bulk of the Uitlanders excepting the actual miners I believe to be Jews ... German Jews who have been in England and figure as British subjects. Many of them are the veriest scum of Europe. The entire mining industry, with the partial exception of the Consolidated Gold Fields (Rhodes) is in their hands, the Dynamite Monopoly, the illicit Liquor Traffic are theirs, they and Rhodes own or control the press,

[1] Hobson to Scott, Cape Town, n.d.
[2] Hobson to Scott, Johannesburg, 27 Aug 1899.
[3] *M.G.*, 28 Sept 1899 (*The War in South Africa*, pp. 10–14).
[4] Hobson to Scott, Johannesburg, 27 Aug 1899.

manipulate the slave market, and run the chief commercial businesses both in Johannesburg and Pretoria. These men will rig the politics when they have the franchise. Many of them have taken English names and the extent of the Jew power is thus partially concealed. I am not exaggerating one whit. I think I can prove this.[1]

Here were the conspirators: the German Jews of the Rand.[2] The allegation was not new, but for Hobson the definite and tangible connexion between economic pressure and political action was. He made very little of it while he was in South Africa – by the time his later despatches reached England the pages of the *Manchester Guardian* were full of news of the first campaigns of the War, to the exclusion of all else. But on his return (his place was taken by a military correspondent) he pressed the anti-capitalist charge with renewed vigour.

Hobson's return to London in October was greeted with the verbal and physical abuse which often befell notorious 'pro-Boers' in that City during the War.[3] Popular jingoism was a phenomenon whose worst effects he had escaped while he was away, and his encounter with it now stimulated him during the next two years to launch a bitter attack on it and to integrate

---

[1] Hobson to Scott, 2 Sept 1899.

[2] Hobson was attacked for his *Judenhetze* by a contemporary, the Rev. J. Guinness Rogers, in *C.R.*, May 1900, pp. 616–17; and his strictures on the Jews have been emphasised by such modern writers as Harvey Mitchell ('Hobson Revisited', in *J.H.I.*, vol. xxvi, no. 3 (July–Sept 1965), pp. 398–404), and Koebner and Schmidt (*Imperialism*, pp. 226–7). The letter quoted above, attacking the Rand Jews in terms stronger than he used in his books, seems to confirm their view. It is difficult to decide where anti-capitalism ends and anti-semitism begins. But it might be more charitable to believe that, in the context of the S. African situation, Hobson's main purpose in mentioning the race of Jewish financiers was to stress the fact that their interests, and hence the gains which would accrue from a British victory, were not, as the pro-War public supposed, British, but 'cosmopolitan'. It may or may not be significant that one of Hobson's closest friends was the Jew Herbert Samuel. Cf. Arnold White's *Efficiency and Empire*, pp. 78–81, which condemns the same 'capitalist Jews' in S. Africa as Hobson, but from an extreme Fabian-type imperialist viewpoint.

[3] Information supplied by Mrs Mabel Scott.

jingoism into his analysis of imperialism. In 1900 a series of articles appeared in the *Ethical World* which were published the next year under the title *The Psychology of Jingoism*.[1] The 'psychology' contained in this work was based upon Le Bon's *Psychologie des Foules*;[2] but its chief importance lies in its scathing account of the forces of irrationalism which seemed to him to be dominant in Britain during the War. His language was intemperate: 'The modern newspaper is a Roman arena, a Spanish bull-ring, and an English prize-fight rolled into one';[3] 'A twelve-month's debauch in these ancient and abandoned stews of savage lust has set back the dial of civilization more points than we care to contemplate.'[4] But he had much justification for his anger; and all the more, it seemed to him, when he considered to what ends this 'coarse patriotism' had been put:

> This conjunction of the forces of the press, the platform, and the pulpit, has succeeded in monopolising the mind of the British public, and imposing a policy calculated not to secure the interests of the British Empire, but to advance the private, political, and business interests of a small body of men who have exploited the race feeling in South Africa and the Imperialist sentiment of England.[5]

Whatever the professed causes of the War, we were in fact fighting, he claimed, 'in order to place a small international oligarchy of mineowners and speculators in power at Pretoria'.[6] These were the men he had discovered in Johannesburg; mainly Jews – 'for the Jews are *par excellence* the international financiers' – and 'of Continental origin'.[7]

> Not Hamburg, not Vienna, not Frankfort, but Johannesburg is the New Jerusalem . . . the industrial and agricultural

---

[1] *Ethical World*, mid-July 1900 to early 1901; *The Psychology of Jingoism*.
[2] On Le Bon, see above, p. 182, fn. 4. Harvey Mitchell, op. cit., makes a comparison between *The Psychology of Jingoism* and J. Schumpeter's 'Sociology of Imperialism', in *Imperialism and Social Classes*.
[3] *Psychology of Jingoism*, p. 29.   [4] Ibid. p. 40.
[5] Ibid. p. 138.   [6] *The War in South Africa*, p. 197.
[7] Hobson, 'Capitalism and Imperialism in South Africa', in *C.R.*, Jan 1900, p. 4.

future of the Transvaal is already hypothecated to this small ring of financial foreigners. . . . Englishmen will surely do well to recognise that the economic and political destinies of South Africa are, and seem likely to remain, in the hands of men most of whom are foreigners by origin, whose trade is finance, and whose trade interests are not chiefly British.[1]

This highly organised group of international speculators, he said, were concerned only to increase their profits by securing a regular supply of cheap – and probably forced – native labour.[2] To do this they had to become the political as well as the economic rulers of the Transvaal gold-fields.[3] To this end they had bought up the organs of public opinion in South Africa, by means of which they could foster race hatred there and, indirectly, in England. 'South Africa presents a unique example of a large press, owned, controlled, and operated in recent times by a small body of men with the direct aim of bringing about a conflict which shall serve their business interests.' [4] Chamberlain, therefore, was not a 'free agent'. 'The generals of finance well know that he is their instrument and not they his.' [5] In South Africa capitalism was 'using' imperialism.

Out of this working example of capitalistic imperialism in South Africa, Hobson formulated a general principle.

The full significance of this evil business in South Africa is only understood when it is recognised as a most dramatic instance of the play of modern forces which are world-wide in their scope and revolutionary in their operation. Those who see one set of problems in Egypt, another in China, a third in South America, a fourth in South Africa, or trace their connexion merely through the old political relations

---

[1] Hobson, *The War in South Africa*, pp. 190, 194, 197. (This chapter first appeared in the *Speaker*, Nov 1899.) Cf. 'Capitalism and Imperialism in South Africa', *C.R.*, pp. 3, 5.

[2] Hobson, 'A Reply to Mr Hosken', *C.R.*, May 1900, p. 661; and *The War in South Africa*, pp. 230–8, 284–5.

[3] 'Capitalism and Imperialism in South Africa', *C.R.*, p. 5.

[4] *The War in South Africa*, p. 206; and cf. *The Psychology of Jingoism*, pp. 107–24.

[5] 'Capitalism and Imperialism in South Africa', *C.R.*, p. 16.

between nations, will be subjected to a rough awakening as
their calculations, based on this old Separatist view, are
everywhere upset. Without seeking to ignore or to disparage
the special factors, physical, economic, and political, which
rightly assign a certain peculiarity to each case, I would insist
upon the supreme importance of recognising the dominance
everywhere exercised by the new confederacy and interplay
of two sets of forces, conveniently designated by the titles
International Capitalism and Imperialism.[1]

In this partnership capitalism was the dominant partner; and its
nucleus was the financier. Round the nucleus there gathered
'certain other allied economic interests': the iron and ship-
building trades; most of the export trades which were 'won over by
fallacious appeals to the Trade which "follows the Flag" '; the
armed services; the aristocracy, seeking positions for their sons;
and the investing public.[2] These interests harnessed for their own
purposes such diverse forces as popular 'race-lust' and genuine
humanitarianism;[3] and together they hoodwinked governments
into implementing the need of international finance to expand
political boundaries 'so as to cover the new areas of economic
interest established by its individual members'.[4] The amount of
political control which finance could exercise over a country
varied according to that country's political strength. In South
America the control was real, but concealed. In South Africa it
was more blatant.

None of this line of reasoning was unique. A large number of
'pro-Boer' Liberals were saying – and some of them had been
saying it before Hobson went to South Africa – that the South
African War was a financiers' war, and pointing to the same
'conspiracy' on the Rand. And William Clarke in the *Progressive
Review* had, a short time before, attributed Western imperialism
in general to the 'international money-power'.[5] For Hobson,
however, the emphasis was new. The British traders and investors
who had surpluses to export were now on the periphery, instead
of at the centre of the imperial nucleus; and the economic forces

[1] Hobson, 'Capitalism and Imperialism in South Africa', *C.R.*, p. 1.
[2] Ibid. p. 16.   [3] Ibid. pp. 15–16.   [4] Ibid. p. 2.   [5] See above, p. 192.

directing foreign policy were now international and sinister instead of domestic and social.

Hobson's visit to South Africa had not begotten the 'economic theory' of imperialism. But its significance was nonetheless considerable. When he sailed for Cape Town, Hobson had seen imperialism as the product of an unjust economic system, which was 'compelling' manufacturers and capitalists to export abroad what would, in a more equitable ordering of society, be consumed at home. His criticism was levelled at the system; to a certain extent individual capitalists were merely the innocent tools of a situation they themselves had not created, or for which they could take only collective responsibility. When he returned, however, the emphasis had changed. For a time he ignored the deeper social causes of imperialism. In the books and articles he wrote in 1899, 1900 and 1901, 'underconsumption' is scarcely mentioned; instead he dealt almost exclusively with the more tangible connexion between capitalism and war. This led him to concentrate his fire on a more limited target: a small group of 'cosmopolitan Jew' financiers. His criticism grew more hostile as its object became more concrete; the problem became more sinister as he talked in terms of a 'conspiracy' instead of impersonal economic forces; and a possible inconsistency, or at least an ambiguity, was set up between two different kinds of economic motivation.

CHAPTER SEVEN

Imperialism: a Study

ALL the different elements of Hobson's imperial theory were now at hand. It remained to draw them together into a more coherent whole. *Imperialism: a Study*,[1] published in the autumn of 1902, combined, in its two main sections, the two approaches to imperialism which Hobson had formulated during the previous four years. Its first part, 'The Economics of Imperialism', elaborated his theory of the causation of expansion. Part II, 'The Politics of Imperialism', dealt with the ethical justification of empire. The whole was designed, he stated in the preface, to help that minority of people 'who are content neither to float along the tide of political opportunism nor to submit to the shove of some blind "destiny", but who desire to understand political forces in order that they may direct them.'[2] His faith in rationalism – in the power of man to apply his reason to the task of bettering his environment[3] – made any notion of 'scientific' or economic determinism repellent to him. Much of his writing was concerned with attacking the various forms of Social Darwinist or 'manifest destiny' doctrines promulgated by the imperialists;[4] and equally repugnant were the fatalistic conclusions about the power of economic forces which at least one contemporary writer read into Hobson's own works.[5] *Imperialism*, therefore, aimed firstly to demonstrate the irrationality of expansion: to show that, by any rational criteria, imperialism was not profitable or beneficial to

[1] References are to the 1st ed. (1902) except where otherwise stated.
[2] Hobson, *Imperialism*, pp. v–vi.   [3] See above, p. 173.
[4] See *Imperialism*, pt. ii, ch. ii; and *Ethical World*, July 1899.
[5] See Hobson, letter in the *Speaker*, 5 July 1902, replying to Dr Crozier in the *Fortnightly Review*, July 1902.

any nation or race, least of all to those in Britain who believed that they gained by it. Secondly, it set out to show why such an irrational policy was supported so enthusiastically and unanimously by those it harmed.

> Seeing that the Imperialism of the last three decades is clearly condemned as a business policy, in that at enormous expense it has procured a small, bad, unsafe increase of markets, and has jeopardised the entire wealth of the nation in rousing the strong resentment of other nations, we may ask, 'How is the British nation induced to embark upon such unsound business?' [1]

Thirdly, it tried to predict the disastrous consequences, in the form of protection, war, social reaction and economic depression, which would arise if this policy were persisted in. And lastly it prescribed (with little hope of its application) a remedy. Here is the argument as it was finally elaborated.

I. THE ECONOMIC ARGUMENT

Hobson conducted his analysis of the economic unprofitability of imperialism on much the same lines as his *Contemporary Review* paper of August 1898. The idea that Britain needed markets for her surplus products and for her expanding population, and that to get these it was necessary to annex more territory because other countries were doing so and pre-empting the markets of the world was, he said, a 'delusion'.[2] Britain was not overpopulated; and, if she were, the new tropical territories did not provide a significant contribution to the area of emigration.[3] The same could be said for commerce. First of all, it was one of 'the commonplaces of the economics of Free Trade, the plainest lessons of enlightened common sense' [4] that even if foreign markets fell into the hands of other protectionist nations, the indirect gains accruing to Britain would still be considerable. Secondly, trade did not follow the flag. Hobson published figures to show that, during the period

[1] Hobson, *Imperialism*, p. 51.
[2] Ibid. p. 76.   [3] Ibid. pp. 47–8.   [4] Ibid. p. 72.

1870–1900, imperial trade was a small and diminishing proportion of our total commerce; that trade with foreign countries was increasing to a far greater extent; and that, of our imperial trade, that with the new tropical acquisitions was 'the smallest, least progressive, and most fluctuating in quantity'.[1] Against any *absolute* increase in colonial trade must be set the expenditure on armaments which an expansionist policy had stimulated. The figures spoke for themselves: military expenditure had risen much more sharply than the colonial trade it was designed to extend and protect; the whole thing was 'nothing else than a huge business blunder'.[2] And more than this: foreign trade as a whole was unimportant, compared with domestic trade. It was only a small proportion of the 'real income'[3] of the nation, and this proportion, per head of the population, was diminishing.[4] If we lost foreign markets, we would not lose a proportionate amount of our income. The assumption that home demand was a fixed amount, and that goods in excess of this must either find foreign markets or remain unsold, was false. 'There is no natural limit to the quantity of wealth which can be produced, exchanged, and consumed within Great Britain except the limits imposed by restricted natural resources and the actual condition of the arts of industry', provided that 'the productive power is disposed in industries which meet the rising demands of the consumer'.[5] The domestic market, therefore, was adequate; if the system was working correctly at home, so that supply and demand went hand in hand, there was no need for foreign markets.[6]

Why, then, did Britain embark on such unbusinesslike ventures? The reason was not what Norman Angell was to call 'sentiment'.[7] 'We must put aside the merely sentimental diagnosis which explains wars or other national blunders by outbursts of

[1] Ibid. I ii.   [2] Ibid. pp. 69–70.   [3] Ibid. p. 30.   [4] Ibid. pp. 33–4.
[5] Ibid. p. 32. In the 2nd ed. (1905) this provision was modified slightly: there was no limit, provided that 'the effective demand for the goods that are produced is so distributed that every increase in production stimulates a corresponding increase of consumption' (p. 26).
[6] In the 2nd ed. Hobson made an exception in the case of exports which paid for necessary imports which could not be produced at home (pp. 29–30).
[7] See below, pp. 221–2.

H

patriotic animosity or errors of statecraft.'[1] Hobson would not accept such irrational explanations. Imperialism must appeal to the rational interest of someone; if not the nation as a whole, then to some group within the nation who could wield political power. South Africa had revealed to him the identity of this group. 'The only possible answer is that the business interests of the nation as a whole are subordinated to those of certain sectional interests that usurp control of the national resources and use them for their private gain.'[2] These sectional interests could be resolved into three 'well-organised' groups. There were those special commercial, industrial and political interests he had listed before:[3] the arms and shipping industries, certain exporters, and aristocrats seeking careers, who were 'able to make a definite impression upon politics' through chambers of commerce, their parliamentary representatives, and organised pressure groups such as the Imperial South African Association.[4] Secondly, there were the investors who were unable to find fields for investment at home, and demanded government protection for their investments abroad.[5] He showed how foreign investment had grown side by side with the 'period of energetic Imperialism',[6] and the enormous capital value of colonial loans. Modern British foreign policy, he deduced from this, had been 'primarily a struggle for profitable markets of investment'.[7] But in the middle of the web lay the financial houses, 'the central ganglion of international capitalism', composed chiefly of 'men of a single and peculiar race', closely organised, and providing for the other diffuse economic interests their 'central guiding and directing force'.[8] Their stake in imperialism was double: as investors, and (chiefly) as financial speculators.[9] It was they who guided policy:

> it is true that the motor-power of Imperialism is not chiefly financial: finance is rather the governor of the imperial engine, directing the energy and determining its work: it does not constitute the fuel of the engine, neither does it generate the power. . . . An ambitious statesman, a frontier

[1] Hobson, *Imperialism*, p. 52.   [2] Ibid. p. 51.
[3] See above, p. 205.   [4] *Imperialism*, pp. 53–5.   [5] Ibid. pp. 56–61.
[6] Ibid. p. 57.   [7] Ibid. p. 60.   [8] Ibid. pp. 63–4, 68.   [9] Ibid. p. 64.

soldier, an overzealous missionary, a pushing trader, may suggest or even initiate a step of imperial expansion, may assist in educating patriotic public opinion to the urgent need of some fresh advance, but the final determination rests with the financial power.[1]

In a later chapter Hobson described how this financial clique exercised its control over foreign policy. It enlisted the support of statesmen and politicians by associating them directly in their business schemes; and by appealing to the conservative instincts of the possessing classes, 'whose vested interests and class dominance are best preserved by diverting the currents of political energy from domestic on to foreign politics'.[2] It secured the acquiescence of 'the body of a nation in a course of policy fatal to its own true interests' by appealing to humanitarian motives, the mission of 'civilisation', but 'chiefly by playing upon the primitive instincts of the race' – the 'spirit of adventure' and the 'animal lust of struggle' (exhibited, said Hobson, in such degenerate forms of spectator sport as professional football).[3] The financiers had under their thumb every means of influencing public opinion. They controlled the Press either directly or through the influence they wielded as controllers of the advertising 'upon which its living depends';[4] they influenced the political machine by their financial contributions,[5] and even the Church and schools by endowments and other monetary contributions.[6] 'He who pays the piper calls the tune.'

Thus do the industrial and financial forces of Imperialism, operating through the party, the press, the church, the school, mould public opinion and public policy by the false idealization of those primitive lusts of struggle, domination, and acquisitiveness which have survived throughout the eras of peaceful industrial order and whose stimulation is needed once again for the work of imperial aggression, expansion, and the forceful exploitation of lower races.[7]

[1] Ibid. pp. 66–7.   [2] Ibid. pp. 102–3, 224.
[3] Ibid. pp. 225–7. Cf. E. Ensor, 'The Football Madness', in C.R., Nov 1898, p. 751.
[4] Hobson, Imperialism, p. 228.   [5] Ibid. p. 229.
[6] Ibid. pp. 229–31.   [7] Ibid. pp. 233–4.

By all these means these men made themselves 'the prime deter-
minants of imperial policy'.

Yet this policy had been shown conclusively (said Hobson) to
be unbusinesslike from the point of view of the national interest,
and still people deluded themselves that 'the use of national force
to secure new markets by annexing fresh tracts of territory is a
sound and necessary policy for an advanced industrial country
like Great Britain'. It was possible for imperialists to argue con-
vincingly that ' "We must have markets for our growing manufactures, we must have new outlets for the investment of our
surplus capital and for the energies of the adventurous surplus of
our population." ' [1] And such arguments were, Hobson saw, not
entirely irrational: for there was, in Europe and America in 1902,
a surplus of products and capital. The United States provided a
clear illustration of the way in which over-production forced
price-cutting, which led to the formation of great trusts and
combines; these further limited the amount of capital which
could be employed within the country, and increased the profits
out of which fresh savings and capital would spring: the result
was pressure for markets and fields for investment. Europe could
only satisfy these demands to a limited extent, for in general
she could provide for herself, and so 'Messrs. Rockefeller,
Pierpoint Morgan, and their associates', who 'needed Imperialism',
used President Theodore Roosevelt to satisfy them elsewhere, in
China, South America and the Pacific.[2] Similarly, in Europe
(without the same degree of 'trustification'), over-production and
surplus capital 'force Great Britain, Germany, Holland, France to
place larger and larger portions of their economic resources outside the area of their present political domain, and then stimulate
a policy of political expansion so as to take in the new areas'.[3] The
facts, he wrote in the *Fortnightly Review*, are beyond dispute.

In Great Britain, Germany, America, France, Belgium,
Holland, Switzerland, the power of producing goods grows

[1] Ibid. p. 76.
[2] Ibid. pp. 78–85. Cf. the 1906 ed. of *The Evolution of Modern Capitalism*,
pp. 256–61, on American trusts and cartels.
[3] Hobson, *Imperialism*, p. 85.

faster than the needs of consumers as exhibited in effective demand, with the result of a continual tendency to over-production ... the trading classes in a nation find that markets which ought in theory to be unlimited are rigidly limited, that they cannot sell all they can produce and wish to sell, that, in a word, there are not enough markets to go round.[1]

The need for financial expansion, therefore, was not an illusion. There was some justification for the claim that 'Imperialism is ... not a choice, but a necessity'.[2]

Where Hobson differed from these imperialist exporters (and from Lenin) was in his denial of the inevitability of this problem. Imperialism was not the only way out of the dilemma of over-production. Equilibrium could be restored between production and consumption, 'If the consuming public in this country raised its standard of consumption to keep pace with every rise of productive powers.' [3] What, in fact, was required was *the fabrication of conditions in which Say's Law would hold good.* For 'With everything that is produced a consuming power is born';[4] the home market was capable of indefinite expansion, if only the present competitive price system were replaced by a system under which goods were distributed 'on a conscious basis of the satis-faction of human needs'.[5] Over-production and over-saving, and hence imperialism, had as their 'tap-root' the maldistribution of wealth,[6] which was also the root of the Social Problem.[7] The solutions for both were one and the same: either an 'extensive', militaristic and ultimately disastrous policy of imperial expansion, or the 'intensive' cultivation of domestic resources, on the basis of a better distribution of wealth.

[1] *Fortnightly Review*, 1 Mar 1902, p. 436.
[2] Hobson, *Imperialism*, p. 78.   [3] Ibid. p. 86.   [4] Ibid. p. 87.
[5] Ibid. 3rd ed. (1938), Introduction, p. xvii.
[6] See ibid. (1st ed.), pp. 88–90.   [7] See above, p. 168.

II. INTEREST AND SENTIMENT

Hobson's theory of imperialism has been superseded by Lenin's; and much criticism of Hobson has, inevitably, been coloured by the use to which Lenin put his economic thesis. But while it is true that the more general significance of *Imperialism: a Study* lies in its contribution to neo-Marxian thought, and that its impact was never so great in any other form, from the point of view of an understanding of English Radical ideology in the early twentieth century it must be studied quite apart from its later modifications. Lenin took from Hobson (with generous acknowledgments) those arguments which related imperialism to capitalism, and moulded them into a theory identifying imperialism with late, or declining, capitalism. He introduced into it the factor of inevitability, and systematised the whole argument into a deterministic form which excluded any possibility of rational choice. Capitalism, he claimed, *had* to over-save; if of its own free will it applied remedial action, 'it would not be capitalism'.[1] Imperialism was not (as Kautsky had maintained) a policy *preferred* by financial capitalism;[2] it was its inevitable 'monopoly stage'.[3] This went far beyond Hobson's argument. Hobson's 'economic interpretation of history' did not conceive at all of 'economics' in the terms implied by Lenin – as an all-powerful underlying historical force against whose laws the actions of men were impotent.[4] For a clear comprehension of his theory, and of its place in the development of Radical 'anti-imperialism' in Britain, it is necessary to establish exactly what Hobson did mean by economic imperialism, and the reasons behind his adoption of this interpretation. This, in turn, may give

[1] V. I. Lenin, *Imperialism, The Highest Stage of Capitalism*, in *Selected Works*, vol. i, pp. 759, 801.
[2] Ibid. i 783–90.
[3] Ibid. i 781.
[4] Hobson cites the Italian economist Achille Loria in support of his contention that economic forces are a powerful determinant in politics (*Imperialism*, pp. 61, 78). But Loria was an economic determinist in the Marxian pattern, and a little later Hobson makes it clear that he cannot follow him quite so far along the materialist path. See Hobson, 'The Possibilities of Popular Progress', in *University Review*, June 1905.

an indication of the basis upon which a judgment of *Imperialism* should be formed.

In reality, there are two 'economic theories' contained in *Imperialism*: a 'conspiracy' theory, and an economic 'model'. The first was the product of Hobson's visit to South Africa, and, except perhaps for his wider application of it, it is no different from the line which other left-wing Liberals had been taking over South Africa for some years. It also bears a strong resemblance to that earlier Liberal approach which tended to see all political problems in terms of 'the interests' versus 'the democracy'. This conspiracy theory attributed to a financial clique the manipulation of imperial sentiment in the interests of their own selfish greed. But this had no essential, integral connexion with the second, more original theory, which placed imperialism at the top of a logically constructed and carefully integrated economic model having at its roots the maldistribution of income. Although Hobson put the financiers at the centre of the imperialist web, they lay outside the bounds of his underconsumption theory. It was not necessary to explain their actions in terms of economic pressures: simple human wickedness would suffice. When the 'cosmopolitan Jews' of the Rand forced Britain into war, they did so because they wanted bigger profits, not because they needed fields for investment. The financiers, therefore, Hobson could strongly condemn on moral grounds; the industrialists and investors, forced into a course of action by circumstances beyond their control, he had, to a certain extent, to sympathise with.

The ambiguity of Hobson's conception of the relationship between these two groups – the international financiers and the over-capitalised investors – has given rise to some misapprehension. Partly, of course, the difficulty lies in the singular unhelpfulness of his 'imperial engine' metaphor.[1] But it also arises from his use of the term 'finance': sometimes it can be taken to cover the whole field of Stock Exchange operations; more often it refers only to his international clique. This ambiguity is due largely to the circumstances in which *Imperialism* was written: in

[1] See above, p. 210.

the first place it was a piece of political propaganda directed against specific contemporary events. It was written in the form of separate articles contributed to a number of different journals: chapter IV on the financiers appeared first in the *Speaker* in November 1901, chapter VI on the under-consumption thesis in the *Contemporary Review* in August the next year. Only later, and probably hurriedly, was it patched together in the form of a book with some pretensions to logical consistency. Hobson's argument in *Imperialism*, in fact, is less carefully constructed than many of his other works. The thesis has little of the clear logical development which marks, for example, *The Evolution of Modern Capitalism*, and its style is more virulent and acrimonious. This is not to say that the argument is inconsistent or self-contradictory: only that, on a careful reading of *Imperialism*, it reveals itself to be less simple and 'scientific' than some commentators have made it appear.

Imperialism has been forced into a mould for which (although by his frequent overstatement and ambiguity he must take much of the responsibility) Hobson did not intend it. Those criticisms, therefore, which have tried to disprove his theory by demonstrating, for instance, that there was no close relationship between the export of capital and the area of British expansion after 1870 are, because they over-systematise Hobson's thought, largely irrelevant. It is true that Hobson failed to prove that, because overseas investment and imperial expansion increased simultaneously in the late nineteenth century,[1] there was a causal connexion between them. It is true, perhaps, that he was guilty of an 'intellectual conjuring trick'[2] in implying (though never explicitly stating) that the coincidence of the two rising graphs pointed such a connexion. But statistics which demonstrate that sums invested in the new tropical areas of the Empire 'were quite marginal to the total overseas investment'[3] do not, in themselves, show Hobson to be wrong. Hobson never denied that most

[1] Hobson, *Imperialism*, p. 57.
[2] D. K. Fieldhouse, ' "Imperialism": An Historiographical Revision', in the *E.H.R.*, vol. xiv, no. 2 (1961), p. 190.
[3] Ibid. p. 199.

foreign investment still went to the United States, South America and the old white dominions.[1] It was not necessary to his argument to do so. His purpose in quoting overseas investment figures was to demonstrate what was undeniable: that this investment had doubled in twenty years, that capitalists therefore were looking around for foreign markets, and that this suggested (what was more dubious but difficult to disprove)[2] that there was pressure at home for such external markets. While there were opportunities elsewhere, capitalists would send their money there; in more highly developed countries there was no need for government protection in the form of political annexation.

> The policy which definitely aims at expanding the British Empire so as to cover all new areas of British economic interest cannot, of course, be consistently pursued. For the strongest forms of international capitalism consist of investments in powerful civilised states with which no interference upon such grounds is possible.[3]

But some of this capital went to 'small, decadent, or new countries', and it was in these areas that 'alien investments exercise a dominant power in foreign policy'.[4] It mattered little how 'marginal' this amount of capital was; from the point of view of the political and imperial aspect of financial expansion, it was sufficient.

The same point which Hobson made about trade – that the proportion which went to the new colonies was small and, from the point of view of the nation as a whole, insignificant – could be applied also to capital; and the same moral could be drawn. There was pressure from below to export a 'surplus', some of it into new fields.[5] Capitalism as a whole was not interested in these marginal

---

[1] Cf. Harvey Mitchell, 'Hobson Revisited', *J.H.I.*, p. 412.

[2] The alternative, of course, is that investors were *attracted* by higher interest rates abroad. See Strachey, *The End of Empire*, pp. 113 ff., for a discussion of this.

[3] Hobson, 'Capitalism and Imperialism in South Africa', *C.R.*, p. 2.

[4] Ibid. loc. cit.

[5] Fieldhouse (op. cit. p. 199) quotes these overseas investment figures for 1911: U.S.A. £688m.; S. America £587m.; Canada £372m.; Australasia £380m.; India and Ceylon £365m.; S. Africa £351m.; W. Africa £29m.; the Straits and Malay States £22m.; other British possessions £33m.

areas, but those traders and investors who *were*, were organised in such a way as to enable them to influence foreign policy in their own minority interests and against the interests of the nation.

This is where Hobson's 'conspiracy' theory is, for him, necessary to bolster up the deficiencies in his 'economic model'. Four years after the publication of *Imperialism* he interpolated into his *Evolution of Modern Capitalism* a section dealing with this small financial conspiratorial clique. The development of industry had, he said, 'favoured the segregation of a financial from a more general capitalist class', and had given it 'a larger and more profitable control over the course of industry'.[1] Cosmopolitan finance, or 'cross-ownership among nations', was not in itself a bad thing. Indeed, he went so far as to say that it was 'by far the most substantial guarantee of the development of a general policy of peace. Economic internationalism is the precursor and the moulder of political internationalism'.[2] But the more general interest of international capitalism was flouted by the minority interest of a small but powerful class within it.

> This obvious result of the community of economic interests [i.e. peace] is ... gravely impeded by certain group-interests of financiers within the several nations which do not coincide with, and are often antagonistic to, the more stable interests of international investors.[3]

The mass of small investors became, in the hands of this clique, nothing more than 'a great capitalist proletariat'.[4] So, in the new introduction which he provided for the third edition of *Imperialism* in 1938, Hobson could on reflexion point out that:

> in arguing the case for maldistribution as the main cause of Imperialism and of the wars which accompany that policy, it is not necessary to contend that capitalism as 'an economic

---

[1] Hobson, *Evolution of Modern Capitalism* (1906 ed.), pp. 235–6.

[2] Ibid. pp. 237–8. Cf. Hobson, *The Importance of Instruction in the Facts of Internationalism* (1913); and *The Economic Interpretation of Investment* (1911), pp. 121–2. Harvey Mitchell (op. cit. p. 415) wrongly takes the last-named work as evidence of a change of view on Hobson's part.

[3] Hobson, *Evolution of Modern Capitalism* (1906 ed.), p. 238.

[4] Ibid. p. 242.

system' benefits by war, but only that certain sections of capitalism with political influence at their disposal favour pushful foreign policies that involve the risk of war.[1]

Hobson escapes, therefore, from any attempt to confine him within the bounds of a self-operating economic system. By keeping his 'conspirators' in the wings, he does not need wholly to rely on 'underconsumption' for his explanation of imperialism. His view is more flexible and less deterministic: it brings on to the stage the conscious will of groups of individual human beings.

Yet he was quite certain that economics lay behind imperialism. If capitalism as such was not the decisive factor, yet certain *capitalists* were. Again and again he maintained that the economic factor was the decisive one. This kind of 'economic causation', however, is not a thing which can be verified or disproved scientifically. It is a historico-philosophical problem, rather than an economic one; it depends upon our view of the relative importance of (for example) psychology, power, altruism or economics as the prime determinant of historical motivation. And this in turn will rest upon our opinion of what kind of factor should be accounted a 'cause': whether it is that consideration which influences the conscious decision of a statesman to take a particular course of action; or the 'underlying' and perhaps subconscious reasons which impel him to think along lines which make this consideration decisive for him; or the external factors which determine what alternative policies shall be open to him; or pressures acting from below which might render his 'free choice' of no account. All these are 'causes' of different kinds, and the selection we make from among them is largely subjective. Hobson chose economic pressures: and it makes little impression on his argument merely to show that, for instance, considerations of strategy were decisive in a government's conscious determination. He would (and did) answer that governments were pawns in the hands of others, and while evidence may come to light which

[1] Hobson, *Imperialism* (3rd ed. 1938), p. xv; and cf. *Imperialism* (1st ed.), p. 380.

reduces the necessity for an economic interpretation, so long as we cannot contradict him on the facts (and his view is so flexible as to make this difficult), we cannot make a final judgment on his choice.

Hobson never denied that other factors were important, in the sense that imperialism would have been impossible without them.[1] In 1917 he wrote:

> In linking up militarism and the policy it serves with capitalism, we must avoid the temptation to over-simplify the issue. The economic interpretation of history so often discredits itself, either by ignoring non-economic factors, or by ingenious endeavours to show that they are economic in the last resort. In claiming, therefore, that militarism and the domestic and foreign policy it serves are moulded and directed chiefly by definite and conscious business aims, I wish to make it clear that this claim does not exclude the operation of other impulses, desires and purposes.

But, he said, the 'guidance and direction' of the patriotic, humanitarian and nationalistic sentiments supporting militarism 'mostly come from the economic motives which fuse with them and exploit them'.[2] This view was challenged soon after the publication of *Imperialism*. The *Political Science Quarterly* in September 1903 regretted that 'he did not develop more fully his evidence as to the existence of an international group of capitalists who mould public opinion and direct public action in order to be able to profit by the fluctuations of the stock market'.[3] And the *Edinburgh Review* complained of Hobson's 'palpable exaggeration':

> It is preposterous to argue, as Mr Hobson seems to do, that British policy is *dictated* by self-interested groups and classes who fatten on the expenditure and extravagance which impoverish the nation. Financiers and millionaires undoubtedly in various ways exercise great influence. . . . But for all this we greatly doubt whether in this country our statesmen are more exposed than formerly to pressure

---

[1] See *Imperialism*, pp. 66–7.
[2] Hobson, *Democracy After the War*, pp. 35, 37.
[3] Paul S. Reinsch in *P.S.Q.*, vol. xviii, no. 3, p. 533.

rendering them unable to act upon their own independent judgment in guarding the real interests of the nation.[1]

From Hobson's point of view, however, the criticism which told most – because it accepted that imperialism was *not* 'guarding the real interests of the nation' – came from a man who was later to be his ally in the Union of Democratic Control.[2] In 1903 Norman Angell published *Patriotism Under Three Flags*, dealing with those expressions of national fervour manifested in the South African War, the American conquest of the Philippines, and the Dreyfus Affair.

The book was ... a blunt challenge to materialistic and economic determinism, the germs of which had long been present in much current interpretation of events and was to gain immense popularity in the next few decades. The challenge was based on the quite simple proposition ... that men are not guided by the facts but by their opinions about the facts, opinions which may or may not be correct.[3]

And this challenge, in the first place, was directed at Hobson. Angell replied specifically to *Imperialism* in his opening chapter:

While it is undoubtedly true that class interests have been served by those policies which are the result of patriotic outbursts ... those interests did not, and could not create the sentiment throughout the numerous classes whose material interests were in no way touched by the national action in the events concerned. The intensity of feeling which embraced in each case substantially the whole nation – a feeling which in every characteristic was non-rational – precludes the idea that it has its origin in or is mainly animated by a limited clique whose motives are intensely rationalistic. At the most, we can assume that the vested

[1] *Edinburgh Review*, Jan 1903, pp. 268–9.
[2] The Union of Democratic Control was founded in the early months of the First World War by Ramsay MacDonald, Charles Trevelyan, Norman Angell and E. D. Morel. Hobson was on its executive committee from the beginning. The U.D.C.'s purpose was to 'secure real parliamentary control over foreign policy'. See Mrs H. M. Swanwick, *Builders of Peace.*
[3] Norman Angell, *After All*, p. 107.

interests merely exploited an already existing sentiment. In that case the factor of greater importance for political students is the all but universal one, not the smaller and incidental.[1]

Hobson had put 'interest' before 'sentiment'; Angell reversed the two – 'the political forces Englishmen call imperialism can flourish independently of financial stimulus'.[2] In England, France and America recently, 'sentimental considerations have dominated those of interest'.[3] So, believing that 'emotional forces within ourselves'[4] had determined the imperial policy of the last decade and not 'rational considerations of interest',[5] Norman Angell proceeded to analyse the psychological roots of those emotional forces. Hobson, in *The Psychology of Jingoism*, had done much the same, and his practical conclusions about national feeling were not inconsistent with Angell's. But on the question of priorities between interest and sentiment, the difference between the two writers was a fundamental one. It was not to be resolved by argument, because it rested on their contradictory opinions of human nature. For Hobson, Angell's interpretation of events (and, incidentally, that of Chamberlain: 'sentiment is one of the greatest factors in all our affairs ... the world is not governed by interest')[6] threatened his deepest convictions and hopes.[7] All these hopes rested upon his own definition of human rationality.

Perhaps a little naïvely, Hobson identified reason with material interest. Every man, if he were rational, must act according to what he regarded as his own material interests; he could not con-

---

[1] Norman Angell, *Patriotism Under Three Flags*, p. 24. The book was published under Angell's baptismal name, Ralph Lane.
[2] Ibid. p. 4.   [3] Ibid. p. 5.   [4] Angell, *After All*, p. 106.
[5] Angell, *Patriotism Under Three Flags*, p. 15.
[6] Quoted in William L. Strauss, *Joseph Chamberlain and the Theory of Imperialism*, ch. v.
[7] Hobson replied to Angell in the introduction to the 3rd ed. of *Imperialism*, pp. xi–xvii: 'though this patriotism has its own basic instinctive origins, it is fed and directed in its activities by economic motives ...' (p. xii). Angell's criticism of Hobson tends to be a little misdirected: he confuses Hobson's 'interest' (of sectional groups) with the 'interest of the nation'. See especially *Patriotism under Three Flags*, pp. 80 *et passim*.

sciously act against those interests. If he did then there was no hope for progress. For the only sure guarantee of reform was real democracy, the people acting in their own collective interest. No one else could be trusted to look after their interests for them.[1] If he were to retain any idealism, therefore, it was philosophically necessary for Hobson to believe that men were fundamentally reasonable.

Yet at the end of the nineteenth century they seemed to be acting *against* their own interests, irrationally. He showed in *Imperialism* and elsewhere how British foreign and colonial policy were detrimental to the national welfare. Not only did trade not benefit; it was positively harmed by a policy that must result in a system of protectionism which would sacrifice 'the customers who take four-fifths of their trade for the benefit of those who take one-fifth'.[2] Imperialism would raise indirect taxation;[3] it would encourage wars and all the dangers which war brought – military expenditure, arms competition, militarism, conscription;[4] it was the 'implacable and mortal enemy of Peace and Economy'.[5] He claimed that it would threaten that other dream of the imperialist – colonial federation.[6] And most ominous of all, it was absolutely inconsistent with democracy and social reform. It maintained a despotism abroad which could not be squared with popular government at home; it drained the public purse of money which might be spent on reform; it diverted public resentment away from domestic grievances.[7] Imperialism, in fact, was the implement of class rule. The vested interests –

> The city ground landlord, the country squire, the banker, the usurer, and the financier, the brewer, the mine-owner, the iron master, the shipbuilder, and the shipping trade, the great export manufacturers and merchants, the clergy of the State Church, the universities and great public schools, the legal trade unions and the services

[1] See Hobson, 'Ruskin and Democracy', in *C.R.*, Jan 1902, p. 112.

[2] Hobson in *Fortnightly Review*, 1 Mar 1902, p. 442; *Imperialism* I v and vii; *International Trade*.

[3] *Fortnightly Review*, 1 Mar 1902, pp. 439–40; *Imperialism* I vii.

[4] Hobson, *Imperialism*, pp. 135–46.

[5] Ibid. p. 146.   [6] Ibid. p. 356.   [7] Ibid. pp. 123, 140, 147–61, 382–3.

had all 'drawn together for common political resistance against attacks upon the power, the property, and the privileges which in various forms and degrees they represent'.[1] Imperialism was part of what he later called the great 'Alliance of Reaction' against democracy.[2] 'Empire Abroad is wedded to aristocracy at home.'[3] The alternative lay between imperialism and class rule on the one hand, and internationalism and popular government on the other.[4] Why, then, had the people chosen class rule?

Norman Angell had replied by saying that they were irrational. Hobson could not accept this. If men were motivated by 'sentiment', if imperialism was really the manifestation of their wishes, then there were no grounds for expecting that they would ever decide in favour of progress. So Hobson had to infer that their real interests had been concealed from them, that they were acting to their own detriment *unknowingly*. If reason, in his sense of 'pursuit of material interest', was to be rehabilitated, then someone must benefit and *his* rationality must be the cause of imperialism. This is why, when he came to the question 'What causes imperialism?', he recast it in the form '*Cui bono?*'[5]

> The disastrous folly of these wars, the material and moral damage inflicted even on the victor, appear so plain to the disinterested spectator that he is apt to despair of any State attaining years of discretion, and inclines to regard these natural cataclysms as implying some ultimate irrationalism in politics. But careful analysis of the existing relations between business and politics shows that the aggressive Imperialism which we seek to understand is not in the main the product of blind passions of races or of the mixed folly and ambition of politicians. It is far more rational than at first sight appears. Irrational from the standpoint of the whole nation, it is rational enough from the standpoint of certain classes in the nation.[6]

[1] Ibid. p. 150.
[2] See Hobson, *Democracy After The War*, ch. v; and cf. *Imperialism*, p. 382.
[3] H. D. Lloyd, *A Sovereign People* (written by Hobson from Lloyd's notes), p. 16.
[4] Hobson, *Imperialism*, p. 181.   [5] Ibid. p. 62.   [6] Ibid. p. 52.

Here lies the real flaw in Hobson's argument. It is no part of our purpose to test his theory by the facts of colonial expansion in the late nineteenth century, to see whether it stands or falls in the case of Egypt or of South Africa or elsewhere: this is one critical approach to the 'economic theory' (albeit an inconclusive one) but it must be left to imperial historians to pursue. We can, however, judge Hobson's ideology as a logical system, for its internal consistency; and treating it on this level we can say this: that his emphasis on 'interest' was not empirically deduced, but rather born of his own *a priori* assumptions; and these assumptions led him into error. For what had *Imperialism: a Study* achieved? It had shown, first of all, that trade was not a good rational reason for imperial expansion, that commerce was not served by the acquisition of new territories. This was all well and good, and it appeared to have demolished *one* economic theory of imperialism, that propagated by the imperialists themselves. If Hobson had stopped there he would have arrived at an adequate (though unoriginal) anti-imperial ideology. But he went further: the seeming unprofitability of empire was as unnerving to him as it would have been to imperialists, because it made the process appear 'irrational'. So he looked around to see whose interests *were* being served by expansion, and hit upon the financial capitalists; and because it was necessary for his intellectualist peace of mind to believe that political phenomena must be the product of rationally considered self-interest, he was forced to make these men, even though they were a small minority, the central driving-force behind imperialism, and not merely its 'hangers-on'. Events in South Africa, throwing into sharp relief the Jewish financier and his conspiracies, hastened this deduction.

But why should such a deduction be necessary? Only because Hobson's 'intellectualism' was so rigid as to make any other unacceptable to him. A more cynical age would read other lessons into his demonstration of the commercial unprofitability of empire. On the basis of the 'sociology' which Hobson professed to have taken account of, but which in fact he had merely used for his own intellectualist ends, we might say today that men do not always act rationally; but it is not necessary even to go this far to undermine Hobson's theory of political causation. For even in so far as men act according to their own interests, they do not always do so upon an accurate calculation of those interests. Hobson assumed, with remarkable naïvety, that only that self-interest which was accurately assessed had any great impact on politics. Because he was so committed to rationalism, because all his reformist hopes rested on it, he gave men far too much credit for percipience. If those who gained by the South African War were *not* those who had brought it on, his argument ran, then those who wished to gain more virtuous ends could not themselves do anything to achieve them.

Yet it is difficult to see how, without this kind of *a priori* assumption, such a deduction could reasonably be drawn from the imperial events of the 1890s. Even in the case of South Africa it is arguable whether Hobson's capitalists really gained from the Boer War, even if initially they thought they would; if they *had* spent money to bring the War on, said Winston Churchill in 1901, then 'they know now that they made an uncommonly bad bargain'.[1] If the financial capitalists could themselves so grossly miscalculate their own self-interest, surely the ordinary commercial capitalists could do so too, and the nation as a whole. For most people in the late nineteenth century thought they would gain by colonial expansion: the Birmingham industrialists who gave evidence to the 1885 Inquiry, for example;[2] governments concerned to safeguard the route to India; Chamberlain looking for 'imperial estates' for future development; the 'man on the top of the Clapham omnibus' for all kinds of less sophisticated reasons. It was a time when apprehension was widespread about Britain's place in the world, about her ability to keep up, economically and politically, with growing nations like Germany and Russia and the United States; and when other nations were fast appropriating the remaining 'waste places' of the earth. There was not the time, nor was the political climate cool enough, for men to assess the profitability of colonies in a calm and dispassionate way. Yet the assessment was made, after a fashion, and the

[1] Churchill in H. of C., 18 Feb 1901; 4 P.D. 89, c. 414.
[2] See above, p. 45.

presumption was always in favour of the profitability of Empire. It entailed a large outlay, and the profits were a long time coming in: but they would probably come in soon, and in any case it was safer to assume so – because if Britain acted on the opposite assumption and contracted out of the 'scramble for Africa', and if other countries stepped in, as they would, and later appeared to gain by it, then it would be too late for Britain to have second thoughts. People who felt this way might have been wrong, and Hobson tried to show that they were: but why should this make them less effective, politically, than those whose arithmetic was more exact?

So we come back to the industrial and commercial capitalists, to those men afraid of India's strategic isolation and to the man in the street: all these groups thought that empire was a profitable proposition. All of them supposed that they were acting in their own or in the national self-interest. All of them were haunted by the spectre of declining exports or of foreign rivalry, and thought that territorial expansion might exorcise this spectre. Perhaps they were mistaken; but there is no reason to suppose that their faulty calculations were any less powerful than the financiers' correct ones. If we do not accept Hobson's intellectualist assumption, therefore, we need not follow him in isolating and emphasising the financial factor. The other, more broadly based factor – uncalculating fear of foreign advantage – furnishes an adequate theory of late-nineteenth-century British imperialism; and it does away with the necessity for a 'conspiracy' theory to back it up.

Yet this is the reason for Hobson's 'economic interpretation of history'. It was grounded in his restricted conception of rationalism, a conception which was, for him at the time, essential to his idealism. Some years later he was to modify his view. In 1938 he admitted that he had been led 'to an excessive and too simple advocacy of the economic determination of history'; he had 'not yet gathered into clear perspective the nature of the interaction between economics, politics, and ethics, needed for anyone who might wish to claim the title of Sociologist'.[1] In 1926 he gave a more 'sociological' flavour to his explanation of political motivation:

[1] Hobson, *Confessions*, pp. 63–4.

The main defect of the economic interpretation of history lies here. Property, beyond the means of subsistence, evidently serves less as an instrument of direct material enjoyment than as a means of prestige and power over other persons. When ... the economic motive enters, and often governs, politics, it is, as a rule, none the less the servant of this instinct of self-assertion.[1]

Elsewhere he borrowed the term 'the will to power' to describe this instinct.[2] Applying it more specifically:

Imperialism in practice ... is mainly the expression of two dominant human instincts, self-assertion and acquisitiveness. To the former the primacy may be accorded, in the sense that individual or collective self-assertion, or lust for power, which inspires men to take or enforce rule over others, uses the arts of acquisition ... as a means to the furtherance of this end.... The general body of evidence ... seems to support the view that power-politics furnish the largest volume of imperialist energy –

yet his conversion was not complete – 'though narrow economic considerations mainly determine its concrete application.'[3]

This, then, is Hobson's 'economic interpretation': it is not deterministic, because it finds in it an important place for man's exertion of his rational will. It can be criticised on several grounds. Hobson's rationalist assumption can be questioned or

[1] Hobson, *Free-Thought in the Social Sciences*, p. 181.

[2] In a paper on 'The Will to Power' delivered to South Place some time in the thirties, where he explains war in terms of it. Property, he says, is merely 'the chief instrument for the embodiment of power and the satisfaction of will to power' (MS. notes in possession of Mrs Mabel Scott).

[3] Hobson, *Free-Thought in the Social Sciences*, p. 193. An interesting parallel with this 'reason *versus* sentiment' doctrine, and one which supports the contention that it has its roots in 'Ethicist' theory, is found in G. H. Perris's *A Short History of War and Peace*. Perris asserts that 'sentiment, opinion, even genius, are factors in social growth of small importance in comparison with hunger, sex, greed of wealth and power, and other primary and universal motives which provide the body-stuff of history'. He attempts, therefore, 'to get beneath more heroic but superficial explanations of events to those roots of material interest in which, as the writer believes, and not in passion or instinct, the causes of war and peace are to be found' (p. 9).

modified (as he himself modified it); or it can be argued – either by pointing the similarities between mid-Victorian 'informal Empire' and late-nineteenth-century imperialism,[1] or alternatively by showing that (for example) strategic considerations were a real and sufficient reason for expansion[2] – that there is no *need* for a special economic explanation of the New Imperialism. But Hobson is not vulnerable to the same criticisms as Lenin. Although his underconsumption thesis provided Lenin with the basis for a neo-Marxian theory of empire, underconsumption did not play the same part in Hobson's thought as it did in the Marxists'. And his solution was radically different. For Lenin there was no solution as such: merely an inevitable revolutionary transition to socialism. Hobson provided a dual solution to a dual problem: first the economic solution – better distribution of wealth; but secondly a political solution:

> The power of the imperialist forces within the nation to use the national resources for their private gain, by operating the instrument of the State, can only be overthrown by the establishment of a genuine democracy, the direction of public policy by the people for the people through representatives over whom they exercise a real control. Whether this or any other nation is yet competent for such a democracy may well be matter of grave doubt, but until and unless the external policy of a nation is 'broad-based upon a people's will' there appears little hope of remedy.[3]

This remedy was identical to Cobden's:

> If you had a thorough representation in Parliament, you could not persuade the people of this country to spend half the money that is now spent under the pretence of protecting them, but which is really spent in order that certain parties may get some sort of benefit out of it.[4]

Hobson's 'genuine democracy' differed widely from Cobden's: it was less individualistic, more 'organic'. But essentially his

[1] Gallagher and Robinson, 'The Imperialism of Free Trade', *E.H.R.*
[2] R. E. Robinson and J. Gallagher, *Africa and the Victorians.*
[3] Hobson, *Imperialism*, p. 382.
[4] Cobden, speech at Rochdale, 29 Oct 1862; quoted above, p. 11.

solution was part of the Liberal, or social-democratic tradition, and not the Marxian one; and as such it was far better suited to the needs of the British Labour movement.

III. THE ETHICAL ARGUMENT

Hobson's strictures on economic imperialism did not lead him to regard all tropical empire, *per se*, as reprehensible. Part I of *Imperialism* was directed against expansion as it was seen in action in 1902, and the warnings contained in the last three chapters of the book applied only to that practical manifestation of the New Imperialism. The greater part of *Imperialism* was taken up with countering the arguments which had come from the other side, arguments which he looked upon as self-deceptive. But because the 'imperial trust' had been abused, it did not follow that there was no justification for any form of trusteeship. On the basis of the principles worked out in his earlier writings, Hobson turned, in a long chapter on the 'Lower Races', to the problems posed by the West's assumption of responsibility for the welfare of tropical peoples; and he was able to contribute to Radical ideology a set of constructive proposals for native government and economic development which bore more resemblance to the ideas of (for example) Sir Frederick Lugard than to those of the Liberal Little Englanders. In the previous chapter we saw how he came to formulate these proposals. Before we leave Hobson we should summarise his final statement of them.

Tropical development, he said, was right and necessary, and for two reasons. First, the extreme 'national rights' argument – as he had maintained before – was invalid. Those people 'in actual occupation or political control over a given area of the earth' were not entitled thereby 'to do what they will with "their own" ';[1] if they failed to utilise their resources then a more progressive power had the right to step in, for the 'general good of nations',[2] or for the 'welfare of humanity regarded as an

[1] Hobson, *Imperialism*, p. 237.
[2] Hobson, 'Socialistic Imperialism', *I.J.E.*

organic unity'.[1] This was a clear extension of the 'organic' socialist scheme he had devised for the State and, as in its more restricted form, it justified some measure of coercion.

> Assuming that the arts of 'progress', or some of them, are communicable, a fact which is hardly disputable, there can be no inherent natural right in a nation to refuse that measure of compulsory education which shall raise it from childhood to manhood in the order of nationalities. The analogy furnished by the education of a child is *primâ facie* a sound one, and is not invalidated by the dangerous abuses to which it is exposed in practice.[2]

But, secondly, even if this were not so, it was in any case impossible to check the exploitation of the tropics. 'That the white Western nations will abandon a quest on which they have already gone so far is a view which does not deserve consideration.'[3] A 'hands off' attitude was unrealistic.

> If organised Governments of civilised Powers refused the task, they would let loose a horde of private adventurers, slavers, piratical traders, treasure hunters, concession mongers, who, animated by mere greed of gold or power, would set about the work of exploitation under no public control and with no regard to the future.[4]

Nations, therefore, had both the right and the duty to interfere with 'lower races'. The only question was one of 'safeguards, of motives, and of methods'.[5]

So far he accepted the main tenet of the Fabian view: that the 'interests of civilisation as a whole' should govern imperial policy.[6] But he differed from the Fabians (and from Benjamin Kidd)[7] in refusing to accept either that a nation could act in so disinterested a way, or that mere expansion, *per se*, was a guarantee of 'international social efficiency'.[8] Whatever the professions of

---

[1] Hobson, *Imperialism*, p. 246.   [2] Ibid., p. 241.
[3] Ibid. p. 242.   [4] Ibid. loc. cit.   [5] Ibid. p. 241.
[6] See Shaw, *Fabianism and the Empire*, p. 24; and see above, pp. 116–17.
[7] Whom he cited on page 238 of *Imperialism*.
[8] Hobson, 'Socialistic Imperialism', *I.J.E.*; and *Imperialism*, pp. 238–9.

imperialists, in practice 'The exclusive interest of an expanding nation, interpreted by its rulers at some given moment, and not the good of the whole world, is seen to be the dominant motive in each new assumption of control over the tropics and lower peoples.'[1] Neither the 'world' nor the natives benefited. There was almost no sign that in any British dependency anything but pure selfishness motivated policy. We had destroyed native institutions and made no attempt to understand or educate the races in our care.[2] Our only concern was to get 'cheap labour' in ways which approximated to slavery.[3] None of the competing imperial races, therefore, could be trusted to subordinate 'its private interests and ends to the wider interests of humanity or the particular good of each subject race brought under its sway'.[4]

The only guarantee of this was the establishment of some mandatory authority – 'some genuine international council', composed not only of the 'great powers' like the Berlin Conference, but 'a body genuinely representative of civilisation' – to which a 'civilising' power could be made responsible.[5] (The significance of this idea as a forerunner of the League of Nations mandate system has been noticed by at least one writer.[6] It is interesting in this connexion to read Hobson's later scornful criticism of the League Mandate in his introduction to the third edition of *Imperialism*.)[7]

After establishing the conditions for a real imperial impartiality, Hobson went on to enumerate the principles upon which genuine trusteeship should be based. There were two general considerations. First, it must aim at the good of the whole world. The first criterion should be 'social utility expanded to its widest range'.[8] Secondly, it must benefit the natives, and to this end it must respect the 'services of nationality, as a means of education and of self-development'[9] (just as Hobson's State, however 'organic', will respect the individual). In other words,

[1] Hobson, *Imperialism*, p. 294.
[2] Ibid. pp. 249–50, and pt. ii, ch. v, on 'Imperialism in Asia'.
[3] Ibid. pp. 260–5.   [4] Ibid. p. 249.
[5] Ibid. pp. 251–2. Cf. Hobson, *The Crisis of Liberalism*, p. 259.
[6] Harvey Mitchell, 'Hobson Revisited', *J.H.I.*, p. 413.
[7] (1938), p. xxiii.   [8] Hobson, *Imperialism*, pp. 245–7.   [9] Ibid. p. 247.

Hobson was broadly stating the principles of Lugard's Dual Mandate; and the same fundamental problem was implied: how to reconcile the two sides of the mandate.

In practical terms this resolved itself into 'the labour problem'. The world economy demanded raw materials from the tropics, but could not induce the native to cultivate them because 'the local conditions are such that from the mere bounty of nature all the ambitions of the people can be gratified without any considerable amount of labour'.[1] If the native could live by sitting under a tree and waiting for the bananas to fall, why should he work? Hobson was aware of the reality of the problem. There were, he said, only two natural economic forces which would solve it; 'the growth of population with increased difficulty in getting a full easy subsistence from the soil is one, the pressure of new needs and a rising standard of consumption is the other'.[2] But these forces were 'somewhat slow', while 'white industrialists are in a hurry to develop the country'.[3] The results were such expedients as forced labour, indentured Chinese labour, bribery of chiefs, the *corvée* and the hut-tax.[4] All these were too high a price to pay for tropical development. Hobson insisted that the problem should be solved more gradually, and with a greater regard for the welfare of the natives.

> Surely it is far better that the 'contact with civilisation' should lead these men to new kinds of industry on their own land, and in their own societies, instead of dragging them off to gang-labour on the lands or mining properties of strangers. It can do this in two ways: by acquainting them with new wholesome wants it can apply a legitimate stimulus, and by acquainting them with new industrial methods applicable to work in their own industries it can educate them to self-help.[5]

[1] Ibid. p. 268 (quoting Professor Ireland). The origins of 'the myth of tropical exuberance', and its persistence throughout the nineteenth century, are described in Curtin, *The Image of Africa*, pp. 60 *et passim*.

[2] Ibid. p. 268.   [3] Ibid. p. 269.

[4] Ibid. pp. 269–91 (Hobson quotes Chalmers' report on the Sierra Leone Hut-Tax War to illustrate the last of them.)

[5] Ibid. p. 292.

In the terms of the debate about West Africa which was starting up in Colonial Office and Liverpool commercial circles, Hobson was on the side of those who opposed the 'plantation policy'.[1]

The keynote of his approach to the problems of native administration was one of *sympathy*. He insisted that the extension of Western contact with 'lower races' should be accompanied by careful study:

> By studying the religions, political and other social institutions and habits of the people, and by endeavouring to penetrate into their present mind and capacities of adaptation, by learning their language and their history, we should seek to place them in the natural history of man; by similar close attention to the country in which they live, and not to its mining and agricultural resources alone, we should get a real grip upon their environment.[2]

Too often Western civilisation had been grafted on to alien institutions with no attempt to 'understand the active or latent progressive forces of the subject race, and to develop and direct them'.[3] Usually this was abortive: 'We are incapable of implanting our civilisation in India by present methods of approach: we are only capable of superficially disturbing their civilisation.'[4] And it was unjustified. Who was to say that the traditional society of China (which he painted in glowing colours)[5] was inferior to that of the West? He saw signs of a more enlightened approach; Basutoland he held up as an ideal of sensible administration.[6] Liberals were beginning to realise the falsity of the view that

> there exists one sound, just, rational system of government, suitable for all sorts and conditions of men, embodied in the elective representative institutions of Great Britain, and that our duty was to impose this system as soon as possible, and with the least possible modifications, upon lower races, without any regard to their past history and their present capabilities and sentiments.[7]

[1] See below, Ch. 8, *passim.*
[2] Hobson, *Imperialism*, p. 256. A footnote (p. 257) commends the foundation of the African Society as 'a move in the right direction'.
[3] Ibid. p. 250.   [4] Ibid. p. 323.
[5] Ibid. pp. 338 ff.   [6] Ibid. pp. 258–9.   [7] Ibid. p. 258.

Indirect Rule in Basutoland, however, merely served as a foil for 'most of our Imperialism', as represented by Rhodesia. The 'sane' imperialism was that which was devoted to the 'protection, education, and self-development' of lower races.[1]

This was Hobson's 'Ethical' theory of empire. It was a constructive policy, in contrast to his economic theory; it was also similar in many respects to the ideas of another group of colonial critics. In the remaining chapters, which will be concerned with this other group, we shall see how it was to work out in practical policy, and where its virtues and its deficiencies lay.

Imperialism begins and ends with a plea for internationalism: for an international federation of nations. Hobson was above all a rationalist, a 'progressive' and an idealist. His dislike of imperialism sprang primarily from his conviction that it was a brake on the evolution of mankind from a primitive, competitive stage to a rationalist, co-operative one. Hence his lengthy refutation of the Social Darwinists in a chapter on the 'Scientific Defence of Imperialism'.[2] Just as in *The Evolution of Modern Capitalism* he had looked forward to a time when competition had been eliminated from the lower, industrial plane and raised on to a higher intellectual and moral level,[3] so in international affairs he hoped that the 'natural selection' of competitive imperialisms might be replaced by the 'rational selection'[4] of international co-operation, and so encourage 'the higher kinds of competition, the struggle of languages, literatures, scientific theories, religious, political, and social institutions, and all the arts and crafts which are the highest and most important expressions of national as of individual life'.[5]

It was this kind of approach which characterised most of his political writing after 1902. For a short time between 1898 and 1902 part of his 'anti-imperialism' had manifested itself in practical criticism of colonial policy. But after 1902 he said very little about

[1] Ibid. p. 259.
[2] Ibid. ii ii.   [3] See above, p. 175.
[4] Hobson, *Imperialism*, pp. 184 *et passim*.   [5] Ibid. p. 198.

this. Occasionally he repeated the broad lines of his 'international social utility' argument *vis-à-vis* colonies;[1] in 1909 he criticised the South Africa Constitution, especially the colour-bar, in some detail;[2] and in 1911 he read a paper to the Universal Races Congress which reiterated the substance, with some elaboration, of his solution to the native labour problem.[3] But in the main his 'anti-imperialism' was diverted into other channels: imperialism was treated as an aspect of two more pressing problems – reaction at home and conflict abroad. Imperialism *per se* he neglected. He was much more concerned with a wider political ideal of his own, a new heaven he was trying to build, or predict, on earth. His declared aim was a synthesis (on the Spencerian model, but without Spencer's individualism) of all knowledge – economic, scientific, sociological, psychological – on the basis of 'evolution', to provide a new 'organic' social philosophy, and so assist in the 'great work of human reconstruction'.[4]

To this end, in informal alliance with L. T. Hobhouse, he ranged freely over the whole field of economics, politics and sociology, uncovering his 'reactionary alliance',[5] developing his welfare economics,[6] elaborating on his own peculiar 'organic' social philosophy and 'Lib-Lab' politics,[7] and dabbling in 'evolutionary' sociology.[8] His whole output after 1896 can be seen as a continuous attempt to formulate a new Progressive philosophy 'upon the newer and higher ground which the 19th century has disclosed'.[9] When he commented on contem-

---

[1] Hobson, *Crisis of Liberalism*, pt. iii, ch. vi; *Towards International Government.*

[2] Hobson, *Crisis of Liberalism*, III v.

[3] Hobson, 'Opening of Markets and Countries', in *Papers on Inter-Racial Problems*, pp. 222–32. The Secretary of the Universal Races Congress, which published this volume, was an Ethicist, G. Spiller.

[4] Hobson, *Crisis of Liberalism*, III vii. There is, of course, a surface parallel here with Comteism.

[5] See Hobson, *International Trade*; *Traffic in Treason*; and *Democracy After the War.*

[6] Hobson, *The Industrial System*; *The Science of Wealth* and *Work and Wealth.*

[7] Hobson, *Crisis of Liberalism.*

[8] Hobson, *Free Thought in the Social Sciences.*   [9] See above, p. 167.

porary politics, it was only to clear the way for this new philosophy. Hence his involvement with the Union of Democratic Control in 1914. *Imperialism* was, primarily, an attempt to describe some of the obstacles on the road to progress.[1] It was the offshoot of an earnest, ambitious, dedicated intellectual movement which was trying to meet the demands of what it regarded as a new age; to respond to a political and ideological 'crisis' of which the New Imperialism was only one symptom of many, and for which the existing radical political parties were inadequate.

Because of its wider preoccupations, therefore, and because of its esoteric and chiefly extra-partisan appeal, this movement could not of itself directly influence colonial policy. Before 1914 it was left to other groups more closely involved with colonial affairs to translate similar attitudes into practical policy: administrators in the field, and certain interested groups of traders and reformers (who are treated in the following chapter). The importance of the New Radicalism lies in the rather more intangible influence it had on the Left's way of thinking. From now on Labour and Radical politicians had to take more account, when considering imperial affairs, of the disturbing idea which Hobson had emphasised: that imperialism was a capitalist phenomenon and hence one which was fundamentally antagonistic to democratic socialism. The more positive side of the Progressive gospel, forgotten by the New Radicals themselves, was – in part – grafted on to Labour policy chiefly by Ramsay MacDonald. When he drifted away from the Rainbow and Ethical group and became more closely identified with Labour, he took with him the practical attitude to colonies he had inherited from his liaison with Hobson. *Labour and the Empire* (1907) is a direct descendant of the Ethical imperial ideology which he and others had formulated during his 'Pro-

[1] An article by Hobson in the *University Review*, June 1905, on 'The Possibilities of Popular Progress', gives a clear exposition of his main preoccupation at this time. The paper is concerned to describe again the economic forces making for reaction, chiefly tied up with capitalist and class interest; but he insists at the outset that these forces are not omnipotent, and that reason and 'the moral aspirations of mankind' can play a 'real part' in determining the 'pace or course' of history.

gressivist' period.[1] The seeds both of the 'myth' of economic imperialism and of one strand of Labour inter-war colonial policy[2] are found in the New Radicalism of the late nineties.

[1] We are not concerned here with the broader aspects of Ramsay MacDonald's socialism; but his work on *The Socialist Movement*, in the Home University Library Series (n.d.), offers striking parallels with Hobson's earlier writings on social reform, and it is at least possible that much of MacDonald's 'evolutionary socialist' doctrine came from Hobson. See especially ch. vi, on 'Socialist Method' (pp. 99 ff.).

[2] See below, Ch. 9.

CHAPTER EIGHT

Liverpool and Africa

H O B S O N and MacDonald had provided for 'progressives' a philosophy of empire which, although it was as critical of the New Imperialism as was the Little Englander attitude of the Radical Liberals, was yet not *too* anti-imperialist to concern itself with constructive policy. As well as a critique of imperialism they had suggested a practical remedy, or at least a number of principles on which a remedy should be based. Yet still Hobson's main concern (as was the Liberals') was with imperialism as a *domestic* rather than a colonial phenomenon, with England rather than Africa. He had pointed the way towards a rethinking of imperial problems, but his vocation he saw as that of a social reformer, and this precluded him from translating into practical policy his imperial philosophy. To maintain a real interest in the problems arising from the government of tropical dependencies, one still had to be an imperialist of sorts. Mary Kingsley, E. D. Morel and John Holt, who are the main subjects of this chapter, were imperialists; but they were imperialists with a difference, and that difference puts them in a tradition which runs closely parallel to, if it is not identical with, that of the New Radicals. It was this 'Liverpool School' – all of them were connected in some way with a section of the Liverpool merchant community of which Holt was the leader – which gave the resistance to the New Imperialism some concrete meaning. Hobson attacked capitalist imperialism; the Liverpool School attacked its manifestations in West and Central Africa – the 'plantation policy', monopoly companies, the exploitation of natural resources for profit, gold-mining, forced labour. Hobson recommended Indirect Rule and the guardianship of native civilisations; the Liverpool School said this could best be done by the methods of the old trading companies. Each reacted in a similar way to the same thing, and each came to the same conclusions about the economic and cultural impact of the white races on the black. The chief difference between them (and there were others which will be pointed out in the course of the chapter) was one of approach: the New Radicals were objective and theoretical, the Liverpool School inductive and 'interested' – altogether less 'intellectual' than Hobson, and the more effective for being so.

I. MARY KINGSLEY AND JOHN HOLT

The colonial ideology of the Liverpool School was drawn from two main sources: from the writings and personal influence of Mary Kingsley, and from John Holt's commercial interest and the philosophy which surrounded it. In the late 1890s these two worked together, after a fashion, to try and formulate an alternative to the New Imperialism in West Africa. When Mary Kingsley died in 1900 they had laid the foundations, at least, for the reformist critique which was to become known in the following decade as 'Morelism'.

Even after her death Mary Kingsley remained the guide and mentor of this Liverpool School.[1] It was her works and her example to which men like Holt and Morel continually referred, and from which they seemed to draw sustenance. It was she who first expressed, in bad English but a racy and captivating literary style, the broad lines of their philosophy. Some of the reasons for

[1] Mary Kingsley's career is remarkable enough to have elicited the attention of a number of biographers and historians. The best analysis of her ideas is an article by J. E. Flint in *J.A.H.*, vol. iv, no. 1 (1963), pp. 95–104; this renders unnecessary any more detailed treatment of her philosophy than we can give here. See also the short 'Note' on her in Hancock, *British Commonwealth Affairs*, ii 2, pp. 330–4; and the biographies by Stephen Gwynn, Olwen Campbell and Cecil Howard. Of these, Gwynn is still the fullest and most useful, although Campbell and Howard make use of materials not available to Gwynn. Nworah, 'Humanitarian Pressure-Groups and British Attitudes to West Africa, 1895–1915' also treats her ideas briefly. None of her papers is extant.

her various tastes, activities and accomplishments can be found, perhaps, in her family background – she boasted of slave-trading and Viking forebears; one of her uncles, Charles, was the novelist, historian and reformer; another, Henry, was also a novelist, and a traveller and adventurer; and her father, George Henry Kingsley, travelled incessantly and nurtured, in himself and in his daughter, a passionate interest in anthropology. But her particular concern for West Africa arose from two journeys she made there between 1893 and 1895. In November 1895 she returned from the second of these journeys, bringing with her specimens of rare tropical fish and voluminous notes on native customs (especially what she called 'fetish'), and a mind full of vivid impressions of the place – impressions of its fertility and its unhealthiness for white men, a strong sympathy and liking for the natives, and rock-hard opinions about traders and missionaries.

She was at once struck by the divergence between these opinions and those of 'imperialist' England. No one could accuse her of anti-imperialism – she called herself 'a hardened, unre-formed, Imperial expansionist,' [1] – but she was dismayed by the jingo temper she saw around her. The people seemed to 'hunger and thirst after nothing but praise of England and they call that Imperialism';[2] they had succumbed to 'windy-headed brag and self-satisfied ignorance . . . the nearest thing an Englishman can have to hysterics'.[3] The real issues were ignored. There was, she complained, 'no general public interested in W.A.';[4] the people were apathetic and smug,[5] and, in so far as they considered the welfare of their African subjects at all, they were content to leave it in the hands of the missionaries. A minority was critical, but unconstructive, 'a great brood of Little Englanders screaming –

[1] *West African Studies* (2nd ed. 1901), p. 431. She advocated the creation of a contiguous belt of territory from the east to the west coasts of Africa (lecture delivered in Mar 1896, quoted in Gwynn, *The Life of Mary Kingsley*, p. 122).
[2] Mary Kingsley to Holt, 21 Sept 1898; in J.H.P., box 16, file 2.
[3] Mary Kingsley, quoted in Gwynn, op. cit. p. 238.
[4] Mary Kingsley to John Holt, 19 Nov 1898; J.H.P., box 16, file 3.
[5] Mary Kingsley to Mrs A. S. Green, n.d.; A.S.G.P., N.L.I., Dublin (microfilm copy in University Library, Cambridge).

I

about the folly of interfering with such a horrid place'.[1] And the direct control of Africa was in no better hands. Chamberlain was concerned merely for 'personal grandeur',[2] and the rest of the Government were interested only in foolish Rhodesian schemes, or in 'China, China, China'.[3] This kind of imperialism, what she called the 'modern form of jubilee Imperialism',[4] worked against the interests of the West Africa she knew. For it played into the hands of the missionaries, and in 1896 the missionaries were her especial *bête noire*. Their bravery she admired, and she always acknowledged that they had an important rôle to play in Africa.[5] But their influence on English public opinion and on the administration of Africa was disastrous, in particular the influence of their ideas about native races. These she considered superficial, sentimental and unrealistic. Going to West Africa with preconceived notions of morality and civilisation – the notions of Victorian Christianity and of Exeter Hall 'emotional' egalitarian humanitarianism – they destroyed the bases of the Africans' morality and civilisation, took away from them the moral restraints which their own religion imposed without replacing them with anything really deep and permanent, and so rendered them rootless.[6] The end-product of this process was the 'educated native' whom Mary Kingsley - in company with many other Europeans on the West Coast – hated and despised. When the missionaries saw the failure of their policy they either blamed other influences, such as the liquor trade, which distracted attention from the real error, or, more disastrously, began to look upon the native as a 'fiend',

[1] Mary Kingsley to Holt, 21 Sept 1898; J.H.P., box 16, file 2.
[2] Mary Kingsley to Mrs Green, 2 June 1899; A.S.G.P. In a letter to Holt (8 Nov 1898) she called Chamberlain 'self-conceited and at the same time a weathercock'; he was concerned only, she said, for 'rapid success'; J.H.P., box 16, file 3.
[3] Mary Kingsley to Holt, 13 Dec, 16 July 1898; J.H.P., box 16, file 2, and box 16, file 3.
[4] Mary Kingsley to Holt, 20 Feb 1899; J.H.P., box 16, file 3.
[5] See Mary Kingsley, *West African Studies*, p. 356. She did not want, as J. E. Flint maintains, to 'eradicate' the missionaries from West Africa (Flint, op. cit. p. 103). Her plan was to put education, if nothing else, in their charge.
[6] Mary Kingsley, 'The Development of Dodos', *National Review*, p. 71.

to be civilised only by means of force. And this, she predicted, would bring back slavery in the guise of compulsory labour.[1] Yet the view of the missionaries, because they monopolised the 'showy big words',[2] triumphed over more common-sense ideas which did not have the same sentimental appeal. Such was the 'New Imperialism'.

We have seen what Mary Kingsley wanted put in its place: a colonial policy rooted in anthropological science, which recognised the functional value of African institutions and the distinctive character of African culture.[3] Europe should not try to impose her own standards on Africa, but rule instead through indigenous institutions.[4] This was the philosophy of 'cultural diversity' which Hobson and MacDonald – approaching the problem from a different direction – adumbrated at about the same time. But for them it was part of a wider theory, depending on the fulfilment of other conditions before it could be implemented in practical policy. The *Manchester Guardian* put the point in 1899: commenting on Mary Kingsley's recommendation that an anthropologist be called in to African councils, it said, 'We heartily agree, but we are inclined to fear that English Imperialism is a little too "ardent" at present for such reasonable counsels to prevail.'[5] Mary Kingsley was more sanguine. She wanted Indirect Rule put into practice immediately; and this led her to side – disastrously for her African ambitions in her lifetime – with the *least* popular factor in West Africa: the Liverpool traders.

Her support for the traders has been called 'fanatical and unbalanced'.[6] Towards the end of her life it was, indeed, to

[1] Mary Kingsley, quoted in Gwynn, op. cit. pp. 233–4.
[2] Mary Kingsley to Holt, 6 Sept 1899 (enclosure); J.H.P., box 16, file 4.
[3] See above, pp. 149–55.
[4] It is worth pointing out that her conception of Indirect Rule was not absolutely rigid. In *West African Studies* (ch. xvii) she advocated the setting up of European towns on the coast to enable the African to choose to take what he wanted from the Western culture presented to him there. Her assumption that he would choose only those aspects which were of real lasting benefit to his own culture was perhaps a dubious one.
[5] Review of Mary Kingsley's *The Story of West Africa* in the *M.G.*, 30 Nov 1899.
[6] Flint, op. cit. p. 96 *et passim*.

become something of a fetish, and to push her other interests into the background:

> I feel more dislike & alarm at the position of the English traders than at the position of the African. The African has done very little to justify his having a voice in affairs, the English trader has done everything ... he is to-day in our Crown Colonies in the same position as the uitlander is in the Transvaal, he pays the money – that keeps the thing going – but he is not a citizen, nothing but a helot ... I do *not* like this, it is gall and wormwood to me worse than down trodden Blacks.[1]

And in the way she presented the mercantile case to the public, it sometimes appeared to be no more than a rehearsal of the old imperialist 'surplus goods' argument. England and Germany, she said, 'have the same habit in their commercial production that they have in their human production – the habit of overdoing it for their own country'; and their surplus manufactures must 'find other markets' – in an expanded West African Empire.[2] Yet though her loyalty to Liverpool was perhaps excessive, and her economics appeared dubious, Mary Kingsley's ideas were (she maintained) founded upon sound anthropological and Indirect Rule principles, and they forged that alliance between Liverpool trade and colonial reform which, in various forms, was to provide one of the main strands in the discussion of African policy after her death.

The practical manifestation of this alliance during her lifetime was her close friendship with John Holt, the founder and owner of the company of West African merchants which still bears his name.[3] Holt kept the interests of Liverpool continuously before

---

[1] Mary Kingsley to Holt, 20 May 1899; J.H.P., box 16, file 4.

[2] Mary Kingsley, *West African Studies*, p. 250; and cf. her lecture to the Liverpool Geographical Society, Mar 1896, partly printed in Gwynn, op. cit. pp. 120–5, which stresses the value of West African expansion to the manufacturing classes of Britain.

[3] See Mrs A. S. Green's obituary of Holt in the *J.A.S.*, Oct 1915, pp. 11–16; Cecil R. Holt (ed.), *The Diary of John Holt* (covering the years 1862–71 only), and (Anon), *Merchant Adventure* (n.d.) – the two latter works printed privately by the Company.

her, as he did later with E. D. Morel. Those interests needed a champion. For the prosperity of Holt's company depended on freedom of trade on the west coast; his method – the traditional method of the Liverpool merchants he represented – was the free exchange with native middlemen at river or coastal stations of Western cloth (or liquor – or arms) for African-produced raw materials. If he were to maintain his level of profit then he had to have free access to native producers. But that access was currently being denied to him in certain parts of West Africa. European plantation enterprises set up to develop the country's natural resources were coming between him and the native; in the Congo, as we shall see, the African was being denied the right to buy and sell on his own account; and monopolies granted to other trading companies were effectively excluding him from many of his old hunting-grounds. In the French Congo the position was particularly serious: in 1899 rubber bought there by one of his agents was confiscated by a French monopoly company, and Holt's attempts to secure legal redress for this flagrant breach of free-trade ethics ended only in failure.[1] In addition, the extravagance of the Colonial Office was putting additional burdens both on the trader, in the form of customs duties, and on the native producer in the form of property taxes. So things were looking black for him. Holt's dissatisfaction with this situation, and the line of policy he impressed upon Mary Kingsley, were clearly dictated by self-interest; but he justified his outlook also on philanthropic grounds. His faith in the value for the African native of free commerce was almost mystical:

> The beneficent daughter of liberty & industry! The giver of human happiness! The creator of wealth! The supporter of social existence! Blessed commerce the friend of the slave the deliverer of the oppressed. . . . Hail God's means of blessing mankind with comfort and joy & hope in this mortal life![2]

We shall examine this elevated creed in more detail a little later.[3]

[1] See S. J. S. Cookey, 'Great Britain and the Congo Question, 1892–1913', p. 68.
[2] Holt to Morel, 7 Jan 1907; E.D.M.P., box F8.
[3] See below, pp. 257–8.

Suffice it to say now that around it revolved Holt's whole philosophy of West African government. He believed in Indirect Rule – the preservation of native institutions, the administration of justice through native chiefs, representation of natives on West African councils.[1] This was a rider to his main free-trade contention. To Holt, Indirect Rule meant *minimum* rule, the old Cobdenite formula of non-intervention and *laissez-faire*. He bitterly attacked (because they threatened his interests) the extravagance of West African administration, the impatience implied in the policy of 'developing our imperial estates', and the concessionary and monopolistic tendencies visible in the Congo and elsewhere. In place of these methods he advocated nothing but the old informal methods of the trading companies, the indirect encouragement of native production by means of 'free exchange'. Incentive and competition were the salvation of the African, the best and kindest way to encourage him to elevate himself.

In his dislike of the 'pushing' imperialism of Chamberlain and the Colonial Office, Holt shared common ground with Mary Kingsley. They came closest together in 1898 over the question of Sierra Leone. The imposition of a hut-tax on the natives there had provoked an uprising which had been suppressed by a British force. In England the affair had led many to suggest that Britain abstain from taking charge of more African subjects, because she had shown herself unable in this instance to control them. This possibility Mary Kingsley – the imperialist in her – regarded with apprehension. If such suggestions could be made and apparently justified by native rebellions, she said, then there must be something wrong with the administration of West Africa. So she looked for the fault: and found it in the system. The trouble stemmed from the fact that the 'English tradition' of maintaining 'the native law-form when that law-form is not too bloodstained to be handled by a Christian gentleman' had been abrogated.[2] The hut-tax was 'abhorrent to the principles of African law'. To the natives it suggested the appropriation of their property. What

[1] See, for example, Holt to Morel, 19 Dec 1901; E.D.M.P., F8.
[2] Mary Kingsley, letter to the *Spectator*, 19 Mar 1898, pp. 407–8.

Britain appeared to be after in West Africa (she wrote a few months afterwards in *West African Studies*) was complete territorial sovereignty there, what she called the *Landeshoheit*; this was what was implied for the African by a property tax. Naturally he objected. But the *Landeshoheit* was of no real use to Britain, and its appropriation was 'devastating what is of use to us, the trade'. The *Landeshoheit*, said Mary Kingsley, should be vested in the chiefs; Britain should confine her control to the *'Oberhoheit'*, or what was implied by the words 'raj' or 'protectorate'.[1] In Sierra Leone they had violated this principle; this was why the natives had rebelled, and why, therefore, the administration of Sierra Leone was troublesome and expensive. Keep to native customary law, in this as in other things, and Africa would advance peacefully and cheaply.[2]

This tied in well with Holt's views as to the value of informal trading contact with native proprietors and the necessity for economy. And Mary Kingsley – challenged by Joseph Chamberlain to provide a viable alternative to the hut-tax system[3] – thought she had found in Holt the solution to her problem. What was needed was something to replace the Crown Colony method of government. That method was extravagant (in terms both of money and of lives),[4] and it was impermanent, changing with every new political breeze in England;[5] but its chief weakness was the quality of its overseers. The Colonial Office personnel – 'those conceited fools' – were ignorant and amateur; they knew nothing of native religion and laws, particularly land-laws.[6] Consequently their administration was heavy-handed. The men who ran Africa, she thought, must be professionals, with an intimate knowledge of the place and its people. But who were the professionals? There were the scientific men, the anthropologists

[1] *West African Studies*, pp. 336–8, 357–8 and ch. xviii.
[2] *Spectator*, 19 Mar 1898.   [3] See Gwynn, *Life of Mary Kingsley*, p. 178.
[4] Mary Kingsley to Holt, 21 and 27 Mar, 26 and 29 Apr, and 21 Sept 1898; J.H.P., box 16, file 1, and box 16, file 2.
[5] *West African Studies*, ch. xv, and the *British Empire Review*, Aug 1899, p. 30. Cf. J. S. Mill, *Considerations on Representative Government*, ch. xviii.
[6] Mary Kingsley to Holt, 21 Mar and 21 Apr 1898; J.H.P., box 16, file 1, and box 16, file 2.

and ethnologists; and she wanted to see these people given a voice in African affairs.[1] But the scientists were not directly concerned with West Africa, they had no *interest* there. Then there were the chartered companies; but although Mary Kingsley admired Goldie, and tolerated the Royal Niger Company *for Nigeria* (much to Holt's chagrin),[2] she disliked the system in general, especially in its Rhodesian form. So all that remained to her was the trader – professional, benevolent and committed in his own interest to the principle of Indirect Rule. The merchants, therefore, must be given pride of place in the administration of West Africa.[3]

At first Holt seemed co-operative.[4] But not for long; and the reason for this highlights a wide and vital divergence between their views. For, however closely they agreed on the question of the Sierra Leone hut-tax, on other matters they were less in accord. Mary Kingsley preached Indirect Rule, but she was not so closely wedded to the idea of *economic* indirect rule as was Holt. She vigorously defended the enterprises of the Royal Niger Company, and of Miller Brothers of Glasgow: in the right place a plantation policy or a Chartered company was good for the African. Neither was she as hostile to government intervention – she commended it so long as it was right-minded. When she championed the traders, therefore, it was not for their *laissez-faire* opinions. It was not 'free trade' as such whose quality and value she stressed – commerce by itself was insufficient – but the

[1] *Fortnightly Review*, 1 Apr 1898, p. 544; and Gwynn, op. cit. p. 272.
[2] Mary Kingsley to Holt, 27 Nov 1897; 2 Feb, 21 Mar, 10 Oct, 2 Nov, 13 Dec 1898; 21 Jan 1899; J.H.P., box 16, file 1 to box 16, file 3. Mary Kingsley defended the R.N.C. against Holt because it had resisted the French, refrained from interfering with the power of the chiefs, and because it was so unfairly abused. See also Mary Kingsley to Lugard, 31 Dec 1897, in Lugard Papers, s. 59, ff. 12–14 (copy).
[3] See *West African Studies*, chs. xiii–xv.
[4] At Mary Kingsley's suggestion he wrote a letter to the *Spectator* advocating that 'the people who pay taxes in West Africa' should have some say in its administration (*Spectator*, 26 Mar 1898; and see Mary Kingsley to Holt, 13 and 19 Mar 1898, J.H.P., box 16, file 1). He meant, of course, the merchants; but he was taken by further correspondents to the *Spectator* to mean the African natives.

men, the merchants. She wanted to see them represented on West African councils, firstly because it was unfair to them to have their interests ignored; but secondly because their intimate, unprejudiced knowledge of local conditions made them the factor least likely to jeopardise the welfare of the natives. If they did not necessarily share her anthropological views, yet their interests (she said) included nothing which would preclude the implementation of those views. They were free from missionary 'cant'. They were familiar with West Africa. And as traders, it was in their interest to treat the natives – their customers – well, to encourage native production and to respect their customs and institutions. 'The traders', Mary Kingsley wrote to Alice Stopford Green, 'do know the nat[ive], they have no fancy notions about his being a man & a brother, & the prosperity of their trade depends on the prosperity of the native.' [1] Trade provided the *material* for a just administration of West Africa: but it would have to do more than buy and sell.

This was asking too much of Holt. He advised Mary Kingsley that merchants had enough to do without becoming involved in administrative work: her scheme did not fit in with his own *laissez-faire* ideal of minimum government.[2] And from this position he would not move, despite Mary Kingsley's exasperated entreaties: 'You great merchant adventurers of England *must* pull yourselves together, and become a fighting force, and a governing force in a region with which your honour is so closely connected as well as your profit. I have no faith in any other party.' [3]

Holt was to get a little more sympathy for his view of things from E. D. Morel a little later; but Mary Kingsley was to know only failure for hers. Eventually, she felt, 'imperialist' England would come round to her way of thinking, stop being gulled by the missionaries and see the trader for the shining paragon he was. 'I know England is good or else she would not always pretend to be.' [4] She set herself to work on this potential merit, preaching to

[1] Mary Kingsley to Mrs Green, 2 June 1899; A.S.G.P.
[2] See Mary Kingsley to Holt, 14 Nov 1898; J.H.P., box 16, file 3.
[3] Mary Kingsley to Holt, 28 Aug 1899; J.H.P., box 16, file 3.
[4] Mary Kingsley to Mrs Green, 2 June 1899; A.S.G.P.

the public in lectures and articles, revealing to the Colonial Offices its errors in Sierra Leone, and trying to persuade Liverpool to take a more active interest in the administration of West Africa, to press for a share in its government or else to set up a body of its own.[1] But she was not a good propagandist. 'I am a negligible quantity', she wrote to Lugard, 'because I am to be trusted to play fair according to my lights';[2] and 'fair play' signified the reckless revelation of unpalatable truths, which was not the easiest road to popularity. Her proud imperial expansionism alienated Little Englanders. 'What is quite clear', proclaimed *Concord*, the pacifist monthly,

> is that Miss Kingsley is a very unwomanly woman, that her language is tainted with the demoralisation of frontier life, that her politics are bad, her economics worse, and her morals, in regard to these public concerns, worst of all. Heaven save us from all such foolish advisers![3]

Her championing of the Liverpool merchants – the heirs of the old slave-traders – was suspect. Her mocking denunciation of the missionaries offended the fondest assumptions of the church-going Victorian's vicarious philanthropy, and of his Christian morality. Other humanitarians attacked 'fetish', the liquor traffic, polygamy, slavery and the nakedness of the African: Mary Kingsley defended them strongly and insolently.[4] And she had no comfort to offer the Unionists. So the general public remained

---

[1] When her scheme to associate Liverpool in the government of West Africa fell through, she tried others. She tried to persuade the merchants to found 'an African Society like the Royal Asiatic Society', which would be 'a great step towards an African Council like the Indian Council' (Mary Kingsley to Holt, 7 Dec 1898; J.H.P., box 16, file 3); but this she abandoned for fear that such a society might 'fall into the hands of the Rhodesian group'. (Mary Kingsley to Holt, 13 Dec 1898; J.H.P., box 16, file 3). Then she tried to get Sir Alfred Lyall to stand as Liverpool trading representative for Parliament; he refused (Mary Kingsley to Holt, 2 Dec 1898; J.H.P., box 16, file 3).
[2] Mary Kingsley to Lugard, 31 Dec 1897; Lugard Papers, s. 59, f. 11.
[3] *Concord*, Apr 1898, p. 60.
[4] See 'The Development of Dodos', *National Review*; and *Travels in West Africa, passim*.

deaf to her pleas. When she turned to the men at the hub of West African politics – the administrators and the Colonial Office – her success was no greater. Lugard she considered antipathetic to her ideas – 'plainly a dreamy partisan of the missionary party'.[1] And in the Colonial Office she found 'everywhere the same thing a hatred to the traders a distrust of them & a rank blank ignorance about West African natives'.[2] When she sailed for Cape Town in 1900 (to nurse Boer prisoners) her failure *vis-à-vis* West Africa seemed complete. She wrote to Mrs Green shortly before her death: 'All this work here, the stench, the washing, the enemas, the bed pans, the blood, is my world. Not London Society, politics and that gateway into which I so strangely wandered – into which I dont care a hairpin if I never wandered again. . . .'[3]

If she had been more diplomatic, not quite so honest and impulsive in expressing her opinions, not so bitterly scornful of the Victorians' sacred cows; if, perhaps, she had not been a woman – she might have had more of the direct influence she wanted. If the Liverpool merchants had been more co-operative, if Holt, in particular, had overcome his dislike of the limelight, and if they had identified their interests with those of the 'scientists' in the way that Mary Kingsley had taught them, they might have constituted a political pressure group which Chamberlain would have had to take some account of. But the chief reason for her apparent failure was the temper of the country at the time. Mary Kingsley called herself an imperialist, and indeed she was. But she continuously railed against the type of 'bragging' imperialism

[1] Mary Kingsley to Holt, 13 Dec 1897; J.H.P., box 16, file 1. Dame Margery Perham (*Lugard*, vol. i, p. 651) asserts that Lugard and she were on terms of close personal friendship, and implies that they carried on a long correspondence with one another. There are only two letters from Mary Kingsley in the Lugard Papers, dated 19 and 31 Dec 1897 (Lugard Papers, s. 59, ff. 6–14 (copies)), neither of them friendly; and to Holt she wrote that Lugard 'irritated' her (J.H.P., box 16, file 1). In Apr 1898 she contributed to the *Fortnightly Review* an article strongly attacking him. If Lugard was well disposed towards Mary Kingsley – as he certainly was after her death – the feeling does not appear to have been reciprocated.

[2] Mary Kingsley to Holt, 19 May 1899; J.H.P., box 16, file 4.

[3] Mary Kingsley to Mrs Green, 11 Apr 1900; A.S.G.P.

which, she said, characterised *The Times* and Flora Shaw;[1] and
she refused to condemn those Little Englanders like John Morley
who were doing the Empire a service by 'pointing out where the
moths are getting into our ermine'.[2] In fact she took neither side
in the contemporary debate over imperialism, because that debate
seemed to be irrelevant to, and to distract attention in a disastrous
fashion away from, the real questions at issue. She put this point
in a letter to John Holt in February 1899: St Loe Strachey and the
other Press men, she said,

> do not care about West Africa *itself* but only about how it
> bears on politics. . . . I fancy if I showed them I cared for
> W.A. quite apart from Imperialism they would think me a
> thundering fool & pay no more attention to me – as it is they
> think I am quite the last thing out in commercial imperialism.[3]

Both sides in the debate thought of imperial affairs in terms of
simple, general moral issues; you were either against it or for it;
and they *used* West Africa merely as an argument for or against
the Empire and its expansion. Consequently, when Africa was
debated in Parliament, unless one of these moral issues was
involved, there was little discussion or dissent. The Nigeria
debates of 1899 were a case in point.[4] To Members of Parliament,
the replacement of one kind of imperial control by another was
an unimportant detail – it was all imperialism. To Mary Kingsley,
this 'detail' was the most important and vital question of them
all.[5]

Yet despite her pessimism, Mary Kingsley's failure was not so
great as she thought. Her antagonism to Lugard and other
permanent officials had blinded her to the good that could come
out of the Colonial Office; and some years later Mrs Green could

[1] Mary Kingsley to Holt, 20 Feb 1899, J.H.P., box 16, file 3; and cf. above,
pp. 241–2.
[2] Mary Kingsley, *West African Studies* (2nd ed.), pp. 418–19.
[3] Mary Kingsley to Holt, 14 Feb 1899; J.H.P., box 16, file 3.
[4] H. of C., 3, 19, 26 and 27 July 1899; and see above, p. 57.
[5] See her article on 'The Transfer of the Niger Territories' in the *British
Empire Review*, Aug 1899, pp. 29–31. The details of this transfer are described in J. E. Flint, *Sir George Goldie*, ch. 13.

write to Holt: 'I was saying the other day to Sir George [Goldie] what a wonder it would be if Mary Kingsley could see the change in the system – the excellent officials, the zeal & ardour of their work, the new hope of keeping the native life & customs going.' [1] Her books became essential reading for West African administrators after 1900, and if her direct influence cannot be traced in the development of colonial policy in the early twentieth century, yet that policy was largely in harmony with her ideas. Her more tangible influence is found among the friends she left behind, men fired with an immense admiration for her, active in West African affairs after her death, and acknowledging her contribution to their thinking. Consciously or unconsciously, they were selective in their adoption of her ideas. But the most important of these ideas survived their reinterpretation by other men. Chief among them was her *empathetic* solution to the problems of tropical government. This solution grew out of her empirical approach. Her thinking had originated in the facts of West Africa, and her recommendations were adapted to the different situations of different countries and races. Thus she rejected the idea that Christianity and Western culture were the cures for all African evils, and advocated a variety of solutions suited to differing environments. So chartered-company rule, for example, was unsuitable for South Africa, but it was *more* suitable for Nigeria. It was not *a priori* right or wrong. But, most important of all, this empiricism involved a detailed study of African society as it existed on the ground, and the preservation of all those native customs and laws which were not demonstrably 'too blood-stained to be handled by a Christian gentleman'. This was the principle of Indirect Rule. We have seen that it was by no means an original concept. But it seemed to be going directly against that principle of African administration which had gained the ear of the Colonial Office in the 1890s: the policy of 'developing the imperial estate' and its concomitant policies of plantation agriculture, native taxation and forced labour.

Mary Kingsley was concerned first of all about the *cultural* implications of 'direct rule', the cultural imperialism of the

[1] Mrs Green to Holt, 20 Feb (year?); J.H.P., box 11, file 7.

missionaries. But the Sierra Leone Hut-Tax War had turned her attention briefly to another aspect of the problem, the question of land proprietorship; and it was this aspect which was to occupy most of the time of her successors. This is where Holt came into his own. For him, and for the other twentieth-century disciples of Mary Kingsley (Morel, Wedgwood, Emmott, Dilke), the root of the African problem was economic, and its solution was indirect *economic* rule. The approach was similar; but the emphasis was different.

II. EDMUND DENE MOREL

The alliance between Mary Kingsley and John Holt was, at best, a loose one. The two were looking at West Africa from different directions – Holt from the point of view of commerce, Mary Kingsley from that of native customary institutions. They saw eye to eye when the two things seemed to coincide, as in Sierra Leone in 1898, but their real interests were very far apart. Mary Kingsley was never so passionately concerned with things economic as was Holt, and Holt took no interest in administration. So they could be of little real help to one another. But Mary Kingsley died in 1900, and Holt lived on; and he found in Edmund Dene Morel a man who was better disposed towards his own peculiar view of African questions. Morel reinterpreted Mary Kingsley in a way which was consistent with Holt's commercial ideology; out of the fusion between the two arose a new and effective policy of colonial government.

Morel's connexion with Liverpool was twofold.[1] Throughout

---

[1] E. D. Morel, born in Paris 10 July 1873; baptismal name Georges Edmond Morel-de-Ville. On his father's death in 1877 he was sent to school in England. He was employed for a time in a Paris bank, then in 1890 he and his English mother came to live in England. From 1890 to 1901 he worked for the Elder Dempster shipping company in Liverpool; afterwards he devoted himself full-time to journalism and humanitarian agitation. He was one of the founders of the Union of Democratic Control in 1914. Died 12 Nov 1924.

There are a number of useful accounts of his career. F. Seymour Cocks,

the 1890s he had worked as a clerk in the Liverpool shipping firm of Elder Dempster. It was while he was here that he first became interested in West and Central Africa. From early on he contributed to various journals articles on African affairs, at first taking the orthodox line of advocating more railway-building and government protection for the 'open door' in Africa,[1] but soon concentrating on abuse rather than neglect in West African policy. A pamphlet he published in 1899 on the Sierra Leone Hut-Tax War took a line similar to Mary Kingsley's,[2] and was the means by which he was introduced to her. In the summer and autumn of 1900 he wrote a series of six unsigned article for the *Speaker* attacking the 'Congo atrocities'; and this led him to become associated with such men as Dilke and Fox Bourne and, in 1901, to resign from Elder Dempsters.[3] His second connexion with Liverpool was less intimate, but happier and more long-standing. Since May 1899 (at the latest) he had known John Holt – whose case in the French Congo he defended vigorously[4] – and he

---

E. D. Morel: The Man and his Work is still helpful, but brief and superficial. A short account of his life is contained in W. S. Adams, *Edwardian Portraits*. R. Wuliger, 'The Idea of Economic Imperialism, with Special Reference to the Life and Work of E. D. Morel' is, despite its title, a straight life of Morel, very largely narrative and chronological. Cookey, 'Great Britain and the Congo Question, 1892–1913' gives a full and excellent account of the history of Morel's Congo Reform Association. Nworah, 'Humanitarian Pressure-Groups and British Attitudes to West Africa, 1895–1915' includes a description of his policies for British West Africa and their impact.

Morel's private papers are in the British Library of Political and Economic Science (L.S.E.) – a vast collection of informative material. Among them is Morel's own manuscript 'History of the Congo Reform Movement' (1912?), unfinished, in box H; this will be referred to here as '*MS. History*'.

[1] *MS. History*, ch. iv; E.D.M.P., H.

[2] E. D. Morel, *The Sierra Leone Hut-Tax Disturbances*, 1899; copy in the J.H.P., box 23, item 42.

[3] The chairman of Elder Dempster was Sir Alfred Jones, Holt's chief trade rival, a Congo concessionaire (Cookey, op. cit. p. 117), and Consul in Britain for the Congo Free State. None of these things endeared him either to Holt or Morel. Morel wrote of his experiences at Elder Dempsters: 'And what of the *atmosphere*? Not an atmosphere of straight commercial dealing. An atmosphere of trickery and deceit, of shiftiness, of neglect: an atmosphere of foul and filthy talk, of gross ideals, and grosser methods' (Morel to Holt, 14 Aug 1906; J.H.P., box 18, file 3).

[4] See Cookey, op. cit. pp. 68 ff.

corresponded regularly with him until 1915: an exchange of information and ideas which was invaluable to the interests of both. Besides this, Holt subsidised Morel's efforts generously, giving financial backing to his journal, the *West African Mail*, and contributing large sums towards his salary and to the Congo Reform Association. With Holt's considerable support, influence and friendship, Morel was able after 1903 to pursue the full-time reformist career which might otherwise have been closed to him.

Holt and Mary Kingsley were the source of most of his ideas. His debt to the latter he freely acknowledged.[1] His first important contribution to the literature of Africa, *Affairs of West Africa*, published in 1902, echoed again and again the more analytical passages in her works, and to Holt he wrote that he was endeavouring, 'though without her knowledge & gifts, to accentuate & emphasise' Mary Kingsley's 'main ideals'.[2] Apart from the advice he gave against further expansion in Africa – 'The country needs political rest' [3] – there was little in it with which she would not have agreed. Here, and in his other books and correspondence, were to be found the same prejudices and opinions. He attacked the same people and the same things: extravagant finance and punitive expeditions,[4] ministerial laxity and the policy of the 1865 Committee,[5] the missionary and his unthinking hostility to liquor and domestic slavery, the missionary-educated native,[6] and the impatience of money-grabbing financiers.[7] Like Mary Kingsley he counselled 'patience' and rule through native institutions and laws.

> I was thoroughly in accordance with what you said yesterday; the policy of building up these native States on indigenous lines; strengthening and consolidating native

[1] Holt wrote to him (7 Oct 1906): 'Truly the mantle of Mary Kingsley has fallen upon you, a worthy disciple.' (E.D.M.P., F8.)

[2] Morel to Holt, 27 Oct 1902; J.H.P., box 18, file 1.

[3] *Affairs of West Africa*, p. 15.   [4] Ibid. p. 19.

[5] Ibid. ch. ii; cf. Mary Kingsley, *West African Studies*, pp. 259–60.

[6] *Affairs of West Africa*, pp. 34, 108–9; see also his *Nigeria*, Introduction; and Morel to Holt, 21 Sept 1910; J.H.P., box 18, file 7.

[7] *Affairs of West Africa*, p. 183 *et passim*.

institutions; & upholding the power of the chiefs, is an admirable one, & should be supported all through.[1]

And he championed the merchants in the same terms: 'commerce is the explanation of our presence in West Africa';[2] the merchant had 'expert knowledge' of the country and so 'should have a voice in the framing of legislation calculated to affect the internal politics, and consequently the commerce of our West African possessions'.[3]

But in his claims for commerce he went far beyond Mary Kingsley, and, indeed, nearly achieved the heights of eulogy reached by Holt. He accepted, also, the rationale which Holt had worked out for his commercial credo, as Mary Kingsley had not done. Holt's philosophy was simple. Trade, he said (with Cobden), was the best guarantee of African self-development. Free exchange with native producers left the native

> a free agent to dispose of his produce to whoever he chooses. This means competition and the survival of the fittest in trade. It also means a variety of minds being continually employed in trying to discover what is best to be done to promote development in every district. There is activity enterprise and energy everywhere. . . .

Under free trade both Europeans and Africans were given the incentive to improve Africa. Monopoly had the opposite effect:

> A monopoly means stagnation and the crushing of the native. He will not be attracted by what the monopolist chooses to offer him in order to induce him to work. He will not produce enough to satisfy the appetite for wealth of the monopolist who will plan & scheme in a variety of ways to compel him to work.[4]

Monopoly only encouraged the native to 'stagnate' and the European to coerce. Free trade encouraged each side, in its own self-interest, to benefit the other.

[1] Morel to Holt, 9 June 1903; E.D.M.P., G (copy-books), vol. 4c, p. 72.
[2] *Affairs of West Africa*, p. 10.
[3] Ibid. p. 23. He suggested this to Lugard; see Morel to Lugard, 4 Nov 1903 (copy), E.D.M.P., G (copy-books), vol. 5c, p. 391.
[4] Holt to Morel, 31 Dec 1901; E.D.M.P., F8.

Lord Curzon's policy is also the correct one for Africa. We must build up native institutions & ally the people to us by a common interest. Their peaceful progress must be due to us. Our reward must be the trade we do with them which should rest on their welfare.[1]

Civilisation by trade: this was the philosophy of the old Manchester and the new Liverpool, and Morel preached it too. 'Commerce', he wrote in *Affairs of West Africa*,

> is the greatest civilising agent. The steps upward in the ethical development of the human race have been synonymous with the spread of commercial relations... such commonplace things as commerce and improved means of communication will do more to benefit the native than any attempts to impose laws and institutions unfamiliar to him.[2]

With its implication of 'minimum government' this was far closer to Holt's ideal than to Mary Kingsley's.

So Holt welcomed Morel's support. So far as his trading interests were concerned, Morel could be of great use to him – more so than Mary Kingsley, for he was more diplomatic and much more 'firm' on the economic question. 'Morel is a great asset,' he wrote to William Cadbury in 1910, 'if we know how to make use of him properly in our West African work.'[3] Both of them saw the New Imperialism and its dangers chiefly in economic terms. Holt feared for the interests of the traders, threatened, as we have seen, by monopolies, concessions and Colonial Office extravagance. The Government appeared to smile on these new departures; it was part and parcel of the new West African policy of 'development', pushed by what Holt called 'stock-exchange sharks', 'blackguardly mineowners' and local officials with a love of 'puff and honour' and 'native-hunting'.[4] 'It all comes', he wrote to Morel in 1906,

[1] Holt to Morel, 23 Apr 1901; E.D.M.P., F8.
[2] Morel, *Affairs of West Africa*, pp. 21–2.
[3] Holt to Cadbury, 20 Aug 1910; J.H.P., box 12, file 7.
[4] Holt to Morel, 3 Oct 1900, 23 July 1901, 13 Dec 1902 and 28 Oct 1906; E.D.M.P., F8.

because of our desperate hurry – we have not the patience to develop slowly as we have done so well on the Coast. . . . It is the East African craze which has now crossed the continent – originally imported from South Africa. We shall soon see the whole country in the hands of a lot of harpies.[1]

The picture Morel painted of the New Imperialism was identical. In 1901 he wrote to Holt:

Times are changing. You have got new impulses, new conceptions of colonial policy and colonial development surging up like a wave over the country. It is patent that they do not conduce to the prosperity or the peace of mind of the merchant community. The merchant is looked upon as out of date, rivals in the shape of concessionaires are appearing everywhere, and everywhere threatening the old order of things, everywhere threatening the merchant and the interests he represents. Then again a strong endeavour is being made to impose upon West Africa a military policy which spells financial embarrassment to the country and a consequent increase of the merchant's burden; and ultimate impoverishment of the British West African possessions. You know the spirit that is in the air, you know the revolution which this mining industry is bringing: you are aware of the host of unsafe guides which are arising right & left to lead the people of this country in the wrong channels, to force on a policy of rush and hurry, brimful [?] of evil and retrogression.[2]

There was a real sympathy here between them. They attacked the same phenomena – the financial aspects of the New Imperialism; and their solution, the commercial one, was the same.

These, then, were the roots of 'Morelism': Mary Kingsley's doctrine of 'Indirect Rule', combined with John Holt's economic emphasis and his free trade-ism But there was another ingredient still to be added, the proprietary one. Mary Kingsley had touched on the question of land ownership in 1898, with reference to

[1] Holt to Morel, 28 Oct 1906; E.D.M.P., F8.
[2] Morel to Holt, n.d.; J.H.P., box 18, file 1. Morel wrote this letter in an effort to persuade Holt to contribute an advertisement to *West Africa*, a weekly journal which Morel edited.

Sierra Leone, and so had Morel. But for both of them at that time this aspect of the West African problem was only an incidental one. Morel was to make it central to his case. By combining, in effect, the Free Trade of John Holt with the *Oberhoheit* of Mary Kingsley, he produced the distinctive synthesis which came to be associated with his name. The factor which stimulated this synthesis was his study of the Congo.

Since 1890 there had been complaints of the way King Leopold II of the Belgians had been conducting the affairs of the Congo Free State. By the Berlin General Act of 1885 he had been given personal sovereignty over the Congo; and despite his professions of altruism he had clearly abused his trust. He had sunk his personal fortune into the country and initially lost by it, and in order to recoup this money he began, in the early nineties, to pursue a policy designed to make the Congo profitable. This policy involved the assumption of absolute ownership over half its area – the *domaine privé* – and a more veiled proprietorship of a further area around Lake Leopold II, the *domaine de la Couronne*. Within this territory the natural resources of the country were reserved to the absolute exploitation of the State, and outside it they were granted in the form of territorial concessions to various monopoly companies for *their* exclusive exploitation. The result was a remarkable improvement in the financial position of the State; but this improvement was effected only by methods which involved hardship and cruelty to the native population. The Aborigines Protection Society was told in December 1890 of atrocities in the Congo; and from then onwards reports came in from missionaries and others of cruelties perpetrated by state officials on natives who omitted to gather the quantities of rubber which the State or the concessionaires demanded, of atrocities (including cannibalism) on the part of native troops employed by those companies, of wholesale massacres and of individual barbarities.[1] Dilke brought up the question in the British House of Commons in April 1897, and asked the Government to press

[1] See Ruth Slade, *King Leopold's Congo*, pp. 175–81; E. D. Morel, *Red Rubber*, sect. i; and Cookey, op. cit. ch. i.

for a new Berlin Conference to redress these wrongs; but no official move was made.[1] In 1900, despite a gesture made by Leopold in 1896 in appointing a Commission to look into the allegations, the situation remained as bad as ever.

Morel's interest in this situation arose from the visits he undertook, while in the employ of Elder Dempsters, to Brussels and Antwerp. In 1898 he first became suspicious of 'the true character of the Congo Free State Govt. & of its proceedings in Africa'.[2] He had discovered that his own firm had been shipping exorbitant quantities of rifles and ball-cartridge into the Congo. On further analysing – with John Holt's help – the 'so-called commercial statistics of the CFS' he found that 80 per cent of the Congo's imports consisted of such items, 'articles which were remote from trade purposes'. Yet the Congo's exports of rubber and ivory were increasing, and for these exports 'the natives were getting nothing or next to nothing' in exchange. There was a discrepancy here. If the Congolese were exporting more, then they should also be importing proportionately more useful articles from Europe. He went deeper, and studied the official bulletins of the C.F.S.; and the truth dawned on him. In the Congo there was no question of free barter. By law the whole territory and its products were owned by Leopold, the natives had no rights at all, and they were therefore slaves *de facto*.[3]

The Aborigines Protection Society before him had for some years been conducting an agitation against the horrors and abuses of the Free State. Morel's propaganda, which began in the *Speaker* in July 1900,[4] was not new; but his approach and emphasis were. From the beginning his offensive was directed against what he considered to be the *economic* tap-root of the problem: the concessionaire system in Central Africa. His basic position he formulated in these words:

At bottom, the problem in one sense, was economic. The

[1] See above, p. 57. See also Dilke's 'Civilisation in Africa', in *Cosmopolis*, July 1896, pp. 21–35.
[2] Morel, *MS. History*, p. 5; E.D.M.P., H.
[3] Ibid. ch. iv; and see Seymour Cocks, op. cit. pp. 68–72.
[4] The *Speaker*, 28 July, 4 and 25 Aug, 1 Sept, 6 Oct and 1 Dec 1900.

basis of the Congo Free State's policy instituted a complete revolution of accepted economics. The material factor governing the relationship of peoples is the exchange of commodities – in other words, trade.[1]

In the Congo freedom of trade had been destroyed; trade itself was illegal over three-fifths of its territory.

> The appeal to commerce to assert its rights was, therefore, doubly justified, and doubly necessary. Justified because the policy of the State was a cynical & outrageous violation of the world's trading rights with an enormous region. . . . Necessary, vital indeed, from the point of view of succouring the native people from their intolerable position. Why? Because by international insistence upon the practical restoration of native rights in the products of the soil & in the freedom of labour, the restoration of native rights to collect & dispose in barter of those products, to trade in them with the outer-world (the most elementary of human rights), could the policy which claimed as the property of a 'State' incarnated in one man, the actual & potential wealth & profit-carrying medium of millions of men, & the labour of those millions of men themselves & of their wives & children; alone be done away with. Because if the right to trade be taken from the natives of tropical Africa & the raw material of commerce thereof converted by law into the raw material of taxation, the natives are automatically reduced from free economic units to pure & simple slaves.[2]

The root cause of the evil, therefore, was the system which robbed the African of his land and forbade him to trade on his own account either with other Congolese or with the outside world: and the only solution was free commerce, based upon a recognition of the native's right to ownership of all the land and its produce.

This was the burden of Morel's case against the Congo Free State; and he argued it relentlessly and consistently during the next ten years. It stimulated the C.F.S. itself to accuse him of

---

[1] Morel, *MS. History*, ch. viii, pp. 10–11; E.D.M.P., H.
[2] Ibid. ch. viii, pp. 13–14.

'base commercial motives', and engendered initial suspicion even among his allies. 'Even Sir Charles Dilke & Mr. Fox-Bourne strongly queried the wisdom of my insistence upon this fundamental issue.' [1] Friends were wary of supporting anything so mercenary as a commercial case. 'Monkswell jibes at the word "trade" and is horrified lest we be thought running a trade idea. He has not grasped the economic question.' [2] Yet Morel's persistence brought many such doubters around to his view. Dilke wrote to him in 1908: 'You showed us that all depended upon the right of the original black inhabitants of the soil to own their own property & carry on trade.' [3] It was Morel's achievement that by 1908 a small but influential group of men were convinced that the morality of imperialism *vis-à-vis* subject races was dependent upon its economic foundations; that one kind of 'economic imperialism' was wrong; and that economics lay at the root of colonial reform.

And Morel's interest, even when he was most immersed in the affairs of his Congo Reform Association, was not confined to the Congo; nor did he limit to the concessionaire régime there the application of his 'trade' principle. What had happened in the Congo, he said, was threatened elsewhere; in British West Africa gold-miners were urging on the Government a similar policy with the aim of getting the 'lazy' native to work, and the Forest Laws of Southern Nigeria were just as abusive of native land-rights as was the Congo system.[4] The Government was surrounded by 'evil counsels';

In the Congo State we see what these counsels lead to when put into practice. All this talk about the puerility of preserving land tenure, the futility of maintaining native institutions, the efficacy of punitive expeditions, the necessity of teaching the native 'the dignity of labour', the cry for territorial concessions, the advocacy of monopoly, and all legislative acts framed in accordance with these views, or with some of

[1] Ibid. ch. viii, p. 14.
[2] Morel to Holt, 5 June 1907; J.H.P., box 18, file 4.
[3] Morel, *MS. History*, ch. viii, p. 15; E.D.M.P., H.
[4] Morel, *Affairs of West Africa*, ch. xix.

them, tend to produce in greater or less degree a state of affairs in tropical Africa similar to that which prevails in the Congo.[1]

Europe's desire for fresh markets, and her industrial need for Africa's raw materials,[2] together with the greed for gold (in 1902 Morel was particularly concerned about the Gold Coast), had 'let loose a flood of ignorant talk about West Africa',[3] and a host of new schemes for the impatient and forcible 'development' of Africa. These schemes contemplated the expropriation of the natives' lands. Such confiscation would be disastrous to real African development, and especially economic development.[4] This could only come about on the basis of native proprietorship.[5]

> In those whose labour is alone available for the cultivation of the land and for the harvesting of its natural wealth, in those is ownership of the land and its products vested; and with those – the people of the land – must the white man negotiate on terms of honest commercial dealing if he would acquire those products of which modern industrialism has need.
> From this fundamental principle which regulates and directs relationships between the white man and the black in the African tropics... there can be no derogation. To retreat a single inch in this regard is to leave the door wide open to the buccaneer, the pirate, and the slaver. ....
> This principle is termed TRADE.
> Trade means barter, or exchange. Between individuals, as between nations, it presupposes, and in practice necessitates, the possession on either side of commodities to sell with which to purchase. In the African tropics the commodities possessed by the inhabitants are the raw products of their plains and their forests, products which they alone can cultivate or gather.[6]

The methods of the modern imperialism of industrial capitalism

---

[1] Ibid. p. 352.   [2] Ibid. p. 22.   [3] Ibid. p. 183.   [4] Ibid. p. 187.
[5] Morel spent much time establishing that in Tropical Africa 'every square yard of the country is *owned*' – communally if not individually – by the natives. See ibid. p. 173.
[6] Morel, *Red Rubber* (2nd ed. 1907), pp. 201–2.

were sabotaging the self-development of the tropical native. That development was dependent on free exchange. And free exchange in turn depended on peasant proprietorship.

Each strand of Morel's argument had its precedents. Sir Thomas Fowell Buxton had anticipated his 'trade' theory in 1840,[1] and Holt was forever preaching it. Mary Kingsley had discussed the question of proprietorship.[2] Dilke and Fox Bourne had agitated for some time against the Congo atrocities. But by combining all these things together into a consistent and (it seemed) watertight theory, Morel was able to make a greater impact than those before him. For the Congo atrocities he had an *explanation* – his general theory. And for the theory – peasant proprietorship and trade versus the concessionaire system – he had powerful evidence and an illustration in the Congo.

This combination of fact and idea gave Morel a great advantage. He could be much more effective in combating the Congo Free State, because he saw the problem not so much in terms of isolated abuses, to be corrected perhaps sporadically by diplomatic action, with little hope of guarantee against their repetition; but as the outcome of a false system, to be reformed once and for all by a drastic but simple and infallible solution. And that solution was consistent with the ideas and interests of a potentially powerful section of English commercial life, who would give him moral and material support. Secondly, in trying to reform the administration of British West Africa, Morel could use the Congo situation to arouse public and official interest in his general schemes. Mary Kingsley had complained again and again of apathy about West Africa, and of complacency about British policy there.[3] Now the Congo scandal came to dispel this apathy. It was presented in such a horrific fashion – with testimonies from missionaries and travellers as to the most brutal atrocities, accompanied by numerous photographs of mutilated Congolese natives[4]

[1] See above, p. 23.   [2] Mary Kingsley, *West African Studies*, ch. xviii.
[3] See above, pp. 241, 251.
[4] See especially (for horror-photographs) Morel's *King Leopold's Rule in Africa* and S. L. Clemens (Mark Twain), *King Leopold's Soliloquy*.

– as both to thrill and to enrage a general public weaned on the 'Penny Dreadful'. And the C.F.S. was a foreign possession, run by foreign personnel, so that criticism of it did not directly harm the Englishman's national *amour propre*. Much of the credit for keeping the Congo in the public eye for so long must go to Morel's own personal journalistic skill and his perseverance; but the nature of the affair was much to his advantage. And while the Congo was in the public eye, with Morel to drive home a general moral applicable to all Africa, West Africa was there too. The Congo forced people to think about the problems of tropical government, and some of this speculation, guided by Morel, was transferred to the British possessions.

III. THE CONGO REFORM ASSOCIATION

Such was the full-blown colonial critique of the Liverpool School, with its triple roots in the Indirect Rule of Mary Kingsley, the Free Trade of John Holt and Congo land policy. Like Hobson's critique it arose out of the New Imperialism of the 1890s, and especially its capitalistic aspect. But the Liverpool School's ideology was not merely a critique, it was a practical policy too; Morel was not content only to write books in splendid academic isolation, but was concerned also to see his recommendations put into practice; and he was no less active as an organiser of political movements than as a writer. The main vehicle for his ideas at this early stage was the Congo Reform Association, and it is worth recounting, very briefly, the Association's history: because it was the concrete manifestation of his ideology, and the means by which that ideology was transmitted to other men, men more prominent and influential in public affairs than himself. These men in turn added new ingredients to the Liverpool philosophy which strengthened it and gave it a broader popular basis.[1]

Roger Casement, for example, whose consular investigation of

[1] Cookey, 'Great Britain and the Congo Question', treats in detail the whole history of British diplomacy *vis-à-vis* the Congo, and in particular the C.R.A.'s part in it.

the Congo Free State in 1903 did most to arouse public feeling against Leopold's methods, brought with him into the C.R.A. that hostility to 'landlordism' which was the inevitable concomitant of Irish nationalism, and which tied in well both with traditional English Radical prejudices and with Morelism. His sympathy for the Congolese natives, he claimed, arose largely out of the same opinions which were to hang him twelve years later; to Alice Stopford Green, the Irish widow of the historian J. R. Green, he wrote in April 1904:

> I think it has been my insight into human suffering and into the wrongs of the spoiler and the ruffian who takes 'Civilisation' for his watchword when his object is the appropriation of the land and labour of others for personal profit and which the tale of English occupation in Ireland so continually illustrates that gave me the deep interest I felt in the lot of the Congo natives.

The Congo situation was, he said, 'a tyranny beyond conception save only, perhaps, to an Irish mind alive to the horrors once daily enacted in this land'.[1] It was Casement, in fact, who first conceived the idea of a Congo Reform Association in January 1904,[2] and who fired Morel's enthusiasm. His engaging, fanatical personality endeared him to Morel; 'He is a man in 10,000,' the latter wrote to Holt in 1904,[3] and six years later, 'I think Casement is about as near to being a saint as a man can be.' [4] They worked closely together all through the 1900s, but in an unequal kind of way, Casement providing the fire and Morel the hard

---

[1] Casement to Mrs Green, 24 Apr 1904, in A.S.G.P., N.L.I., MS. 10464. To William Cadbury he said the same thing: '. . . it was only because I was an Irishman that I could understand *fully*, I think, the whole scheme of wrongdoing at work on the Congo' (Casement to Cadbury, 7 July 1905, in Casement Papers, N.L.I., MS. 8358, item 1). It is interesting, however, to note that Casement, like Morel, had once (in 1884) been employed by Elder Dempster (René MacColl, *Roger Casement*, p. 13).
The story of Casement's mission to the Congo and his relations with the C.R.A. is told in Cookey, op. cit. pp. 77–83 and ch. iv.
[2] See Casement to Morel, 25 Jan 1904, in E.D.M.P., F8.
[3] Morel to Holt, 24 Jan 1904; J.H.P., box 18, file 2.
[4] Morel to Holt, 12 July 1910; J.H.P., box 18, file 7.

work.[1] Casement was too preoccupied with Irish questions to help in the organisation of the C.R.A.; after the publication of his consular report in February 1904 he left this to Morel.[2]

The Association's foundation (with Morel as its secretary) was announced (appropriately enough) in Liverpool on 23 March 1904,[3] and it continued in existence until 16 June 1913.[4] Its purpose was stated in a 'Preliminary Announcement' issued before its formal inauguration:

> To secure for the natives inhabiting the Congo State territories the just and humane treatment which was guaranteed to them under the Berlin and Brussels Acts.
>
> 1. By the restoration of their rights in land, and in the produce of the soil, of which pre-existing rights they have been deprived by the legislation and procedure of the Congo State.
>
> 2. By the restoration through the exercise of a just and humane administration of their individual freedom, of which individual freedom both men, women and even children have been deprived through oppressive and unlimited taxation. . . .[5]

[1] The familiarity of their relationship is illustrated by the nicknames they used for each other in their correspondence after Sept 1904: Casement called Morel 'Bulldog' and signed himself 'Tiger' or, more rarely, 'Roddie' – this in an age when even the use of the surname, unadorned, was a mark of intimacy. 'Bulldog' and 'Tiger' describe well the tenacity of the one and the ferocity of the other.

[2] See Casement's letters to Morel, 1904 to mid-1906, E.D.M.P., F8. To Morel he left a mystery the reasons why he could not actively assist in the organisation of the C.R.A. – 'I am not going to go over those reasons to you, my dear bulldog – but it is sufficient to me to know that they are over-whelmingly sound' (Casement to Morel, 25 Jan 1904; E.D.M.P., F8). But to Cadbury he wrote: 'I am only a broken reed to lean on – and just at present I am up to my Eyes in an Irish question which is causing me grave anxiety on behalf of others. The Congo question is very near my heart – but the Irish question is nearer – and I have a fight on hand so near home here that for some time I shall not be free to help or advise Morel.' (Casement to Cadbury, 7 July 1905; Casement Papers, N.L.I., MS. 8358, item 1). He was also in financial difficulties at this time.

[3] Seymour Cocks, op. cit. pp. 101–2.

[4] 'Notice of Dissolution', in E.D.M.P., F4, box 4.

[5] 'Preliminary Announcement' of the C.R.A. in E.D.M.P., F4, box 1.

These principles together formed a colonial policy of general
application, and to them Morel secured the allegiance of a large
minority of important public figures, with widely differing views
on every other question. This he did by insisting that the Association should be entirely non-sectarian and bipartisan. Such an issue
as this could too easily be used by parties or churches for political
or sectarian ends; Mary Kingsley had chided Strachey of the
Spectator for not caring about 'West Africa *itself* but only how it
bears on politics',[1] and Morel wanted to make certain that the
Congo Reform movement was free from such irrelevant and
enervating associations. Before a parliamentary debate on the
Congo in 1903 he wrote to Holt: 'Let us do all we can to do away
with the idea that the thing is a party question';[2] and he deplored
the attitude of Fox Bourne in thinking (he said) of himself and
his Aborigines Protection Society first 'and the Congo natives
afterwards'.[3] He even went so far as to try to prevent the missionary organiser Grattan Guinness from opening a meeting
with a prayer, on the ground that 'It would at once give it a
religious flavour, which would do it harm.' [4] His fastidiousness
in this respect was amply repaid. The list of his supporters is
impressive both for their social and political distinction and for
the variety among them. He was able to reconcile such conflicting
personalities as those of the missionary Grattan Guinness and the
godless Fox Bourne, and Members of Parliament from all parties
and all sections – Dilke,[5] Samuel, Wedgwood, Channing,

[1] See above, p. 252.   [2] Morel to Holt, 24 Apr 1903; J.H.P., box 18, file 1.
[3] Morel to Casement, 8 Mar 1903, E.D.M.P., G (copy-book), vol. 5d,
p. 417. Fox Bourne, of course, was afraid that the C.R.A. might steal some
of the A.P.S.'s thunder.
[4] Morel to Holt, 3 Feb 1904; J.H.P., box 18, file 2.
[5] Dilke was at first afraid for the effect the C.R.A. might have on the
traditional humanitarian organisations. 'Morel, no doubt, can do a great
deal; but there has for several years been a most crying case, & excellent
appeals based on it have been sent far & wide by the Aborigines Protection
Society, by the Anti-Slavery Society, and recently by Stead's International
Association. . . . So that [it] is very doubtful, whatever energy is thrown into
the matter, whether more could be done by the new Association than to
bleed & kill the Anti-Slavery Soc^y. & the Aborigines Protection Soc^y . . .'
(Dilke to Casement, 12 Feb 1904; Casement Papers, N.L.I., MS. 13073).

MacDonald, Sir Gilbert Parker. His net was spread wide, and he caught some big fish. Among those who served on the C.R.A.'s executive body (besides these politicians) were Lords Beauchamp, Aberdeen, Listowel and Mayo; the Bishops of Southwark and Liverpool; Sylvester Horne, John Clifford, R. J. Campbell and John Scott Lidgett among the nonconformists; the journalists Harold Spender and St Loe Strachey; a handful of Gladstones, Buxtons, Wilberforces and Foxes – powerful names in humanitarian circles; and John Holt, Alfred Emmott and William Cadbury representing industry and commerce.[1] Conan Doyle and Mark Twain lent their pens to the cause.[2] And Morel had the public support of Sir Harry Johnston,[3] and the private sympathy of Sir George Denton, Sir William MacGregor and Sir Percy Girouard among colonial administrators.

These men helped to wean the movement away from its exclusive identification with Liverpool trading interests. Through them other ideological factors became associated with the central body of 'Morelist' doctrine: the old-fashioned humanitarianism of the missionaries and philanthropists, for example, and the newfangled ideas of the 'single taxers', Wedgwood and Girouard. These last, with their emphasis on land-values as the key to social and economic problems, were clearly particularly receptive to Morel's anti-landlordism.[4] In its final form, Morelism had become

[1] List in E.D.M.P., F4, box 4.
[2] See Sir A. Conan Doyle, *The Crime of the Congo*, and Clemens, *King Leopold's Soliloquy*. Conan Doyle was 'converted' by Morel's *Red Rubber* (see Doyle to Morel, 10 July 1907, in E.D.M.P., F8), Twain by a visit from Morel (see Morel's Introduction to Clemens, op. cit.). Joseph Conrad, with first-hand experience of Central Africa, was sympathetic to the cause. He wrote to Casement, 17 Dec 1903: 'There can be no doubt that his [Morel's] presentation of the commercial policy and the administrative methods of the Congo State is absolutely true' (Casement Papers, N.L.I., MS. 13073). His short novel, *Heart of Darkness* (1902) gives a terrifying picture of the Congo situation.
[3] Johnston was at first dubious, but on 3 Apr 1905 he wrote to Casement: 'I have at last seen my way clear to join the Congo Reform Association; I mean, I have become convinced that Morel's accounts are no more exaggerated than your dispatches' (Casement Papers, N.L.I., MS. 13073). In 1906 he wrote the Introduction to Morel's *Red Rubber*.
[4] See below, p. 303. Nworah places much emphasis on the influence of Henry George on Morel's policies for British West Africa, through Wedg-

a broad and many-sided philosophy; but still its central theme was simply and firmly the one which Morel had drawn, at the turn of the century, from Mary Kingsley, Holt and the Congo.

Its immediate practical impact is hard to gauge. By its sustained campaign of propaganda, in the Press, in pamphlets and at organised meetings, and by means of Morel's indefatigable efforts to secure the support of influential men and organisations for his cause, the C.R.A. was largely instrumental in stimulating the Belgian Parliament to take over the control of the Congo State in 1909: this was its primary object, and here it was successful. But the new Belgian Congo was not concession-free, and the diplomatic sanctions which Morel had demanded against the C.F.S. were never applied. How influential the British agitation was, compared (for example) with Vandervelde's agitation in Belgium itself, is largely a matter for speculation. And it has been suggested that even without Morel's influence the Congo's wastefulness 'would in any event have necessitated a change of system'.[1] In this matter it is difficult to extricate Morel's impact from the tangle of other pertinent factors. The same can be said of his impact on English opinion, which has more relevance to our purpose. Morel had brought the general issue before the public; Putumayo later showed how widespread it was – 'It is *EDM* versus Leopold all over again & the same *Root* policy under both Tyrants . . .' wrote Casement from South America; 'Land confiscation the key in both cases.' [2] But Morel himself soon lost all faith in the power of public opinion to influence external policy, and this led him in 1914 into the Union of Democratic Control with Hobson, Angell and MacDonald. In Parliament, however, his influence was more tangible. His hand is seen immediately in the Commons debate on the Congo of May 20 1903, when Alfred Emmott gave great emphasis to the evils of the *system*, not merely its abuses, and besought Members to 'stand at the back of our John Holts, and

---

wood (op. cit. pp. 303–8); but it is clear that those policies derived from his Congo ideology, and predated any knowledge he may have had of Henry George.

[1] Hancock, *British Commonwealth Affairs*, ii 2, p. 180.
[2] Casement to Morel, n.d. (April 1911?); E.D.M.P., F8.

men of that kind'.[1] Morel, in fact, had briefed him the day before.[2] From 1903 there were annual debates on the Congo, and Morel provided Emmott, Dilke, Herbert Samuel, Sir Gilbert Parker, Francis Channing, Ramsay MacDonald and Josiah Wedgwood with a flood of facts and figures to use in their speeches.[3] In 1906 a formal pressure group was organised, with Ramsay MacDonald as its chairman.[4] Behind the Congo lobby Morel was all the time controlling affairs, stressing 'earnestly' to its members the principle 'that the thing to fight is the system itself',[5] and making certain that they kept to the straight and narrow path of Morelism.

And these men did not confine their Morelism to the Congo. Dilke applied it more widely in a paper he composed shortly before his death on 'Indentured and Forced Labour'.[6] MacDonald's *Labour and the Empire* (1907) is strongly redolent of Morel as well as of Hobson.[7] And several Congo Reformers were soon to find themselves in high places, whence, perhaps, they could hope to influence the colonial policy of the Liberal Government: Samuel and Emmott both became members of that government, the latter as Colonial Under-Secretary. Wedgwood sat on the Northern Nigeria Lands Committee of 1908[8] and on the West African Lands Committee of 1912–16,[9] and here he pursued a line which was a curious amalgam of Morelism and Henry George. These committees, in fact, provide the most impressive evidence of Morel's achievement. He himself was a member of the second of them (and Holt and his son gave evidence), and his insistence on the preservation of native land-rights met with little opposition from its other members. They all agreed and reported that, whatever the details of West African land-law, it should rest on the 'fundamental basis' of 'the preservation, with such defini-

---

[1] 4 P.D. 122, c. 1311.
[2] Morel to Emmott, 19 May 1903; E.D.M.P., G (copy-book), vol. 2c.
[3] See E.D.M.P., *passim*.
[4] See MacDonald to Morel, 21 Feb, and Morel to MacDonald, 28 Feb 1906; E.D.M.P., F8 and G8.
[5] Morel to MacDonald, 13 Mar 1906; E.D.M.P., G8.
[6] Printed in *Papers on Inter-Racial Problems*, pp. 312–22.
[7] See especially pp. 17–20, 98–100.   [8] P.P. (1910), xliv.
[9] Their report was never published. Draft in Colonial Office Library.

tions and modifications as may be found necessary, of existing native customs with regard to the use and occupation of the land'.[1]

Sir Harry Johnston had no doubts about Morel's influence. When *Red Rubber* was published he wrote to him: 'You have made a great hit with your book – perhaps greater than you realise. I have heard it discussed in rather high political circles, and even by prominent officials, who are not wont to be readily moved.' [2] Two years later he told him:

> Your great crusade has had an enormous effect on the future of the African. Your words and theories have been studied in Uganda, throughout the coastlands of West Africa and by the educated Kaffirs, as well as by civilised governments. I do not doubt that much of the recent trend of the Colonial Office policy has been inspired by you.[3]

Among men connected with Nigeria (which Morel visited in 1910) there is strong evidence of a real personal influence. Goldie disappointed Morel by refusing to join the C.R.A. because (he said) he had failed to provide an alternative to the Free State system.[4] But Lugard was more sympathetic;[5] and, despite Holt's doubts about Lugard and implacable hostility to the Crown Colony system, Morel exchanged long and informative letters with him.[6] It is too much to say that *The Dual Mandate in British Tropical Africa* was directly influenced by Morel's works, or his administration of Nigeria by Morel's recommendations, but there are similarities between them; and Lugard – to Holt and Mary Kingsley the embodiment of all West African evils – was at

---

[1] P.P. (1910), xliv, Report, para. 16.
[2] Johnston to Morel, 23 Dec 1906; E.D.M.P., F8.
[3] Johnston to Morel, 8 Sept 1908; E.D.M.P., F8.   [4] E.D.M.P., F8.
[5] See Morel to Holt, 13 Oct 1903; E.D.M.P., G, vol. 5c, p. 270.
[6] Not many of which are extant either in the Morel or the Lugard papers. But see E.D.M.P., G, vol. 5c, and F9; also Lugard to Casement, 28 July 1911, in Casement Papers, N.L.I., MS. 13073 (Miscellaneous). John Holt came to like Lugard better shortly before his death. 'Your scheme of Government', he wrote to him on 8 Feb 1914, 'commends itself fully to my idea of what is sound and good. I love your ideal of working with the native rulers for the government of their country' (J.H.P., box 11, file 5).

K

any rate now back in the Liverpool School's good books. Sir Percy Girouard also corresponded with Morel and Wedgwood,[1] and his memoranda to the Nigerian Lands Committee – criticising their report for not recommending a specific declaration reserving the produce of the land to the natives, and citing the Congo as an example of the danger of declaring 'vacant' lands crown possessions – tallied closely with their views.[2]

Yet if these men *were* influenced by Morel, Morel's importance in this regard was not in inaugurating a *new* policy. That policy, of preserving native land-tenure, was to a great extent the 'traditional' Colonial Office line. Rather he helped to prevent a reaction setting in against it, to stem the tide of agitation on behalf of a new 'plantation' system. He and Holt together wanted only a return to the old methods of informal, commercial imperialism, a *return* to Indirect Rule.

IV. MORELISM VERSUS THE DUAL MANDATE

We shall have something more to say about the impact of Morelism on British Colonial policy in the next chapter: about its virtues and its shortcomings in the later part of the twentieth century. In many respects it was to prove deficient. But before we leave the Liverpool School and turn to other things we must take note of one incident in its history which was to point its deficiency even before the Congo Reform Association ended its career, an incident which seriously undermined its consistency and compromised its internal logic. For the traffic in ideas was not all one-way. In the second decade of the new century Morel's own somewhat rigid imperial ideology was to bend a little under the pressure of circumstances and of persuasion, and the factors which led to this virtual betrayal of his principles are so instructive as to deserve recounting at some length.

The weakness of Morelism lay in the Congo situation itself.

[1] E.D.M.P., F9; and Wedgwood Papers (Barlaston, Staffs.), *passim*, especially letter of 20 Nov 1908.
[2] P.P. (1910), xliv, Girouard's second memorandum, paras. 16–20.

The problem was this. However simple the explanation for the Congo atrocities appeared – monopoly and land-alienation – it soon became clear that the *solution* involved more than a mere restoration of native land-rights. The Congo was far too disorganised to return to, or to adopt, a system of peasant proprietorship and free trade immediately Leopold's power had been destroyed. As Casement reminded him in October 1905:

> Remember, that if the native was first robbed of his rights in land, his freedom as a human being, and his enjoyment of the products of his industry by a mere stroke of the pen, that consummate theft has since been elaborated by 15 years of comprehensive and carefully developed labour. You cannot undo the work of those 15 busy years by a stroke of the pen![1]

Morel accepted this. 'A steady patient healing process,' he wrote to Goldie in 1907, would be necessary after the present system had been overthrown. But this, he said, should not dissuade them from making the attempt. 'The Congo is not going to run away.' And the essential prerequisite for such a reform, the immediate object to be aimed at, was still the 'stroke of the pen'. Belgium must take over the Congo and reverse the existing economic system; 'the cardinal necessity of the situation is, precisely, the re-establishment of freedom and commerce'. *After that*, native prosperity could be slowly and carefully built up, until it had returned to 'the normal' – peaceful and profitable trading with native producers.[2]

Yet even here he was to encounter obstacles. They were presented to Morel in three forms; first, by doubts expressed by many of his contemporaries as to the ability of the native to develop on these lines sufficiently to satisfy the demands of the outside world; secondly, by the failure of the traders to take the opportunity afforded by Leopold's demise to demonstrate the possibilities of the trade approach; and thirdly by the conditions of the post-Leopoldian Congo, which were so poor as to resign Morel to a 'second-best' solution.

[1] Casement to Morel, 22 Oct 1905; E.D.M.P., F8.
[2] Morel to Goldie (copy), 12 July 1907; E.D.M.P., F8.

During the Congo agitation, Morel's stand on the principle of native rights in land had been firm and uncomplicated. Legally, *all* the land in West Africa, even land termed 'vacant' or 'waste', belonged to the natives; and only by recognising their rights, by permitting free trade with the Africans, and by assisting them to improve their technical methods, could African agriculture and industry be developed without friction. Morel chiefly looked at the problem from the point of view of the native and the merchant, and in so far as he ever considered the claims of 'humanity' in general (or what Hobson called 'international social utility'), he assumed that this method would, in the long run, be most beneficial to them also. This is why he stressed the foolishness as well as the wickedness of the concessionaire system, and the Congo, exhausted after a few years of forcible 'development', confirmed his opinion that the interests of the world, as well as of the natives, were best served by the policy of peasant proprietorship. Permanent African prosperity, and consequently the prosperity of Liverpool and the world, could not be *forced* by plantation schemes, however profitable they appeared in the short run.

But this attitude in its extreme form clashed with another trend of thought, which in every other way closely resembled Morelism – in its concern for the native and its opposition to the financial exploitation of Africa. This was the view – partly a reaction away from the *laissez-faire* attitude which would preserve all 'national' rights regardless of what a people did with its territory – that misuse or neglect of the land justified imperial intervention, in the wider interests of 'the world'. This was Benjamin Kidd's view, and the Fabians'; and Hobson, although hedging it round with safeguards, accepted it in principle.[1] In essence it was identical to Lugard's 'Dual Mandate' idea: colonising powers held a mandate on behalf both of the natives and of humanity at large; and sometimes these two might seem to conflict.

Morel, concerned chiefly with the first mandate, reconciled it almost casually and incidentally with the second only by assuming that the general interest would follow automatically and unconditionally from the particular interests of the natives; by assuming

[1] See above, pp. 230 ff.

that if the natives were looked after, then the world would naturally benefit, by trade. The gradual increase of European trade with African peasant proprietors was the only – and a sufficient – return for colonial enterprise. This view was founded upon a confident faith in the African, in his ability to develop his own resources sufficiently to satisfy the growing needs of European industry for those resources. Morel was aware of the increasing European demand for tropical products, but he attributed any attempt to satisfy that demand by means which transgressed his principles to unreasonable impatience. African production, on a basis of peasant proprietorship, and stimulated by Western advice and the stimulus of trade, *could* keep pace with European industrial growth.

Among Morel's sympathisers, however, there were those who were more sceptical of the natives' abilities. One of these was Sir Harry Johnston, a pillar of the Congo agitation, and a frequent correspondent of Morel's. Johnston in 1907–8 was worried especially by recent events in Liberia,[1] and by the suspicion that perhaps the African might be unfitted to develop his own country. He suggested to Morel that, in the case of sparsely populated lands, it was wrong to 'lock up the potential wealth of that country for the benefit of a people whose mode of life was of a very low order and of no use to the mass of humanity'.[2] The ownership of such territories should be vested 'in the government of the country'; this was, he conceded, 'awfully like what Leopold maintains', but the difference lay 'in the application of the theory'.[3] Morel's gospel, he said, was acceptable 'as *our ultimate standard of right-dealing*'. But it was not universally applicable. His experience had shown him that the Negro was inherently lazy, that he lacked 'esprit de corps and sympathy with other negroes', and that he disliked 'sustained work EXCEPT WHEN ASSOCIATED WITH THE EUROPEAN or mixed with foreign blood'. He was a subject race; why? 'It is *not* only the inherent

[1] He published a book on Liberia in 1906. At this time he was associated with two Liberian companies (see R. Oliver, *Sir Harry Johnston*, p. 342).

[2] Johnston to Morel, 28 June 1907; E.D.M.P., F8.

[3] Johnston to Morel, 29 May 1908; E.D.M.P., F8.

wickedness of the white man, the delight of the mentally superior race to impose servitude on the mental inferior.' [1]

> The great difficulty about large regions such as the Congo is that if you vest in the natives *entirely* the *whole* of the rights to uncultivated land and the products thereof, you may be giving to a parcel of ignorant and brutish savages the fee simple over vast territories that they are quite incapable of turning to account in the general interest of the whole State.[2]

Such thoughts, he said, gave him 'qualms that I am a bit of a humbug in preaching consideration for the Negro *only*'.[3] There were wider considerations – the second part (in effect) of the Dual Mandate. Local African rights were all very well; 'But all states must now regard themselves as members of a vast Human Confederation and no one of them can demean itself selfishly so as to injure the other members.' [4] And in the interests of humanity as a whole, it was right that the colonial power should become the fiduciary owner of uncultivated land and, in that event, be allowed to 'grant concessions for working State property on lines which shall be advantageous to the general Native community: where of necessity is the harm?' In other words, Leopold's system should be readopted, but administered on more benevolent lines. 'The fact that wicked Leopold represented this fiduciary authority grossly, abominably misused his self-constituted trust does not invalidate the theory in my eyes as a working arrangement.' [5]

Morel's replies to Johnston (while ignoring most of his points) denied that he was claiming that the African had a right to unoccupied land – 'What would be the good of vesting rights, for example, in a native population where there is no native population!' [6] – and maintained that they were, in fact, in agreement on

[1] Johnston to Morel, 8 Sept 1908; E.D.M.P., F8.
[2] Johnston to Morel, 10 Oct 1908; E.D.M.P., F8.
[3] Johnston to Morel, 8 Sept 1908; E.D.M.P., F8.
[4] Johnston to Morel, 10 Oct 1908; E.D.M.P., F8.
[5] Ibid. loc. cit.
[6] Morel to Johnston, 21 Oct 1908; E.D.M.P., F8; but cf. above, p. 264, fn. 5.

essential points; but there was a clear difference between them of outlook and approach. Johnston was looking at Africa from a different viewpoint, a 'dual' viewpoint, which took into account the interests of the 'vast human confederation' as well as of the natives themselves. And his view of the African was not so optimistic as to allow him to assume, as Morel did, that what the native *wanted* was what the world *needed*. Morel's excessively simple 'trade' solution was arousing scepticism within his own camp: a scepticism born of a new, post-Cobdenite view of international society. And one specific, practical flaw in his argument Morel had been made to take account of: the point that recognition of native land-rights was not a universal solution, that there was need, in some instances, for an imperial government to take into its possession, in trust, African lands and their products, just as Leopold had claimed to be doing.

The unwillingness of the merchants to co-operate with him increased Morel's disillusion. The Liverpool traders were as divided as ever they were in Mary Kingsley's day, and when he looked elsewhere for men to demonstrate the virtues and possibilities of free trade in Africa, he met only with rebuffs. To Herbert Shaw of the Newcastle and Gateshead Chamber of Commerce he wrote in 1909: 'Of course, what I think should be done is the creation of a British Trading Company in the Congo, and I don't see why the Newcastle Chamber of Commerce should not lead the van and form such a Company. It is the obvious thing that needs doing.' [1] But Shaw replied that there was little chance of this;[2] the traders – 'a miserable crowd' [3] – had failed Morel as they had failed Mary Kingsley. He was forced to look in other directions for the economic assistance which he felt must be given by Europe towards the Congo's recovery and development. It was at this time that Sir William Lever, the soap

[1] Morel to Shaw, 13 Sept 1909; E.D.M.P., F8.
[2] Shaw to Morel, 13 Sept 1909; E.D.M.P., F8.
[3] Morel to Mrs Green, 7 Mar (?)1909: 'All that I pray and hope for is that wherever Fate may direct my footsteps it will be away from West African mercantile interests, from Mary Kingsley's "trade lords", who, with one or two exceptions, are a miserable crowd.' (A.S.G.P., N.L.I., Uncatalogued file.)

manufacturer, brought himself to Morel's attention with another African problem. Morel saw in Lever a man who, if he would not work his system, would at least not abuse the system he had opposed throughout his career; and when Lever was granted by the Belgian Government a concession in the Congo which approximated closely to Leopold's concessions, Morel decided to waive his principles on the grounds that a bad system, in the hands of a good man, was better than none.

Lever first corresponded with Morel in July 1910. A shortage of raw palm-oil had led him to apply to the Colonial Office in 1907 and 1909 for grants of land in Nigeria and Sierra Leone on which to build depericarping mills;[1] these grants would involve a monopoly within a radius of ten miles around the mills and the right to build monorails; and the Colonial Office had turned down his application. Baffled by this opposition to his schemes he wrote to Morel to ask whether *he* had had anything to do with it. He had not, he assured Morel, demanded any rights over the land or its produce, but merely a guarantee that, if he set up mills – which had yet to be proved profitable – no one else would, for a period of years, be allowed to build others nearby. The natives would not be compelled to sell through Lever Brothers, and their rights would be unaffected.[2] Morel could see nothing objectionable in the scheme. It seemed to him to be 'eminently reasonable' and 'full of the greatest potentialities for Southern Nigeria', and he wrote to his contacts at the Colonial Office, Charles Strachey and Sir Walter Egerton, on Lever's behalf.[3] On this first acquaintance Morel had been 'favourably impressed' by Lever;[4] and he advised him, now that he was about to become 'a great power in

[1] Hancock, *British Commonwealth Affairs*, ii 2, p. 190.

[2] Lever to Morel 25 July, and Morel to Chas Strachey 17 Aug 1910 (giving an account of an interview with Lever); E.D.M.P., F8.

[3] Morel to Strachey 17 Aug 1910; E.D.M.P., F8. Strachey's reply was that, in fact, Lever had asked much more of the C.O. in 1909, and it was up to Lever to make the next move (Strachey to Morel 20 Aug 1910). Lever re-applied, but still got no satisfaction from the C.O., who would only offer him the 'ludicrous' offer of a monopoly within a five-mile radius (Lever to Morel 27 Apr 1911; E.D.M.P., F8). The C.O. was in this instance more anti-monopoly than Morel.

[4] Morel to Holt, 21 Sept 1910; J.H.P., box 18, file 7.

West African affairs', to read Mary Kingsley's *West African Studies* for guidance.[1]

But his faith in Lever was a little misplaced. Morel admired him for his treatment of his employees at Port Sunlight[2] – an example of enlightened capitalism comparable with Cadbury's Bournville – and he had a very high opinion of his integrity and character; and this blinded him to the contravention of his principles which Lever was contemplating. Morel did not know it yet: but Lever's views on the African native were very different from his. He believed, first of all, that the natives should be dispossessed of their lands if they did not use them properly:

> I sometimes wish that all native chiefs ... were made dukes. In my opinion we should then take the sensible view that this land was for development and the advancement of civilisation, and just as we will not tolerate a duke keeping his land for his own pleasure, or to lock it up, and have passed laws that make this impossible in the U.K., so I can never understand why a black man should be allowed to assume a different attitude, and neither develop his own land nor allow other people to do so.[3]

And secondly (says Professor Charles Wilson),

> He was equally unimpressed by the arguments in favour of tribal organisation. Natives should be treated as 'willing children', housed, schooled, doctored, and moved from place to place as might be required. Above all, they should be taught the value of regular habits and of working to time. Under such a regime, how could they fail to become both healthy and industrious, and how then could they fail to be happy?[4]

This was exactly the attitude – 'the land for those who can use it' plus 'the dignity of labour' – which Morel saw at that time as the

---

[1] Morel to Lever, 23 Sept 1910, E.D.M.P., F8; and see Morel's eulogy of Lever's enterprise in *Nigeria*, pp. 54–5.

[2] Morel to Ernst Vohsen, 7 Nov 1912; E.D.M.P., F9.

[3] Lever, quoted in Charles Wilson, *History of Unilever*, vol. i, pp. 166–7.

[4] Ibid. i 167.

K2

most dangerous to the welfare of Africa. Before his departure for Nigeria late in 1910 he wrote to Holt:

> I agree with you that West Africa is only in its infancy. The increasing demand for tropical products will bring it more and more into the public gaze. The great fight now, which has been looming on the horizon for the last five years and which is now fairly raging behind the scenes, is whether the policy of allowing natives to develop these productions for their own benefit assisted by technical instruction from the Administration, or whether the other selfish and immoral and eventually stupid policy of taking the development out of the natives' hands and running it in the interests of European speculators with hired native labour, is going to win the day.[1]

He did not realise that Lever was on the other side. But soon this was to become obvious to Morel. For in April 1911 a Concession in the new Belgian Congo for which Lever had been angling since 1909[2] was granted to him, and the terms of the concession clearly transgressed Morel's principles.

'La Société Anonyme des Huileries de Congo Belge', under the control of Lever's Company, was granted the right to the leasehold of 750,000 hectares of land, and to the freehold of as much territory within this area as it occupied and developed.[3] This in itself was ominous. And four days after the ratification of the concession Lever revealed his mind to Morel. The negro, he said, could not organise, develop and open up large tracts of country; Liberia demonstrated this. The land should be put in the hands of those who could.

> The land of the world, in any part of the world ought to be in the possession of those people who can develop it and its resources. I do not agree therefore with you because I think that whether a man is a Duke or a Nigger he ought to stand the same in the eyes of his fellowmen & be judged by his ability and willingness to make use of God's earth. . . .

[1] Morel to Holt, 17 Oct 1910; J.H.P., box 18, file 7.
[2] Wilson, op. cit. i 167.
[3] Hancock, op. cit. ii 2, p. 194; and Wilson, op. cit. i 168 ff.

I think that your advocacy of the black man's interest can be made more helpful to the black man if whilst fighting with all your power against brutal & inhuman & inconsiderate treatment for the black man you do not build a halo round the black man & convert him into a kind of being which it will take hundreds of years of intercourse with the white man to become.[1]

Morel could not accept this. Throughout 1911 he tried to persuade Lever of the error of his ways. He insisted that not only was a concessionaire system unjust, it was also inefficient and uneconomical. 'Where a man owns his land and is his own master, he will make that land produce tenfold more than in cases where it belongs to somebody else and he is a mere labourer working on it at a fixed wage', and consequently, he said, 'the former system is better for humanity at large since it ensures a larger production'.[2] But Lever disagreed that peasant proprietorship could satisfy the needs of the world. The native could not manage the higher forms of agriculture, and the world demanded that large-scale agricultural undertakings replace small farms.[3] This was the point at issue. Granted that the native *could* develop on Morel's lines, could he develop fast enough?

Morel was forced to concede that African development would be quicker under a plantation system. But this, he still maintained, would be detrimental to the native if not to the world. Holt wrote to him in April:

My own feeling is that Lever is going too fast in that direction, he would be doing greater good to the native, if he would instruct him first of all, by simple machinery, to be invented for the purpose, how to produce a larger amount of grease products, by hand labour.[4]

That is, progress was to be deliberately and artificially retarded while the natives caught up. Morel communicated this view to

[1] Lever to Morel, 18 Apr 1911; E.D.M.P., F8.
[2] Morel to Lever, 19 Apr 1911; E.D.M.P., F8.
[3] Lever to Morel, 21 Apr 1911; E.D.M.P., F8.
[4] Holt to Morel, 26 Apr 1911; E.D.M.P., F8.

Lever. Our duty was to train the native to make the land increasingly valuable to himself.

> I would, as trustee for my native wards, put that before
> everything else, even if economic development took a little
> longer, believing that in so doing I was responding to
> the dictates of Imperial duty and adopting a course which
> would ultimately prove of most benefit to the world at
> large.[1]

By stressing the 'ultimate' rather than the immediate benefits to the world of his policy, Morel was now making those benefits seem more distant, and so was appealing to Lever's altruism rather than his interest. He still believed Lever was wrong, but he admitted that the alternative policy would retard the economic development of Africa.

Despite his doubts (and although a few months earlier he had attacked a new company, the Congo Rubber Plantations Ltd, for a scheme very similar to Lever's),[2] Morel made no public protest against Lever's concession. Many of his sympathisers expressed surprise at this silence. The (newly amalgamated) Anti-Slavery and Aborigines Protection Society issued a report on the concessions which made gloomy prognostications as to the dangers which might arise from them;[3] and Consul Ernst Vohsen of the *Deutsche Kongo-Liga* complained in strong terms of Morel's weak acceptance of the Lever Monopoly. His *volte-face* certainly appeared surprising. Partly it might be accounted for by the fact that Lever was actively and generously supporting the C.R.A. financially. It has been suggested that his contributions were in the nature of a bribe,[4] and the possibility cannot be discounted or

---

[1] Holt to Lever, 1 May 1911; E.D.M.P., F8.

[2] See Morel's correspondence with C.R.P. Ltd, in E.D.M.P., F8.

[3] Dec 1911, signed by John Harris. Copy in E.D.M.P.

[4] In July 1911 Lever contributed £100 to the C.R.A. (letter to Morel, 24 July 1911; E.D.M.P., F8); a fact which 'Morel did not reveal' to Vohsen (Cookey, 'Great Britain and the Congo Question', p. 350). Recently K. K. D. Nworah (without citing evidence) has revealed that in 1910 Lever gave Morel a cheque for £100 to support his African journey. Nworah points a sinister implication: there may, he says, have been 'an *arrière-pensée*. Although this cannot specifically be proved, the documents suggest that

disproved. But the mere fact that Lever gave money to Morel's cause does not in itself suggest corruption, and corruptibility does not tie in well with Morel's character. There is no evidence that he succumbed to any such temptation while the Congo Reform movement was in its hey-day, and his earlier support of Lever over Nigeria and Sierra Leone appears to have been spontaneous. There are adequate explanations elsewhere for his connivance in Lever's schemes. The excuse he offered to Vohsen was that they had to make the best of a bad job.[1] The principles behind the Congo scheme were, he agreed, unsound. But the concession was a *fait accompli*, so that protest would have been useless. Vandervelde – the leader of the Belgian parliamentary campaign against the old C.F.S. – had accepted it. And, besides this, the Congo was in such a debilitated condition that he considered *any* enterprise would benefit the natives, and Lever's character was such that in itself it guaranteed a humanitarian policy. It was these two considerations that determined both Morel's and John Holt's attitudes towards the Lever monopoly: their concern for the plight of the Congo, where native society had been so far disrupted as to make a solution on native lines impossible, and their joint admiration for Lever. Holt, after recounting all his doubts in a letter to Morel, was forced to make this *caveat*: 'It is something, however, to have a man like Lever, making an attempt to do the thing he is taking in hand.' [2] They trusted the man enough to let him violate the very foundations of their principles.

Yet after this Lever affair, neither Morel nor Holt were as confident as they had been even of their principles. Speaking of the Gold Coast Concessions ordinance, Morel wrote to Holt in October 1912: 'I fully realise that it is impossible to attempt to arrest industrial development, even if one were convinced that its arrest would be for the benefit, in certain cases, of humanity'. He

money changed hands'. And Morel might have needed Lever's support for his ambition to stand as parliamentary candidate for Birkenhead. (Nworah, op. cit., p. 528; and cf. p. 541.)
  [1] See Vohsen to Morel, 7 Nov, Morel to T. Buxton, 28 Feb, Morel to Vohsen, 7 Nov 1912; in E.D.M.P., F8–9.
  [2] Holt to Morel, 26 Apr 1911; E.D.M.P., F8.

was no longer certain about the question; 'My mind is largely in a state of flux concerning it'. He was not sure what was best for the Congo – 'I have failed to see clearly, what is going to be the economic outcome of these privileges granted to Lever. I mean from the native point of view.' [1] And Holt's ideas, too, were undergoing a change. He wished Lever, he said, 'every success'; his schemes were novel – 'but the man is a genius, and we have to do with a fresh set of ideas which are quite strange to us but which may turn out to be the very best thing for Africa and the advancement of her people'.[2] In January 1913 he was even more enthusiastic about these 'new ideas':

The African Merchant must altogether alter his vision. . . . He must take bigger views because Lever is come with an absolutely fresh mind full of big ideas which will mean the development of Africa on scientific lines – a complete economic revolution in fact and one which we shall have to follow or fall back in the race.[3]

And when Morel appears to have expressed alarm at this opinion, Holt replied: 'I do not like concessions any more than you do . . . but we have to do with other minds, and many other sets of ideas. Mine are old-fashioned ones.' [4] In retirement, the man who had been the bastion of the African free-trade stronghold for twenty years was losing his faith.

By 1912, therefore, the thinking of the Liverpool School, personified in Morel and Holt, had undergone modification. No longer was it uncompromisingly anti-Crown Colony and anti-Concession; the realities of the West and Central African situation had forced upon it a more realistic attitude. Even if, ideally, Morel still preferred an Africa independent, developed by peasant proprietors with the kindly help of European instructors, and providing the wants of European industry by means of trade on its own terms with unfettered Liverpool merchants, yet he was willing to recognise the impracticability of this policy and to

[1] Morel to Holt, 7 Oct 1912; E.D.M.P., F8.
[2] Holt to Morel, 17 Nov 1912; E.D.M.P., F8.
[3] Holt to Morel, 15 Jan 1913; E.D.M.P., F8.
[4] Holt to Morel, 13 Feb 1913; E.D.M.P., F8.

accept a second-best: *enlightened* Crown Colony administration and *enlightened* concessionaires. In the circumstances of the years immediately before the First World War he had to cut his losses and co-operate with an imperfect system in order to achieve the greatest possible good for Africa.

Morelism – the doctrine that African development could best be secured on African lines – originated in a non-partisan reaction against the impatient, monopoly-capitalistic exploitation of tropical countries revealed in the Congo and elsewhere at the turn of the century. It was born originally of Mary Kingsley's concern for the *cultural* impact of European imperialism on native races – for the disruptive effects of the forcible imposition of Western standards upon alien civilisations and tribal structures – and of Liverpool's alarm at the threat which newly favoured monopolistic ideas presented to their traditional methods of trading, methods which they believed to be for the good of the African as well as of themselves. It became stereotyped into a rigid economic doctrine, the doctrine of peasant proprietorship, Indirect Rule and free commerce, in the hands of E. D. Morel. What Morel, Mary Kingsley and John Holt were objecting to was what Hobson and Ramsay MacDonald deplored: capitalistic exploitation of tropical resources, the unthinking and arrogant sweeping away of 'backward' cultures on the assumption that they could and should be replaced by a European-grown civilisation, and (the down-to-earth manifestation of all this) forced native-labour, or wage-labour on Western industrial lines – 'the East African craze which has now crossed the continent – originally imported from South Africa'.[1] The system was the same in Rhodesia, the Congo and Putumayo; it was the fruit of the New Imperialism; and the result was everywhere identical. The solution for Morel, therefore, lay in abolishing the system and replacing it by its antithesis – indirect instead of direct rule, free trade in place of monopoly, peasant instead of company proprietorship. The argument was a curious mixture of various attitudes and strands of thought: anti-capitalism, anti-militarism,

[1] Holt quoted above, p. 259.

anthropological empiricism; the old-fashioned Cobdenism of *laissez-faire* and free competition, a nostalgic reactionary idealism (looking back to the 'good old days'),[1] a pinch of Henry George, especially in the attitude of Josiah Wedgwood; and a strong flavour of 'self-help'. But it all boiled down to a basically simple solution, one of those simple panaceas for complex problems which were so popular at the end of the nineteenth century and the beginning of the twentieth.[2] Like the Single Tax, the various socialisms and Norman Angellism, Morelism was a one-sentence answer to a two-volume question; and this accounted for its success – as a critique. The Congo Free State was, as we have seen, overthrown, and among the personnel and servants of the Colonial Office before and after the First World War an attitude prevailed of hostility towards plantation policies.

But as practical policy the simple solution was not quite so effective. The adherence to it of influential men ensured that the worst excesses of the plantation system would not be repeated, for the Colonial Office paid scrupulous regard to the preservation of native land-laws in the second decade of the new century. Yet the idealistic demands of the Liverpool School that native economic development be left to the natives themselves, with the friendly help of Western technologists and incentive supplied by the traders, was found to be unrealistic. In part the stumbling-block was that the traders failed Morel and Mary Kingsley, just as they had failed on the Niger in 1841 to demonstrate the viability of the trade solution. However 'wholesome' their commerce might be, it was *unprogressive*. Liquor was possibly as harmless to the natives as Mary Kingsley had claimed, but it conferred no economic benefit on West Africa,[3] and the merchants were unwilling to organise themselves in such a fashion as to prove that trade was a good and sufficient way to develop Africa

[1] Compare Hobson's idealisation of traditional Chinese society – 'a huge nest of little free village communes, self-governing, and animated by a genuine spirit of equality' (*Imperialism*, pp. 337–42) – with the Liverpool School's similar idealisation of African tribal and communal life.

[2] And, of course, not only then: cf. C.N.D. See John Morley, *Notes on Politics and History*, pp. 12–13.

[3] See J. E. Flint in *J.A.H.*, vol. iv, no. 1 (1963), p. 99.

industrially. More important, however, was the effect of that world demand of which Morel, unlike Hobson, took little or no account. The needs of an industrial world-community dictated a more drastic approach, and that was the approach of Lever Brothers.

Morel and Holt, preoccupied with the system, found the basis of Lever's enterprises abhorrent to them. But while this basis was similar to Leopold's, Lever's methods were not; and this – not the system – made all the difference. Leopold's methods were exhaustive of the land and its products, and therefore, in the long run, unprofitable even from a purely European point of view. Lever was more 'scientific' and far-seeing, and so his system was (says Sir Keith Hancock) 'more moderate in its demands upon Native land and labour'.[1] The realities of the world industrial situation made the trade approach unfeasible, because too slow; and Morel in 1912 was coming to see this – 'I fully realise that it is impossible to arrest industrial development...'.[2] Hence his wavering position immediately before the War. As he began to suspect then, his limitation was just that preoccupation with the *system* which formed the backbone of his agitation. When the system was no longer abused, it lost its terrors, and with safeguards it could work with little detriment to the African. In so far as Morel failed, it was first of all because of his idealism, which blinded him to the necessity of compromising with world demand in order to meet the second condition of the Dual Mandate; and secondly because of his dogmatism, which prevented him from admitting (as Mary Kingsley had done) that different kinds of economic development might be suited to different countries.

At bottom, however, Morel's 'anti-imperialism' was an antipathy to the New Imperialism, just as was Hobson's and the Liberals'. All of them saw something different in this New Imperialism, and this explains the variety, not so much of their interpretations of the problem, as of their solutions to it. Liberals saw it in terms of jingoism, expense and militarism; Hobson in terms of jingoism, social reaction and capitalism: all of them looked primarily at its domestic manifestations, and prescribed

[1] Hancock, op. cit. ii 2, p. 181. [2] Morel quoted above, p. 285.

their remedies accordingly. Hobson and MacDonald looked incidentally, but only incidentally, at its effects on the colonies themselves, and so parenthetically prescribed a solution for this aspect also. Mary Kingsley and Morel, on the other hand, were concerned almost exclusively with the New Imperialism as colonial policy, and so it was natural that the most practical suggestions *vis-à-vis* the Empire itself should come from them. But these suggestions were practical chiefly in so far as they were critical. The positive side of Morel's philosophy was his call for a return to the old, commercial imperialism, and this was less effective, because less realistic, than his criticisms of existing policy. His anti-imperialism was relevant to the early twentieth century; his imperialism, it seemed, was not.

CHAPTER NINE

The Twentieth Century: Radicals and Africa

LIKE Joseph Chamberlain's orchids, the imperial critiques of Hobson and Morel had been bred in a hot-house atmosphere. They had grown out of a short period of intense controversy, during which certain colonial issues were greatly magnified and their implications made to appear unnaturally alarming. There was no saying at the time how long this state of affairs would last. Certainly a Liberal would have had to be optimistic in the extreme to predict, in 1900, a landslide victory for his party six years later. Yet this is what happened; and Hobson's and Morel's tropical plants were left to flower in the cooler climate of a Liberal-run Empire. How would this affect their utility and relevance, and the colonial thinking of the broader body of Liberals and socialists?

I. PARLIAMENT: THE EMPHASIS CHANGES

Their weapons had been forged in response to a specific situation, and in the first decade of the new century the situation changed. The change can be seen as early as 1902. After the end of the South African War those aspects of imperialism which had antagonised Radicals in the first place became already less pressing. Popular jingoism was dampened by the lingering frustrations of the last months of the War, and the electorate of 1906, by contrast with that of 1900, appeared (to Liberals) sober and reasonable. Capitalistic imperialism changed its form; still active, as it seemed, in tropical and southern Africa, it was nevertheless no longer a domestic problem of the kind characterised by the Jameson Raid and the 'machinations of the Randlords' prior to the War: no longer a sinister force endangering the security of the nation by involving it, against its real will, in conflict with rival great powers. Chamberlain, the arch-enemy, had resigned in 1903 and his grander imperial schemes were given no chance to mature. The new government of 1905 was tainted more than a little, perhaps, with the spirit of Liberal imperialism, but it had had (for ten years at least) no tangible connexion with the New Imperialism which had so riled the Radicals in the 1890s. Their demands would be considered sympathetically by the new Colonial Secretary and Under-Secretary, Elgin and Churchill, and some of those demands (withdrawal from Somaliland, abolition of Chinese Labour, prohibition of West African concessions) were implemented as soon as was practicable.[1] Imperial policy was changing, despite Chamberlain's plea for 'continuity',[2] and so criticism of that policy had to change too. It was no longer so easy to take a straightforward condemnatory line against imperialism; the rôle of the Radical was now that of a reformer within the walls, rather than an assailant outside.

There was still some anti-imperialism. Hobson continued to inveigh, in Cobdenite fashion, against the capitalist-imperialist interests which were subverting the *national* interest, and his economic theory was taken up again later by H. N. Brailsford and Leonard Woolf. But for Hobson and Brailsford it was now a matter less of colonial import than of domestic and European politics, and Leonard Woolf's analysis of the economic motive in Africa was, initially, very much less rigid even than Hobson's.[3] In Parliament the Labour Party and a few Liberals carried over

[1] See R. Hyam, 'The African Policy of the Liberal Government, 1905-9', *passim.*
[2] H. of C., 19 Feb 1906; 4 P.D. 152, c. 153.
[3] For Hobson, see above, pp. 235-7. H. N. Brailsford's *The War of Steel and Gold* saw economic factors at the root of arms rivalries and the 'struggle for the balance of power'. Leonard Woolf, in *Empire and Commerce in Africa* and *Economic Imperialism*, differed from Hobson in attributing imperialism to a capitalist *frame of mind*, and not to capitalist necessity. In *Imperialism and Civilisation* his emphasis changed to a more orthodox Hobson–Leninist one.

into the post-Chamberlainite era their campaign against capitalist exploitation in the colonies. Chinese labour gave them a magnificent opportunity: it was an unexpected bonus, visible proof that they had been right all along. 'What excited such intense indignation about Chinese labour in this country', said Herbert Paul in 1906,

> was the fact that it was the sign and symbol of that gigantic swindle, that colossal fraud, the policy of the late Government in South Africa. Five and a half years ago the people of this country were humbugged and deceived . . . but their eyes were now open to the fact that the policy of the late Government was engineered in South Africa by bloodthirsty money grubbers . . . mostly of foreign extraction, without honour, without conscience, without country, without God. . . . They saw now . . . that the war was a sweaters' war, a war for cheap labour.[1]

Throughout Balfour's administration this was still the lynch-pin of the Radicals' case. The only difference was that it was gaining converts. Many who had kept quiet during the War, or who had actively supported the war policy, came more and more to accept in some degree the anti-capitalist argument. By 1903 Sir John Gorst – a Tory – had developed a strong distaste for the 'dirty gold from the reefs of the Transvaal';[2] and even Winston Churchill, who in 1901 had scorned the idea that the War was motivated by capitalists,[3] was four years later prepared to admit that the mine-owners exerted 'tremendous influence', often adversely, over the Press and the Colonial Office.[4] The Congo and the South African native-labour question provided more material for anti-capitalists to work on.[5] This economic line of

---

[1] H. of C., 19 Feb 1906; 4 P.D. 152, cc. 201–2.
[2] H. of C., 24 Mar 1903; 4 P.D. 120, c. 78.
[3] H. of C., 18 Feb 1901; 4 P.D. 89, c. 414.
[4] H. of C., 22 Mar 1905; 4 P.D. 143, cc. 842–3.
[5] Examples of Radical anti-capitalism are too numerous to list in detail, but they are found in the S. African debates of 19 and 24 Mar and 30 July 1903; 16–17 Feb, 21 Mar, 5 May and 21 July 1904; and 17 Feb and 22 Mar 1905. A curious exception to the otherwise unanimous hostility of Radicals and Liberals to Chinese labour is A. B. Markham, who had been in the fore-

argument was becoming a popular and even a respectable one. But it was not the same as anti-imperialism; and indeed we shall see that there was *less* anti-imperialism in Parliament, even among Labour M.P.s, after the Boer War than before. It was replaced on the Left by criticism, along constructive lines, of the *details* of colonial policy.

The reasons for this are not difficult to find. In the first place, the old guard of Liberal Little Englanders found its forces much depleted in the new Parliament of 1906. Sir William Vernon Harcourt had died in 1904, and Labouchere retired to a Florentine villa in the following year. Two other prominent Radicals, Burns and Morley, were absorbed into Campbell-Bannerman's government and their cabinet positions effectively silenced them on African affairs. With the departure of these men, and the demise of the party of 'forward' imperialism, went the old 'Peace, Retrenchment, Reform' doctrine which had led its adherents to take so little interest in the affairs of the tropical empire – except to demand its evacuation. Now and again there was a recrudescence of the 'traditional' Liberal line: the only significant occasion was in April 1914, when a handful of M.P.s begrudged money spent in East Africa on the grounds that 'charity should begin at home' – in the English Midlands or in Scotland.[1] But such isolated outbreaks were untypical. Earl Winterton noted the change: 'In the old days a proposal to vote a single penny to any colony or dependency was met with an outburst by hon. Members below the Gangway, but I am glad to see that they are conspicuous by their absence today.'[2] The Little Englanders had gone; and to

front of the attack on capitalist cartels in S. Africa during and after the War, yet strongly supported the Chinese Labour Ordinance; see 4 P.D. 120 (cc. 85 ff.), 138 (cc. 827 ff.) and 152 (cc. 604 ff.).

Bertrand Russell was another who was converted to pacifist anti-capitalism after 1900 – though in a somewhat unorthodox fashion; see his *Autobiography*, vol. i (1967), p. 146; and also a letter of 1905 quoted on p. 176: '... though Balfour governs the Empire, Werner governs Balfour'.

[1] Debate on the East Africa Loans Bill, 7 Apr 1914; 5 P.D. (Commons) 60, cc. 1849–58 and 61, cc. 49–51; speeches of R. L. Outhwaite, James Hogge and F. H. Booth.

[2] 5 P.D. (Commons) 60, c. 1836; and cf. Sir Clement Hill in H. of C., 29 July 1912; 5 P.D. (Commons) 41, c. 1674.

fill their places there appeared men like J. M. Robertson, a colleague of Hobson's and an Ethicist; Josiah Wedgwood, once a member of Milner's 'Kindergarten' and soon to become an African land-reformer à la Morel; and Ramsay MacDonald, also apprenticed in the school of Hobson and the Ethicists, with a train of new Labour M.P.s – some of them more willing than their predecessors to concern themselves with empire – behind him.[1] Nearly all those M.P.s who gave them their consistent support were newly elected in 1906 – the Liberals Percy Alden, William Byles, Harold Cox, Herbert Paul and T. Edmund Harvey, and the Labourites Thomas Summerbell, James O'Grady, Stephen Walsh and John Ward. None of these men was fashioned in the old Liberal mould, least of all the socialists (O'Grady, Walsh and Ward were even accredited with 'imperialist' tendencies);[2] nor were those who remained from the old Parliament to take an active part in colonial debates – Gorst, Dilke and Sir Gilbert Parker. So far as discussion of imperial questions was concerned, the character of the Radical Left had undergone an almost total transformation.

Then again, the situation was less conducive to a purely Anglocentric preoccupation. Most Radicals before 1902 had been against the tropical Empire because of what it did to England – because it impoverished her or involved her in war. After 1902 this might have been no less true, but it was less blatantly so. The Boer War had identified imperialism with jingo mobs, social reaction and war; afterwards there was nothing to do this in quite the same way. The imperial debate, therefore, was freed from the distraction of the 'Greater Britain/Little England' controversy which had bedevilled the Radical approach in earlier days, and turned into other channels. More time could be devoted to Africa *per se*. The question was no longer 'should we have an empire?', but 'what should we do with the empire we have?' The new,

---

[1] By G. D. H. Cole's computation, 30 Labour Party M.P.s and 25 'Lib–Labs' or miners were elected in 1906 (*British Working-Class Politics 1832–1914*, pp. 281–7).

[2] See *M.G.*, 20 Dec 1934, p. 10 (Ward), and 18 Mar 1929, p. 7 (Walsh); and *The Times*, 11 Dec 1934, p. 11 (O'Grady).

enlarged limits of Britain's South African possessions, for example, became accepted, and the South African issue now turned on the question of how best to guarantee the welfare of their indigenous inhabitants. This question gradually became isolated from the welter of issues which had obscured it before and during the War. South Africa had always had a 'race problem': but to all but a very few the term had been applied exclusively to the British–Dutch antithesis. Now it came to embrace in addition the native and 'coloured' races, and soon it was to become repolarised around a black–white axis. Similarly, debates on East and West Africa were conducted with the problems of native labour and land-tenure, rather than that of expansion, chiefly in mind. The native question had been elevated for the first time to the forefront of the Radical case.

Perhaps there was another, less creditable reason for the Radicals' more compromising approach to imperial questions. The old Liberals had only been peripherally interested in the Empire: chiefly they resented the way it detracted from domestic reform. Labouchere's 'main objection' to Somaliland campaigns was that 'they were an absolute waste of money, and heaven knows there were many social improvements for which we required money in England'.[1] Yet this very fact pointed to a way in which the Empire might be made more attractive to Radicals, attractive enough for them to take a constructive interest in its government. Thomas Lough said in 1903 that 'what he contended for was that these countries should be developed with some regard to the trade we got out of them';[2] and if colonial expansion and development could be shown to be profitable, then Radicals might not be so careless of the Empire's welfare. The Lancashire cotton famine of 1902 pointed the relevance of colonial development to working-class interests in a way that Chamberlain's propaganda to the same end had failed to do. It was estimated that 700 cotton mills were working short time by 1903,[3] and the reason was a shortage of raw cotton from the main source of supply, the southern states

[1] H. of C. 8 Mar 1905; 4 P.D. 142, c. 771.
[2] H. of C., 2 Mar 1903; 4 P.D. 118, c. 1197.
[3] Gerald Balfour in H. of C., 24 July 1903; 4 P.D. 126, c. 228.

of America, and 'American speculation based on that shortage'.[1] In 1902 Lancashire manufacturers combined with operatives to found the British Cotton Growing Association, in order to explore the possibilities of developing alternative sources of supply within the Empire. Reports prepared for the Government encouraged the belief that West Africa, and later East Africa, were suited to cotton cultivation,[2] and the approval of all sections of the House of Commons for government aid to such enterprises was secured in April 1905.[3] The attitude of Philip Snowden – Labour M.P. for Blackburn – to the East Africa Loans Bill of 1912 is significant. He objected to all its clauses except one: 'As a member for a Lancashire constituency which consumes more raw cotton than any country in the world I cannot but look with approval upon the proposal to grant a loan for the development of cotton growing in East Africa.'[4] Imperial cotton-growing schemes were clearly as much in the interests of workers as of mill-owners. If East Africa could be shown to be useful for such purposes, then it might reconcile many Radicals to the African railway enterprises their predecessors had so reviled. It might also help to unite Labour M.P.s with more 'imperially minded' colonial reformers on the basis of a common interest. In this instance Friedrich Engels' earlier judgment could contain a grain of truth:

> You ask me what the English workers think about colonial policy. Well, exactly the same as they think about politics in general: the same as the bourgeois think. There is no workers' party here, you see, there are only Conservatives and Liberal-Radicals, and the workers gaily share the feast of England's monopoly of the world market and the colonies.[5]

[1] P.P. (1910), lxvi, p. 67.   [2] P.P. (1904), lxxxvii; (1908), lxx; (1910), lxvi.
[3] H. of C., 5 Apr 1905; 4 P.D. 144, cc. 550–70.
[4] 5 P.D. (Commons) 40, c. 94.
[5] Engels to Kautsky, 12 Sept 1882; printed in Marx and Engels, *On Colonialism*, p. 340.

II. THE RIGHTS OF MAN

Whatever the reasons, Radical critics of colonial policy in the 1890s did become more 'imperially minded'. They took more interest than hitherto in the minutiae of African government, and their interest was informed and constructive. A glance at the African debates in Parliament after 1902 will illustrate the transition, and reveal the main lines of Radical criticism.

So long as the Unionists were in power, and continued to spend money on railways in Uganda, punitive expeditions in Somaliland and 'development' elsewhere, there could still be found Radicals who, after the old style, would condemn their 'extravagance', scoff at the suggestion that trade would benefit, and plead the prior claim of the poor of England to the country's charity. One example of many will serve as illustration.

> He [John Burns] believed in freedom's cause, and in the saving of the people who were unemployed at this moment, to whom these £6,000,000 of money would be an inestimable boon. . . . This Uganda policy was a link in the long chain of rash, costly, deadly Imperialism that involved this country in the most costly war of modern times . . . the only asset would be two long rusty steel ribbons stretching from Mombasa to Victoria Nyanza abandoned in despair because our policy of universal grab had landed us in trouble nearer home.[1]

Before 1906 this kind of attitude was still a common one. And when African native affairs were raised the Radical approach was scarcely more constructive. The native question remained, primarily, a labour question, and parliamentary discussion of it continued to devolve around the 'exploitation' theme so dear to Labour members.[2] When Keir Hardie treated forced labour and the like he was concerned mainly with blackening the capitalists,

[1] Burns in H. of C., 11 Dec 1902; 4 P.D. 116, cc. 956 and 958. Other examples are found in the debates on E. Africa, 9 and 15 Dec 1902, 2 Mar and 10 Aug 1903; and on Somaliland 24 Feb 1904 and 7–8 Mar 1905; especially in the speeches of Bayley, Broadhurst, Bryce, Burns, Buxton, Gibson Bowles, Dilke, Labouchere, Lloyd George, Lough and Bryn Roberts.
[2] See above, Ch. 4, Sect. iii.

and with voicing the grievances of British workmen who, he said, wanted to work in South Africa and now found they could not.[1] But, even as early as this, one or two others were showing concern for the natives themselves, irrespective of their significance for the capital–labour struggle; and Sir Charles Dilke – always the most enthusiastic champion of native rights – gave to the labour question a new perspective when he introduced a debate on the subject in March 1903:

> If it were true, as the Secretary of State told them, that this was not merely the native labour question, but the labour question as a whole – the fact that white labour would not compete with black labour, and if they were compelled for all time to rely on this servile class – a class which was never to rise, even in the persons of its most chosen citizens, out of its dependent position, and never to obtain anything in the nature of citizenship – they were discussing something which was not the labour question, but the whole future of South Africa.[2]

The discussion which ensued marks the point at which the Boer War debate began to be superseded by a different and wider controversy. By a few Radicals the 'native problem' was seen to be far more urgent than the question of Boer or British predominance because, as Bryce pointed out in 1905,

> The natives were in the vast majority in South Africa; and when they begin to speak English or to arrive at a common dialect they would begin to realise their power and be a far more important element in the country than they were at the present moment.[3]

In the debate of 24 March 1903 three speakers, Sir John Gorst, Herbert Samuel and Dilke (a Conservative, a Liberal Imperialist

[1] e.g. Hardie in H. of C., 19 Mar 1903 (4 P.D. 119, cc. 1251–5) and 24 Mar 1903 (4 P.D. 120, cc. 113–15); also Broadhurst, 16 Feb 1904 (ibid. 129, cc. 1574–9); Fenwick, 17 Feb 1904 (ibid. 130, cc. 67–72); Burns, 17 Feb 1904 (ibid. 130, cc. 93–102) and 22 Mar 1905 (ibid. 143, cc. 857–9); Bell, 22 Feb 1904 (ibid. 130, cc. 637–9) and 5 May 1904 (ibid. 134, cc. 624–7); and Crooks, 22 Feb 1904 (ibid. 130, cc. 648–51).

[2] H. of C. 24 Mar 1903; 4 P.D. 120, c. 71.

[3] H. of C., 27 July 1905; 4 P.D. 150, c. 641.

and a suspect Radical) consistently argued from the point of view of the native. He should not be forced to work under conditions uncongenial to him; he should not be subjected to the injustice and indignity of a 'colour-bar'; he should be allowed to retain and cultivate his own land and live his own life; and, if the South African whites persisted in their illiberal practices, then Britain had the right to impose her will on them – a right 'to insist that British ideas as well as colonial ideas should be consulted in the settlement of the native question'.[1]

The emergence of the 'Congo scandal' was to consolidate this Afrocentric approach and give it a new direction. On 20 May 1903 the same trio which had been so prominent two months before in the South African debate – Dilke, Gorst and Samuel – drew the attention of politicians, almost for the first time,[2] to those questions of monopoly and the exploitation of native lands which were to provide one of the main themes for colonial reformers in later years.[3] On the same occasion the doctrine of Morelism was introduced fully fledged to the Commons by Alfred Emmott, the mouthpiece of the Liverpool trading interest: 'He believed these atrocities to be the direct, necessary, and inevitable result of a wrong system . . .';[4] and Emmott pressed home the same argument in subsequent debates.[5] The lessons to be drawn from the Congo situation could not be confined to that

[1] H. of C., 24 Mar 1903; 4 P.D. 120, cc. 68 (Dilke), 75 (Gorst) and 80–5 (Samuel).

[2] Concern over the Congo had been expressed in Parliament as early as 1897 (see above, p. 57). Questions were raised about atrocities and trading rights there in 1900 and 1902 (4 P.D. 79, c. 1215; 108, c. 1545; 114, c. 1357; and 116, cc. 1143–4); but these were the only occasions before 1903 when these matters were raised. In 1903, by contrast, there were seventeen parliamentary questions, one large-scale debate (20 May) and two smaller debates (17 Mar and 10 Aug) on the Congo question.

[3] 4 P.D. 122, cc. 1289–1331. The motion presented by Samuel at the beginning of this debate was framed by Morel.

[4] Ibid. c. 1310; and cf. above, pp. 271–2.

[5] e.g. H. of C., 9 June 1904 and 3 Aug 1905. The Radical attitude to the Congo was not quite unanimous. Certain Irish nationalists felt that Grey's protests to Leopold were a sign only of covetousness and Protestant bigotry, and defended the C.F.S. The only English M.P. to do so in quite so uncompromising a way was the Catholic Hilaire Belloc.

IN THE RUBBER COILS.

Scene—*The Congo "Free" State.*

Punch *joined the ranks of the Congo Reformers in November 1906*

part of Africa. Dilke, Gorst and the Liberal Cathcart Wason all used the Congo to illustrate the unwisdom of concessionary policies in East Africa. 'It was to be regretted that into several of these protectorates there had been introduced the principle of concessions – the very system, although doubtless in a mitigated form, which had been condemned in the Congo Free State.' [1] The seeds were here already of a new approach to African problems. After 1905 it was to become the common approach of Radicals. Their arguments were all to do with native rights, and they fell into two broad categories: those concerned with land and labour, and the case against the colour-bar.

The first was fostered by the increasing momentum of the Congo Reform campaign. Morel's arguments against concessions were persuasive, and they were applied more and more to the British Colonies. The very suspicion of a 'concession' aroused the immediate concern of the Commons: concessions in Sierra Leone to the British West African Produce Company,[2] reports of a trading monopoly held by Elder Dempsters,[3] land-alienation in the Malay States,[4] concessions to Lever Brothers in Sierra Leone and Nigeria.[5] Often Members of Parliament were more vigilant over such things even than Morel. The same kind of concern was shown too for those native tribes whose lands were being taken from them by white settlers in East and southern Africa. In Natal and in the East African Protectorate the best lands were (it was claimed) being 'jobbed away in freehold for the purposes

[1] Dilke in H. of C., 10 Aug 1903; 4 P.D. 127, c. 701. Sir John Gorst said much the same thing on 6 Aug 1903 (ibid. 127, c. 115); and on 20 June 1904 Cathcart Wason based his case against a proposed Jewish settlement in British East Africa on his opposition to 'the stupidity of allowing concessions to be given without having regard to native rights'. 'All the trouble in the Congo', he said, 'was due to the same fact.' His book *East Africa and Uganda, or, Our Last Land* puts his case against land syndicates in general and the proposed Jewish settlement in particular.

[2] 4 P.D. 163, cc. 1320–3; 165, cc. 386–7; 166, cc. 1548–9; 167, cc. 125 and 1021–2; and 171, c. 556 (1906).

[3] Ibid. 174, c. 354 (1907).

[4] Ibid. 183, cc. 514 and 712 (1908).

[5] 5 P.D. (Commons), vols. 46–8, 51–2, 56, 58, *passim* (questions), and debates on 31 July and 12 Aug 1913, ibid. 56, cc. 785–865 and 2401–8.

of speculation',[1] and the natives pushed around at the mere whim of voracious settlers.[2] It was being said against us, declared Edmund Harvey, that 'while we talk very much about shouldering the white man's burden, we take great care to secure for ourselves the black man's land'.[3] Wedgwood was particularly worried about the land problem. His own solution – an amalgam of Morelism and Henry George – was that all lands not already irrevocably alienated should revert to the State, and then be granted out only on short leases. In this way speculation for large artificial profits would be rendered impossible, and the value of the land would always – in the short term by the income derived from a 'fair rent' and in the long term through the land's reversion to the State at the expiry of the lease – accrue to the country and all its inhabitants.[4] In applying the doctrine of the 'Single Tax' in this way to Africa, Wedgwood was alone in Parliament, and his efforts to implement his grand schemes got scanty support from his fellow Radicals.[5] Nevertheless, his contributions to colonial debates were symptomatic of the new sophistication which was beginning to enter into the Radicals' discussions. Partly through the agency of Morel, their attention had become more sharply focused on the economic and social structure of Africa herself.

A corollary of the land question was the problem of native labour. One of the motives behind the alienation of tribal lands, said Edmund Harvey, was the effort to 'force the natives out of their reserves in order that there might be a more adequate supply

[1] Outhwaite in H. of C., 7 Apr 1914; 5 P.D. (Commons) 60, c. 1851.

[2] See also the debates on S. Africa of 27 July 1905 (Bryce), 28 Feb 1906 (Robertson), 11 Mar 1907 (Alden) and 13 May 1908 (Alden); and on E. Africa, 20 July 1911 and 28 July 1914.

[3] H. of C., 28 July 1914; 5 P.D. (Commons) 65, c. 1157.

[4] See Wedgwood's essay on 'Native Lands and Crown Colonies', in *Essays and Adventures of a Labour M.P.* (1924), pp. 116–29; and also his parliamentary speeches on E. Africa, 28 May 1908, 27 July 1909, 29 June 1910, 24 June 1912 and 14 Apr 1914.

[5] No one supported him in the protracted efforts he made, in Apr 1914, to amend the East African Loans Bill so as to prevent money being spent on a railway which passed mainly through freehold land, thus profiting (he said) only the settler landowners.

of labour for the planters'.[1] Again, the point was starkly illustrated by the Congo. 'Forced labour' was the other great threat to the welfare of native races which arose out of capitalist exploitation. The Radicals' case against it was drawn from three sources. There were the old anti-capitalist arguments which Labour had contributed to the Boer War debates, and which Hobson had implemented. There was the agitation of the humanitarian societies, which had a number of prominent deputies in the Commons,[2] and whose literature from the early years of the new century displayed a marked change of emphasis away from 'legal' slavery and the slave trade towards more general labour questions.[3] And, lastly, there was the Congo Reform movement, to which belonged nearly all those who were most vigilant about forced labour in the British colonies.[4] A paper by Sir Charles Dilke, read posthumously to the 'First Universal Races Congress' of 1911, is typical of the Radicals' approach: of their concern that the *de jure* slavery which earlier humanitarians had successfully combated was being replaced by *de facto* servitude – by the 'general recrudescence of slave conditions in disguise'.[5] In South Africa they saw the mine-owners trying to secure cheap labour from China or Central Africa and 'inducing' their own Kaffirs to

[1] H. of C., 28 July 1914; 5 P.D. (Commons) 65, c. 1154.
[2] Dilke was a vice-president of the Anti-Slavery and Aborigines' Protection Society, Byles and Harvey were on its committee, and Cox and Cathcart Wason ordinary members. The Society's parliamentary committee consisted of J. C. Lyttelton, Noel Buxton, Ramsay MacDonald and (from 1912) Edmund Harvey (Reports of the A.S. and A.P.S., *passim*).
[3] See *The Aborigines Friend, The Anti-Slavery Reporter* and (after 1909) the journal of the amalgamated society. San Thomé was their first concern, after which they discussed every form of forced labour.
[4] Among those who were most active against the Congo in Parliament, and who also sought to reform British colonial administration, were Alden, Dilke, Cathcart Wason and Wedgwood (Liberals), Parker (Unionist) and MacDonald (Labour). A large number of M.P.s concerned themselves with the Congo but not at all with other parts of Africa. Between 1906 and 1914, 23 Unionists, 27 Liberals and 6 Labour members put parliamentary questions on the Congo.
[5] Sir Charles Dilke, 'Indentured and Forced Labour', in *Papers on Inter-Racial Problems*, pp. 312–22.

work for them by means of poll- and hut-taxes.[1] In the Congo and West Africa forced labour took the form of the concessionaire system;[2] in the East African Protectorate the native was compelled to work for the white man by the gradual erosion of his only alternative means of subsistence, his tribal lands and hunting-grounds.[3] In the New Hebrides there was indentured child labour;[4] elsewhere, the *corvée*. All these came under Radical fire. If they were not slave-systems on the old pattern, they were the modern capitalist equivalent. Mine-owners and concessionaires, said Radicals, were endeavouring to create in Africa 'one universal black proletariat' for the white man's industry[5] – 'to use the natives purely as the "Nethinim", the hewers of wood and drawers of water'.[6] This should not be tolerated under the British flag.

By and large the 'land and labour' argument was confined to Liberals. Apart from MacDonald, Labour M.P.s took little active interest in the Congo[7] (although they made it clear that they were behind the reformers in this matter),[8] or in questions of land ownership. The Party showed less concern about 'capitalist monopolies' and 'forced labour' in the tropics than might have been expected from them.[9] Its main contribution to the discussion

[1] See the Commons debates on Chinese labour, 19–23 and 28 Feb, and 14 Mar 1906; and on S. African natives, 13 May 1908.

[2] There were parliamentary debates on the Congo every year between 1903 and 1913. On W. Africa, see above, p. 302. Labour conditions in the Portuguese possessions of San Thomé, Principé and Angola were also frequently discussed.

[3] See especially the debate on E. Africa of 28 May 1908.

[4] See the Commons debate on the New Hebrides Convention, 12–13 Feb and 11 Mar 1907.

[5] Dilke, 'Indentured and Forced Labour', op. cit.

[6] Alden in H. of C., 11 Mar 1907; 4 P.D. 170, c. 1354.

[7] MacDonald was the only Labour M.P. on the committee of the C.R.A. He spoke three times in Parliament on the Congo, and put nine questions. The only other substantial speech on the Congo by a Labour Member came from George Roberts in Feb 1908.

[8] See Arthur Henderson in H. of C., 22 July 1909; 5 P.D. (Commons) 8, c. 641.

[9] Their case on native labour generally followed traditional lines: vilifying capitalists, sympathising with white labourers out of work. A socialist outside the parliamentary party who did take a real and deep interest in native labour problems was, of course, Sydney Olivier, Governor of Jamaica from

L

of the 'native question' after 1906 was not the argument based on the economic position of the African. It was the more purely moral case for equal rights, and it was increasingly directed rather against racial prejudice and political oppression than against industrial servitude.

On India, for example, Keir Hardie (who visited the sub-continent in 1907) concentrated on such issues as the 'colour-line', education and local self-government.[1] On South Africa Labour M.P.s were the most forward of those who attacked the colour-bar and pleaded for equal treatment of white and black. Nearly everyone in the House of Commons agreed that the exclusion of natives from the South African franchise was evil; Arthur Balfour was almost alone in declaring bluntly that 'We have to face facts; men are not born equal, the white and black races are not born with equal capacities: they are born with different capacities which education cannot and will not change.'[2] Others were more egalitarian. But it was the Labour M.P.s who were willing to press their egalitarianism to a division. The debate on the South Africa Constitution Bill in 1909 was very largely *their* debate. Theirs was the amendment which sought to excise from the Bill that clause which restricted the franchise to men of 'European descent';[3] many of the speeches were from the Labour benches, and all took the theme first stated by George Barnes, that those 'insulting words' in the Bill would 'set the seal of racial inferiority upon the masses of the people of South Africa, and . . . commit us to a new principle in local government and human rights'.[4] The House of Commons, said Hardie,

---

1907 to 1913. See his *White Capital and Coloured Labour*, published by the I.L.P. in 1906; 'The Government of Colonies and Dependencies', in *Papers on Inter-Racial Problems*; and Margaret Olivier (ed.), *Sydney Olivier: Letters and Selected Writings*.

[1] See Hardie's *India, Impressions and Suggestions*, which contains the meat of the arguments of all his many parliamentary speeches on India.

[2] H. of C., 31 July 1906; 4 P.D. 162, c. 799.

[3] Moved by Barnes, 19 Aug 1909; 5 P.D. (Commons) 9, c. 1553. Twenty-eight Labour M.P.s voted for it, including the tellers, out of 57. Three voted against it. (Ibid. cc. 1603–4.)

[4] Ibid. c. 1555.

'should not assent to the setting up of the doctrine that because of a man's misfortune in having been born with a coloured skin he is to be barred the possibility of ever rising to a position of trust'.[1] The line was familiar. It was the old legalistic liberalism of 'human rights' once again.[2]

III. THE IMPERIAL STANDARD

Concern in Parliament for the welfare of the African was growing. But so far there was nothing remarkable in the Radicals' arguments on his behalf, little that could not have been said equally well fifty or a hundred years earlier. They had reverted, after the abnormality of the 1890s, to the orthodox humanitarianism of the past, flavouring it with just a dash of newly concocted land theory. But at least their attention was focused more directly on Africa; no longer did they reject the Empire out of hand. Especially significant is the Labour contingent's abandonment of its old working-class parochialism. The amount of interest taken by Labour members in the Empire is illustrated by the number of parliamentary questions put by them between 1906 and 1914: 300 on India, 200 on South Africa, 175 on the British West Indies and British Guiana, 50 on West Africa, 40 on Egypt and the Sudan, 20 on East Africa, 20 on Malta, 20 on the Pacific Islands, 10 on Malaya and the Straits Settlements, 10 on the Congo, and 6 (only) on the white dominions.[3] O'Grady's contention was broadly justified, that 'the party with which he

[1] Ibid. c. 1575.

[2] This was the line taken by parliamentary Radicals over the 'colour-bar' issue: abstract and idealistic. Outside Parliament, however, Sydney Olivier, with considerable practical experience in the multi-racial West Indies, discussed the question at a much deeper and more knowledgeable level – and came to roughly the same conclusions. His *White Capital and Coloured Labour* is the most impressive analysis by any socialist at the time of racial problems in the colonies and the United States.

[3] These are approximate figures only. In the cases of India and the West Indies, they are a little misleading in that the questions nearly all came from one or two M.P.s who took a special interest in those countries. On other issues, interest in the Party was more broadly based.

sat had been taunted with the fact that they cared very little about Empire, but they cared as much for the Empire as any Member of the House'.[1]

Not only did they take an interest in the colonies; they also professed a kind of imperialism, taught them by MacDonald. MacDonald had shared with Hobson his rejection of the old Manchester atomistic view of world society.[2] The demands of international morality, he said, were pre-eminent over the claims of 'nationalities'. Because the rights of man were universal and all-important, they could justify the abrogation of national liberty. Applied to the British Empire, this principle meant that the central imperial authority should be able to intervene in the internal affairs of any of its constituent dominions, if it could be shown that that dominion was not adhering to a specified 'Imperial Standard' of political conduct. The Imperial Standard was the most original concept to come out of the pre-war colonial debates.

In *Labour and the Empire*, published in 1907, MacDonald expounded it more fully and applied it specifically to South Africa.[3] For South Africa it was particularly useful. In the 1906 and 1909 debates on the Transvaal and South African constitutions, the problem of the franchise was one on which there was a large measure of concurrence. Nearly everybody agreed that civilised Africans should be given political equality with Europeans. This was not the point at issue. The question was whether it was desirable or possible to try to force egalitarianism down the throats of an unwilling colonial legislature, at the risk of destroying all chances of an amicable federation. The choice was between two Liberal principles: self-government and democracy. Winston Churchill was aware of the dilemma. The 'great principle of self-government', he admitted, was 'not a moral principle, and when it comes into collision with moral principles I think upon occasion it should be over-borne'. But on *this* occasion he felt constrained to override other considerations:

[1] H. of C., 20 July 1906; 4 P.D. 161, c. 633 (Debate on India).
[2] See above, pp. 185–6.
[3] Pt. ii chs. 2–4, and (on S. Africa) pp. 54–9.

self-government is a fundamental maxim of Liberal colonial policy. It is the master-key of many of the problems which embarrass and perplex us. The responsible government of a Colony is a great gift: it is, I think, the greatest and best gift that we can bestow – the bestowal of Home Rule upon a distant community, to live their own life in their own way, to develop their own civilisation according to their own ideals, through the agency of a representative Legislative Assembly and an Executive responsible thereto. It sounds familiar, does it not?[1]

Indeed it was familiar, and for most Liberals it was a compelling argument.[2] To combat it, the left wing had to deny the efficacy of Home Rule as a universal panacea, and to make out a case for even stricter imperial control than the 'Imperialists' themselves wanted.

Some of them argued that, because the majority of the population of South Africa was excluded from the franchise, it could not rightly be called self-government.

The Transvaal was not a self-governing colony. It was an oligarchically governed colony. The great majority of the people of that colony had no voice in the Government. We had endowed a minority of the population with the power to govern all the rest.[3]

Others held that South Africa's dependence on imperial troops

---

[1] H. of C., 28 Feb 1906; 4 P.D. 152, c. 1238.

[2] Together, of course, with the argument that Article VIII of the Treaty of Vereeniging ('The question of granting the franchise to natives will not be decided until after the introduction of self-government') limited their action with regard to the Transvaal; and that the S. African colonies would not accept federation upon any other basis than the one outlined in the South Africa Constitution Bill. Many Liberals were also persuaded that the colonies would come to take a more enlightened view after federation through their closer relations with Cape Colony, whose native policy, said Dilke, 'compared with Natal, was as heaven to hell' (4 P.D. 162, c. 771). Churchill was confident that 'we shall see in the next few years a distinct and powerful forward movement in South Africa in the direction of the admirable system which prevails in the Cape Colony' (4 P.D. 167, c. 1133).

[3] Harold Cox in H. of C., 19 Aug 1907; 4 P.D. 181, c. 225. Cf. Byles in H. of C., 28 Feb 1906 and 16 Aug 1909; 4 P.D. 152, c. 1212; and 5 P.D. (Commons) 9, cc. 1031–2.

rendered her responsible to British opinion. If she found herself in difficulties, said J. M. Robertson, like an inter-racial war, then she would 'call for the employment of the whole forces of the Empire' to safeguard her interests. It was bad policy to give a country *carte blanche* to get herself into situations from which Britain would have to extricate her.[1] Dilke reminded the House of the trust which Britain held for the Indians in South Africa.[2] R. W. Essex spoke ominously of the effects of the Bill elsewhere: 'in many and many a distant home and palace in India this day's debate will be read and pondered over, and all over the world the question is rapidly growing as to how long the intolerant domination of the proud white is going to last'.[3] But more often Radicals pleaded MacDonald's broader kind of imperialism:

> If we were to have an Empire we must have something that corresponded to a political unity, and if we were going to have that then the parts of the Empire that shared in the glory, pretension, and honour of belonging to it must, as a *quid pro quo*, allow some central authority to take charge of the traditions, the honour, and the reputation of the whole.[4]

A few Liberals followed his lead, most notably Dilke and Seely (before the latter's Radicalism was muted by his elevation to the Colonial Under-Secretaryship). Despite the 'Anglo-Saxon' imperialism of *Greater Britain*, Dilke had seen by 1906 that the Empire as it existed was a multi-racial one, and this he regarded as one of its greatest merits. 'Our glory was that we had welded together races who were proud to live under us'; they could not

---

[1] H. of C., 28 Feb 1906; 4 P.D. 152, c. 1217. This was a particularly forcible argument during the Rand Strike of 1914: we had a right to interfere, said Wedgwood, because 'it is the British Army that has provided the steel at the bottom of the heel of General Smuts' (H. of C., 12 Feb 1914; 5 P.D. (Commons) 58, c. 397).

[2] H. of C., 13 May 1908; 4 P.D. 188, c. 1230.

[3] H. of C., 19 Aug 1909; 5 P.D. (Commons) 19, c. 1635.

[4] H. of C., 4 Aug 1906; 4 P.D. 162, c. 1815 (on the Transvaal Constitution). The first intimation of this doctrine is found in MacDonald's argument in favour of British intervention in Natal, 29 Mar 1906 (4 P.D. 154, c. 1646). On 2 Apr he declared that 'Natal was not merely responsible to herself... but to the whole Empire' (4 P.D. 155, c. 249).

treat the Empire as a 'white Protestant Empire', for if they did, then 'the whole fabric would collapse'.[1] Therefore, he said, Parliament 'must impress on the Rand that it had something larger than the Rand to look to – not only the future of South Africa as a whole, but also the position of the Empire as a whole'.[2] Seely put the same point impressively.

> A spirit seemed to have grown up in the last year or two that the British Empire was a thing which had no common principle, that it was to be bound together by other means or no means at all. If they were bound to abandon the principles upon which the Empire was founded, better a thousand times the Empire were shattered to pieces ... we must hold fast to the principles of Empire and, if necessary, assert them from the home country. All lesser matters might be left to the other parts of the Empire; but to the guiding principles of Empire, namely, justice, law, and mercy, we must ever hold fast.[3]

But chiefly this was the special contribution of Labour, MacDonald's 'imperial' answer to the old-style nationalism of the Liberals. Labour M.P.s reverted to it again and again, in justification for their overriding the claims of colonial self-government, in order to protect the rights either of disfranchised natives or of exiled trade unionists.[4] In April 1914 F. W. Goldstone, with the support of the whole party, could move

> That, in the opinion of this House, the rights of British Citizens set forth in Magna Charta, the Petition of Right, and the Habeas Corpus Act, and declared and recognised by the Common Law of England, should be common to the whole Empire, and their inviolability should be assured in every self-governing dominion.[5]

[1] H. of C., 31 July 1906; 4 P.D. 162, cc. 769 and 772.
[2] H. of C., 17 Dec 1906; 4 P.D. 167, c. 1098.
[3] H. of C., 2 Apr 1906; 4 P.D. 155, cc. 254-5.
[4] e.g. 5 P.D. (Commons) 9, c. 1597; 58, cc. 367-9 (MacDonald), and 18, c. 1019 (O'Grady); and see the *Labour Party Conference Report* for 1914, pp. 94-7.
[5] H. of C., 1 Apr 1914; 5 P.D. (Commons) 60, c. 1270.

By this time the Imperial Standard – however ineffective – had become a firm tenet of Labour Party policy.

It was a kind of imperialism. An Irish nationalist taunted those who wished to interfere in the affairs of South Africa with being 'the real Empire-Builders', seeking to 'recede back to the middle ages and to shackle themselves to the remnants of a feudalism from which we are emerging in this country'.[1] Certainly it was a good deal more 'imperially minded' than the Little Englandism of the old school of Liberals, or the apathy of pre-1900 Labourites. It might so easily have gone another way. Labour might have donned the mantle of Harcourt and Labouchere and become the anti-imperialists of the later 1900s – there was plenty in contemporary socialist ideology to justify such an approach.[2] At the time of the Boer War there had been little to suggest that Labour would grow to love the Empire, even this high moral Empire of its imagination. If it had gone the way of the neo-Marxists and identified *all* imperialism with capitalism, then it could not have considered anything but a non-imperialist alternative. If it had done what one delegate at the 1906 Labour Party Conference wanted it to do, and concentrated exclusively on domestic matters,[3] then it could have made no contribution at all to imperial discussions. Instead it followed the advice of another speaker, who 'hoped such a narrow-minded policy would not be adopted, because anything they could do to assist the Labour group to broaden their own minds they ought to do. . . . As they would be legislating for the empire, they ought to know the needs of the empire.'[4] Labour M.P.s never compromised with the militarism and aggression they saw as the hallmarks of the New Imperialism. They never shared its Kiplingite enthusiasm for pageantry and military glory. They attacked capitalist exploiters

[1] Arthur Lynch in H. of C., 1 Apr 1914; 5 P.D. (Commons) 60, c. 1299. The Nationalists rarely looked further than their Irish noses; they saw everything from the point of view of the Anglo-Irish dispute. Cf. above, p. 300 fn. 5.

[2] See above, Ch. 4.

[3] J. Cunliffe at the 1906 Labour Party Conference, objecting to a proposed imperial tour by Labour M.P.s *Labour Party Conference Report*, 1906, p. 47.

[4] Ibid. loc. cit.

as strongly as ever. They chided the Government for failing to concede more in the way of local self-government to India.[1] They sympathised with the aspirations of the Indian National Congress[2] (MacDonald was even offered its presidency).[3] Yet none of these things led them to a blanket rejection of empire. In the House of Commons they preached an alternative imperialism which was unparochial, but above all, based not on power but on ideals.

IV. INDIRECT RULE

The rights of man, preservation of African property in land, and the Imperial Standard: these were the main themes of Radical criticism between 1906 and 1914. The old anti-imperialism of the pro-Boers had been superseded by a line which was at once more concerned with tropical empire for its own sake, and more informed. In several of its aspects we can trace the influence of the New Radicals and E. D. Morel, and the tangible participàtion of the latter. But only very faintly. By and large the impact of these men's more central ideas was hardly visible in Parliament. Labour's traditional case against 'capitalistic imperialism' gained nothing in sophistication from Hobson's analysis of it, and its incidence declined in the relatively placid years (for Africa) following the Boer War. Anti-imperialists had given way to colonial reformers. In part this transformation itself can be attributed to Morel and his disciples. They had told Parliament what needed reforming. But the direction which constructive criticism took in the Commons did not follow at all closely the path of Indirect Rule and 'peasant proprietorship' which the New Radicals and the Liverpool School had assiduously marked out

[1] See Hardie's *India, Impressions and Suggestions,* and the *I.L.P. Conference Report* for 1910, pp. 82–4, and 1911, pp. 103–4.

[2] A resolution to this effect was passed by the 1908 I.L.P. Conference (*Report,* 1908, p. 66).

[3] An official letter from the I.N.C. offering him the presidency, and dated 3 Aug 1911, is preserved in the MacDonald Papers; also a letter from Morley advising him to refuse such an offer (22 Feb 1911).

for it in the early 1900s. J. M. Robertson, Hobson's colleague at
South Place, paid due obeisance to the principle of Indirect Rule
in 1906. 'It was very commonly held', he said, 'as a condition of
the well-being of any nation that its political development should
be sequent and continuous.' This was widely admitted for
European nations; yet when men were put in charge of 'lower
races' they were found ready to 'tear up those races by the roots,
to make an end suddenly of the system of tribal law, and to impose
upon them all at once the methods of a superior race'.[1] Edmund
Harvey asked that the backward races of the Empire be given
'an opportunity to go forward, each in its own way, to develop,
not a cheap imitation of our civilisation, but some healthier stage
which will naturally follow on their own'.[2] One or two other
Liberal M.P.s made the same plea,[3] and Ramsay MacDonald, in
the books he wrote after 1906, repeated this 'Ethical' viewpoint.
It was wrong, he said, to try to 'elevate' native races by forcing
them into 'moulds of British thought and British notions of
excellence', into 'new grooves' which the native mind 'does not
fit and can never fit'.[4] A visit to India in 1909 confirmed him in his
opinion as to the unwisdom of this policy; 'The source of most
of our failures is a lack of sympathetic imagination'.[5] This he
described as the 'Imperialist' approach. The democratic and

[1] H. of C., 28 Feb 1906; 4 P.D. 152, c. 1214.
[2] H. of C., 27 June 1912; 5 P.D. (Commons) 40, c. 607–8.
[3] William Byles deprecated the destruction of the 'communal system of
land owning' in Africa, which 'in many ways was a far better system than the
system of the private ownership of land that we had in this country' (4 P.D.
152, c. 1214). Cathcart Wason defended the House Rule System in Nigeria
on the grounds that 'The rule of the chiefs is the whole foundation of the
government of the country, and if we once upset their rule and sway over
the people it will be a very serious matter indeed' (5 P.D. (Commons) 28,
c. 1323). And J. S. Higham gave fulsome praise to the way 'we were adapting
our teaching to native customs and habits' in southern Nigeria.
[4] Labour and the Empire, pp. 19, 99.
[5] The Awakening of India, p. 218. A tribute to MacDonald's own 'sympathetic imagination' is found in a letter from an Indian in the MacDonald
Papers, dated 25 June 1912: 'you have won my soul by so wonderfully
catching the soul of India in a moment as it were as evidenced in your
book. . . . I cannot shake off my idea that you are a Hindoo reborn in western
flesh.'

socialist approach was to 'develop native civilisation on its own lines'.[1] So the teaching of Mary Kingsley and Hobson on the subject of 'cultural relativism' was not entirely forgotten. But when it came to questions of practical administrative policy, Radicals paid little attention to it in Parliament. The common line of argument was that deriving from the much older doctrines of 'human rights', racial equality and free labour. The attitude of Josiah Wedgwood, one of the most prominent negrophiles in the Commons, illustrates this – and suggests an explanation. He wrote in 1941:

> I always opposed that school of thought which supports indirect rule through the native chiefs; and I pressed instead for direct rule by the Colonial service till natives were fit for liberty. In this I differed from E. D. Morel. I want to train the poor natives up to self-government, to teach them English, to start some political franchise however limited, for Europeans, for Indians, and for Africans on a common electoral roll.[2]

The difficulty was that Indirect Rule was a policy originally formulated for West and Central Africa, which were almost the whole extent of Mary Kingsley's and Morel's early interest in the continent. For West Africa it appeared a viable proposition. The preoccupation of Parliament after 1906, however, was not here, but with eastern and southern Africa, whose situation and climate put them in a different category altogether. West Africa was indisputably a black man's country; East Africa was being claimed for the white man, and the presence there of settler communities, European and Indian, complicated the issue. It rendered more inexorable and more rapid the Westernisation of the country. The Hilton Young Report of 1929 conceded that

> Whether modern European civilisation, so largely dependent for its maintenance and progress on a system of private property and the money-seeking motive, represents, in spite of its greater material comforts, something which in a true

[1] *Labour and the Empire*, p. 19. Cf. his *What I Saw in South Africa*, p. 119.
[2] Lord Wedgwood, *Memoirs of a Fighting Life*, p. 185 (referring to Kenya).

sense is better than the communal organisation of the primitive African tribes, is a matter for philosophical speculation.

But for East Africa, it said, the question was purely academic, because 'for better or worse' the process of Europeanisation 'has everywhere been started and cannot be stopped'.[1] The concept of Indirect Rule *could* be applied to this situation, and it was, by the Hilton Young Commissioners themselves. But first it had to become a little more sophisticated: to compromise, on the economic level, with plantation agriculture,[2] and to fit itself, politically, for a 'dual' society.[3] Before 1914 parliamentary Radicals (with the possible exception of Wedgwood)[4] do not appear to have reached this degree of sophistication. The simple form of Indirect Rule preached by Morel – 'peasant proprietorship' and African self-elevation through informal trading contacts – was patently impracticable in East Africa, and much more so in the south. At the Colonial Office after 1911 Lewis Harcourt was tackling the problem of African economic development in much more positive – and Chamberlainite – a way.[5] Radicals could no longer insist on the rigid and permanent preservation of tribal organisations and native agricultural methods: instead they set

[1] *Report of the Commission on Closer Union of the Dependencies in Eastern and Central Africa*, 1929 (Cmd. 3234), p. 19.

[2] Ibid. pp. 44–71. When considering what type of economic development would most benefit the Africans, said the Report, 'the consideration of abstract principles is not sufficient' (p. 60). In many cases plantations would teach the African 'regular habits of work', and bring the prosperity which could provide him with necessary medical and educational services (pp. 58, 60, 63–4; and cf. below, p. 319). What was wanted was rigid control over labour conditions, and the provision of native reserves which would provide the African with an alternative means of subsistence.

[3] Ibid. pp. 77–84. The Report advocated parallel political development for both native and non-native communities, for the native built on the foundation of his own traditional institutions, and leading gradually from segregated local self-government to eventual native participation in the central (Western-type) government.

[4] Who, as we have seen, wanted the land given to the charge of the State and not to peasant proprietors (above, p. 303).

[5] See the Commons debates on the Colonial Estimates of 20 July 1911, 27 June and 29 July 1912, 31 July 1913 and 28 July 1914.

themselves the task of erecting safeguards against economic abuse, and securing the active political participation of those Africans who – 'for better or worse' – had already been forced into the torrent of modern European civilisation.

So in those parts of Africa called 'white men's countries' things had gone too far for a rigid application of Indirect Rule. In West Africa the situation was different. Indeed, Indirect Rule was already being implemented there by Sir Frederick Lugard, following the advice of his predecessor, Sir George Goldie. The latter's sentiments accorded very closely with Mary Kingsley's. In 1898 he had advocated for Nigeria 'the general policy of ruling on African principles through native rulers'; he advised that the colonial administration take care to assume only the *Oberhoheit* of a territory, and leave the *Landeshoheit* in the hands of native authorities; and he suggested the founding of European 'cities of refuge' on the coast to which Africans disaffected with tribal life could flee:[1] the very words are reminiscent of *West African Studies*.[2] And Lugard's own policy for northern Nigeria, of ruling through the chiefs and respecting native land-rights, was easily compatible with Morel's. The principle seemed to have triumphed in one part of Africa at least. Later it was to spread, and to become the most widely accepted 'general principle' behind what was always, in fact, chiefly a pragmatic colonial policy. From the point of view of posterity, Mary Kingsley, Morel and Hobson appear to have been on the right lines in West Africa with their 'indirect' approach to the problems of colonial government.

But not quite. There are striking similarities; yet in many ways their own brand of Indirect Rule was very much less sophisticated than the policy as it was subsequently preached and practised. It had serious flaws. One has already been touched on – its apparent inability to meet the demands of the second provision of the Dual Mandate; the inadequacy, from a world-economic point of view, of Morel's scheme of peasant proprietorship. Europe could not,

---

[1] Goldie, Introduction to C. F. S. Vandeleur, *Campaigning on the Upper Nile and Niger* (1898); quoted as an appendix to Dorothy Wellesley and S. Gwynn, *Sir George Goldie*.

[2] See, for example, above, pp. 243, fn. 4, 247.

it seemed, afford to wait for Africa slowly and laboriously to raise her production on pre-industrial lines. Her impatience was graphically described by Sir Harry Johnston in 1920:

> It somehow shocks the sense of fairness of hard-headed White or Yellow people that semi-savages should be driving ill-bred sheep, scraggy cattle or ponies hardly fit for polo over plains and mountains that are little else than great treasure-vaults of valuable minerals and chemicals; or that they should roam with their blow-pipes and bows and arrows through forests of inestimable value for their timber, drugs, dyes, latices, gums, oil-seeds, nuts or fruits; be turn-ing this waiting wealth to no use, not allowing it to circulate in the world's markets. Whatever a few poets – dreamy enthusiasts sure of bed and board, theorists who write in a spirit of perversity – may pretend, the world at large is arriving at a pitch of intolerance of the lotos eater. It wants him to can or cask his lotos berries and ship them overseas in exchange for manufactured goods.[1]

Hobson had said much the same thing long before, and Ramsay MacDonald repeated him in 1907: Europe had a right to demand an exchange of goods from the tropics – 'The world is the inheritance of all men.' [2] And tacit approval, at least, was given to this idea by all those Labour M.P.s who connived in the imperial cotton-growing schemes of the 1900s.[3] If they never thought explicitly in terms of 'the world's' interests, at least they felt that their *own* interests justified colonial development. Europe's need, it appeared, was too pressing – or her appetite too voracious. Morel, of course, had held that it *could* be satisfied by peasant proprietors: men worked better for themselves than for foreign shareholders. But we have seen how Johnston and Lever dis-abused him of this idea, for the Congo at least.[4] The choice was

[1] Sir H. H. Johnston, *The Backward Peoples and our Relations with Them*, p. 59.
[2] MacDonald, *Labour and the Empire*, p. 98. Sydney Olivier made the same point in ch. 13 of *White Capital and Coloured Labour*; no race, he said, had a sacred right to exclude strangers from its territory, so long as they conducted themselves inoffensively.
[3] See above, pp. 296–7.   [4] See above, Ch. 8 sect. iv.

between indirect economic rule and industrial development; it seemed that the two could not be reconciled.

From the point of view of the Africans, even, there was a case for saying that a plantation system on Lever's lines was more beneficial to their welfare. That welfare demanded improvements in 'nutrition, health and education', which depended on a rising revenue, which in turn depended on increased productivity; and this could only be achieved along Western lines.[1] This was how the argument ran. And more than this: some held that industrial development was dependent also on *social* change. 'The steady reduction of poverty which has characterised the West in the last century and a quarter,' writes one modern commentator, resulted from 'the coming together in Western society of a whole series of institutions and attitudes, all of which were necessary to the nineteenth century's outburst of economic activity.... It is, therefore, *a priori* likely that any underdeveloped society which wishes to develop will have to transform itself to be as like as possible in attitudes and institutions to Western Europe and its offshoots.'[2] This is no place to argue the merits or demerits of the system of peasant proprietorship. The question was debated at length in the 1930s and 1940s; and though some persisted in maintaining the profitability of peasant production,[3] on balance the advocates of plantation development got the better of the argument.[4] Suffice it to say that plantations were not necessarily beneficial only to capitalists, as they seemed to be in the 1890s and early 1900s; nor was peasant proprietorship the only or the best way of promoting African interests. Later British policy came to recognise this: that the choice between the two, in Lord Hailey's words, should

[1] Hancock, *British Commonwealth Affairs*, ii 2, p. 175 (paraphrasing A. D. A. de Kat Angelino's *Colonial Policy*, The Hague, 1931). This was also a common argument before 1914. Cf. Sydney Olivier, 'The Government of Colonies and Dependencies', *in Papers on Inter-Racial Problems*, pp. 298–300.

[2] Maurice Zinkin, *Development for Free Asia* (1956), p. 99; and cf. Hailey, *An African Survey*, p. 1465.

[3] See Dr I. C. Greaves, *Modern Production among Backward Peoples* (1935), cited in M. Perham, *Native Administration in Nigeria*, p. 321.

[4] See, for example, Perham, op. cit. pp. 320–4; and Hailey, op. cit. pp. 980–3.

'depend on local circumstances rather than on general principles'.[1]

Much the same is true of Indirect Rule in its political and cultural aspects. Again, it is no part of our purpose to pass judgment on it. But it is worth noting that, in so far as the Indirect Rule of the inter-war period was unsatisfactory, Morel's and Hobson's versions were more so, because more uncompromising. Morel's ideal had been the old West Africa of informal trading-contact; Hobson's was the administration – or non-administration – of Basutoland.[2] Each of these ideals of Indirect Rule was too extreme, too static. In part their deficiencies arose from a still defective anthropology.

Mary Kingsley, Morel and Hobson had all deprecated the imposition of Western culture on alien peoples. Their disapproval of it derived from their 'cultural agnosticism' – their scepticism as to the superiority of Western civilisation; and from Mary Kingsley's half-formed conception of the functional value of social institutions. This was an improvement on older anthropological assumptions. But perhaps it was *too* respectful of alien cultures, too conservative in its opposition to change. Certainly if it had been applied to Europe it would have appeared reactionary in the extreme – the maintenance of aristocratic privilege because the transition to anything more egalitarian would be socially painful. And for a 'Progressive' to advocate Radical reform for his own people but something more gentle for others savoured a little of condescension. Some Africans found it patronising. Dame Margery Perham quotes one of them: 'We do not wish for any special treatment. We do not wish to be protected; we want to be allowed to make our own mistakes, and to work out our own salvation, as you did.'[3] Whether the 'special treatment' approach was right or wrong, it seemed at best over-kind, and at worst hypocritical – 'an excuse for leaving the African very much as he is, and leaving him to deteriorate in his own way'.[4] Moreover, the form of Indirect Rule favoured by Hobson and Morel was impracticable in the conditions of the twentieth century, even

[1] Hailey, op. cit. p. 706.   [2] See above, p. 234.
[3] M. Perham, 'Some Problems of Indirect Rule in Africa', in the *J.R.S.A.*, vol. lxxxii (1934), p. 700.
[4] W. M. Macmillan, reported in ibid. p. 703.

for West Africa. If it had ever existed in the past, the happy communal life of the tribal African certainly did not exist in the same form then; the very fact of contact with Europeans had modified it, for good or ill, and must continue to do so. Even if the will had been there – 'What government has the power and the knowledge to prevent men from adapting their culture to the many and drastic changes we have made in their environment?' [1] Change of some sort was inevitable. So the study of complete indigenous cultures, however interesting and rewarding it might have been scientifically, was of little use from a practical, administrative point of view. For purposes of colonial government anthropology had to be not only functionalist and relativist, but concerned also with the phenomenon of culture-*contact*. 'It is more important', said Lord Hailey, 'to study the reactions of the African to the rapid changes in cultural and material environment to which he is being subjected, than to attempt any analysis of his character based on his traditional customs or beliefs.' [2]

This was widely admitted by English and American anthropologists in the 1930s. It was Malinowski who directed British anthropology towards an examination of culture-change, and students of Indirect Rule followed step.[3] But before 1914 little was seen of this new anthropological approach. The diffusionist hypothesis, perhaps, pointed the way: if similar cultural traits in different peoples were the result of propagation, and not of indigenous growth, then contact was an ethnological reality.[4] One

[1] M. Perham, 'A Re-statement of Indirect Rule', in *Africa*, vol. vii (1934), p. 325.
[2] Hailey, op. cit. p. 32.
[3] For the study in America of culture-contact, see F. Boas, 'The Methods of Ethnology', in the *American Anthropologist*, n.s., vol. 20, no. 4 (1920), pp. 311–21; for the same in England, see B. Malinowski, *The Dynamics of Culture Change* (1961 ed.), and the articles cited on p. 165 of that book; for Indirect Rule and culture-change, see, for example, L. P. Mair, *Native Policies in Africa*.
[4] See above, p. 149. A diffusionist who was not a functionalist, however, would tend to regard acculturation as a mechanical process, a straightforward appropriation of a new cultural trait in place of an inferior one – which was not the approach of later proponents of culture-contact theory. See Lowie, *The History of Ethnological Theory*, p. 245.

or two anthropologists in the early 1900s suggested that 'the difficulties arising from the clash of cultures, and the modification and gradual defecation of native customs and beliefs under the influence of civilisation' might be worth investigating.[1] But few took up the suggestion, and paid close attention to the dynamics of the process itself. Certainly they did not do so in time for Hobson and Morel to reap the benefits. In so far as these two latter treated at all the phenomenon of acculturation, it was in order to demonstrate its evils. It was the worst aspects of Western civilisation which were being conveyed to the African in the 1890s; their solution was to stop cultural proselytising altogether.

Hence their hatred of the 'educated African' (though this was a long-established prejudice among Englishmen on the West Coast). In a way the problem of the educated African was the practical manifestation of the deficiencies of their approach, of their neglect of culture-contact. He existed; but he could not easily be fitted into the traditional pattern of African society – 'what scope . . . can the rudimentary Ibo groups offer to one of their tribe who has spent ten years at American universities accumulating academic qualifications?' [2] It was this body of Westernised Africans which had the deepest suspicion of the motives behind Indirect Rule, and resisted it most fervently.[3] And the educated African was to win through. Indirect Rule needed *time* for its fulfilment. Most men in the 1920s and 1930s thought they had time.

> We have assumed that it will be towards some form of representative parliamentary government that a united Nigeria will some day aspire. We may also assume that for a people so backward and so divided in religion and culture, and who never knew any unity but that imposed by Britain upon this arbitrary block of Africa, that day will be very distant. We have, therefore, an interval within which to

[1] See E. S. Hartland in *Man*, vol. i (1901), p. 91; and A. C. Haddon in the *J.A.I.*, vol. 33 (1903), p. 18 (on 'Contact-Metamorphism').

[2] Perham, *Native Administration in Nigeria*, p. 361.

[3] See the contributions of Africans to a discussion at the Royal Society of Arts, 27 Mar 1934, summarised in *J.R.S.A.*, 18 May 1934 (vol. lxxxii), pp. 702–10.

build up, as a foundation for unity and democracy, that wide and active citizenship which we neglected to prepare in India. . . .[1]

But they were not to have such an interval. Hence the failure of Indirect Rule, and the triumph of its Europeanised African opponents.

Such criticisms were levelled at the Indirect Rule of the 1930s; but they were much more valid for that of Hobson and Morel. For the Indirect Rule which became the orthodoxy of British policy between the wars differed considerably from theirs, and even from Lugard's. Some at least of the old flaws had been ironed out. Colonial administrators had learnt from Malinowski, and perhaps more from observation, that a rigid preservationism was no more viable in West Africa than elsewhere. Their enlightenment was encouraged by the International African Institute, founded in 1926 to bring together the District Commissioner and the professional exponent of culture-contact theory.[2] In Nigeria and Tanganyika Sir Donald Cameron was relaxing the rigidity of Indirect Rule:

> In some measure we have departed from the intentions and principles of Lord Lugard . . . in drifting into the habit of mind that a 'feudal monarchy' of this [Nigerian] kind . . . is the be-all and end-all of Indirect Administration. . . . It is the avowed intention of the Government that the natives should not 'stay put'.[3]

By Cameron's time Indirect Rule no longer meant 'preserving and stereotyping indigenous institutions in their traditional form'; rather it looked to 'their evolution towards representative organs of democratic local government'.[4] Culturally, too, it was abandoning the attempt to preserve, like anthropological museum-

---

[1] Perham, op. cit. p. 361.

[2] See Kroeber, *Anthropology Today*, pp. 847–9 (article by Daryll Forde).

[3] Sir Donald Cameron, quoted in Perham, op. cit. p. 331.

[4] R. E. Robinson, 'Why "Indirect Rule" has been replaced by "Local Government" in the Nomenclature of British Native Administration', in *J.A.A.*, vol. ii, no. 3 (July 1950), p. 14. See also Perham, 'Some Problems of Indirect Rule in Africa', in *J.R.S.A.*, 27 Mar 1934, p. 699.

pieces, the customs and practices of native races, and was seeking instead to promote their 'progressive adaptation . . . to modern conditions'.[1] In other words, in its most advanced form Indirect Rule was not a policy of static non-interference, but a way of breaking the African in, slowly and gently, to modern civilisation.

V. CONCLUSION

This was something very different from what Morel and Hobson had envisaged. Their own policy for Africa was less dynamic, more *laissez-faire*. They seemed to have fallen prey to that 'quasi-romantic tendency to value a primitive institution in proportion as it differs from our own';[2] certainly their efforts were directed more towards pointing the excellence of alien cultures than to a balanced assessment of them. The practical defects of their approach were to show through in the following years – early and clearly in East and South Africa, later but no less clearly in the west. And if we were to accept the advantages of hindsight we could, perhaps, indict them for their immoderacy. But it was understandable that their reaction should be extreme, and of no small value to posterity that it was so. For the situation as they saw it in Africa in 1900 was not conducive to moderation. The inroads of the white man there were bringing only suffering and social disruption. If Europeans went to Africa for gain, then they were purposely callous; if they went there to 'spread the blessings of civilisation' then their good intentions were neutralised by their ignorance and their Eurocentrism. There had to be a reaction against the impatient culture-chauvinism of the New Imperialism. Few men had thought before of its sociological implications in the way that Mary Kingsley and Hobson did; if they saw only its bad side, it was because the novelty of the idea lent it an exaggerated importance. Their extremism was a necessary counter to the extremism of the alternative policy, which seemed in the 1890s to have won over the Colonial Office. Only when their point had

[1] Mair, *Native Policies in Africa*, p. 56.
[2] Perham, *Native Administration in Nigeria*, p. 315.

been made, and people had been made aware of the difficulties attendant upon the 'civilising mission', could the pendulum of colonial policy settle somewhere between the two extremes: take account of the difficulties without capitulating to them.

And the difficulties *were* taken account of in the 1920s, more so than before: by colonial administrators, as we have seen, and even by those whose profession was proselytism – the missionaries. William Vincent Lucas, for example, Bishop of Masasi between 1926 and 1945, accepted fully the functionalist hypothesis of the anthropologists, the evidence they produced of the disruptive effects of acculturation, and found theological sanction for his insistence on preserving the structure of African culture. 'The Zulu who becomes a Christian', he wrote, 'in no way ceases to be a Zulu, but his life is raised to a higher and supernatural plane as a Zulu Christian' [1] – *gratia non tollit naturam sed perfecit*. This contrasted strikingly with his predecessors' arrogant identification of Christianity with English civilisation. Not everyone was to accept in the same way the relativist approach. Sir Philip Mitchell, later Governor of Kenya, satirised its alleged impracticality:

if an inhabitant of a South Sea Island feels obliged on some ceremonial occasion to eat his grandmother, the anthropologist is attracted to examine and explain the ancient custom which caused him to do so: the practical man, on the other hand, tends to take more interest in the grandmother. The one calls it aviophagy and the other murder: it depends on the point of view.[2]

But by and large informed opinion about African government had

[1] W. V. Lucas, 'The Christian Approach to Non-Christian Customs', in Rev. E. R. Morgan (ed.), *Essays Catholic and Missionary* (1928), p. 118.

[2] *Africa*, vol. iii, no. 2 (Apr 1930), p. 217. Mitchell, of course, was being less than fair. W. H. R. Rivers, a pioneer of functionalist studies, had pointed out the serious ramifications attendant upon the British Government's abolition of head-hunting expeditions in the Solomon Islands; but his solution was not to preserve the custom, but rather to replace it by something which would fulfil the same social functions more innocuously – canoe races and the ceremonial use of pigs' heads instead of human skulls (*Essays on the Depopulation of Melanesia*, pp. 93–109).

become rather more respectful of the findings of 'science', and more willing to be guided by them. This the imperial criticism of the 1890s had achieved.

It would be wrong to attribute it, or the policy of Indirect Rule, entirely to those three or four critics who have been given most prominence in this book. Indirect Rule and the philosophy behind it would probably have arisen without their assistance. There are adequate explanations for its origins elsewhere: precedents in Fiji, the Gold Coast and Sarawak; the situation of Northern Nigeria in 1900;[1] visible social conflict in Africa; and the general mood of disillusionment with existing methods which pervaded Radical circles in the 1890s. This last was perhaps the most important factor, and it was not of Hobson's or Morel's creation. The New Imperialism, with its jingoism, its gold-lust and its disregard for African rights, had itself revealed a fundamental crisis of colonial ideology; it asked its own questions about the relations between primitive peoples and the industrial West, and to a great extent supplied its own answers. Hobson and Morel had only to elucidate and emphasise them. Their rôle was to give expression to already existing doubts; and this they did articulately and effectively. Yet this in itself was of considerable importance. By voicing as they did the imperial disquiet of the time they made it more coherent. Occasionally their work had a direct and specific impact on policy – through Mary Kingsley's books, or the Congo Reform movement. Less tangibly, but possibly more important, their writings helped to promote among Radicals a deeper rethinking of the problems – economic and cultural – of colonial trusteeship.

Not in any readily definable sense did they influence English Radical attitudes after 1906. Those attitudes were determined largely by the exigencies of the contemporary imperial situation. In the 1890s imperialism seemed to mean mercenary, aggressive jingoism, so Radicals restricted their attention to these aspects, and neglected the purely colonial connotations of the 'new' phenomenon. The New Radicals and the Liverpool School looked

[1] See Robinson, 'Why "Indirect Rule" has been replaced by "Local Government" ', *J.A.A.*, p. 13.

a little further into the problem than Liberals and Labourites, and gave some attention to questions of African 'development': these two groups came up with an imperial ideology which appeared, at the time, more relevant to the deeper implications of imperialism and to the situation in Africa. Yet this ideology itself was a product of its time, a response to a challenge peculiar to the 1890s, more transient than its authors suspected. This became apparent during the first decade of the new century. Hobson had been too timid of the potency of imperialism, Morel and Mary Kingsley too closely occupied with only one of its many aspects. So the central features of their philosophies were found to be less serviceable than certain of their adiaphora. The doctrine of Indirect Rule and the imperial claims of the Western economy, whatever their effect on policy, only hindered Radical criticism in Parliament. For since Vereeniging the situation had altered: the imperial problem was no longer seen to be expansion, war and the exploitation of countries where white men could not live. The predominant theme of parliamentary discussion had become instead the political and economic structure of settler colonies. MacDonald and Wedgwood were concerned to plead the case in Africa not of European industry but of native races, and of native races who, it seemed, could not well be governed 'indirectly'. Here Hobson and Morel offered little guidance. Their ideas were hardly more relevant to these issues than the Cobdenites'. The challenge was different, and so the response had to change too. It returned to older, well-tested humanitarian lines.

But the fact that it was humanitarian and not Little Englander, that anti-imperialists had now given way to colonial reformers, was in some measure due to Hobson and Morel. Their greatest contribution to parliamentary criticism was to make it more Afrocentric and interested: to render the Liberals' indictment of forced labour and land alienation more informed, and to free Labour from the uncompromising anti-imperialism of the past. This produced a new situation in the House of Commons, very different from that of the 1890s. 'Before World War I', writes a modern historian, 'the Labour Party had developed a strong anti-colonial sentiment, as expressed in J. A. Hobson's *Imperialism: a*

Study, but it had evolved no concerted colonial policy';[1] yet the striking feature of the pre-war period is that this was not so. Hobson's *Imperialism* was not an expression of Labour sentiment. In so far as it influenced Labour policy, it was not in the direction of anti-imperialism. The 'capitalist' theme of its first section was employed by neo-Marxists elsewhere as an indictment of imperialism *in toto*, and by socialists in England as a revelation of the motives behind foreign policy; it was also used to implement Labour's attack on colonial exploitation. But Hobson was not an anti-imperialist in the way his plagiarists were, and his chief contribution to Labour Party policy was to encourage, indirectly, an alternative imperialism which enabled the party, even before 1914, to contribute positively and constructively to colonial debates. On questions of native labour, the franchise and imperial intervention, Labour had had a colonial policy, clearly pursued in Parliament, ever since 1906. It only needed the adherence to it, at the end of the war, of Wedgwood and Morel, bringing with them that concern with the land problem which was lacking hitherto, to fit the Labour Party for the imperial discussions of the 1920s.[2]

It was during these years between Vereeniging and Sarajevo that Radicals had learnt to come to terms with the African Empire: not to condemn it out of hand like their predecessors, but to accept, for the time at least, its existence and the responsibilities which accrued to it. They criticised the way Britain was administering it, but not the fact that she did administer it. They looked forward to its emancipation, but accepted the opinion of the experts that emancipation could not be immediate. As late as 1943 the Labour Party was able to declare that 'for a considerable time to come' the African colonies would 'not be ready for self-government'.[3] Before 1914 they rarely even mentioned the possibility. India and Egypt should be guided, slowly, towards

---

[1] R. G. Gregory, *Sidney Webb and East Africa*, p. 82.

[2] Morel joined the I.L.P. in Mar 1918; Wedgwood in Apr 1919.

[3] *The Colonies. The Labour Party's Post-War Policy for the African and Pacific Colonies* (Mar 1943), p. 2. For this attitude they were chastised by the British Communist Party: see *The Colonies: the Way Forward*, published by the executive committee of the Communist Party, pp. 52–6.

local self-government:[1] but India and Egypt were different, more 'civilised'. Africa was still in her minority, and had a long way to go yet under the tutelage of her British guardians. That tutelage must be benevolent – respectful of native laws and customs, vigilant in its defence of human rights – but it must continue. So despite the impact of the 'anti-capitalist' indictment of imperialism, and its subsequent incorporation into a revolutionary political ideology, for Radicals in Britain it did not imply revolution. Their own solution to imperial problems was pragmatic, gradualist, even conservative: and Hobson and Morel had helped to make it so. In a way they might be said to have imperialised Radical criticism of empire.

[1] On Egypt Labour M.P.s said very little. Grayson spoke in the Egyptian debate of 30 July 1907 (4 P.D. 179, cc. 873–5), and Gill on 23 Apr 1913 (5 P.D. (Commons) 52, cc. 435–8), but neither advocated independence. On India, see Georges Fischer, *Le parti travailliste et la décolonisation de l'Inde*, p. 38.

Epilogue

There was a spirit abroad during the 'nineties which, looking back to them now, makes it seem as if quite a different England had come into existence from that of the jubilee decade; an England no longer content to tread the paths of peaceful and solid progress, but whose mood had come to resemble the irresponsible aggressiveness of a man who has taken rather more than he can stand of some unaccustomed vintage, and who, without any serious thought of having to make his words good, goes about flaunting his capacity to take on and vanquish all comers.[1]

THE jingoistic national temper of the 1890s was the stimulus behind much of the left-wing speculation about empire described in the preceding pages. A quiet imperialism might have gone unnoticed; a noisy one sowed doubts and fears and resentments which gave rise to counter-doctrines and alternative policies. Liberals were bewildered by jingoism; the New Radicals worried themselves about its implications for democracy and progress; and the Liverpool reformers deplored its irrelevance to the real, practical issues and the way it distracted attention away from them. They may all have taken it too seriously. Looking back on the 1890s with the hindsight of the subsequent decades, we can see that they were over-apprehensive of its significance, for jingoism was a passing phase, and the intoxication of the nineties was soon to be relieved by the hangover brought on by John Bull's 'having to make his words good' in South Africa, and a comparative sobriety afterwards.[2] Yet it was this transient

---

[1] Esmé Wingfield-Stratford, *Before the Lamps Went Out*, p. 73. Cf. L. A. Atherley-Jones, *Looking Back*, p. 111.

[2] 'In the years of reconciliation on imperial matters, the noisy extremes of the days between the Jameson Raid and the Relief of Mafeking might be seen for what they were: an ostentatious deviation from a norm of sober responsibility towards colonial duty.' (A. F. Madden, in *C.H.B.E.*, iii 353–4.)

phenomenon, and the things which accompanied it – Joe's 'sharp tongue' and vulgar aggressiveness, his war-mongering schemes in Africa, the 'coarse' imperialism of brag and cynical stock-jobbing, the *panem et circenses* domestic policy of the Government:[1] in fact, the flags and bugles of late nineteenth-century imperialism – which stimulated the Radicals' anti-imperialist reaction.

To those Radicals with Liberal tendencies – Hobson included – imperialism had appeared as a threat to their ideals, a rude awakening out of the dream their predecessors had dreamt, and which Lowes Dickinson's fictional Liberal could still dream as late as 1908:

> I see the time approaching when the nations of the world, laying aside their political animosities, will be knitted together in the peaceful rivalry of trade; when those barriers of nationality which belong to the infancy of the race will melt and dissolve in the sunshine of science and art; when the roar of the cannon will yield to the softer murmur of the loom, and the apron of the artisan, the blouse of the peasant be more honourable than the scarlet of the soldier; when the cosmopolitan armies of trade will replace the militia of death; when that which God has joined together will no longer be sundered by the ignorance, the folly, the wickedness of man; when the labour and the invention of one will become the heritage of all; and the peoples of the earth meet no longer on the field of battle, but by their chosen delegates, as in the vision of our greatest poet, in the 'Parliament of Man, the Federation of the World.' [2]

Imperialism appeared, if not to give the lie to Cobden, at least to

---

[1] The *panis* most vociferously demanded at the turn of the century – old age pensions – was never granted, only promised by Unionists; and even then it was made to appear dependent in some way on an imperialist or protectionist policy. In Aug 1899, for example, Henry Chaplin, M.P., opined that 'the shilling duty [on corn] would produce two millions or more, and that would be a nice little nucleus for any modest scheme of old-age pensions proposed, and well worth considering' (speech at Stockton on Tees, reported in *The Times* 12 Aug 1899).

[2] G. Lowes Dickinson, *A Modern Symposium*, pp. 26–7. Cf. Cobden's Manchester speech of 15 Jan 1846, quoted above, pp. 14–15.

necessitate a reappraisal of this Cobdenite vision. England was
Free Trade, yet still there was war and aggression. Why? The
tradition of Cobden and Bright could not supply an answer. For
that tradition was not so much anti-imperialist as *un*-imperialist;
when the liberal dream had been conjured up long ago, it was out
of the materials to hand at the time, and imperialism (as it
appeared at the end of the century) was not among them. Consequently in the 1890s the Empire, if not outside the range of the
Radicals' experience, was outside the range of their ideals. No
account was taken of it in their vision of the future. So there was
a gap in Radical ideology: the Left had no workable, progressive
philosophy of empire – only a non-imperialism; and this deficiency
became glaringly apparent in the late nineties. This was the
deficiency which Hobson and his colleagues set out to remedy.

How they remedied it has been described above. The Radical
philosophies of empire which came out of the New Imperialism
seemed eminently realistic (though no less 'progressive' for that),
because they were based upon different assumptions, approaches
and ideologies. Perhaps too much has been made of the 'self-
confidence' of the Victorians; maybe not all Victorians were as
arrogant as we like to paint them, not so cock-sure of the
superiority of British democracy, British Free Trade and British
Christianity as panaceas for all the evils of the world. Such a concept seems ripe for another 'historiographical revision'. But
however this may be, in so far as the Victorians *were* self-confident
and naïve in their social and international outlook, the New
Radicals and the Liverpool reformers would have nothing to do
with them and rejected their assumptions. The number of idols
smashed by Hobson and Mary Kingsley would have made
Cromwell envious: individualism, charity, nationality and
laissez-faire were all subjected to Hobson's iconoclasm; and Mary
Kingsley attacked in no less summary a fashion temperance,
missionaries, the catechism, monogamy and even the wearing of
trousers. Such irreverence was necessary before an empirical
solution could be found for the problem of empire. England had
to be taught that the world could not be made in her image, that
the problems of civilisation and race and social and economic

development were more complex and difficult than she had fondly imagined. To a great extent, of course, Hobson and Mary Kingsley were shadow-boxing; if a large part of the British public still retained their old arrogance, those who administered the Empire did not share it to the same degree. The Indian Mutiny had taught them the futility of the simple British-pattern method of cultural imperialism; Henry Maine and Fitzjames Stephen had communicated some of their own disillusionment with Liberalism (especially *vis-à-vis* India) to others;[1] and mid-Victorian optimism had been on the wane for some years. But if there was less of the old naïve approach to tropical colonial problems than there had been, there was as yet nothing to replace it on the Left of British politics, and this left the door open for more cynical and less altruistic colonial policies to creep in. Hobson and Mary Kingsley had to stamp on what remained of the old assumptions before they could construct an alternative to the New Imperialism. This alternative, once formulated, was altogether more humble: Indirect Rule implied a greater respect for alien customs and cultures, the kind of humility which is contained in Ramsay MacDonald's *Awakening of India*.[2] English civilisation was not the only civilisation; England had as much to learn from Asia and Africa as they from her, for peoples were more varied, and world-civilisation more mysterious, than the bourgeois Victorian – the coffee-broker, say, of Eduard Douwes Dekker's *Max Havelaar*[3] – liked to think.

This was one bourgeois assumption destroyed, so far as the new Left was concerned; others followed; and soon – by 1902, let us say, the year in which both *Imperialism: a Study* and *Affairs of West Africa* were published – the broad outlines of a new approach to empire had been laid down, for such of those

[1] See J. P. C. Roach, 'Liberalism and the Victorian Intelligentsia', in *C.H.J.*

[2] Published in 1910. See especially pt. III ch. viii; and above, p. 314.

[3] 'Multatuli' (Eduard Douwes Dekker), *Max Havelaar* (first published 1860, English translation by Baron Alphonse Nahüys, 1868); a bitter indictment of forced and unpaid labour in Dutch Java, and of the expropriation of native possessions there, together with a brilliant satire on the Dutch Calvinist middle-class which tolerated such conditions.

who were not imperialists by Chamberlain's definition to take up
and use, if they so wished. These philosophies were themselves
based upon certain assumptions, assumptions which in many
respects bear a striking resemblance to the old ones. Hobson's
faith in human rationality and his dichotomy between the people
and the (capitalist) interests, and Morel's simple free-trade
idealism, all had a strong Cobdenite flavour. Lenin was right in
labelling Hobson a bourgeois. This is why both he and Morel,
despite their anti-capitalism, formed part of a distinctively English
tradition which was a natural development from nineteenth-
century Radical Liberalism to twentieth-century democratic
socialism. But there was much in their thought which was either
antagonistic to, or omitted from, Cobdenism: and chiefly, perhaps, the principle illustrated by Hobson's dictum, 'the land to
those who can use it'. His doctrine of social utility, and his internationalism which was so different from Cobden's because it was
less atomistic and more 'organic', provided the basis for a colonial
ideology which seemed more in touch with the early twentieth-
century world-industrial situation than Cobden's. The world was
an economic unit, and, to some extent, economic exigencies
traversed national boundaries. Such a doctrine could very easily
lead to abuse, and Hobson was hard put to it to find ways in which
such abuse could be prevented: and his conclusions were so
pessimistic as to neutralise the effect of his social utility principle.
Such a principle was viable if...; and Hobson listed a number of
essential safeguards (international control, redistribution of
wealth, and so on) whose implementation seemed highly improbable in the 1900s. Morel, on the other hand, took little or no
account of the world-economy, and the demands of that economy
had to be forced on his attention by Johnston, Lever and others.
Consequently when in 1912 he began to pay some attention to the
fact of the inexorability of industrial progress, which was what was
implied in a wider view of the world economy, it did untold
damage to his 'pure' theory. By compromising it he seemed to
deny its total validity, for if it had been put forward originally as
the universal cure for all colonial complaints, a general law
applied to particulars, and if in one particular case it need not hold

good, why should the general law still be valid? The new Radical theories of empire had their intrinsic weaknesses. Hobson's was too 'realistic', perhaps, to be consistent with a practical reformism; Morel's too idealistic and over-simple to be realistic.

Each was the outcome of a special and ephemeral situation. Consequently when the situation changed after 1906, certain aspects of these ideologies became redundant. 'Cosmic utility' was never a concept of any practical use to an advocate of native interests, and so it was ignored by Radicals in favour of a principle approximating more closely to 'native paramountcy'. On the other hand, for those colonial issues most prominently in view during the latter half of our period, the policy of economic and political Indirect Rule was scarcely more serviceable. Progressives in Parliament preferred a more old-fashioned egalitarian approach to native questions: it was found to suit eastern and southern Africa better. Similarly, 'peasant proprietorship' came to be regarded rather as an obstacle to African industrial development than as a painless way of furthering it. Morel was, perhaps, too deferential to African sensitivity. Karl Marx had also wept over the suffering caused to primitive communities by the uprooting of their economic and social structures; but he saw that the torment was necessary: 'The question is, can mankind fulfil its destiny without a fundamental revolution in the social state of Asia? If not, whatever may have been the crimes of England she was the unconscious tool of history in bringing about that revolution.' [1] And the Africans themselves, when given the choice, opted for pain and progress. On all these counts the theories of Hobson and Morel proved less permanent than other and less sophisticated ideas.

Yet their significance is far from negligible. Indirect Rule was endorsed by the Colonial Office for West Africa and, in a modified form, for Kenya and Uganda. Wedgwood and others took up the anti-concession cry, and effectively. The Labour Party became 'imperially minded', and came to accept the implications of trusteeship in a way which had once seemed improbable.

[1] Marx, 'The British Rule in India' (*New York Daily Tribune*, 25 June 1853), printed in Marx and Engels, *On Colonialism*, p. 39.

The yardstick of progressive opinion ceased for a while to turn on the issue of 'independence', and became instead the question of native land and labour. Hobson and Morel had a hand in all this. Yet what gives the Radical imperial thinking of these years its greatest import is the 'myth' of economic imperialism it helped create. The financial advantages of and necessity for colonial expansion had been advertised, by imperialists themselves, long before 1900; but at the turn of the century events in China, South Africa and the Congo magnified the capitalist element in imperialism and pointed sinister and fearful implications. Morel and Hobson threw these implications into sharp relief, and their propaganda greatly strengthened the case of those Radicals who wished to purge the Empire of such elements, to make it less mercenary. By socialists outside England, however, this policy became regarded as futile, because Hobson's analysis of colonial expansion was interpreted more rigidly and his term 'capitalistic imperialism' was read as a tautology. For Marxists it not merely described but also defined 'imperialism' –

> Imperialism: The highest and last stage of capitalism, characterised by the domination of large monopolies, by the struggle between large capitalist countries for sources of raw materials, markets and foreign territories, and the exploitation of other peoples; all of which leads to unceasing wars of aggression for a new partition of the world,[1]

and in this garb the word passed into the language of Soviet diplomacy. If myths are a force in world affairs, then the ramifications of this one are indisputable; and Hobson, unwittingly, helped to shape it.

The New Imperialism made a dent in the course of British history; but not half so big a dent as the reaction to it. However superficial and ephemeral was the new jingoism, however unimportant capitalist imperialism in Africa and however abortive the Imperial Zollverein agitation, the ideological movement which

[1] *Slovar' russkogo yazyka* (Dictionary of the Russian Language), published by Akademiya Nauk S.S.S.R., Moscow, 1957. I am grateful to Mr Christopher Barnes for the translation.

these things provoked on the Left was, arguably, more significant in the long run than the thing itself. Chamberlain would have been distressed by the irony of it. For it was his New Imperialism which had forced Radicals to come to terms with the imperial situation, and by so doing paved the way for, or at least determined some of the characteristics of, the post-imperial age that followed. The new anti-imperialism was not directly responsible for the emancipation of the British Empire. Britain eventually got out of Africa and Asia because she had to – because of her changed status and strength after the Second World War, and because of the pressure of nationalist movements in the colonies. But the propaganda of these nationalist movements, the way in which emancipation was effected, the conduct of colonial policy before, and the tyranny of the anti-imperial concept since, were all in some degree influenced by the ideas which Radicals had worked out in the 1890s and early 1900s, in response to the situation of that time as they saw it.

M

Bibliography

I. MANUSCRIPT SOURCES

John Burns Papers, British Museum, London.

Sir Henry Campbell-Bannerman Papers, British Museum, London.

Roger Casement Papers, National Library of Ireland, Dublin.

Lord Courtney Papers, British Library of Political and Economic Science, London School of Economics.

Sir Charles Dilke Papers, British Museum, London.

Fabian Society Papers, 11 Dartmouth Street, London S.W.1.

Viscount Gladstone Papers, British Museum, London.

Alice Stopford Green Papers, National Library of Ireland, Dublin.

J. A. Hobson–C. P. Scott correspondence, in the possession of *The Guardian*, Manchester.

John Holt Papers, John Holt & Co., Liverpool.

Lord Lugard Papers, Rhodes House, Oxford.

Ramsay MacDonald Papers, in the care of Mr David Marquand, M.P.

E. D. Morel Papers, British Library of Political and Economic Science, London School of Economics.

Passfield Papers (Sidney and Beatrice Webb), British Library of Political and Economic Science, London School of Economics.

Lord Ripon Papers, British Museum, London.

Lord Samuel Papers, House of Lords Record Office, Westminster.

George Bernard Shaw Papers, British Museum, London.

Graham Wallas Papers, British Library of Political and Economic Science, London School of Economics.

Lord Wedgwood Papers, Wedgwood Works, Barlaston, Stoke on Trent, Staffs.

II. GOVERNMENT PUBLICATIONS

Parliamentary Debates, 4th and 5th series.

Report of the Select Committee on Aborigines (British Settlements), P.P. (1837), vii (1).

Report of the Select Committee on Africa (Western Coast), P.P. (1865), v (1).

Second Report from the Select Committee on British South Africa, P.P. (1897), ix.

Report by Sir R. E. R. Martin, K.C.M.G., on the Native Administration of the British South Africa Company, P.P. (1897), lxii.

Report to the Board of Trade on Cotton Cultivation in the British Empire and in Egypt, P.P. (1904), lxxxvii (Cd. 2020).

Report on the Quality of Cotton grown in British Possessions, by Professor W. R. Dunstan, P.P. (1908), lxx (Cd. 3997).

Memorandum on the subject of Government Action in Encouragement of Cotton Growing in Crown Colonies, P.P. (1910), lxvi (Cd. 5215).

Report of the Northern Nigeria Lands Committee (1908), P.P. (1910), xliv (Cmd. 5102).

West African Lands Committee, Evidence and Draft Report, 1912–16. Never published. Copy in Colonial Office Library.

Report of the Commission on Closer Union of the Dependencies in Eastern and Central Africa, 1929 (Cmd. 3234).

III. PERIODICALS

The Aborigines' Friend

The American Anthropologist

Annual Register

The Anti-Slavery Reporter

The Anti-Slavery Reporter and Aborigines' Friend

The Clarion

Concord

The Contemporary Review

Cosmopolis

The Economist

Edinburgh Review

The Ethical World

Fabian News

Fortnightly Review

The I.L.P. News

The Independent Review (from Apr 1907, *The Albany Review*)

The Inquirer

The Investors' Review

The Journal of the Anthropological Institute of Great Britain and Ireland

Justice

The Labour Leader

Man

Manchester Guardian

The New Age

The Nineteenth Century

The Pall Mall Gazette

The Positivist Review

The Progressive Review

The Reformer   *The Times*
Reynolds's Newspaper   *West Africa*
South Place Magazine   *West African Mail*
The Speaker   *Westminster Gazette*
The Spectator

IV. PRIMARY PRINTED SOURCES

Aborigines Protection Society, *Transactions*.

[Angell, Norman] Ralph Lane, *Patriotism Under Three Flags*, 1903.

Anti-Slavery and Aborigines Protection Society, *Annual Reports*.

Baden-Powell, R. R. S., *Aids to Scouting for NCOs and Men*, 1900.

Bannister, S., *Humane Policy; or Justice to the Aborigines of New Settlements essential to a due Expenditure of British Money, and to the Best Interests of the Settlers*, 1830.

Bentham, Jeremy, *The Works of Jeremy Bentham*, ed. J. Bowring, 1843, vols. iii and iv.

Bérard, Victor, *L'Angleterre et l'Impérialisme*, Paris, 1900.

Boas, Franz, 'The Methods of Ethnology', in *American Anthropologist*, n.s., vol. 20 (1920), p. 311.

Bourne, H. R. Fox, *The Story of Our Colonies*, 1869.

— *Matabeleland and the Chartered Company*, 1897.

— *Blacks and Whites in South Africa*, 1900.

— *The Native Question in South Africa*, 1900.

— *The Claims of Uncivilised Races*, 1900.

— *The Aborigines Protection Society: Its Aims and Methods*, 1900.

— *Expéditions de Représailles* ('*Punitive Expeditions*') *en Afrique*, Paris, 1902.

— '*Civilisation*' *by War*, 1905.

— *Notes on Egyptian Affairs* (5 pamphlets), 1907–8.

Brailsford, H. N., *The War of Steel and Gold*, 1914.

Bridges, Horace J., *et al.*, *The Ethical Movement, Its Principles and Aims*, 1911.

Bright, John, *The Public Letters of the Right Hon. John Bright, M.P.*, ed. H. J. Leech, 1885.

— *Selected Speeches of the Rt. Honble John Bright, M.P., on Public Questions* (Everyman ed., n.d.).

— *Speeches on Questions of Public Policy by the Right Honourable John Bright, M.P.*, ed. Thorold Rogers, 1869.

Bryce, James, *Impressions of South Africa*, 3rd ed., revised, 1899.

— *The Relations of the Advanced and the Backward Races of Mankind*, 1902.

Buchanan, Robert, 'The Voice of "The Hooligan" ', in *Contemporary Review*, Dec 1900.

Burrows, H., and Hobson, J. A. (ed.), *William Clarke, a Collection of his Writings*, 1908.

Buxton, Thomas Fowell, *The Remedy; being a Sequel to the African Slave Trade*, 1840.

Carpenter, Edward, *Civilisation, Its Cause and Cure*, 1889.

Clarke, Sir Edward, *Public Speeches 1890–1900*, 1900.

Clemens, S. L. [Mark Twain], *King Leopold's Soliloquy*, 2nd impression, 1907.

Cobden, Richard, *Speeches on Questions of Public Policy by Richard Cobden, M.P.*, ed. John Bright and Thorold Rogers, 2 vols., 1870.

Communist Party of Great Britain, *The Colonies, The Way Forward*, 1944.

Congreve, Richard, *India*, 1857.

Lord Cromer, *Modern Egypt*, 1908.

— *Political and Literary Essays*, 1913.

Cust, R. N., *Notes on Missionary Subjects*, 1889.

— *Essay on the Prevailing Methods of the Evangelization of the Non-Christian World*, 1894.

Davidson, Morrison, *Africa for the Afrikanders: Why I am a Pro-Boer*, 1902.

Davis, W. J., *The British T.U.C.: History and Recollections*, 1916.

[Dekker, Eduard Douwes] 'Multatuli', *Max Havelaar* (English ed.), 1868.

Dicey, Edward, 'After the Present War' in *Nineteenth Century*, Nov 1899, pp. 693–707.

Dickinson, G. Lowes, *A Modern Symposium*, 1908.

Dilke, Sir Charles, *Greater Britain*, 1868.

— 'Civilisation in Africa', in *Cosmopolis*, July 1896.

— 'Indentured and Forced Labour', in *Papers on Inter-Racial Problems*, 1911, pp. 312–22.

Doyle, A. Conan, *The Crime of the Congo*, 1910.

Durkheim, Émile, *The Rules of Sociological Method*, 1912.

East London Ethical Society, *Reports*.

Fabian Society, *Resolutions of the Fabian Society* (Fabian Tract no. 70), 1896.

— *Fabianism and the Fiscal Question* (Fabian Tract no. 116), 1904.

Lord Farrer, 'Does Trade Follow the Flag?', in *Contemporary Review*, Dec 1898, pp. 810–35.

Froude, J. A., *Oceana*, 1886.

Gardiner, A. G., *Prophets, Priests and Kings*, 1908.

Giddings, Prof. Franklin Henry, *Democracy and Empire*, New York, 1900.

Gooch, G. P., *The War and its Causes*, 1900.

Green, James, *Causes of the War in South Africa, from the American Lawyer's Standpoint*, Worcester, Mass., June 1900.

Green, Joseph J., *War: Is It or Is It Not Consistent with Christianity?*, 1901.

Greenwood, Frederick, 'Sentiment in Politics', in *Cosmopolis*, Nov 1896, pp. 340–54.

— 'Machiavelli in Modern Politics', in *Cosmopolis*, Aug 1897, pp. 307–22.

Greenwood, Frederick, 'The Cry for New Markets', in *Nineteenth Century*,
    Apr 1899, pp. 538–46.
Earl Grey, *The Colonial Policy of Lord John Russell's Administration*, 1853.
Hardie, J. Keir, *India, Impressions and Suggestions*, 1909.
— *Keir Hardie's Speeches and Writings*, 1928.
Harrison, Frederic, *Memories and Thoughts*, 1906.
— *The Creed of a Layman*, 1907.
— *National and Social Problems*, 1908.
Hirst, F. W., *et al.*, *Oxford Essays in Liberalism*, 1897.
Hirst, F. W., Murray, G., and Hammond, J. L., *Liberalism and the Empire*,
    1900.
Hobhouse, Emily, *The Brunt of the War, and Where it Fell*, 1902.
Hobhouse, L. T., *Democracy and Reaction*, 1904.
— *Liberalism*, 1911.
Hobson, J. A., and Mummery, A. F., *The Physiology of Industry*, 1889.
Hobson, J. A., *Problems of Poverty*, 1891.
— *The Evolution of Modern Capitalism*, 1st ed., 1894; revised ed., 1906.
— *Problem of the Unemployed*, 1896.
— *John Ruskin, Social Reformer*, 1898.
— 'Free Trade and Foreign Policy', in *Contemporary Review*, Aug 1898.
— 'Capitalism and Imperialism in South Africa', in *Contemporary Review*,
    Jan 1900.
— 'The Testimony from Johannesburg', in *Contemporary Review*, May 1900.
— 'The Pro-Consulate of Milner', in *Contemporary Review*, Oct 1900.
— 'The Ethics of Industrialism', in Stanton Coit *et al.*, *Ethical Democracy*,
    1900.
— *The Economics of Distribution*, 1900.
— *The War in South Africa: Its Causes and Effects*, 1900.
— *The Psychology of Jingoism*, 1901.
— *The Social Problem: Life and Work*, 1901.
— 'Socialistic Imperialism', in *International Journal of Ethics*, vol. xii (1901).
— 'Ruskin and Democracy', in *Contemporary Review*, Jan 1902.
— 'A Restatement of Democracy', in *Contemporary Review*, Feb 1902.
— 'The Scientific Basis of Imperialism', in *Political Science Quarterly*, vol. 17
    (1902), pp. 460–89.
— *Imperialism, A Study*, 1st ed., 1902; 2nd ed. (revised), 1905; 3rd ed.
    (revised), 1938.
— *International Trade: An Application of Economic Theory*, 1904.
— 'The Possibilities of Popular Progress', in *University Review*, June 1905.
— *Canada Today*, 1906.
— (ed.) H. D. Lloyd, *A Sovereign People*, 1907.
— Introduction to Ruskin, *Unto This Last*, 1907.
— *The Crisis of Liberalism: New Issues of Democracy*, 1909.
— *The Industrial System: An Enquiry into Earned and Unearned Income*, 1909.

Hobson, J. A., *The Economic Interpretation of Investment*. (London, *Financial Review of Reviews*, 1911).
— 'Opening of Markets and Countries', in *Papers on Inter-Racial Problems*, 1911.
— *The Science of Wealth*, 1911.
— *The Importance of Instruction in the Facts of Internationalism*, 1913.
— *Work and Wealth: A Human Valuation*, 1914.
— *Traffic in Treason*, 1914.
— *Towards International Government*, 1915.
— *Democracy after the War*, 1917.
— *Richard Cobden, the International Man*, 1918.
— *Free-Thought in the Social Sciences*, 1926.
— 'The State as an Organ of Rationalisation', in *Political Quarterly*, vol. ii, no. 1 (1931).
Huxley, T. H., *Evolution and Ethics and Other Essays*, New York, 1898.
Increased Armaments Protest Committee, *Empire, Trade and Armaments. An Exposure*, 1896.
Independent Labour Party, *Annual Reports*.
Independent Labour Party, City Branch, *Imperialism, Its Meaning and its Tendency*, May 1900.
International Ethical Union, *Manifesto of the First Congress of the International Ethical Union*, 1896.
Jebb, Richard, *Studies in Colonial Nationalism*, 1905.
Johnston, Sir H. H., *The Uganda Protectorate*, 2 vols., 1902.
— *Liberia*, 2 vols., 1906.
— *Views and Reviews from the Outlook of an Anthropologist*, 1912.
— *The Backward Peoples and Our Relation with them*, 1920.
Kebbel, T. E., 'England at War – a Supplement', in *Nineteenth Century*, Mar 1898, pp. 337–44.
Kidd, Benjamin, *The Control of the Tropics*, 1898.
— *Social Evolution*, 1894.
Kingsley, Mary, 'The Development of Dodos', in *National Review*, Mar 1896.
— *Travels in West Africa*, 1897.
— 'Liquor Traffic with West Africa', in *Fortnightly Review*, Apr 1898.
— 'The Transfer of the Niger Territories', in *The British Empire Review*, Aug 1899.
— *West African Studies*, 1899.
— 'Life in West Africa', in W. Sheowring (ed.), *The British Empire Series*, vol. ii (1899), pp. 366–80.
— *The Story of West Africa*, 1900.
Kipling, Rudyard, *Poems, 1886–1929*, 1929.
Labour Party, *The Colonies. The Labour Party's Post-War Policy for the African and Pacific Colonies*, 1943.

Labour Representation Committee (Labour Party), *Annual Reports*.
Le Bon, Gustave, *The Crowd: a Study of the Popular Mind* (English translation), 1896.
— *The Psychology of Peoples* (English translation), 1899.
— *Bases scientifiques d'une philosophie d'histoire*, 1931.
Lecky, William, *The Map of Life*, 1899.
Lenin, V. I., *Imperialism, the Highest Stage of Capitalism* (1922), in Lenin, *Selected Works* (Foreign Languages Publishing House, Moscow, n.d.), vol. i, pp. 707–815.
London Ethical Society, *Constitution and Reports*.
Lucas, W. V., and James, E. O., *Christianity and Native Rites*, 2nd ed., 1950.
Lord Lugard, *The Rise of our East African Empire*, 1893.
MacDonald, J. R., 'The Propaganda of Civilisation', in *International Journal of Ethics*, vol. xi, no. 4 (1901).
— *What I saw in South Africa*, 1903.
— *Labour and the Empire*, 1907.
— *The Awakening of India*, 1910.
— *The Socialist Movement*, n.d. (1911).
Marx, K., and Engels, F., *Selected Works* (Foreign Languages Publishing House, Moscow), 1962.
— *Capital* (F.L.P.H., Moscow, 1961 ed.), vols. i and iii.
— *On Colonialism* (F.L.P.H., Moscow, n.d.).
Masterman, C. F. G., *et al.*, *The Heart of the Empire*, 1901.
Methuen, A. M. S., *Peace or War in South Africa*, 1901.
Mill, John Stuart, *Principles of Political Economy*, 1848.
— *Dissertations and Discussions Political, Philosophical and Historical* (4 vols.), 1859–75.
— *Considerations on Representative Government*, 1861.
— *Letters of John Stuart Mill*, ed. H. S. R. Elliot, 1910.
— *The Earlier Letters of John Stuart Mill, 1812–1848*, ed. Francis E. Mineka, Toronto, 1963.
Moffat, Rev. J. S., 'The Native Races', in *Nineteenth Century*, June 1900, pp. 890–8.
Morel, E. D., *The Sierra Leone Hut-Tax Disturbances*, Liverpool, 1899.
— *Trading Monopolies in West Africa: a Protest against Territorial Concessions, by E.D.M.*, 1901.
— 'The Belgian Curse in Africa', in *Contemporary Review*, Mar 1902.
— *The Affairs of West Africa*, 1902.
— *The British Case in French Congo*, 1903.
— *The Congo Slave State*, 1903.
— *King Leopold's Rule in Africa*, 1904.
— *The Congo Horrors*, 1904.
— *The Scandal of the Congo*, 1904.
— *The Treatment of Women and Children in the Congo*, 1904.

Morel, E. D., *The Commercial Aspects of the Congo Question*, 1904.
— *The New African Slavery*, 1904.
— Preface to Pierre Mille, *Le Congo Léopoldien*, 1905.
— *The Development of Tropical Africa by the White Races: Two Divergent Policies*, 1905.
— *Red Rubber: The Story of the Rubber Slave Trade on the Congo*, 1906; revised ed. 1919.
— Preface and appendices to S. L. Clemens, *King Leopold's Soliloquy. A defence of his Congo Rule* (2nd impression), 1907.
— *The Future of the Congo*, 1909.
— *Great Britain and the Congo. The Pillage of the Congo Basin*; with an introduction by Sir A. Conan Doyle, 1909.
— *Nigeria, Its Peoples and Its Problems*, 1911.
— *Truth and the War*, 1916.
— *Africa and the Peace of Europe*, 1917.
— *The Black Man's Burden*, 1920.
Morley, John, *Notes on Politics and History*, 1913.
— Article on 'Auguste Comte', in *Encyclopaedia Britannica*, 14th ed., 1929.
Morris, William, *Selected Writings and Designs*, ed. Asa Briggs, 1962.
Motte, Standish, *Outline of a System of Legislation, for Securing Protection to the Aboriginal Inhabitants of All Countries Colonised by Great Britain . . . ,* 1840.
Ogden, H. J. (ed.), *The War Against the Dutch Republics in South Africa, its Origin, Progress and Results*, 1901.
Olivier, Margaret (ed.), *Sydney Olivier: Letters and Selected Writings*, 1948.
Olivier, Sydney, *White Capital and Coloured Labour*, 1906.
Papers on Inter-Racial Problems, 1911.
Pearson, Karl, *National Life from the Standpoint of Science*, 1901.
Perris, G. H., *Blood and Gold in South Africa*, 1902.
— *A Short History of War and Peace*, 1911.
Peyton, Rev. W. W., 'The Crucifixion and the War in the Creation', in *Contemporary Review*, Oct 1900, pp. 518–31, and Dec 1900, pp. 835–57.
Reich, Emil, *Imperialism*, 1905.
Reitz, F. W., *A Century of Wrong*, with an introduction by W. T. Stead, 1900.
'Ritortus', 'The Imperialism of British Trade', in *Contemporary Review*, July 1899, pp. 132–52, and Aug 1899, pp. 282–317.
Rivers, W. H. R., 'The Government of Subject Peoples', in A. C. Seward (ed.), *Science and the Nation*, 1917.
— *Essays on the Depopulation of Melanesia*, 1922.
Robertson, J. M., *The Fallacy of Saving*, 1892.
— *Patriotism and Empire*, 1899.
— *Wrecking the Empire*, 1901.

Lord Rosebery, *Miscellanies, Literary and Historical*, 1921.

Ruskin, John, *Unto This Last*, 1862.

— *The Crown of Wild Olive*, 1866.

Samuel, Herbert, *Liberalism, its Principles and Proposals*, with an introduction by H. H. Asquith, 1902.

Seeley, J. R., *The Expansion of England*, 1883.

Shaw, George Bernard, *Fabianism and the Empire*, 1900.

— Preface to *John Bull's Other Island*, 1909.

— *The Intelligent Woman's Guide to Socialism and Capitalism*, 1928.

Sheowring, William (ed.), *The British Empire Series*, vol. ii, *British Africa*, 1899.

Smiles, Samuel, *Self-Help*, 1859.

Smith, Adam, *The Wealth of Nations*, 1776.

Smith, Goldwin, *The Empire*, 1863.

Socialist International, *Compte rendu sténographique non officiel de la version française du cinquième Congrès Socialiste International, tenu à Paris du 23 au 27 septembre 1900*, Paris, 1901.

South Place Ethical Society, *Reports*.

Statham, F. Reginald, *South Africa and the Transvaal: The Story of a Conspiracy*, 1899.

Stead, W. T., *The History of the Mystery, Review of Reviews* Annual for 1897.

— *Joseph Chamberlain, Conspirator or Statesman?*, 1st ed., 1899; 2nd ed. (with a new preface), 1900.

— Preface to F. W. Reitz, *A Century of Wrong*, 1900.

de Thierry, C., *Imperialism*, with an introduction by W. E. Henley, 1898.

Trades Union Congress, *Annual Reports*.

Tylor, E. B., *Researches into the Early History of Mankind and the Development of Civilization*, 1865.

— *Primitive Culture*, 2 vols., 1871.

Union of Ethical Societies (The Ethical Union), *Reports*.

Wallace, Robert, M.P., 'The Seamy Side of "Imperialism" ', in *Contemporary Review*, June 1899, pp. 782–99.

Wallas, Graham, *Human Nature in Politics*, 1908.

Wason, J. Cathcart, *East Africa and Uganda, or, Our Last Land*, 1905.

Watson, William, *The Poems of William Watson*, 1905.

Webb, Sidney, 'Lord Rosebery's Escape from Houndsditch', in *Nineteenth Century*, Sept 1901, pp. 366–86 (reprinted as Fabian Tract no. 108).

Webb, Sidney and Beatrice, *The Decay of Capitalist Civilisation*, 1923.

Wedgwood, Josiah (Lord), *Essays and Adventures of a Labour M.P.*, 1924.

White, Arnold, *Efficiency and Empire*, 1901.

Woolf, Leonard, *Empire and Commerce in Africa*, 1919.

— *Economic Imperialism*, 1920.

— *Imperialism and Civilisation*, 1928.

V. AUTOBIOGRAPHY AND MEMOIRS

Angell, Norman, *After All*, 1951.
Asquith, Margot, *The Autobiography of Margot Asquith*, 2 vols., 1920–2.
Atherley-Jones, L. A., *Looking Back: Reminiscences of a Political Career*, 1925.
Bax, Ernest Belfort, *Reminiscences and Reflexions of a Mid and Late Victorian*, 1918.
Blunt, Wilfrid Scawen, *My Diaries*, 1919.
Buxton, T. F., *Memoirs of Sir Thomas Fowell Buxton, Baronet, with Selections from his Correspondence*, ed. Charles Buxton, 1848.
Channing, Sir F. A., *Memories of Midland Politics 1885–1910*, 1918.
Clarke, Sir Edward, *The Story of My Life*, 1918.
Gooch, G. P., *Under Six Reigns*, 1958.
Viscount Grey of Fallodon, *Twenty-Five Years, 1892–1916*, 1925.
Haldane, Richard Burdon, *An Autobiography*, 1929.
Harrison, Frederic, *Autobiographic Memoirs*, 1911.
Hewins, W. A. S., *The Apologia of an Imperialist*, 1929.
Hirst, F. W., *In the Golden Days*, 1947.
Hobson, J. A., *Confessions of an Economic Heretic*, 1938.
Hobson, S. G., *Pilgrim to the Left*, 1938.
Holt, Cecil R. (ed.), *The Diary of John Holt*, Liverpool, 1948.
Johnston, Sir H. H., *The Story of My Life*, 1923.
Mill, John Stuart, *Autobiography*, 1873.
Morley, John (Viscount), *Recollections*, 1917.
Lord Samuel, *Memoirs*, 1945.
Webb, Beatrice, *Our Partnership*, ed. Barbara Drake and Margaret Cole, 1948.
Wedgwood, Josiah (Lord), *Memoirs of a Fighting Life*, 1941.

VI. BIOGRAPHY

Adams, W. S., *Edwardian Portraits*, 1957.
Arch, Robert, *Ernest Belfort Bax, Thinker and Pioneer*, n.d. (1927).
Bassett, Arthur Tilney, *The Life of the Rt. Hon. John Edward Ellis, M.P.*, 1914.
Bowle, John E., *Viscount Samuel; a Biography*, 1957.
Brailsford, H. N., *The Life-Work of J. A. Hobson* (lecture delivered 15 May 1947, published 1948).
Campbell, Olwen, *Mary Kingsley, a Victorian in the Jungle*, 1957.
Cocks, F. Seymour, *E. D. Morel: The Man and His Work*, 1920.

Cole, G. D. H., 'J. A. Hobson' (Obituary), in the *Economic Journal*, vol. 50 (June–Sept 1940), pp. 351–60.
Cole, G. D. H., 'J. A. Hobson', in *New Statesman*, 5 July 1958.
Cole, Margaret (ed.), *The Webbs and their Work*, 1949.
The Marquess of Crewe, *Lord Rosebery*, 1931.
Dictionary of National Biography, Supplements, 1901–11 (3 vols., 1912), 1912–21 (1927), 1922–30 (1937), 1931–40 (1949), 1941–50 (1959).
Dod's Parliamentary Companion, 1896–1914.
Dugdale, Blanche E. C., *Arthur James Balfour*, vol. i, 1936.
Lord Elton, *The Life of J. Ramsay MacDonald, 1866–1919*, 1939.
Evans, Howard, *Sir Randal Cremer, his Life and Work*, 1909.
Firth, R. (ed.), *Man and Culture: An Evaluation of the Work of Bronislaw Malinowski*, 1957.
Fisher, H. A. L., *James Bryce*, 1927.
Flint, J. E., *Sir George Goldie*, 1960.
— 'Mary Kingsley – A Reassessment', in *Journal of African History*, vol. iv, no. 1 (1963).
Fraser, Peter, *Joseph Chamberlain*, 1966.
Gardiner, A. G., *The Life of Sir William Harcourt*, 1923.
Garvin, J. L., and Amery, Julian, *The Life of Joseph Chamberlain*, 4 vols., in progress, 1932–51.
Gooch, G. P., *Life of Lord Courtney*, 1920.
Green, A. S., Obituary of John Holt, in *Journal of the African Society*, Oct 1915.
Gwynn, Stephen, *The Life of Mary Kingsley*, 1932.
Gwynn, Stephen, and Tuckwell, Gertrude, *The Life of the Rt. Hon. Sir Charles Dilke*, 1917.
Hamilton, M. A., *Sidney and Beatrice Webb*, 1933.
Hammond, J. L., *C. P. Scott of the Manchester Guardian*, 1934.
Howard, Cecil, *Mary Kingsley*, 1957.
James, Robert Rhodes, *Rosebery*, 1963.
Jenkins, Roy, *Sir Charles Dilke: A Victorian Tragedy*, 1958.
— *Asquith*, 1964.
Kent, William, *John Burns, Labour's Lost Leader*, 1950.
Lockhart, J. G., and Woodhouse, the Hon. C. M., *Rhodes*, 1963.
Luke, W. B., *Sir Wilfrid Lawson*, 1900.
MacColl, René, *Roger Casement*, 1960 ed.
Marett, R. R., *Tylor*, 1936.
Morgan, Kenneth O., *David Lloyd George*, Cardiff, 1963.
Morley, John, *The Life of Richard Cobden*, 1879.
Oliver, R., *Sir Harry Johnston and the Scramble for Africa*, 1957.
Owen, Frank, *Tempestuous Journey: Lloyd George, His Life and Times*, 1954.
Pall Mall Gazette, *The House of Commons in 1906*.
Perham, Margery, *Lugard: The Years of Adventure, 1858–98*, 1956.

— *Lugard: The Years of Authority, 1898–1945*, 1960.

Russell, G. W. E., *Sir Wilfrid Lawson, a Memoir*, 1909.

Spender, J. A., *The Life of the Right Hon. Sir Henry Campbell-Bannerman*, n.d. (1923).

Strauss, W. L., *Joseph Chamberlain and the Theory of Imperialism*, Washington, D.C., 1942.

Thomson, Malcolm, with Frances, Countess Lloyd-George of Dwyfor, *David Lloyd George, the Official Biography*, n.d.

Thorold, Algar Labouchere, *The Life of Henry Labouchere*, 1913.

Trevelyan, G. M., *The Life of John Bright*, 1913.

Walker-Smith, D., and Clarke, E., *The Life of Sir Edward Clarke*, 1939.

Wallace, Elisabeth, *Goldwin Smith, Victorian Liberal*, Toronto, 1957.

Wedgwood, C. V., *The Last of the Radicals*, 1951.

Wellesley, D., and Gwynn, S., *Sir George Goldie, Founder of Nigeria*, 1934.

Who Was Who, vols. 1–5 (1920–61).

Young, Kenneth, *Arthur James Balfour*, 1963.

VII. SECONDARY WORKS

Adams, W. Scovell, *Edwardian Heritage*, 1949.

Ajayi, J. F. A., 'Henry Venn and the Policy of Development', in *Journal of the Historical Society of Nigeria*, vol. i, no. 4 (Dec 1959).

Annan, N. G., *The Curious Strength of Positivism in English Political Thought* (L. T. Hobhouse Memorial Trust Lecture no. 28, Oxford, 1959).

Arendt, Hannah, *The Origins of Totalitarianism*, 2nd ed., 1958.

Barker, Sir Ernest, *Political Thought from Spencer to Today*, 1915.

Baylen, Joseph O., 'W. T. Stead and the Boer War: the Irony of Idealism', in *Canadian Historical Review*, vol. xl, no. 4 (1959), pp. 304–14.

Bealey, F., and Pelling, H., *Labour and Politics, 1900–1906*, 1958.

Bodelsen, C. A., *Studies in Mid-Victorian Imperialism*, 1924.

Briggs, Asa, *Victorian People*, 1954.

Brunschwig, Henri, *French Colonialism 1871–1914*, English ed., 1966.

Burrow, J. W., *Evolution and Society*, 1966.

Cairns, H. A. C., *Prelude to Imperialism*, 1965.

The Cambridge History of the British Empire:
> vol. ii, *The Growth of the New Empire, 1783–1870*, 1940.
> vol. iii, *The Empire–Commonwealth, 1870–1919*, 1959.
> vol. viii, *South Africa*, 2nd ed., 1963.

Cole, G. D. H., *British Working-Class Politics 1832–1914*, 1941.

— *A History of Socialist Thought*, vol. iii, *The Second International*, 1956.

Cole, Margaret, *The Story of Fabian Socialism*, 1961.

Cookey, S. J. S., 'Great Britain and the Congo Question, 1892–1913', London Ph.D. dissertation, 1964.

Curtin, Philip D., *The Image of Africa, British Ideas and Action, 1780–1850*, 1965.

Ensor, R. C. K., *England 1870–1914*, 1936.

Faber, Richard, *The Vision and the Need; Late Victorian Imperialist Aims*, 1966.

Fairchild, H. N., *The Noble Savage*, New York, 1928.

Fieldhouse, D. K., ' "Imperialism": An Historiographical Revision', in *Economic History Review*, vol. xiv, no. 2 (1961).

Fischer, Georges, *Le parti travailliste et la décolonisation de l'Inde*, Paris, 1966.

Freedman, R. (ed.), *Marx on Economics*, 1962 ed.

Furnivall, J. S., *Colonial Policy and Practice*, 1948.

Galbraith, J. S., 'The Pamphlet Campaign on the Boer War', in *Journal of Modern History*, vol. xxiv, no. 2 (June 1952).

Gallagher, J., 'Fowell Buxton and the New African Policy', in *Cambridge Historical Journal*, vol. x, no. 1 (1950).

Gallagher, J., and Robinson, R. E., 'The Imperialism of Free Trade', in *Economic History Review*, vol. vi, no. 1 (1953).

George, K., 'The Civilized West looks at Primitive Africa, 1400–1800', in *Isis*, vol. xlix (1958).

Gregory, Robert G., *Sidney Webb and East Africa*, University of California Publications in History, vol. lxxii (1962).

Grenville, J. A. S., *Lord Salisbury and Foreign Policy*, 1964.

Guiral, Pierre, 'Observations et Réflexions sur un Prophète de la Décolonisation', in *Études Maghrébines* (Paris, 1964), pp. 211–16.

Hailey, Lord, *An African Survey*, 2nd ed., 1945.

Halévy, Élie, *Imperialism and the Rise of Labour*, 2nd ed., 1951.

— *The Rule of Democracy*, 2nd ed., 1952.

Hancock, W. K., *Survey of British Commonwealth Affairs*, vol. ii, *Problems of Economic Policy 1918–1939*, Pt. 1 (1940), Pt. 2 (1942).

Hobsbawm, E. J., 'Fabianism and the Fabians, 1884–1914', Cambridge Ph.D. dissertation, 1950.

Hofstadter, Richard, *Social Darwinism in American Thought*, 1944.

John Holt & Co., *Merchant Adventure*, Liverpool, n.d.

Hoskin, David, 'The Genesis and Significance of the 1886 "Home Rule" Split in the Liberal Party', Cambridge Ph.D. dissertation, 1963.

Hyam, R., 'The African Policy of the Liberal Government, 1905–9', Cambridge Ph.D. dissertation, 1962.

Keynes, J. M., *The General Theory of Employment, Interest and Money*, 1957 ed.

Knaplund, P., *Gladstone and Britain's Imperial Policy*, 1927.

Knorr, Klaus E., *British Colonial Theories 1570–1850*, 1944 ed.

Koebner, Richard, 'The Concept of Economic Imperialism', in *Economic History Review*, vol. ii, no. 1 (1949), pp. 1–29.

— *Empire*, 1961.

Koebner, R., and Schmidt, H. D., *Imperialism, The Story and Significance of a Political Word, 1840–1960*, 1964.

Kroeber, A. L. (ed.), *Anthropology Today*, Chicago, 1953.

Langer, William L., 'A Critique of Imperialism', in *Foreign Affairs*, vol. 14 (Oct 1935), pp. 102–19.

— *The Diplomacy of Imperialism, 1890–1902*, New York, 1935.

Le May, G. H. L., *British Supremacy in South Africa, 1899–1907*, 1965.

Legge, J. D., *Britain in Fiji, 1858–1880*, 1958.

Lovejoy, A. O., *The Great Chain of Being*, Cambridge, Mass., 1936.

Lowie, R. H., *The History of Ethnological Theory*, 1938.

McBriar, A. M., *Fabian Socialism and English Politics 1884–1918*, 1962.

Mair, L. P., *Native Policies in Africa*, 1936.

Malinowski, B., 'Ethnology and the Study of Society', in *Economica*, vol. ii (1922), pp. 208–19.

— 'Practical Anthropology', in *Africa*, vol. ii (1929), pp. 23–39.

— 'The Rationalization of Anthropology and Administration', in *Africa*, vol. iii (1930), pp. 405–29.

— 'Native Education and Culture Contact', in *International Review of Missions*, vol. 25 (1936), pp. 480–515.

— 'Introductory Essay on the Anthropology of Changing African Cultures', in *Methods of Study of Culture Contact in Africa*, International Institute of African Languages and Cultures Memorandum xv (1938).

— *The Dynamics of Culture Change, An Inquiry into Race Relations in Africa*, ed. Phyllis M. Kaberry, New Haven, Conn., 1965.

Mellor, G. R., *British Imperial Trusteeship 1783–1850*, 1951.

Mitchell, Harvey, 'Hobson Revisited', in *Journal of The History of Ideas*, vol. xxvi, no. 3 (1965).

Morgan, Kenneth, *Wales in British Politics, 1868–1922*, Cardiff, 1963.

Neill, Stephen C., *The Christian Missions, Pelican History of the Church*, vol. 6, 1964.

Nemmers, E. E., *Hobson and Underconsumption*, Amsterdam, 1956.

Nworah, K. K. D., 'Humanitarian Pressure-Groups and British Attitudes to West Africa, 1895–1915', London Ph.D. dissertation, 1966.

Oliver, R., *The Missionary Factor in East Africa*, 1952.

Parsons, Talcott, *The Structure of Social Action*, New York, 1937.

Pease, Edward, *History of the Fabian Society*, 1916.

Pelling, H., *A Short History of the Labour Party*, 1961.

— *The Origins of the Labour Party, 1880–1900*, 2nd ed., 1965.

Penniman, T. K., *A Hundred Years of Anthropology*, 1935.

Perham, M., 'A Re-statement of Indirect Rule', in *Africa*, vol. vii (1934), pp. 321–34.

— 'Some Problems of Indirect Rule in Africa', in *Journal of the Royal Society of Arts*, vol. lxxxii (1934), p. 689.

— *Native Administration in Nigeria*, 1937.

Radcliffe-Brown, A. R., 'On the Concept of Function in Social Science', in *American Anthropologist*, vol. xxxvii (1935), pp. 394–402.

Roach, J. P. C., 'Liberalism and the Victorian Intelligentsia', in *Cambridge Historical Journal*, 1957.

Robinson, R. E., 'Why "Indirect Rule" has been replaced by "Local Government" in the Nomenclature of British Native Administration', in *Journal of African Administration*, vol. ii (1950), pp. 12–15.

Robinson, R. E., and Gallagher, J., *Africa and the Victorians*, 1961.

Schneider, M. P., 'Underconsumption and Imperialism', Cambridge M.Sc. dissertation, 1959.

Schumpeter, J. A., 'The Sociology of Imperialism', in *Imperialism and Social Classes*, English ed., 1951.

Schuyler, R. L., 'The Rise of Anti-Imperialism in England', in *Political Science Quarterly*, vol. 37, no. 3 (Sept 1922).

Semmel, Bernard, *Imperialism and Social Reform*, 1960.

Shannon, R. T., *Gladstone and the Bulgarian Agitation 1876*, 1963.

Slade, Ruth, *King Leopold's Congo*, 1962.

Slotkin, J. S. (ed.), *Readings in Early Anthropology*, 1965.

[South Place Ethical Society], *A Short History of The South Place Ethical Society*, 1927.

Stansky, Peter, *Ambitions and Strategies*, 1964.

Stock, Eugene, *History of the Church Missionary Society*, 3 vols., 1899; 4th vol. 1916.

Stokes, Eric, *The English Utilitarians and India*, 1959.

Strachey, John, *The End of Empire*, 1959.

Swanwick, Mrs H. M., *Builders of Peace, Being Ten Years' History of the Union of Democratic Control*, with a foreword by E. D. Morel, 1924.

Thornton, A. P., *The Imperial Idea and its Enemies*, 1959.

— *Doctrines of Imperialism*, New York, 1965.

The Times, The History of The Times, vol. iii, *The Twentieth Century Test, 1884–1912*, 1947.

Tsiang, Tingfu F., *Labour and Empire*, Columbia University Studies in History, no. 106, New York, 1923.

Tyler, J. E., *The Struggle for Imperial Unity*, 1938.

Wilson, Charles, *The History of Unilever*, 1946.

Wingfield-Stratford, Esmé, *Before the Lamps Went Out*, 1945.

Winslow, E. M., 'Marxian, Liberal, and Sociological Theories of Imperialism', in the *Journal of Political Economy*, vol. 39, no. 6 (Dec 1931).

— *The Pattern of Imperialism*, 1948.

Wuliger, R., 'The Idea of Economic Imperialism, with Special Reference to the Life and Work of E. D. Morel', London Ph.D. dissertation, 1953.

Young, G. M., *Victorian England: Portrait of an Age*, 1960 ed.

Index

Aborigine question, *see* Native races

Aborigines, Select Committee on (1837), 21–2, 25

Aborigines Protection Society: philosophy, 50–5; on South Africa, 65, 67–8; on the Congo, 260, 261, 269

Acculturation, *see* Cultural imperialism; Cultural relativism; Culture-contact; Ethnocentrism

Africa, *passim*; importance of, xi; scramble for, 1–2, 54, 227; de-colonisation of, 337. *See also* East Africa; South Africa; West Africa; Native races

African Society, 234 n, 250 n

Alden, Percy, 295, 303 n, 304 n, 305 n

Alexander, William, 40 n

American colonies, 6–7

American Indians, 50

American parallels with South African War, 66

American War of Independence, 5, 8

Angell, (Sir) Norman, 209, 221–2, 224, 271, 288

Anglocentrism, *see* Ethnocentrism

Anglo-Saxon imperialism, 37

Anthropological Institute, 147, 154

Anthropology and ethnology, 52, 175; mid-Victorian, 29–30; late Victorian, 146–9, 150, 151; Mary Kingsley's, 154–5, 241–9 *passim*, 288, 320; twentieth-century, 321–322, 325

Anti-capitalism, *see* Capitalist imperialism

Anti-imperialism, xii, 2–3, 337; early and mid-19th-century, 5–19 *passim*, 33; Liberal, 58, 76, 84–94, 332; Labour, 95–104 *passim*, 124–

137 *passim*; Positivist, 159; Hobson's, 157, 181–4 *passim*, 190–230 *passim*, 236–8, 239, 337; Mac-Donald's, 186–8; Mary Kingsley's opinion of, 241–2, 252; decline of, 292–7, 313, 327–9. *See also* Capitalist imperialism; Economic theory; New imperialism

Anti-Slavery and Aborigines Protection Society: parliamentary Committee, 304 n

Anti-Slavery Society: philosophy of, 50–2; and the Congo, 269 n

Apathy towards problems of colonial government: Manchester School's, 12–13, 19; Liberals', 57, 64–6, 68–70, 73, 84, 93, 94, 138; Labour's, 96–7, 105, 137, 138

Aristocracy and Empire, 12, 113, 205, 210, 224. *See also* Interests

Armaments: expense of, 7, 10, 11, 16, 192, 197, 209; increase of, 139–40, 192, 196, 223. *See also* Retrenchment

Armaments industry, 210

Armed Services, 205. *See also* Interests

Armenian question, 18, 70, 87, 186

Arms traffic, 22, 245, 261

Arnold-Forster, H. O., 46 n, 61

Ashanti Wars, 57, 69, 85, 96, 134

Ashley, W. J., 109 n

Asquith, H. H., 58 n, 60, 80, 81, 111, 121

Australasia, 50, 118

Baden-Powell, R. R. S., 88

Balfour, Arthur, 60, 195, 293, 294 n, 306

Bannister, Saxe, 23

Greenwood, Frederick, 40, 82 *n*, 144
Grey, Sir Edward, 58 *n*, 76 *n*, 80, 81
Grey Declaration (1895), 70–2, 73
Guinness, Rev. H. Grattan, 269
Gurdon, Sir W. B., 68 *n*

Hailey, 1st Baron, 319, 321
Haldane, R. B., 80, 81 *n*, 111, 118,
  161
Harcourt, Lewis, 316
Harcourt, Sir William Vernon, 58 *n*,
  68, 69, 141, 312; and retrenchment,
  86; on 'stock-jobbers', 62; quarrel
  with Rosebery, 72, 82; resignation
  (1898), 60; conduct on Jameson
  Raid Inquiry, 72–4 *passim*; death,
  294
Hardie, James Keir, 101, 156, 162 *n*;
  electoral defeat of (1895), 105;
  opposes Boer War, 92 *n*, 124–9
  passim; on native labour, 131,
  132 *n*, 298–9; on the colour-bar,
  69, 306–7; on India, 306, 313 *n*
Harrison, Frederic, 41 *n*, 90 *n*, 182;
  on political economy, 143–4, 158;
  on overproduction, 193
Hartland, Edwin Sidney, 154, 322 *n*
Harvey, T. Edmund, 295, 303, 304 *n*,
  314
Hawkesley Telegrams, 60–2, 72–3.
  See also Jameson Raid
Hegelianism, 141. *See also* Bosanquet,
  Bernard
Henley, W. E., 36–7, 90 *n*
Hewins, W. A. S., 109 *n*, 121 *n*
Hicks-Beach, Sir Michael, 195
Higham, J. S., 314 *n*
Hilton Young Report (1929), 315–16
Hirst, F. W., 64, 70, 82 *n*, 88 *n*, 92–3
Hobhouse, L. T., 141, 142, 200 *n*, 236
Hobson, J. A., 88 *n*, 112, 125 *n*, 129,
  155, 272, 291, 295, 314, 331–2;
  biography, 156 *n*; and the New
  Radicals, 139, 156–66 *passim*;
  social theory, 168–76, 239; under-
  consumptionist theory, 130, 168–
  170, 171 *n*, 198–9, 206, 213, 215–19
  passim, 229; in South Africa, 63,

200–6; indictment of capitalist imperialism (the 'economic
theory'), xii, 41, 64, 101, 104, 114,
130, 131, 134, 190–1, 194 *n*, 195–
230, 287, 289, 292, 304, 313, 327–
328, 336; and colonial government
(the 'ethical theory'), 28 *n*, 116–17,
176–90 *passim*, 230–5, 239, 243,
276, 287, 288 *n*, 290, 308, 315–28
passim, 332–6 *passim*; and rationalism, 172–5 *passim*, 179, 207, 210,
221–9, 235, 334; and international
affairs, 122–3, 235–7 *passim*, 271
Hobson, S. G., 105, 110, 124, 129,
  162
Hodgkin, Thomas, 50, 52
Holt, John, 94, 239–40, 271, 273 *n*;
  West African policy of, 244–6,
  257–8, 274; and Mary Kingsley,
  246–9, 254; and Morel, 254–60,
  266, 274; and the Congo, 245, 261,
  270; gives evidence to the West
  African Lands Committee, 272;
  attitude to Lever's concessionary
  schemes, 283–90
Home, Henry, 29 *n*
'Home Rule', and the Transvaal
  Constitution Bill (1906), 309. *See
  also* Nationalism
Home Rule Split (1886), effect on
  Liberal Party, 17–18; and Rosebery, 60, 70
Human Rights: possession of
  colonies contrary to, 6, 8; Exeter
  Hall's defence of, 52, 54; and
  Southern and East Africa (post-
  1906), 306–7, 313, 315, 329, 335;
  justifies imperial intervention, 308.
  See also Native races
Humanitarianism, xi; early, 5, 9, 21–
  22, 138; jingo impatience with, 39;
  used by capitalism, 205, 211; and
  the Congo Reform Association,
  270; and native labour, 304;
  Radicals' reversion to after 1906,
  307, 327. *See also* Aborigines
  Protection Society; Anti-Slavery
  Society; Exeter Hall; Missionaries